The Church Unfinished

The Church Unfinished

Ecclesiology Through the Centuries

Bernard P. Prusak

Paulist Press
New York/Mahwah, N.J.

Cover design by Cindy Dunne
Book design by Lynn Else

Library of Congress Cataloging-in-Publication Data

Prusak, Bernard P.
The church unfinished : ecclesiology through the centuries / Bernard P. Prusak.
p. cm.
Includes bibliographical references and index.
ISBN 0-8091-4286-4 (alk. paper)
1. Church—History of doctrines. 2. Church. I. Title.

BV598.P78 2004
262'.009—dc22

2004007376

Published by Paulist Press
997 Macarthur Boulevard
Mahwah, New Jersey 07430

www.paulistpress.com

Printed and bound in the
United States of America

Contents

Acknowledgments

I wish to thank my son, Bernard George Prusak, for his reflective reading of my manuscript and for his very insightful and substantive editorial recommendations, which so enhanced my work. I wish to thank my daughter, Alice Susanne Levine, for the discussions that deepened my awareness of young women's hopes and expectations regarding the Church of the future. As parents and educators, I and my wife, Helen, rejoice to see our faith become young again in a new generation. I am thankful for her love.

Bringing a manuscript to publication involves much dedicated work by an editorial staff. In that regard, I am indebted to Christopher Bellitto, the Academic Editor at Paulist Press, for his invaluable contribution. I likewise wish to remember Douglas Fisher, the editor who guided my manuscript through the process of its acceptance and earlier development. I also thank my copy editor, Susan O'Keefe, and the entire production team at Paulist Press. Finally, I wish to acknowledge the proofreading assistance of Sandy Haney, who has completed her graduate studies at Villanova University.

To my students

Introduction

The Spirit "by the power of the Gospel makes the Church become young again and perpetually renews her."[1] These words from the Second Vatican Council's Constitution on the Church invite deeper reflection. What does it mean to say that the two-thousand-year-old Church can be rejuvenated or become young again? Barring tragedy, being young is to have more future than past. Having more life in front of one than behind involves more than simply having more time left. It means being open to hoping and dreaming, to thinking about new possibilities for the future, and even to being adventurous. One's worldview has not become overly fixed by the past. Yet to be young *again* is not simply to be young. One who is young again has the benefit of experience. Youth is not lost upon such persons, for they know themselves and know enough to value the present both for itself and as the primary point from which they live into the future. In that regard, being young at heart is an attitude that even the old can keep alive and cultivate in the world around them.

It seems fitting that the council convened by Pope John XXIII, who saw a need for *aggiornamento* or updating the Church and for "reading the signs of the times," should have spoken of the Church as becoming young again. That perspective is certainly consonant with the tone of Pope John's opening address at the first session of the council: "In the daily exercise of our pastoral office, we sometimes have to listen, much to our regret, to voices of persons who, though burning with zeal, are not endowed with too much sense of discretion or measure. In these modern times they can see nothing but prevarication and ruin. They say that our era, in comparison with past eras, is getting worse, and they behave as though they had learned nothing from history, which is, none the less, the teacher of life." Despite his age, and precisely because of his knowledge of the Church's long history, John looked to the future with a youthful heart of hope: "We feel we must disagree with those prophets of gloom, who are always forecasting disaster, as though the end of the world were at hand. In the present order of things, Divine Providence is leading us to a new order of human relations which, by [humans'] own efforts and even beyond their very expectations, are directed toward the fulfillment of God's superior and inscrutable designs."[2]

The council's representation of the Church as becoming young again was actually not a new idea but a retrieval of a very early image. The visionary work known as *The Shepherd of Hermas*, written in Rome between 90 and 145, symbolically portrayed the Church as an old woman who became progressively younger and more beautiful (Visions 1–4). The barely one-hundred-year-old Church first appeared as old and haggard because of the stark problems she faced, such as deacons who were plundering the livelihood of widows and orphans (Parable or Similitude 9), and false prophets (Mandate 11). She was rejuvenated by those who heeded Hermas's proclamation of one final repentance in what was then considered the last days. Over eighteen hundred years later, the Second Vatican Council revived the vision of the Church becoming young again, in the context of its commitment to renewing the Church.

Like all living realities, the Church as the Body of Christ within history has a past, a present, and a future. There has, however, been a persistent tendency to underestimate the scope or importance of the future. Some early Christians interpreted the final time of fulfillment proclaimed by Jesus as an immediately imminent, chronological end time. In his Second Epistle to the Thessalonians (3:6–12), Paul admonished those who presumed that no work or effort was required of them because they believed the end of the world and Jesus' second coming were at hand. In the letter known as First Clement (ch. 23), which the Church of Rome sent to the Church of Corinth shortly after the year 97, and in Second Clement (ch. 11), a homily probably preached in Corinth after 125, we read that some Christians were complaining because the things they had heard in their youth, and then awaited day after day, had not happened. They were counseled to endure patiently in hope. Similarly, the canonical Second Epistle of Peter (written in Peter's name, probably between 100 and 125, decades after he had died in Nero's persecution) refers to persons who mockingly ask, "Where is the promise of his coming? For ever since our ancestors died, all things continue as they were from the beginning of creation" (3:3–4).[3] The epistle reminded its readers that creation involves a process brought into being by God's word (3:5–6). A day of fire and judgment is said to be coming, but in the Lord's eyes a thousand years are like one day (3:7–8, 10–13). What some considered a "delay" is declared to be the Lord's generous patience giving time for repentance (3:9).

Unlike Christians of earlier centuries, we no longer measure creation in terms of thousands of years. Our consciousness of the past far exceeds anything our ancestors could conceive, for we have come to understand that our present time is about fourteen billion years after that numinous moment called the Big Bang. The planet we inhabit, Earth, is about four-and-a-half-billion-years old, and it orbits around a star called Sun at the outer edge of a galaxy so vast that light traveling at 186,000 miles a second takes a hundred thousand years to traverse it. And our galaxy is only one of millions. We trace the remote beginnings of the life process on our planet to amino compounds that emerged about three-and-a-half- to four billion years ago. Those who study the evolutionary development of humanity use the term "*Homo*" for a genus that spans over two million years. As *Homo sapiens* humans, we are said to belong to a species that has existed more than fifty thousand years. We have discovered ice-age artifacts from thirty-five to twenty thousand years ago that reveal how much humans of that time were like us in their concerns and artistic expression. Truly, our era has the most expansive time-and-space horizons humans ever imagined.

Despite the early and medieval premonitions, the world has not ended. And the Church has dynamically grown, adapted, and developed while ever carrying its good news into that world over the course of two millennia. In the chapters ahead, we will consider how different eras shaped what the Church has become. Knowing where we have come from, and how we came to where we are, can provide insight regarding the options and responsibilities confronting what is now truly a world Church—present on every continent, amid all cultures, and beginning a third millennium. Appreciating that there is evidence of development in the ongoing life of the Church, and that there have been nuanced changes in the Church's theological self-understanding and self-definition over the past two millennia, can open one to seeing possibilities for creative development in the future of the Church guided by the Spirit who enables it to become young again.

"Horizons change for a person who is moving. Thus the horizon of the past, out of which all human life lives and which exists in the form of tradition, is always in motion." In historical consciousness, "this motion becomes aware of itself."[4] In our time, we are more and more confronting the challenge of relating the relatively short period of *explicit* revelation chronicled in the Bible to God's ongoing self-giving revelation over the entire course of creation and human existence. Given that the oldest written biblical tradition, which includes the Yahwist creation story of Genesis 2, is dated to the time of David and Solomon, the biblical period is only about three-thousand-years old. The fact that our past extends far beyond our biblical and historical horizons opens us to the possibility that our future may be even more vast. What God is seeking to accomplish through the process we call creation, through the event of Jesus of Nazareth—the Word become fully human—and through the community called Church, may be more complex than ever previously imagined. While affirming that there must be continuity in the Church's essential nature and mission, we might at the same time ask what could be different and new in the future of the Church described as becoming ever young.

It is more and more apparent that God's creation is not absolutely fixed and determined but permeated by both lawfulness and a degree of randomness and chance that leaves room for human freedom and creativity amid the laws of nature. Vatican II's Constitution on the Church in the Modern World affirmed that God has endowed humans with a certain autonomy for shaping the world.[5] Walter Kasper believes that this acknowledgment "signifies the final breakthrough of a new definition of the relationship between the church and the modern history of freedom." The council broke away from an earlier restoration mentality that undervalued and polemicized against the modern history of freedom, and instead recognized that the modern demand for autonomy "can find its justification in the Christian message itself."[6] We might ask whether the council's formal recognition of the fact that God has risked entrusting creation to human freedom has any implications for traditional presumptions about the order and structure of the Church. Does accepting that humans are called to be partners with God in shaping the future of this world also signal a need to be more discerning about the presumption that certain new possibilities for the future of the Church have been definitively excluded by a divinely established order? The tendency to presume that nothing new or unexpected could develop in the unfolding future of the Church might close us to the presence of the Spirit in our midst and in our time. It might not leave room for God to work through us for the future. It might fail to recognize that our time, as much as any past time, is an opportunity for God's creative activity and grace.

In this light, the Church's leadership would do well to nurture a renewed eschatological attitude that embraces a genuine openness to the newness and surprise of the future. That eschatological attitude "must be able to chart a course that contains some degree of continuity between past, present and future while at the same time leaving room for the important elements of change and transformation."[7] Given that the Spirit makes the Church become young again, the Church should not be conceived as so predetermined by the past that its future simply has to be more of the same. As the bearer of a *living* tradition keeping the memory of Jesus alive, the community called Church does benefit from the prejudgments or predispositions positively implanted within the tradition by Jesus and sustained by the Spirit.[8] However, its future decisions and practice are not simply a "given" completely evident from the past. Within the vast final time inaugurated by Jesus of Nazareth, we have to live with a trust that is open to possibility and to newness. Within the Church conceived as a dynamic reality, faith may empower a struggle to bring forth what may now be just a dream. In that regard, one might keep in mind Pope John Paul II's invitation to reenvision the role and function of the papacy, expressed in his encyclical *Ut unum sint*.[9]

As it lives into the future, the Church's relationship to Jesus grounds and permeates the decisions through which it responds to the needs of the world. In the process of deciding what it should do in the here and now, and in acting in the here and now, the community called Church not only maintains its continuity with Jesus but also reshapes its own self-understanding and reconstitutes itself. Engaged in a critical dialogue with ongoing human history, and drawn on by the Spirit, the two-thousand-year-old Church is reshaped and becomes young again precisely through its creative efforts to proclaim the good news in such manner that it will be heard and received in every time and culture.

We may wonder what the Church will become in this millennium. Widening our speculative horizons, we might further wonder what Christians five thousand years from now will think about this period in the Church. In that distant future, the first three thousand years of the Church will likely be regarded as the period of primitive Christianity. The Second Vatican Council will be perceived as an ancient event, much as the Council of Chalcedon in 451 appears to us. Seen from that perspective, our era may well be the springtime of a still young Church—although some fear that our era of industrial pollution and nuclear, chemical, and biological weapons might become a self-imposed endtime.

To have hope for the future is to recognize the need for the world to be "otherwise." It is to recognize the need for action to recreate the values and structures whereby humans have shaped a world filled with injustice, poverty, hunger, hatred, violence, and suffering. If humanity is to survive into the distant future, it must face up to the overwhelming problems of a technological world wherein humanity is more and more threatened by its own autonomy. In an era in which humans have the power to destroy all life on this planet, it is imperative that we acknowledge the brokenness and ambiguity of our human freedom. Now more than ever, it is crucial that humans learn how *not* to use power, or rather, learn to exercise power the way God does, motivated by self-giving love and empowering the creativity of "others."

Christianity proclaims the centrality of the cross, the event in which Jesus profoundly expressed and revealed God's self-emptying or kenotic giving of self on our behalf (Phil 2:7), so that evil will never have the last word. That is the horizon within which the Church must work out its own self-understanding and mission in the new millennium. The Church's self-definition cannot, then, be shaped by a proclamation of God in terms of power and control and by an emphasis on authority. Rather, the Church must be reshaped by its proclamation of the God who ever seeks to empower the powerless and to overcome the suffering of the victims of our history—accomplishing that by the power of a transforming love that chose to suffer the vulnerability and defenselessness of the cross. God invites the community called Church and the entire human community to act with that transforming love. The Church is rejuvenated by sharing in the adventure of the Spirit sent by the God who has endowed humans with freedom and creativity. The Church risks becoming a negative sign if it is less open to newness and possibility than God who created a universe that has taken billions of years to evolve.

As the community called Church, we should seek to know and to appreciate our past. To value our past, however, does not require that we simply repeat it. Faith, hope, and love look beyond "what is" to "what is *yet* to be realized." That includes consolation, generosity, and loving care for the distressed and sorrowful, and mercy and patience for the sinful and hesitant. It does not exclude the joys of walking with those whom one loves under a starry sky or of feeling the wind upon the sea. It is never to be self-satisfied with what one has done.

It is in such a framework that we launch an effort to trace the creative visions of those who in past eras shaped the dynamic, living reality of the Church. They struggled to keep alive the way of Jesus in many different times and situations, adapting and improvising as they moved along. They lived out their faith in the manner required by their time and then passed it on to us to do the same. Their story is the one we now carry forward.

The tradition of faith and the shape of the Church are not inert elements simply passed along. Rather, they involve the dynamics of choice and performance; they must be practiced and lived in new times and situations. How we live out and thereby hand on the traditions of faith and the shape of the Church received from those who preceded us is crucial to those who in some distant future will look back to us as the unfinished Church in a world becoming. In that regard, we are called prayerfully to ponder what new insights God's Spirit, ever present in our midst, might be drawing the Church toward. We must ask which dimensions of the ever-young Church are not predetermined and unchangeable, but have arisen from past decisions that God is patiently expecting us to reconsider. To that end, this book puts the present period of the Church in vast historical context.

1
Jesus' Community of the Unexpected, Circa AD 28–30

The Church comes from Jesus of Nazareth, whose humanity was related to the very particular time and place of the Roman Empire and of the Jewish people in whose midst he lived, worked, and died. In the light of resurrection faith, we believe that Jesus' time-conditioned way of being human revealed the divine life he shared with the one he called *Abba* and with the Spirit, and that his unique relationship with God has meaning for all humanity, in every time and place.

There would be no Church without Jesus. One may, however, ask how the Catholic Church of today, in all its complexity, is related to the intentions of Jesus. In the past, it was emphasized that he established the Church as an organized institution and explicitly determined all the structures or patterns that it would ever require to meet the needs of any century. But there is evidence indicating that the Church has "come from" Jesus in a much more complex manner. The details of its organization and of its earliest responses to particular needs appear to have been worked out by Jesus' disciples under the guidance of the Spirit in the postresurrection period. Such a developing mode of origin suggests that the Church is still an unfinished community, always living in a tension between the "already" of the past and the "not yet" of an uncontrollable future, wherein the Spirit ever confronts us with the possibility of the "new."

This chapter will consider the kind of community Jesus gathered through what he did and said during his lifetime. An understanding of the manner in which the Church then came from his way of living and dying, and from his resurrection, might also clarify the deeper possibilities open to the Church in our own time. In short, we will be considering here the christological presuppositions of ecclesiology.

Unfolding Revelations of a Hidden Presence

Jesus of Nazareth did not, of course, invent the realities of human community and caring. Such dynamics had emerged among humans long before him. As a human affected by history, living in a particular time and place, Jesus did not and could not cast aside what was already there. His activity presupposed the positive contributions of previous human development, although what he did and said would also clarify in retrospect the deepest meaning of human potential and creativity. Jesus proclaimed the reign of the God that his fellow Jews had long before come to know. His way of living ultimately made clear that the human potential for goodness, for caring, and for love had, since the beginning, been significative of the inbreaking of the divine love of God. Jesus' life was ministerial because it helped others to comprehend concretely the full meaning of a way of living that had always been possible for all humans. His way of living and dying proclaimed that it really is safe to love because we have all first been loved by God, and that when we give of ourselves for one another, we are responding to and imaging God's love for us.

The inbreaking of unconditional divine love that Jesus concretely proclaimed, not only by what he said, but especially by what he did, transformed those who opened their lives to him. He gathered a community of persons who were bonded together in their experience of his distinctive vision. Yet we must not forget that Jesus himself lived and worked within the community of Israel, as did his earliest followers. Even the later separation of church and synagogue never severed all those bonds. Thus, in its relationship to Jesus, the community called Church always stands in relationship both to a long process of human development and to that particular community called the Jewish people, rooted in the faith of Abraham and Sarah.

The community called Church has roots that stretch deep and wide. We shall see that it arose from the persons whom Jesus gathered, but that it was not born in a single moment with one particular shape clearly decided by him. As Vatican II's Constitution on the Church (*Lumen gentium* 2–5) suggests, the Church "gradually grows" in stages within history, having its remote origin in the very moment of creation. Its genesis involves a dynamic process which began long ago when that self-giving fullness of Love we call God shared life by creating.

Although creation might appear to be an exercise of almighty power, a deeper faith reflection sees it as an act of love. What God *does* expresses what God *is*—God's creating thus expresses the essence of a God who is self-giving Love.[1] Admittedly, such conclusions about God's motive for creating and about the meaning of creation are drawn with hindsight, looking backward through the event of Jesus of Nazareth. For if Jesus on the cross is the image of the invisible God (Col 1:15), then surely God is not primarily power but rather a self-giving and compassionate fullness never diminished in self-giving—an infinite Love always having just as much to give. As Love in freedom, God always loves freely and with a fidelity to the beloved that gives rise to compassion. In loving us, God freely chooses to be affected by us and to be vulnerable to our suffering, as revealed by the cross.[2] In that light, the act of creating was only the beginning or the first moment of an ongoing process of relationship. God created so that "others" might exist and live in relationship, both among themselves and with God, the very Source of all possibility and the Ground of our freedom to love.

The way one perceives God operating in the world deeply influences one's understanding of Jesus and the Church. In our time, to believe that God became human in Jesus of Nazareth is understood to mean that God freely chose to share both our human creativity and our struggle within this evolving process that our faith calls creation. God did not assume a static human nature, but rather became a human with a history. Through the full humanity of Jesus, God has participated in our efforts to create lasting meaning, values, and relationships of love, which are the stuff of positive human development.

In Jesus, God offered anew and in an unsurpassable way the self-giving relationship initiated in the very act of creating. In the very fullness of his humanity, Jesus was the definitive revelation and self-communication of God. What he did and said ultimately actualized the divine plan of love and mercy (Eph 1:3–11). In him, God's initiative of self-revelation, inviting us to be friends both with God and with one another (Exod 33:11; John 15:14–15), achieved its fullness.[3]

Yet Jesus was likewise humanity's free response to God's self-giving. In the fullness of his human freedom, he irrevocably accepted God's gift of self and actualized the possibilities it offered to all humans. That was not accomplished automatically, in a flash, but through the effort of decisions made amid the events of life.

The way that Jesus always said "yes" to God in the struggle of his life continues to have deep meaning for our own experience of and relationship to God. We believe that a relationship with God does not diminish human potential but enhances it. It opens us to possibility in a way that calls forth our deepest creative effort. For the God who created human freedom and possibility would not seek to obliterate human creativity. Rather, God's saving presence is experienced precisely through our efforts to make the future of our world more human.[4]

No human could ever *earn* a relationship with God. That has always been a gift offered to humanity by the God who created out of the motive of love. Such a gift calls for gracious acceptance. But within this world the divine gift of self in love and the free response it invites sometimes seem hidden and overwhelmed. Human freedom has produced both love and hatred, goodness and evil, hospitals that marvelously extend lives and concentration camps that destroy them.[5] Creation is a place of grand possibility, yet ours is also a broken world in which plans and often lives are shattered. Often we do our best, and it isn't enough. As the fully human, self-emptying or *kenotic* (Phil 2:7) presence of God in such a world, Jesus was like us in all things but sin (Heb 4:15—5:8). His "yes" to the God he called *Abba* unfolded through the struggle of his life and was sealed by his trust while dying. "In Christ God was reconciling the world to himself, not counting [humans'] trespasses against them" (2 Cor 5:19). In Jesus, God shared our struggle, and we shared in its transformation.

God's love for us does not flow from any need, since God lacks nothing. Yet because God is Love and loves us, God has freely chosen to be affected by us. Freely choosing to have a task in common with humanity,[6] God initiated a set of possibilities for an evolving process to which humans are invited to contribute, to become cocreators of the future. God likewise chose to share our struggle of freedom within an evolving creation that was not absolutely complete and perfect at the beginning. Such a view reflects what St. Irenaeus already held in the second century: both individual humans and humanity are not created complete but have to grow and develop from childhood into maturity.[7] Effortless perfection would not enhance the freedom of human creativity.

Jesus' divinity need not be understood as making him immune to the struggle or even to the seeming absurdities so often experienced in human life. As God become fully human, he was not just a superpowerful divinity in human disguise, simply on a mission to restore a perfection which humans had lost at the beginning. Grace, or a relationship with God, was a gift always offered, and always inviting response, since the very moment of creation. Thus, in his way of being human, Jesus definitively actualized the crucial possibilities that God's love had always offered humanity. His deeds and words proclaimed the presence of the quiet power of "God's reign" by gathering and revealing the full intensity and depth of human potential. The power of his quiet love would prove to be victorious even over the negative forces that sought to overwhelm him by crucifying him—an initiative carried out by a few who judged Jesus a threat to their established power. In a world where it helps to know that you are loved no matter what, the victory of Jesus' quiet love offered hope and courage to others to join in his "way." As a divine way of being human and a human way of being divine, Jesus revealed the fullness of our own possibilities. Through him we retrospectively realize that all humans have always been invited to his way of living. Moreover, because of the way Jesus lived and died, it can never be said that God's creation has been overcome by our sinfulness.

Vatican II spoke of the Church as a Mystery revealing the hidden presence of God's love for humanity, or a Sacrament that effects what it symbolizes, union with God and unity among humans (*Lumen gentium* 1). As Mystery, the community called Church reveals not what is completely unknown but rather something about which there is always more to know. It effectively reveals the presence of a triune, relational God who offers and invites relationship—a God who is experienced ever more deeply by those who seek to respond, but who nonetheless remains infinitely unfathomable and inexhaustible. The Church thus continues to do what Jesus did. Just as he, in his full humanity, actualized both God's love for us and humanity's union with God, the Church continues to make that love and union historically tangible through a fully human community, the people of God. Like Jesus, the Church cannot be separated from the long process wherein humans developed community among themselves, or from that particular culmination of divine-human community within the consciousness of the people called Israel.

Human Openness to a Quiet Invitation

As a sign and cause of union with God and unity among humans, the Church must celebrate what is valuable in human development because it is inseparably built upon it. The human effort to love and to understand life existed long before there was a Church. Humanity's search for meaning was a question implanted by God, opening humans to their answer: the hidden presence of that self-giving God who wants to be found in the midst of our freedom.[8] Our own finite experience, in which every answer becomes a new question, can lead us to the realization that there is something beyond our horizon.

Recognizing the ubiquitous but hidden presence of God's love, for which the Church is itself a sign, the Church must nurture the restless search for God. In a preoccupied world, busy with everyday survival, where many avoid asking those ultimate questions by which we are drawn toward God, it is important for the community called Church to ask the right questions. It is as important that the answers offered by Christian faith be not simply memorized, but rather personally appropriated as responding to the deepest questions of our lives. A great tragedy occurs when persons do not understand how the tenets of their faith are relevant to the search for meaning that has always been part of human experience. Those of us who have been taught about God since early childhood, and who are accustomed to gathering in special places of worship, must not forget that, in our relationship to that reality called God, we are heirs to the insights of a long human search for understanding. The response that ancient humans gave to that search, implanted in all of us since the beginning, has become our legacy, which we must pass on in a way that will make sense to a new generation.[9]

Religious and spiritual dimensions still fascinate even persons who for various reasons are not attracted to the Church.[10] This fascination indicates the need to do theology "from below" in a way that begins from human experience and its openness to the question of God. For if the religious openness of human existence is not engaged, what is said will not have the benefit of a resonant reception in the contemporary experience of life. People cannot simply be told what to believe; what they hear must draw them to reflect about the depths of their own experience of life. Even Jesus' teaching and meaning had to find acceptance among the persons of his time. A small group of Jews said yes to him because of the experience brought about within them by what he did and said.

Salvation has always been an interpreted experience. As various communities of believers remembered Jesus, in the process that ultimately produced the Gospels, specific memories of him came back as the communities needed them in their struggle to express his meaning in the different contexts of their own experience. Over the centuries that followed, there has been a continual interaction between what those communities remembered and what others later experienced. New experiences set the recollections in a different light.

"Revelation is the saving activity of God as both experienced and expressed in words."[11] It takes place in a long process of events. Since it is an interpreted experience, determining what constitutes the salvation that Jesus brings is impossible without taking into account how it relates to us in the here and now. That is why Christians bring no glad tidings to the "pagans of today" if they simply inform them that Jesus was the fulfillment of all the ancient promises to Israel. The good news of Jesus has to mean something for the present experience of life. It is not proclaimed by authoritarian talk about a gospel, scripture, or past tradition. Its language must be intelligible within the present "epochal horizon of the intellect."[12] That is to say, it must be (as it always has been) thought out within the bounds of interpretative models that reflect and are linked to the horizon of current experience.

In that regard, we do not simply look within the biblical tradition for ready-made answers about our present situation. Our task is to understand the scriptures in a way which illuminates "the world in front of the text," not just the one behind it. We must come to grips with the question that gave rise to the text and also bring to light new aspects of the question from our own historical context.[13] We must rediscover the message of the gospel in what it means to us, and then express our reflections in a language that corresponds to our experience of reality. There is likewise the crucial element of performance. The notes on the score of a symphony come alive in their being interpreted and played by an orchestra; the gospel message comes alive in our efforts to live it in our time.

The earliest human encounter with the personal reality we call God may have been actualized implicitly and prereflectively in some prehistoric gesture of openness to the needs of another human. So we may hypothesize, again looking back through Jesus' revelation of God. Although the potential for caring and for finding meaning beyond our individual lives and beyond the boundaries of all human life has always involved an openness to God, initially that was not reflectively recognized or conceptually articulated. That is to say, human openness to the God who is Love was expressed in humans' love for one another, even before humans developed any explicit concept of God or explicitly realized that they were being invited to respond to God's love. The way humans treat one another has always been indicative of their opening or closing of self to a relationship with God (1 John 4:20).[14]

As members of a Church which celebrates sacraments, we can understand that certain human actions symbolically mediate a deeper, hidden, mysterious presence that transforms us. Something more, hidden behind what is seen or done, is made present through such actions.[15] In that way, an encounter with God was hidden or implicit in a prehistoric human's expression of care for an "other." An openness to the God who is Love was profoundly expressed, although probably still without reflective realization, when someone first dared to show kindness to strangers, or perhaps when some anonymous person first risked her or his own life to save another's. The question and experience of God finally became explicit as humans reflected on the depth of their own potentialities in dealing with life and one another.

We do not know who first reflectively dealt with the anger and confusion which often follow that "awe-full" moment we call death. Nor can we say how long humans were in existence before someone raised the more ultimate questions about life and death that such a moment produces.[16] We can only imagine a man or woman comforting an "other" who was mourning the death of someone deeply missed and still loved, in a time when humans seem to have lived only an average of eighteen years, often dying because of violence.

In that light, the fossils of Old Stone Age humans, first discovered in the Neander Valley of Germany, reveal much about the spirits that once enlivened those bones. Some remains indicate that even severely maimed Neanderthals were cared for until they died at an old age, despite the fact that they might not have been economically useful.[17] The offerings of food, tools, red ocher, and perhaps even flowers (indicated by traces of pollen) discovered in Neanderthal burial sites of sixty thousand years ago supply evidence that respect and care for the living carried over into a respectful relationship with the dead. Such rituals expressing concern for the dead existed some fifty-seven-thousand years before the Bible began to be written.

To come to a conscious realization that one's meaning lies beyond oneself and beyond all the limitations of one's historical situation is not a neutral moment.[18] Consciously acknowledging and accepting that one is loved by an "Other" who is the source of one's own ability to love fosters a powerful new dimension of freedom. It becomes the source of an empowerment to choose and to live out distinct caring possibilities among the many options that life presents. That is one dimension of what the term "created grace" has traditionally sought to express.

We do not know when, in the thousands of years before any book of the Bible was written, some human first wondered about the source of our ability to love and to care and looked beyond the boundaries of life. Perhaps such gentler thoughts were overpowered by awe before the uncontrollable forces of nature such as thunder and lightning, which were often seen as divine manifestations, and before the strength of warriors whose power in a community brought a certain order where there seemed to be chaos. When experience and understanding finally came to explicit realization of some divine relationship to human development, it tended to be expressed through symbolic myths or stories. Some myths (such as the *Enuma elish*) spoke of gods warring among themselves and being brought to order by another god with a mighty sword. In that perspective, human jealousy and violence simply seemed to reflect what existed even among the gods.

Another vision broke through the mists of time and found written expression in the book we call "Genesis." Using symbolic elements, such as a garden, trees of life and knowledge, and a serpent, its writers proclaimed a God who has always intended a creation of goodness. And they made clear that their own experience of the everyday world was often quite in contrast to God's intention. In our world, humans have come to know not only good but evil, and guilt and shame. Humans kill their brothers and sisters; Cains have always been killing Abels. The human- and time-conditioned words of those writers were perceived as telling the truth in a special way: their words expressed the presence of God to their community with such intensity that they were preserved as the "word of God."[19]

The growing collection of such words and stories became foundational for a community with a distinctive story or conscious view of reality. In that way, the Hebrew Scriptures represent a faith community's reflective growth in understanding. They speak of a God who is merciful and gracious, slow to anger, and rich in kindness and fidelity (Exod 34:6), a God who freely chose to enter a covenant and to be affected by human history. The God of the Hebrew prophets was a mighty God who nonetheless cared for widows and orphans. The people who felt loved by that God could not forget the humble and the lowly. Those who told the story of a God who loved them and led them to freedom when they were strangers in an alien land were not to mistreat the lowly or the strangers in their own midst (Exod 22:21, 23:9; Lev 19:34; Deut 24:14–22).

Jesus Came Eating and Drinking

Every historical community constructs a symbolic world of stories, metaphors, and rituals to express and preserve its identity. Such symbolic activity intends to precipitate an "affective engagement," which binds individual members to the total community.[20] Some symbols look to the past, seeking to represent a foundational act and to evoke powerful feelings of participation in its effects. Others look to the future, seeking to bring persons to new horizons and possibilities.

The exodus story of the Jewish people's liberation from Egypt is relived each year in a symbolic meal that effects a renewed experience of that event (Exod 12:1–13:10). As a symbol of freedom, that meal has a subjective effect on its participants; it reconstitutes them as members of a community "passing over" from slavery to freedom.

The Passover meal has always remembered and made present what had once already happened. There was another symbolic meal that Judaism hoped *would* happen. The "Apocalypse of Isaiah" (Isa 24–26), probably inserted about the fourth century BC, looked forward to a feast with juicy, rich food and pure, choice wine (Isa 25:6–9; cf. 55:1–3; Jer 31:11–14), celebrating the ultimate liberation of God's people from that long line of invaders (Assyrians, Babylonians, Persians, and then Greeks) who had occupied their land. As an eschatological symbol of a new future, that meal would celebrate God's people being once and for all saved from death and tears.

During the time of Jesus' ministry, the priestly group known as Essenes was still living a self-imposed exile in the wilderness by the Dead Sea, protesting their loss of the high priesthood in Jerusalem about two centuries earlier. The Essenes refused to participate in the Jerusalem temple sacrifices, believing that God was instead present in their priestly *Yahad* or community as it celebrated sacral meals in the settlement we call Qumran.[21] The Dead Sea Scrolls, discovered in the 1940s, indicate that the Essenes expected they would host a meal like the one described in Isaiah, celebrating Israel's liberation from foreign rule. They anticipated that the incumbent high priest at Jerusalem, whom they considered a usurper, a puppet appointed by the Roman prefect or procurator, would be ousted and the Jerusalem temple purified. But the Essenes' hopes were not realized. The Romans demolished their settlement shortly before the destruction of Jerusalem in AD 70.

The appendix to the Essene Rule, found in the first cave at Qumran, forbade persons with bodily defects—such as the paralyzed, lame, blind, deaf, or dumb—to take part in assemblies of the community (1 QSa 2:3–10). Nor were any women allowed to be present since they were considered defective from their very birth. The awaited meal celebrating liberation by God's Anointed would be presided over by the Essenes' high priest along with the victorious Anointed One, or Messiah. They would be surrounded by priests, in order of honor, and by officers from the Anointed's army, according to rank. Only unblemished sages and dignitaries of repute would share the bread and lightly fermented wine blessed by the high priest and the Anointed on that solemn occasion (1 QSa 2:11–22). That was the Essene version of the banquet with fine wine and rich food described in Isaiah 25:6–9.

Jesus gathered his closest friends to share a meal, and particularly bread and wine, on the night before he died. That was not, however, the first time he celebrated such meal fellowship, nor was it the last time his friends did so. As a Jew living in a particular historical moment, Jesus had inherited perspectives on eating and drinking that developed long before his birth. But he also expanded or stretched the symbolic meaning that humans and Judaism had already created for meals. His frequent sharing of meals was distinctive in the way it included those whom others of his time specifically excluded. The various sources that were blended together in the Gospels, including the Markan (2:15–17) and Lukan (15:2) traditions, and the collection of Jesus' "sayings" known as "Q" (German "*Quelle*" or Source), used by both

Matthew (11:16–19) and Luke (7:31–34), all preserve the memory of a Jesus who regularly ate and drank with sinners and outcasts, such as the tax collectors who served the Roman occupation. Such sharing at table was an "enacted prophecy" wherein Jesus lived out the praxis of the kingdom or reign of God which he proclaimed.[22] Symbolically celebrating the inauguration of God's kingdom or reign, Jesus' meals would, in a challenging way, also become foundational for the community called Church.

Like the Essenes at the Dead Sea, Jesus saw a need to cleanse or renew what was happening at the temple in Jerusalem, believing that the final time, or *eschaton*, had begun. The love and mercy of his *Abba* did not need the temple to become present; they could be experienced among those sharing a meal with him. But Jesus' version of the meal celebrating the liberation of God's people (Isa 25) actualized a vision quite different from that of the Essenes. His ministry specifically embraced the blind, lame, lepers, deaf, poor (Matt 11:4–5; Luke 7:22), and sinners. His small company of followers did not exclude women, who were also important figures in his parables. In the Fourth Gospel (4:7–42), Jesus' disciples are said to be surprised because they find him speaking with a Samaritan woman at a well. That woman, living with a man who was not her husband, then proclaims Jesus to her town.

The symbolic dimensions of Jesus' behavior look back to a time thousands of years before the biblical period. For Jesus was indebted not only to a tradition of symbolic meals within Judaism but also to those unknown prehistoric persons who had invented hospitality. Whoever it was that first used meals as a mode of sharing and communication contributed a great deal to the development of human relationships.

Bread is an artificial substance in the sense that someone first had to blend its ingredients and create it. We who buy our loaves wrapped in plastic, often with additives baked in to retard spoilage, must struggle to imagine some prehistoric person baking the first rather flat loaf of bread on the red-hot rocks around a fire (1 Kgs 19:6) and offering it to a neighbor. Once that trusting guest bravely ventured a taste, the recipe was shared and the meaning of bread—life-giving nourishment, the "staff of life" (Lev 26:26: "staff of bread")—was passed along to others. Someone likewise learned to make wine and discovered what it could add to a meal or a celebration. Bread and wine came to have an even deeper meaning when they were shared and offered as a gift in hospitality. They became symbols of mutual trust, caring, and friendship (Gen 43:26–32, 31:51–54; Ps 41:9; John 13:18). That deeper meaning was a human creation that we reenact whenever we share a cup of coffee, a picnic, or a banquet with fine wine in long-stemmed glasses.

Jesus and his followers were indebted to a longstanding human tradition wherein people receive and share a gift of food that nourishes them together. The same is still true whenever Jesus' disciples gather to eat and drink in remembrance of him, except that Jesus himself has become the gift, present in our midst through the elements of a meal that is salvific.

Inviting and Welcoming the Unexpected

In Mark (2:15–17), Jesus' response to those who criticize him for eating with tax collectors and sinners is that he is one who heals. By eating and drinking with such guests, he claimed to be renewing their relationship with God. The merciful love of the God whom he called *Abba* was thereby made tangible to those whom some considered worthy only of judgment. By eating and drinking with them, Jesus restored hope to sinners, bringing out their deeper potential and the possibility of a different future for them. Jesus also challenged his brother and sister Jews to stretch their own self-understanding. His aim was the restoration, in some sense, of Israel, symbolized by his call of the Twelve. Now "[a]nyone who cherished such a goal was ipso facto intending to leave behind a community, a renewed Israel, that would continue his work."[23] The covenant with God would impel the community he gathered to seek to include, rather than exclude, those considered lost. The reign of God which he proclaimed called his brother and sister Jews into a new relationship with the wider human community. By responding to "an invitation to a new way of being Israel,"[24] they would come back into an authentic, renewed relationship with their God—bringing others with them. It is worth remarking that to pray "your kingdom come" requires openness to the possibility of a different future in human relations.

As Luke suggests (7:36–50, 14:1–24, 15:1–32), Jesus may have told many of his parables while at table, thereby clarifying the meaning he intended for his meal fellowship.[25] He spoke of a son who wasted the inheritance that his father gave him (Luke 15:11–32). Having been reduced to working on a pig farm, an undesirable situation for a young Jew, the son decided to return from his exile, hoping his father would pity him and give him a job. Hearing that his son has come back home, the father runs out to meet him, without first asking whether the son is sorry. He orders a banquet to celebrate the renewed relationship with his son who was lost but came back, and dresses him in a new set of clothes. That sparks a protest from an older, ever-faithful son who had stayed home working diligently (Luke 15:25–32). He complains that the father had never offered a banquet for him and his friends.

The upshot of the parable is that no person is a throwaway for the God whom Jesus called *Abba*. The sinners and outcasts with whom Jesus ate and drank were thereby being reconciled with the God whose reign he was proclaiming. Like a shepherd looking for one lost sheep, like a woman searching for a lost coin, or like a father welcoming home his prodigal son who had been exiled on a pig farm, that God celebrated being reunited with those who had been lost. Acting in the name of that God, Jesus understood his own mission to be one of seeking, welcoming, and saving the lost. That is precisely the message in the story about Jesus inviting himself to Zacchaeus's house (Luke 19:1–10). Unfortunately, like the righteous older brother of the prodigal son, some resented the fact that Jesus ate and drank with "sinners and outcasts" and held them and Jesus in contempt.

Jesus' parables were cryptic stories told so that their hearers might reconsider their presuppositions and prejudices about the world; in this way, parables intended "to articulate and bring to birth a new way of being the people of God."[26] Jesus' behavior was itself a parable. Those with whom he ate and drank became aware of a new future breaking into their present. Such is also the point of the story of the woman caught in adultery. Jesus restored a future to a woman who had no reason to hope, given that many wanted her stoned to death (John 8:3–11).

Being with Jesus was a joyful experience, like being with the groom at a wedding. As a result, his disciples could not fast while they were with him, unlike the disciples of John the Baptist and the Pharisees (Mark 2:18–20). In the parables about wedding feasts in Luke (14:12–24) and in Matthew (22:1–14), the guests are ultimately invited off the streets. They include the good and bad, the poor, maimed, blind, and lame. Admittedly, however, Matthew's version of the parable, with its tone of violence and a veiled reference to the destruction of Jerusalem in the year 70, appears to reflect the post-70 tensions between the Jewish Christian community and the wider Jewish community that did not accept Jesus as the risen Anointed.[27]

The historical Jesus compared those who found his behavior unacceptable to children refusing to play games in the marketplace (Matt 11:16–19; Luke 7:31–34). They would play neither "wedding" with him nor "funeral" with John the Baptist who came neither eating nor drinking: "We played the flute for you, and you did not dance; we wailed, and you did not mourn." In this passage, almost unanimously considered an authentic or historical saying of Jesus, he himself summarizes the reaction to his activity: "Look, a glutton and a drunkard, a friend of tax collectors and sinners!"

Even today, whom one chooses to eat and drink with is significant. Jesus' invitation to "play wedding" was itself the message. His eating with sinners, the marginalized, and outcasts made them happy because they felt loved by the God he called *Abba*. And the parables invited his audience to see God's merciful love present in their midst in unexpected persons and places. A Samaritan (Luke 10:25–37), and not the priest or Levite, stopped to help the man who had been mugged on the road to Jericho.

Unlike Jesus' audience, most of us are not Jewish, so the parable about a "good Samaritan" might not confront us with the challenging impact it originally had. How might Catholic Christians of our time react if asked who was neighbor to a man who had been mugged, either a bishop and a theologian who passed by without stopping, or a young homosexual of color who stopped to help? If we recognize that the Samaritan, or a young homosexual of color in our culture, might be perceived as a threat or an enemy to the identities we possess, an even deeper confrontation with the unexpected emerges from the depths of the parable. We might be offended by the fact that it is in the nature of God to love even those whom we might think unworthy of love. And what if their love for God is shown to be greater than ours and if they are the neighbor who reveals God's love for us?

By eating and drinking with those whom others considered undesirable, Jesus, like the Good Samaritan, did too much of a good thing. The message inherent in his behavior at meals was that God's love is unconditionally offered to all. The God whom Jesus called *Abba* was like a farmer who sowed seed everywhere, not just in soil guaranteed to produce a profitable yield, and then looked forward to the bountiful harvest that does finally come (Mark 4:3–8; Luke 8:5–8; Matt 13:3–8). God is also like the owner of a vineyard who gives workers who labored only from 3 or 5 p.m. into the evening the same wage promised those who had worked from early in the morning (Matt 20:1–16). In terms of our world's standards, that kind of God might be an apt candidate for foreclosure and a farm auction, or for boycotts by a union. The love of the God whom Jesus experiences as *Abba* is recklessly extravagant and not bound by the rules we might consider important. But that is the nature of a gift.

God's Presence in a Temple Not Made by Human Hands

In the villages and towns where he taught, Jesus established small communities of followers, distinct groups who, as his surrogate family,[28] adopted his *praxis*, his way of "being Israel."[29] Some New Testament passages (1 Cor 3:16–17; 2 Cor 6:14—7:1; Eph 2:18–22; 1 Pet 2:4–9) speak of the followers of Jesus as the "house" or temple of God in a new spiritual sense. That would be consistent with the fact that Jesus, like John the Baptist at the Jordan or the Essenes at the Dead Sea,[30] did not need the temple to encounter the presence of God. Moreover, Jesus did not impose the Levitical rules of ritual purity by which the Pharisees made their meals comparable to those of the priests in the temple (Mark 7:1–15). For Jesus, what comes from within a person shapes her or his relationship with God.

In Mark (2:18–22), Jesus' disciples are described as feasting while he is with them, like friends of the bridegroom at a wedding, instead of fasting like the disciples of John and the Pharisees. The subsequent sayings about not putting new patches of unshrunk cloth on an old cloak or new wine into old wineskins, lest they tear or burst, intimate that the reign of God proclaimed by Jesus requires a new container: "one puts new wine into fresh wineskins" (Mark 2:22).[31] God now dwells not just in a stone temple "made with hands," but within a temple "not made with hands" (Mark 14:58; cf. Matt 26:61 and John 2:19), that is, within the community of unexpected persons gathered around Jesus.[32] In Jesus' work "the Temple was being rebuilt."[33] He and his followers were the new temple. Jesus developed his own distinctive version of the perspective that God can be present in a living community rather than in a stone temple (John 4:21).

With the fuller understanding that came after the resurrection, Matthew explicitly proclaimed what had been implicit in Jesus' activity: in him "God is with us" (Matt 1:23). "The place of encounter with God is not the Temple of stone but Jesus himself."[34] And Jesus is still present in the living temple that is his community of disciples: "For where two or three are gathered in my name, I am there among them" (Matt 18:20). As 1 Peter 2:5 declares, Jesus' followers are "like living stones...built into a spiritual house, to be a holy priesthood, to offer spiritual sacrifices acceptable to God through Jesus Christ."

The divine presence in Jesus' meal fellowship, as described by the Synoptics, was hidden. Some saw only a "glutton and a drunkard" (Luke 7:34). By contrast, the Fourth Gospel uncovers and makes clear the divine presence. The Johannine Jesus changes water into choice *new* wine for a wedding at Cana, which, like the resurrection, was on the third day (2:1). That first "sign," revealing his divine "glory" (2:11) so that it could be *seen* (John 1:14), takes place outside Jerusalem, rather than on Mount Zion where the feast of liberation with fine wine was supposed to be celebrated (Isa 25:6). Placing the Cana story just before the cleansing of the temple, the Fourth Gospel effectively joins two passages that are signs of an emerging new order.[35] Its inauguration culminated with the "hour" of glory that was Jesus' death and resurrection (John 2:4, 12:23–27, 13:1, 17:1). The wedding feast looks ahead to that "hour" which "has not yet come" (2:4), but which would "gather into one the dispersed children of God" (John 11:52). Jesus' disciples would then experience the crucified but risen Christ's "glory" as God's miraculous gift within their own community. And, like Mary at Cana (John 2:3–5), they would always have to be completely open to God guiding their community in history.[36]

"The reign of God must have a *people*."[37] It is "a chosen race, a royal priesthood, a holy nation, God's own people" that proclaims "the mighty acts of him who called [us] out of darkness into his marvelous light" (1 Pet 2:9).

Shapes of Church: Varied Interpretations of Jesus

Since one's interpretation of Jesus influences one's model of Church, it is important to remember that how one understands

Jesus depends on how one reads the scriptures. Vatican II's Constitution on Revelation, *Dei verbum* (7, 19), adopted the perspectives of the Pontifical Biblical Commission's 1964 *Instruction on the Historical Truth of the Gospels (Sancta Mater Ecclesia).*[38] It presupposes that two stages preceded what was finally written about Jesus in the Gospels (the third stage). First, there were the words and deeds of Jesus, what he himself actually did and said. Second, there was the oral apostolic preaching about him. That involved a development beyond Jesus' own deeds and words since it included the fuller understanding of his meaning that came with the light of the resurrection event and the coming of the Spirit. Finally, there was what the evangelists wrote about Jesus as they composed the Gospels. What they wrote reflected what their communities were believing. Their Gospels therefore proclaimed what Jesus meant in the life of different communities.

Unity in diversity was crucial in the apostolic period. The varying life experiences of different communities (Palestinian Jewish disciples, Hellenistic Jewish disciples, and Gentile disciples) caused their faith in Jesus to be expressed in different terms and frames of reference. As recent biblical scholarship has shown, the New Testament represents a merging of divergent strands that interpreted Jesus from the perspectives of various postresurrection communities of disciples. Various traditions about the one Jesus of Nazareth were blended together or placed side by side. For example, Paul and Mark viewed the life of Jesus as a kenosis (an emptying or humbling: Phil 2:6–8) while others viewed it as an epiphany or manifestation of glory (John 1:14, 2:11). Despite the diversity in their expression of his meaning, all who formed Jesus' community were united by their experience of him; they were themselves a letter of Christ written by the Spirit "on tablets of human hearts" (2 Cor 3:2–3).

Section 19 of Vatican II's Constitution on Revelation emphasizes the historicity of the four Gospels and that they faithfully hand on what Jesus really did and taught. It explains that in writing these Gospels the authors selected certain of the many things that had been handed down, either orally or already written; some things they synthesized, others they explained in relation to the situation of the Churches. Retaining the form of proclamation, the authors have always communicated the genuine truth about Jesus.[39] That truthfulness runs deeper, accordingly, than a collection of facts. The Gospels did not simply report events; they interpreted their significance. As proclamations or testimonies of faith, intended to generate a similar commitment in their readers, the Gospels blended history and theology, facts and faith.

The Gospels are an indispensable source for learning about the earliest responses to Jesus and what he offered and evoked, since they gathered up particular, communal faith experiences of Jesus in a time of crystallization or formation. As faithful and reliable witnesses, they report how the earliest congregations experienced Jesus and interpreted his story in the light of their experience of his resurrection and the coming of the Spirit. The application of contemporary methods of biblical interpretation enables us to distinguish the memories of what Jesus did and said from those various communities' faith understanding, on the one hand, and from the authors' own theological contributions to what was finally written, on the other.

Those who experienced Jesus as risen, and therefore present in a new way, had to rethink their memories of him. In that process, Jesus now spoke through them. Although the verbal expressions through which the Gospels present the teachings of Jesus are all completely true in substance, some of the sayings attributed to him are not authentic, in the sense that they do not simply preserve the words of the historical Jesus. Such *inauthentic* sayings may synthesize developments that became clear only after the resurrection, capturing the intentions of Jesus by blending a historical memory or fact with the fuller understanding of faith. The Gospels always tell us the truth but sometimes in this more complex manner.

In the end, then, what one finds in the Gospels is not just a biography of Jesus, but also what he came to mean for the lives of early Christians through the prayerful reflection of diverse communities of believers. The Christian Scriptures have such communities as their source and environment, as their cause and their intended effect. The Gospels came from and through the community called Church. That must be kept in mind as we proceed in our discussion of Jesus' relationship to the Church.

Ultimate Trust in the Quiet Power of Love

In the traditions that shaped the gospel picture, Jesus is remembered as a healer who spontaneously responded to the needs of others. Jesus was himself the "miracle" of unmerited love and forgiveness, renewing God's covenant in a way that included persons some considered unclean. Refusing to legitimize his own power and authority, he always acted in a way that benefited others whom he thereby made happy.[40]

Conscious of a prophetic mission, Jesus taught with authority but in a way that valued persons above the Sabbath (Mark 2:27), that did not impose ritual purifications (Mark 7:15), and that rejected legalism (Luke 13:14–16). He was more interested in the relationships that the law was intended to nurture, love of God and neighbor (Mark 12:29–31), particularly the poor and weak in the concrete circumstances of life. He proclaimed a kingdom of God that freed persons to risk living in a way that actualized the deepest possibilities of human existence. In that kingdom, there is concern for the poor, hungry, and sorrowful who weep. Its ultimate goal is fullness and laughter (Luke 6:20–21).

People gathered around Jesus during his lifetime because he was one who strengthened hands that were weak and knees that were feeble (Isa 35:3). To those whose hearts were fearful his behavior proclaimed, "Be strong, do not fear!" (Isa 35:4). Jesus' ministry actualized what Isaiah proclaimed: "Here is your God. He will come with vengeance, with terrible recompense. He will come and save you" (35:4). By talking to, eating with, and celebrating life with outcasts, the marginalized, and sinners, Jesus actualized God's kind of "vengeance," enabling powerless persons—such as the woman caught in adultery (John 8:3–11)—to no longer fear those who wanted them to be frightened and to tremble. Jesus offered a new future to those who seemed hopeless: the poor, captives, and blind (Luke 4:18–19; Isa 61:1–2).

One who takes the side of those whose knees are trembling has thereby judged the actions of those who want others to feel valueless and afraid. Those powerful enough to make hands shake and knees knock quickly realize that a person who can overcome such fear by his very presence is dangerous to their interests. He is really more powerful than they are, but in a different, quieter way. Yet they can apply their kind of power to be rid of him.

No matter what later theological reflections may have predisposed us to think, the Gospels do not require a view of Jesus coming to his death passively, as if it were simply predestined. Rather, Jesus ultimately was condemned to death because of what he did and said. His meal fellowship with the marginalized and outcasts, his statements about the temple (Mark 15:29, 38; John 2:19) combined with a "cleansing" variously attested by all four Gospels, his attitude toward legalism, and his very style of teaching all seem to have been contributing factors. Jesus' religious message made him threatening both to the high priest of his time and to the Roman procurator who appointed that priest or extended his term in office.

A previous crisis of misunderstanding and rejection in his Galilean ministry may well have influenced Jesus' decision to go to Jerusalem. His death on the cross, as a criminal condemned to capital punishment, seemed to indicate even deeper failure. Mark (14:33–34) and Matthew (26:37–38) present a Jesus who is distressed, agitated, and saddened before the prospect of his violent death by execution. Luke's Gospel, which is usually circumspect in its descriptions, has a passage (not found in the oldest papyrus manuscripts) saying that Jesus was anguished or in agony, and his sweat became like drops of blood (22:44). Matthew (27:46) follows Mark (15:34) in having Jesus on the cross pray, "My God, my

God, why have you forsaken me?"—the first verse of Psalm 22, which in its entirety is a prayer of trust. Whether Jesus truly prayed this verse in dying is open to question; but it does appear truly to represent how he died: in distress but with complete trust in the God he called *Abba*.[41] The theme of trust is likewise found in the verse from Psalm 31, "into your hands I commend my spirit," which Luke (23:46) placed on the dying Jesus' lips. Trust is also in the prayer that the cup (of death) be removed from him if it be the Father's will, found in all three Synoptic Gospels (Mark 14:36; Matt 26:39; Luke 22:42; cf. John 12:27). To say that Jesus trusted in the face of death would seem to presuppose his experience of an inner struggle.

During his lifetime Jesus engendered trust in what he proclaimed by deed and word. But like every human life, his own life had an unfinished quality before his death.[42] The claims implied in his message and behavior could be misinterpreted or even appear to be unlimited pride or blasphemy. Only his way of dying, with complete trust and love, followed by his resurrection, removed the ambiguity and made it clear that absolutely nothing had or could separate him from the God he called *Abba*. Only then was the extent of Jesus' unity with God fully perceived by his disciples. The community of the unexpected had to await that moment to become the Church.

A Jesus Understood in Retrospect

The focus or meaning of any human life is by no means given or complete at the beginning. Creating one's meaning as a person involves both an individual process of decision and effort and a communal interaction. These processes are finalized and complete only at the end of life, in death, and ultimately at the end of human history.[43]

As the one who revealed God by the very way he was human, Jesus had to decide to continue to love even in the face of his absurd kind of death. That was, we can imagine, no easy effort.

Despite what was happening to him, he freely and decisively rejected the options of despair and hatred. In dying Jesus lived out what he had proclaimed; he loved even his enemies. After the resurrection event, and in light of the way he had faced death, Jesus' disciples could affirm that he had overcome the sinful condition of human existence and had always lived in total openness to God. Only then did they fully perceive the meaning of what he offered in his life and death.

Long before Jesus, the Hebrew prophets had nurtured the conviction that God was offering humans a qualitatively new future. Jesus of Nazareth entrusted his future, and the future of all for whom he cared, to that God. Sharing in the horizon of Judaism, Jesus saw himself as a participant in the end time or final definitive action of God within history. He seems to have understood his prophetic ministry as God's definitive offer of salvation, unconditionally extended to all in the final time, the *eschaton*, understood not simply as the end of space-time but as the final overcoming or defeat of evil and the fulfillment of Israel's history. As summarized by Mark (1:15), Jesus proclaimed the good news of God: "The time is fulfilled, and the kingdom of God has come near."

Jesus may not have known when the "end" would take place (Mark 13:32), finally consummating God's reign with the coming of the Son of Man (Mark 13:26). It is probable that he tended to think it would be soon, but he offered no timetable.[44] We who live almost two millennia later can witness that the *Parousia*, or coming of the Son of Man as expected by Jesus and the earliest Christians (2 Thess 2:1–2; cf. 1 Thess 3:13), has not yet arrived. But the fact that Jesus expressed himself in the perspectives of his own era does not negate the power of the expectation that he generated. Jesus opened people to a new future already beginning, the "reign of God" breaking in through his own ministry (Luke 17:21).

The very way that the Gospels preserve the term indicates that Jesus spoke of a coming Son of Man. Exactly what "Son of Man" meant in the various types of sayings within the Gospels is a matter of great discussion. The two "future" sayings—in which the Son of Man will acknowledge or deny those who acknowledged or denied Jesus (Luke 12:8–9; cf. Matt 10:32–33), and will be ashamed of anyone who was ashamed of Jesus and his words (Mark 8:38; Luke 9:26)—indicate a continuity between Jesus' ministry and that of the *coming* "Son of Man," although Jesus is not explicitly identified as that figure.[45] In the final consummation of the reign of God already initiated and actualized by what Jesus did and said, the Son of Man will simply seal one's acceptance or rejection of the definitive offer made by Jesus. Although he may have differentiated between himself and the one who would come at the end, Jesus was confident that the Son of Man would consummate the reign of God already breaking through his own healing ministry to the blind, lame, lepers, and deaf. In that ministry, "the dead are raised, [and] the poor have good news brought to them." (Luke 7:22; Matt 11:5). Through their experience of the resurrection, Jesus' disciples came to understand that he himself was the coming Son of Man, and the expectations linked to that figure were then assigned to him. In the new life that followed his way of living and dying, a new future or new creation had tangibly broken through. Although that future has come to be perceived as much more extensive and complex than originally imagined, Jesus' disciples continue to believe in his central role in it.

Jesus was not designated as the coming Son of Man, or as God's Anointed, independent of his own history. It was the Jesus who had been faithful to his *Abba* even in suffering who was "made" God's Anointed, either by his being predestined to come again (Mark 14:62; Acts 3:20–21), or by the resurrection itself (Acts 2:36). And his uniqueness did not depend on the titles that were given to him; rather, the titles were transformed by being applied to him. His own significance and distinctiveness shaped their very meaning. As Edward Schillebeeckx observes, "[T]he meek and gentle messiah is not a Christian 'topsy-turvy' version of the Jewish idea of the messiah but a reaching out, under the pressure of the reality that was Jesus."[46] That is why the blind men who cry out "Son of David" in the Synoptic Gospels proclaim a merciful healer and not a powerful earthly ruler.[47]

During Jesus' lifetime, some of his closest disciples may have hoped that he would be an Anointed or Christ of earthly power. Jesus is remembered as correcting some of the Twelve, who apparently projected their desire for power onto his ministry (Mark 10:35–45; Matt 20:20–28; Luke 22:24–27; Acts 1:6). Even the Twelve fully understood only in retrospect that Jesus would be an Anointed who suffered. Unlike Saul, David, and Solomon, he was not anointed by a male prophet or priest (1 Sam 10 and 16; 1 Kgs 1), but by a woman, and in preparation for his death (Mark 14:3–9; Matt 26:6–13; John 12:1–8).

With the hindsight of resurrection faith, Mark's Gospel synthesized historical memories about the disciples' expectations with the postresurrection community's clearer understanding of the risen Jesus as God's "Anointed." Thus the historical core of Simon Peter's confession of Jesus as the "Anointed" in Mark 8:27–33 may very well be found in verses 30 and 33: "'You are the Messiah [Anointed].'…'Get behind me, Satan….'"[48] During his ministry, Jesus may have rebuked Simon for calling him the Anointed, because it was then intended in the sense of a politically powerful king like David. As the passage presently reads in the full text, the Markan Jesus does not reject the title, because "Anointed" has become inseparably related to his death and resurrection (8:29–31). Mark has Jesus insist on secrecy about his being the Anointed (8:30) and then has him predict his death and resurrection (8:31). Only during his cross-examination by the high priest (Mark 14:61–62) shortly before his death does the Markan Jesus openly admit to being the Anointed. He then immediately proclaims the postresurrection faith of Mark's community, about seeing "the Son of Man seated at the right hand of the Power and coming with the clouds of heaven." Mark's synthesis does tell us the truth. The kind of Anointed that Jesus is could be clearly understood and proclaimed only at the end, in the light of his death and resurrection. Simon, called Peter or "Rock," did have to rethink his expectations and to accept what had originally been unthinkable for him, a *suffering* Anointed.

Mark synthesized fact and faith, history and theology. Matthew (16:13–23) will further transform the Markan account of Simon Peter's confession into a revelation.[49] He alone adds a saying reflecting Simon's postresurrection role as the Rock upon which the crucified but risen Jesus *will* build his faith community: "[Y]ou are 'Rock' *[Petros]*, and on this rock *[petra]* I *will* build my church [assembly] and the gates of Hades [death] will not prevail against it." Peter's full comprehension or faith understanding of Jesus' meaning, upon which the community called Church *will* be built, likewise comes through Jesus' death and resurrection.

Did Jesus Foresee the Church in His Future?

Jesus' view of the future did not preclude his being the source of the Church. However, choosing a starting point for relating the Church to Jesus does involve a certain selectivity regarding the important dimensions and moments of his life and ministry. In the "traditional" approach of more recent centuries, Catholics were taught that Jesus founded the Church as a monarchical, hierarchical society and guaranteed its unity precisely by giving Peter a primacy in which he was to be succeeded by the bishops of Rome.[50] Such conclusions were grounded in a reading of selected gospel texts as being literally historical or authentic sayings, in particular Matthew 16:18–19 ("[Y]ou are 'Rock,' and on this rock I will build my church"). There was also an unquestioned presumption that the existing leadership patterns of the Church were directly traceable to a Jesus who knew the entire future.[51]

Such perspectives on the Church were rooted in a "high descending Christology" wherein the emphasis was on Jesus' divinity. The Fourth Gospel especially, in its final form, laid the foundation for this approach. The Johannine Jesus speaks with sinners (4:4f.), but there is no emphasis on his eating and drinking with them. He is not called "a glutton and a drunkard, a friend of tax collectors and sinners" (Matt 11:19; Luke 7:34). Nor is his divinity "hidden." Rather, John's Jesus manifests his "glory" through signs, such as changing some 120 to 180 gallons of water into fine wine at a wedding in Cana (2:1–11). His humanity is the manifestation or epiphany of the divine glory he had with the Father before the world began and to which he returns through the hour of the cross (1:14, 17:5).

The Fourth Gospel was written at the end of the first century during a time of debate with the synagogue, when Christianity and Judaism were separating. That context, in which Jewish Christians found themselves sometimes unwelcome in the synagogues (John 8:31, 9:22, 12:42), coincided with the time when the interpretation of Jesus in Christian faith had come to the inescapable conclusion that he was to be given the title "God" (John 1:1, 20:28; Heb 1:8). As Raymond Brown observes, a kind of monochromatic portrayal protects the Johannine Jesus from whatever could be a challenge to his divinity by those Jews who refused to accept him as God's Anointed.[52] The Johannine Jesus foresees which follower would go bad (6:70–71); he also cannot pray that the hour of suffering pass because he has come to that hour intentionally (12:27). No one takes his life from him; he has power to lay down his life and to take it up again (10:18; cf. 18:6). He experiences no distress in the garden but instead is clear about all that will happen to him (18:4). He dies having consciously fulfilled all the prophecies: "It is finished" (19:30). The Fourth Gospel single-mindedly proclaims the deeper truth of Jesus' divinity, which could be discerned only with the hindsight of resurrection faith. Such a Johannine perspective became the later traditional emphasis. Throughout early Christianity and into the time of medieval scholasticism, that gospel portrait of Jesus was ever further developed.

In the thirteenth century, Thomas Aquinas maintained that Jesus had three kinds of knowledge. First, Jesus was said to have beatific vision, since his humanity already had to enjoy the vision of God that he enabled the blessed to attain after death. Second, Jesus was said to have infused knowledge, meaning that the Logos or Word had already instilled all the intellectual concepts that Jesus' possible intellect had the potential to know. Third, Jesus also had to have acquired or empirical knowledge whereby he grew in understanding, because his agent intellect was continually transforming the experiential data coming through Jesus' senses into intellectual data.[53] Because of his beatific vision and infused knowledge, Jesus knew all things in the Word: "whatsoever is, will be, or was done, said, or thought, by whomsoever and at any time."[54] He could wonder about what was new and unfamiliar only in his acquired or empirical knowledge.[55] That kind of Jesus could not have any fear regarding the uncertainty of future events, only the kind of fear that arose when unavoidable bodily pain appeared on his horizon (*Summa Theologiae* 3, q. 15, a. 7, resp.). In that regard, he could have avoided future evils by the power of his Godhead, but instead voluntarily assumed fear and sorrow to show the reality of his human nature (3, q. 15, a.7, ad 2 and 3). Able to prevent his passion and death, he died voluntarily and in control. The violence inflicted on him did not take away his life; he succumbed only when he willed to die. "He preserved the strength of his bodily nature, so that at the last moment he was able to cry out with a loud voice: and hence his death should be computed among his other miracles" (3, q. 47, a.1, ad 2).[56] An omniscient Jesus who died in that way would be presumed to have left behind a well-organized and instructed community prepared for all eventualities, a structured Church (*Summa Contra Gentiles* 4, 74, 76). That presupposition was largely unquestioned in recent centuries.

Fully believing that Jesus is true God and true man, as proclaimed by the creeds of the early councils, from Nicaea to Chalcedon, our faith seeks understanding in a contemporary frame of reference. Our theological questions reflect our experience of what it means to be human. Does believing that Jesus is "God become human" require that Jesus as human had to know the entire future? If Jesus knew the entire future, would he have been fully and truly human in the way we understand what it means to be human? Would he have been free the way we understand humans to be free? Would he have truly shared human creativity without the need to improvise? How we answer such questions influences the way we respond to others. More to the point, did Jesus know the whole future and consciously intend to found and organize the Church as a hierarchical structure? Did Jesus know that Peter would later be considered the first in a long line of popes? Did he determine how others would later claim collegial succession to the Twelve?

Many Christians have learned the formula of the Council of Chalcedon (451) that in Jesus there are two natures and one person. That council further insisted that the full divinity and full humanity of Jesus are not to be separated or divided and likewise are not to be confused—since the distinction of natures is not annulled by the union. The later Council of Constantinople III (680–81) taught that Jesus had two wills and two activities, human and divine. Contemporary theology's struggle with the issue of Jesus' knowledge reconfronts the same issues. "As history takes its course, and cultural changes occur, the teachings of the Council of Chalcedon and Constantinople III must always be actualized in the consciousness and preaching of the Church under the guidance of the Holy Spirit." Having made that observation, the International Theological Commission in 1979 declared that theologians must devote their full attention to perennially difficult questions, "for example, the questions relative to the consciousness and knowledge of Christ."[57]

In our time, to suggest that Jesus did not know the future is not to deny his divinity but to reassert one's faith in the fullness of the incarnation. In the fullness of Jesus' humanity, God truly participated in the struggle of human freedom. In that regard, biblical and theological analyses do not require the presupposition that Jesus had to know the entire future, including all the details of how he would die. The clarity about the details of Jesus' death and resurrection found in the passion and resurrection predictions in Mark 8:31, 9:31, and 10:33–34 are traceable to the postresurrection community of faith. If Jesus had been that clear, then the disciples' fearful confusion after his arrest and execution, and their initial refusal to believe that he was risen, would be incomprehensible.[58] Whether the historical Jesus focused on the meaning of his death has been a matter of debate. The sayings' "source" ("Q") used by Matthew and Luke contains no saying in which Jesus reflects on his future death or which attributes any salvific meaning to it.

The death and resurrection predictions as finally formulated in Mark (8:31, 9:31, 10:33–34) include the fuller, faith understanding of the disciples who had experienced the risen Jesus' transforming influence after his death. Their new perspective on the climactic importance of his death and resurrection was blended with a core historical memory, wherein Jesus realized that what he was saying and doing had become threatening and had put him on the path to death: "The Son of Man is to be betrayed into human hands" (Mark 9:31; cf. Luke 9:44).

If the present form of the passion and resurrection predictions is not purely historical, but rather includes a postresurrection faith understanding wrapped around a historical core, we can allow that the historical Jesus came to realize the possibility that he would be killed for what he did and said, not through some special divine foresight, but by seeing the reactions that his behavior drew. His deeds and words, which flowed from his intimate experience of closeness with God as *Abba*, had made him threatening to some who wielded power in Jerusalem. His conscious and courageous decision not to back off but rather to continue in the mission to which he felt called involved a creative struggle, the need to improvise in response to an increasingly difficult and dangerous situation. It also required an ultimate trust in the possibilities that God as *Abba* offered his future. It seems questionable or even dubious to base that trust on some clearly foreseen guarantee of resurrection available to Jesus through a divine supply of detailed foreknowledge. Taken too far, such an interpretation would diminish the fullness of the incarnation as a transforming participation in the human condition and its struggle.

Jesus was not immune to the hard decisions that ordinary people confront in their lives. As the Epistle to the Hebrews tells us, "we do not have a high priest who is unable to sympathize with our weaknesses, but we have one who in every respect has been tested [tempted] as we are, yet without sin" (4:15). In that regard, the fully human Jesus need not be considered automatically sinless. In fact, an automatically sinless Jesus runs the risk of not being authentically human as well as divine. It seems more advisable to affirm that for him, as for us, the decision to be honest, faithful, and caring entailed an exertion of the freedom whereby one defines the self that one ultimately wants to be, amid the harsh realities of the world as it is. In that light, Jesus' death was not simply a mere episode or a suffering temporarily assumed. "Whatever else was happening in Gethsemene *[sic]* and on the cross, we can be sure that Jesus was not merely pretending to struggle through prayer to maintain his obedience."[59] He was not "playacting."[60] Jesus' "loud cries and tears, to the one who was able to save him from death" indicate that, "[a]lthough he was a Son, he learned obedience through what he suffered" (Heb 5:7–8). Amid the catastrophe of facing seeming failure, feeling the utter powerlessness of a human condemned to death, Jesus had to decide once and for all to remain faithful to his *Abba* by continuing to trust in love.[61] In his death, as in his life, Jesus never wavered in his relationship to the God whose reign he proclaimed. That way of "living into" and facing his death gave it redemptive significance. In the light of his resurrection, Jesus was seen to have overcome the sinful condition of human existence by the way he lived and died in utter openness to God. The postresurrection community of disciples, proclaiming a crucified but risen Jesus, was grounded in that free, historical decision of Jesus.

In our time we have come to understand more clearly that God has freely chosen to depend on human creativity and to work through the particularity of time and place, even in the very act of relating to us in Jesus. So we can affirm without fear that, in the incarnation, God became present through a Jesus who was so fully human that he shared our limitations regarding knowledge of the future. Such a theological perspective coincides with Vatican II's recognition that there was development between what Jesus did and said and what the Gospels said about him after the resurrection.

To explain how Jesus could be divine and yet fully share the human condition and its struggle, contemporary Catholic theologians see Jesus having a consciousness of sonship, or an experience of closeness to God as *Abba*. His consciousness of his divinity remained prereflective and unthematized, like the consciousness of self one has when one's attention as a subject is focused outward.[62] A mother who gets up in the middle of the night to take care of a sick child acts as mother without thinking self-defining thoughts about herself. In her concern for her child, she acts as a loving mother without reflexive, self-defining conclusions such as, "I am a caring mother." Jesus, similarly, was focused on "others" rather than on himself. In the deeds and words that flowed from his experience of God, Jesus was intent on proclaiming the reign of God—with whom he felt an intimate closeness and to whom he prayed as *Abba* (Mark 14:36)—and not on proclaiming his own meaning via titles. It seems that the historical Jesus did not make statements about himself as God (Mark 10:18); rather, in all his deeds and words "Jesus is aware that he is acting as God would."[63] In his humanity, Jesus "lived out" the essential nature of God and of the divine person at the core of his identity—"in radical self-giving to the other."[64] Jesus' divinity, however, remained hidden and did not overwhelm the fullness of his humanity during the course of his life and ministry. Only in the light of his resurrection did it become clear that the proclaimer of God's reign was himself to be proclaimed as divine in the faith of the post-Easter community.

Within a "low ascending Christology," which fully affirms Jesus' divinity but which begins from his humanity and draws upon the Synoptic Gospels for its portrait of the historical Jesus, a broad spectrum of Catholic scholars now interprets Jesus' profound sense of intimate relationship with God in terms of his *Abba* experience, rather than a beatific vision as proposed by Aquinas.[65] As Raymond Moloney has noted, it is significant that the International Theological Commission's 1985 statement entitled "The Consciousness of Christ concerning Himself and His Mission" makes no reference to beatific vision.[66] In contemporary Catholic theology, Jesus' experience of God is understood not as some extrinsic relationship but as integrated within Jesus' created spiritual nature and having a historical development, which is not to be underestimated.[67] The special "relation to God" which permeated Jesus' consciousness found expression in his deeds and words. The sense of closeness to God permeating Jesus' self-consciousness was the motivating source of all the unexpected things he did and said.

The incarnation was an event in which the divine presence was incorporated in the full freedom of a complete humanity immersed in the struggle of history. Citing the Third Council of Constantinople, Vatican II's Constitution on the Church in the Modern World (22) reminds us that Jesus "worked with human hands...thought with a human mind...acted with a human will, and with a human heart...loved." In such a perspective, the image of the invisible God (Col 1:15) was a Jesus who did not foresee and predict every detail of his death and resurrection, although he gradually realized that what he was doing and saying would result in his being placed into the hands of those wanting to be rid of him (Mark 9:31). He gathered disciples and appointed or chose the Twelve, whom he envisioned sitting "on twelve thrones, judging the twelve tribes of Israel" when the reign of God reached fulfillment (Matt 19:28; Luke 22:28–30). Looking back after the resurrection event,[68] Mark says that Jesus instilled a sense of mission in the Twelve, his companions whom he sent *(apostellē)* to preach and to have authority to expel demons (3:14–15; cf. 6:7).

Among the Twelve, Simon called Peter is the most prominent, followed by Andrew, James, and John.

The Jesus we have portrayed from the sources does not seem to have formulated precise plans for the structure of a Church that was to last for millennia. Nor did he specifically determine how others would claim succession to the Twelve. As we shall see in the next chapter, something was left for his disciples to decide and to do regarding those specifics, although Jesus' own approach to life and death provided guidelines or a trajectory for those with resurrection faith. He offered a new future to those whom he encountered in his time and entrusted his own future to his *Abba*. The resurrection clarified the full meaning of his life and death, but his style of life had already contributed to the meaning of his death.

That Jesus went to his death with unshaken confidence is crucial.[69] As noted in the 1979 statement of the International Theological Commission,[70] his "existence for others" developed through the historical struggle and questions of his life. "[A]t the last supper and in Gethsemane he seems to have faced death as one entrusting himself to a situation and a future that were still to some extent unknown....[S]uch limits to his knowledge and foreknowledge are precisely part of his being human and not an ugly imperfection from which Jesus must be miraculously preserved."[71] At the end he trusted that his *Abba's* reign would come, even though he himself confronted seeming failure. The Jesus who had lived "for others" now willed to make an ultimate gift of himself, confident that, through his being for others even in dying, the God he called *Abba* would bring forth final salvation, the eschatological reign. He who offered hope to others, especially by eating and drinking with them, never lost hope himself nor his resolve to be for others even in death. During his lifetime, Jesus shifted attention away from himself to the reign of his *Abba*. After his resurrection, the community of his disciples could explicitly and unambiguously proclaim what had always been implicit in his deeds and words, that he himself had been the presence of God's saving love in their midst. In Jesus "God is with us" (Matt 1:23).

The findings of the New Testament sources are best represented by the idea (also put forward by Vatican II's Constitution on the Church, *Lumen gentium* 2–5) that the Church came into existence in stages. It had an "extended establishment...which extends to the entire activity of Jesus, earthly as well as exalted."[72] As Schillebeeckx observes, "The resurrection is the start and the abiding foundation of the Church's life. The Church is founded upon a salvific act of the risen Jesus, but not unrelated to what Jesus said and did in his life here on earth."[73] The developments between the community gathered around Jesus during his lifetime and the Easter faith congregations proclaiming the risen Christ mirror the stages that Vatican II recognizes in the development of the Gospels: there was a difference and yet continuity between Jesus' words and deeds, what was preached about him, and what was finally written in the Gospels. In proclaiming the reign of God, the historical Jesus was inviting his people to renewal, "to a new way of being Israel." Jesus, "as a good first century Jew, believed that Israel functioned to the rest of the world as the hinge to the door; what he had done for Israel, he had done in principle for the whole world. It makes sense, within his aims..., to suppose that he envisaged his followers becoming in their turn Isaianic heralds, lights to the world. But they would be people with a task, not just an idea."[74] The Church is the "sequel" to Jesus.[75] It is what the community that Jesus gathered *became* through his death and resurrection. The regathering of Jesus' community, through the Easter experience of his disciples, and the new understanding and proclamation of Jesus by that community are likewise part of a new history, an eschatological event that will always be.[76]

Continuing the Way of Jesus Who Came to Serve

It has been established by now, if it was not clear already, that Jesus lived in service to others. "His words and actions brought divine pardon to those who felt they were beyond redemption. He never drove away the lepers, children, sinful women, taxation agents, and all those anonymous crowds of 'little people' who clamoured for his love and attention."[77] In their efforts to express the meaning of Jesus' death, his disciples would remember how he lived *for others*: "For the Son of Man came not to be served but to serve." In Mark (10:35–45) and in Matthew (20:20–28), that saying is addressed to the Twelve, who are indignant about a request that James and John, the sons of Zebedee, should sit at Jesus' right and left in a kingdom of glory. In Luke, the saying about service is kept within the Last Supper tradition, where Jesus reminds the Twelve, who are arguing about which of them should be regarded as the "greatest," how those who are served at table are usually greater than the servants. He says, "I am among you as one who serves" (Luke 22:27; cf. 12:37). The Fourth Gospel (13:1–15) tells of Jesus putting on an apron and washing feet, and then instructing the disciples to do what he has done. The message is clear. For Jesus' community and its leaders, service and not domination is primary.

As has also been established, Jesus' service was linked to his meals, which extended the boundaries of fellowship by including sinners and outcasts (Mark 2:15; Matt 11:19; Luke 7:34). The saving mercy and unconditional love of the reign of God which Jesus proclaimed was thereby actualized. For some, however, Jesus' behavior was unsettling and its claims were rejected. Eating and drinking with sinners and outcasts was not easily or universally recognized as an anticipatory sign of the coming of God's reign. That Jesus himself did see it that way is supported by the way he chose to celebrate a Last Meal with the Twelve, during which he reaffirmed his continuing trust that God's reign was breaking through his ministry. Despite the seeming failure of his ministry, which had brought him to the brink of ultimate rejection, Jesus remained confident that he would again drink wine and rejoice with his disciples in the kingdom, which would come even though he faced death: "Truly I tell you, I will never again drink of the fruit of the vine until that day when I drink it new in the kingdom of God" (Mark 14:25; Luke 22:18; Matt 26:29). A broad scholarly consensus considers this saying, preserved in the Last Supper tradition but never used in later liturgies, to be historical or authentic.[78]

It was fitting that the Jesus who lived to serve others, and who healed sinners' relationship with God by eating and drinking with them (Mark 2:17), should use a meal to signify his willingness to accept death when it seemed inevitable. Such continued celebration of meal fellowship in the face of death symbolically proclaimed his renewed intention to serve, or to give himself, by accepting death. He would continue to serve others by completely giving himself, dying with utmost fidelity, trusting in his *Abba*, whose kingdom would come as he had always proclaimed. The words of eucharistic institution thus proclaim the complete truth about Jesus' giving of self at his farewell meal, even though the variations within the scriptural traditions (1 Cor 11:23–25 and Luke 22:19–20 vs. Mark 14:22–24 and Matt 26:26–28) reflect the retroactive influence of postresurrection liturgical formulas. Like humans long before him, Jesus used a meal to symbolize and celebrate his care and trust, but in the deepest mode of self-giving even to death.

The Fourth Gospel omits an explicit institution of the Eucharist in its portrayal of the Last Supper. Having already related the Eucharist to Jesus' wondrous feeding of the crowds gathered to hear him (ch. 6), its version of Jesus' last meal fellowship (chs. 13—17) begins with his putting on an apron and washing feet before the meal. The Jesus of this Gospel then speaks at length about love, instructing his disciples to live his *way*: "I give you a new commandment, that you love one another. Just as I have loved you, you also should love one another. By this everyone will know that you are my disciples, if you have love for one another" (13:34–35). The writer of the Fourth Gospel thereby distilled the deepest truth about the way Jesus lived and went to his death. That way of living was to be imitated by Jesus' disciples.

With the light of resurrection faith, they were to be united with Jesus like the branches on a vine: "Abide in me as I abide in you" (John 15:4).

Remembering that final supper and the death and resurrection that came after it, and looking to the future in hope, Jesus' disciples would do what he had done. This is the key point. Those who sought to live his "way" gathered in homes where they broke bread and ate their meals "with gladness" (Acts 2:46), praying, "*Maranatha*"—"Our Lord, come!" (1 Cor 16:22; cf. Rev 22:20; *Didache* 10:6). The bread and wine used in those assemblies did not simply nourish or gladden one for daily existence but made tangible the presence of the one who was to come, the risen Jesus, now called Lord and God's Anointed. "The Resurrected resumes the eucharistic community with his disciples that was interrupted by his death. [Jesus] is now with and among his own in a new way—in the sign of a meal."[79] Bread and wine had been given a new meaning or significance by Jesus and his way of living and dying. They now made him present and offered a share in his "new life." Those who celebrated Eucharist, or thanksgiving, by breaking bread together (Acts 2:42) did what Jesus had done and thereby proclaimed his death and resurrection until he comes (1 Cor 11:26).

Prior to celebrating such a vision, Jesus' disciples passed through a dark night, only after which there dawned the realization that their Jesus was a suffering servant. "Historically speaking, the hard core of the tradition suggests that all the disciples somehow or other let Jesus down."[80] The community of the unexpected had been held together by his presence, so the seeming failure of his arrest and death caused those whom he had gathered around him during his ministry to scatter to some degree. They experienced a crisis because Jesus had not left them with all the answers, especially about the meaning of his crucifixion. They had to work out their understanding or interpretation from their memories of the way he had lived and from their experience of what followed his kind of death. They came to realize that their continued relationship with a Jesus who was still living and not among the dead (Luke 24:5) required that their way of living reflect his "way." In short, they would have to be open to the unexpected the way he had been.

Jesus proclaimed, "the Son of Man came not to be served but to serve." With the hindsight of Easter faith, it seems that the postresurrection community added "and to give his life a ransom for many" (Mark 10:45; Matt 20:28), thereby proclaiming the complete truth. Through their experience of the Easter event, the disciples of Jesus realized what had previously been hidden in the ambiguity of Jesus' fully human struggle: that the path which led him to the seeming failure of crucifixion would culminate in God raising him from the dead. They finally comprehended how profoundly all his efforts had always been related to God. As the 1964 Instruction of the Pontifical Biblical Commission observes, "After Jesus rose from the dead…his divinity was clearly perceived."[81]

Through his being for others or "pro-existence" in life and death, Jesus incarnated or humanly expressed God's love and compassion for humans. His particular and time-conditioned deeds and words were the deeds and words of God become human in our midst. Now the Church had to exist because there always has to be a community or assembly both *proclaiming* Jesus, and what his life, death, and resurrection proclaimed, and *seeking to live* as he did, in radical openness to his God and all outcasts and sinners. At bottom, there is no difference between proclaiming Jesus and seeking to live as he did. For it is only by seeking to live as he did that he can be truly proclaimed. The Church is thus called to make Jesus' love, service, and offer of union with God tangible in the deeds and words of his community of disciples. Filled with the Spirit sent by Jesus, communities of disciples, in different historical moments and situations, thereby live the "way" of Jesus who now permanently dwells in their midst as the risen Christ (Matt 18:20).

Communities Facing the Future with Creative Fidelity

In proclaiming God's reign, Jesus effected an experience of hope, gathering into his community of the unexpected even persons whose future appeared to hold little possibility. He himself then died as an outcast, with his divinity hidden beneath the "kenotic" (Phil 2:7) powerlessness of his full humanity. Joseph Ratzinger vividly describes Jesus' dark night of faith, "On his lips was the bitter taste of abandonment and isolation in all its horror."[82] Yet despite the fact that there was no help that Jesus could touch or feel, he trusted that he was still in God's hand and in utmost emptiness did not let go of that hand.[83] The verses from Psalms 22 and 31 which the Synoptics put on the dying Jesus' lips tell us the truth: he prayerfully entrusted himself and all his efforts to his *Abba* (Mark 14:36). Nothing would separate him from the God he called *Abba*.[84]

Jesus' humanity has now been emphasized, but his divinity must be as well. In this light, Jesus' self-giving death should not be interpreted simply as a vicarious satisfaction offered to God by a sinless one making amends for human sin, but as a "trinitarian event." The *Abba* to whom Jesus prayed remained inseparably united with him in the Spirit of Love, as Jesus, the Word become human, hung on the cross.[85] Since God had freely chosen to become an ally in our vulnerability and suffering, the entire Trinity participated in and was affected by our human struggle—through Jesus, who in his fully human freedom chose irrevocably to love and to forgive, despite what humans were doing to him. Jesus lived out the "love of enemies" that he had proclaimed during his ministry (Matt 5:44; Luke 6:27). God's transcendent, self-giving love was incorporated in and worked through Jesus' unfaltering, trusting, human love. In his once-and-for-all decision to continue to love, no matter what the cost, Jesus absolutely vindicated God's risk-filled fidelity to human freedom.

At the moment of the crucifixion, God was not powerless but omnipotent in love, and so freely chose to be vulnerable and defenseless.[86] Having chosen to share our struggle in a transforming way, in and through Jesus, God faithfully preserved the freedom of creation, so that both Jesus and those who condemned him to death lived out their free choices. The loneliness and powerlessness of Jesus' death by crucifixion were undeserved and absurd for one who had spent his life proclaiming God's unconditional love and empowering the marginalized and powerless. Yet it was precisely through Jesus' free decision to be for others, even as he was dying defenseless upon the cross, that God had the last word about such seeming failure and absurdity.[87] The seeming failure of Jesus dying on a cross was not made into a success by the fact that God raised Jesus from the dead. Rather, *the resurrection made clear the success that had already taken place on the cross*, where the utterly defenseless and vulnerable Jesus reaffirmed his love for God and all humans, including those who were crucifying him. "God's transcendent overcoming of human failure is historically incorporated in Jesus' never-ceasing love for God and [humans], during and in the historical moment of his [seeming] failure on the cross."[88] The fully human Jesus hanging on the cross was a success in the triumph of his love. His final and irrevocable decision transformed the absurdity he suffered into a victory, made clear in the Easter event. The resurrection revealed the salvific reality hidden within his dark night of faith on the cross. As the other side of the cross and the kind of life that led to it, Jesus' resurrection was human *and* divine love's triumph over destructive power. God's trust in creation and human freedom were not in vain. In and through Jesus, compassionate love prevailed. "The God who personally died in Jesus Christ fulfilled the pattern of love beyond all expectation, and in so doing justified that human confidence which in the last resort is the only alternative to self-destruction."[89]

Mary Magdalene came to the tomb "while it was still dark" and found it empty (John 20:1). Jesus was not among the dead, but living (Luke 24:5). Death and darkness had not overcome life and light (John 1:4–5). Jesus' resurrection on the day we call Sunday marked a new "day one" (Greek text of Mark 16:2; Matt 28:1; Luke 24:1; John 20:1), like the "day one" (Hebrew text) at the beginning of creation when God said, "Let there be light" (Gen 1:3–5). In the dawn of that Sunday after Jesus' death, the new "day one" of Jesus' risen life initiated a renewed creation in which light would never be overcome by darkness, nor life by death (John 1:1–9; cf. Gen 1:3–5). Jesus was the new Adam, or the new human, of that renewed creation (Rom 5:5–19). His resurrection irrevocably opened up the possibility of a qualitatively new future lived in the light of the Easter resurrection. In the light of the resurrection, Jesus' disciples would be called to face the future with his creative fidelity.

During the time of his public ministry it seems clear that Jesus had most closely associated Twelve of his disciples with himself and his work toward a renewed Israel (Matt 19:28; Luke 22:28–30). Yet despite their sharing in his ministry and his Last Supper, Jesus' arrest and crucifixion caused the Twelve, now become Eleven, to falter (Mark 14:27–30; Luke 22:31–34). Even the resurrection was something that they initially doubted and would not believe (Matt 28:17; Luke 24:11, 41; Mark 16:11, 13–14; John 20:9, 25–27). But as the Eleven searched for the meaning of Jesus' death amid the events of Good Friday, the Church had begun to emerge in a more explicit way.[90] As the Eleven and the community gathered around them were reconstituted by their shared experience of Jesus as alive and by their Spirit-filled consensus in resurrection faith, the Church was definitively born.

The appearance narratives in the Gospels tell us about the resurrection experience inasmuch as it grounded the faith of an already-existing Church. They stress that the risen Jesus became present in the midst of the Eleven *gathered together* (Luke 24:33f.; John 20:19f.; Mark 16:14f.). The communal or "ecclesial" resurrection faith of the Eleven *gathered together* was the matrix of the community called Church, in the midst of which Jesus will always be present (Matt 18:20).

Jesus' disciples were not immune to experiences of failure or a lack of understanding. All four Gospels, it is to be recalled, present a Peter who denied he even knew Jesus.[91] But with the resurrection event, the self-manifestation of the Risen One, something different broke through; a new Spirit emerged. Peter himself appears to have been instrumental in bringing the Eleven to their collegial acceptance of the risen Lord (1 Cor 15:5; Luke 22:32, 24:34 [cf. 24:9–12]; Mark 16:7; John 20:2–9). But his own coming to full understanding should not be detached from his dialogue with the other members of the "Eleven." Likewise, the role of Mary Magdalene and the other women as witnesses to Jesus' resurrection and as participants in the dialogue of witnesses must not be underestimated, especially given that in Matthew and John the risen Jesus first appeared to them (Matt 28:9–10; John 20:14–18; cf. Luke 24:10–11).[92]

The appearances of the risen Jesus established and legitimized the official position of the Twelve, and others, as authoritative figures with a mission (1 Cor 15:3–7).[93] Their initial nonrecognition of the risen Jesus, followed by the recognition that it was the same Jesus whom they had known before his death (Luke 24:16, 31; John 20:15–16), indicates that Jesus was raised into a radically different, transformed mode of existence. His new mode of existence was not simply a resuscitation into the same kind of life. The first witnesses came to understand their experience of the risen Jesus through a process of reflection, in which they identified the Jesus they had known with this new experience of him. In other words, "[t]he experience of the resurrected was situated in another field than that of corporal vision. It was situated on the ground *[en el terreno]* of faith."[94] After the Eleven and others were "overwhelmed" by Jesus in their fear, nonrecognition, doubt, and disbelief, a transforming moment of recognition, mission, and authorization followed (Matt 28:16–20). Taken by storm through the disclosure that was their Easter experience, and seized by the Spirit, they now began to proclaim the risen Jesus who "appeared" to them as one united with God. Reconstituted as Twelve (Acts 1:26), the symbolic meaning of the Twelve was reestablished: they now symbolized Israel renewed and regathered as a christological people.[95] They became foundational, communal witnesses, consciously empowered to advance the cause of the risen Jesus. He (Matt 28:18–20; Mark 16:15–20) or the Spirit (Luke 24:48–49; Acts 1:8; John 14:26—16:16) would always be with them in their mission.

The relationship which the Eleven had with the risen Jesus to whom they "returned" was quite new. But there was also a continuity with the earthly Jesus and the way he had lived and died. Existing for others had been the very essence of his being. Those who now proclaimed the risen Christ were expected to live that "way." As the Fourth Gospel makes clear, even Peter's pastoral authority was given him because of his love for the risen Jesus, emphasized three times (21:15–17) to counter his three denials. And like Jesus the good shepherd (John 10:11), Peter would also lay down his life for Jesus' flock (John 21:18–19).

During his ministry, Jesus had lived to reconcile sinners with his *Abba*. Now his death and resurrection established a sense of eschatological forgiveness and peace, a *shalom* that radically opened his broken community beyond itself (Luke 24:47; 1 Cor 15:17; 2 Cor 5:18; John 20:19–23). Such forgiveness, reconciliation, and peace could not remain the personal prerogative of a few; they had to be shared with all humans. Thus, for Peter and the Eleven, for Mary Magdalene (John 20:2, 18 [cf. 10:3, 20:16]; Matt 28:10; Luke 24:9–10), and for Paul (Acts 9, 22, 26), the deputation to proclaim the risen Christ who "died for our sins" (1 Cor 15:3–5) was inseparable from their own conversion to that risen Jesus, in which they came to full insight and acceptance. Their sense of mission was grounded in their own personal and yet communal experience of the merciful salvation which Jesus offered through the resurrection event.

The work of Peter and the Twelve, of Paul, of Phoebe called "deacon" of the church at Cenchreae, of Prisca and Aquila in whose home an assembly or church met, of Andronicus and Junia (or Julia) called prominent apostles (Rom 16:1–7), and of the many other men and women who joined in proclaiming the risen Lord was ultimately rooted in the life and ministry of a Jesus who came not to be served but to serve (Mark 10:45). Their efforts to gather and to serve Spirit-filled communities in the time after the resurrection would have to be creatively open to the future and the unexpected, in the way Jesus had been.

From Jesus to Church: The Nuances of Development

The emerging Church did not stress unchangeability or a fixity of structures positively predetermined by an immutable divine decision. To the contrary, it was still open-ended, and had to be. Jesus had chosen the Twelve and had left an emphasis on service or "pro-existence," but he did not otherwise predetermine the development of his community. His followers had to live the way he had, with love and creative trust amid the dynamics of mutability and diversity. Open to God's universal presence, the early communities were tentative, provisional, and free to experiment in regard to their own order and structure, and in relation to the particularities of various moments and contexts. That was reflected in the diversity of their theological and structural expressions. It seems that God chose to depend on human freedom and creativity, as moved by the Spirit, to contribute to the "becoming" of the Church.

Some Gospel passages indicate that the Easter event deputized the Twelve to proclaim the risen Jesus to the whole world (Matt 28:18–20; Mark 16:15), without making reference to the intense struggle and debate (Acts 11:1–3; 15; Gal 2:1–14) that preceded the full admission of Gentiles into the community called Church. No reliable historical source describes the Twelve actually exercising missionary endeavors all over the world or directly appointing successors.[96] The existing New Testament evidence suggests that they enjoyed great significance primarily for the Jerusalem community (Acts 1:12—2:14). Many others had to come forward to assume the task of proclaiming Jesus to the world. Only later did the perspective emerge which holds that leaders within numerous Christian communities throughout the world had been deputized by and were therefore in direct succession to the Twelve.

Even if Jesus had entrusted the Twelve with the remembrance of his death at the Last Supper, the New Testament does not make clear whether only they could preside at the Eucharist, or who would succeed them in that function. There is no scriptural text that even makes reference to one of the Twelve actually presiding at the Eucharist. The writers of the New Testament were more interested in the unity that the Eucharist effects than in specifying who presides at it. In that regard, Karl Rahner has observed that a realistic view of biblical theology does not allow the conclusion that in New Testament times a special power for the celebration of the Eucharist was recognized, such that it was reserved only to a few and conferred by the laying on of hands. This is not to deny that the postresurrection communities quickly became aware that the normal celebration of Eucharist had to take place under recognized or appointed leaders.[97] As other leaders were later designated with the consent of their communities, their role in presiding at the Eucharist had to be clarified.

Despite the fact that the Council of Trent in the sixteenth century linked the words "Do this in remembrance of me" in 1 Corinthians 11:24–25 and Luke 22:19 with the institution of the Twelve as priests,[98] contemporary Catholic scholarship has recognized that the emergence of ecclesial leadership involved a complex historical development. Although the later Church attaches great importance to ordination, it has "little place" in the New Testament.[99] The various postresurrection communities initially maintained their continuity with Jesus amid theological and structural diversity. As more and more persons came forward in different times and places to carry on the mission first entrusted to the

Twelve, the communities felt free to use a variety of leadership structures.

In the following chapters we shall consider how collegial groups such as overseers *(episkopoi)* and elders *(presbyteroi)* emerged and then gradually evolved into what we know as bishops and priests. The patterns which prevailed were later strengthened in their permanence by being retroactively traced back *directly* to Jesus, or to some specific action by the Twelve. The saying "Do this in remembrance of me," from the Pauline/Lukan Last Supper tradition, was assigned in retrospect as the moment in which Jesus instituted the Twelve as priests and bishops. But contemporary biblical scholarship indicates the need for rethinking the conclusion that Jesus *explicitly* initiated a chain of ordination to pass on the power to preside at the Eucharist from the Twelve to designated successors. That reconsideration, however, in no way denies the fact that others had to succeed to the mission of the Twelve.

From the Protestant Reformation until the mid-twentieth century, Catholic theologians considered it crucial to defend the position that Jesus himself founded or instituted the Church as a society that had all the means necessary to achieve its goals, especially hierarchical authority for unity and sacraments for sanctification.[100] Such perspectives were themselves the product of historical development, but they predetermined the way that the origins of Church were interpreted.

The historico-critical method of biblical interpretation officially began to be accepted in Catholic scholarship with Pius XII's 1943 encyclical on biblical studies, *Divino afflante Spiritu*. As we have seen, such biblical methodology then received fuller sanction at the Second Vatican Council. The Constitution on Revelation acknowledged the development between what Jesus did and said and what the postresurrection community said and wrote about him. However, such perspectives were not prevalent within Catholicism when Alfred Loisy's book *The Gospel and the Church* was published in Paris in 1902. His statement "that Jesus did not systematize beforehand the constitution of the Church as that of a government established on earth and destined to endure for a long series of centuries" sparked a strong reaction.[101]

Loisy actually had no intention of denying a continuity between Jesus' ministry and the Church. Rather, in opposition to Adolf von Harnack, he clearly maintained that, on the basis of Jesus' resurrection, there had to be a visible and structured society called Church in order to continue the proclamation of the kingdom which Jesus announced as "a society." According to Loisy, "Jesus foretold the kingdom, and it was the Church that came; she came, enlarging the form of the gospel, which it was impossible to preserve as it was, as soon as the Passion closed the ministry of Jesus."[102]

For Loisy, the Church of the present represented a continuity in growth, development, and adaptation from the circle of Jesus' disciples, like a child become an adult: "[T]he Catholic Church as a society founded on the gospel, is identical with the first circle of the disciples of Jesus if she...is in the same relations with Jesus as the disciples were...and if the actual organism is only the primitive organism developed."[103] The Church organized as a hierarchical society would thus be an organic development from the seeds already planted by Jesus. Loisy maintained that Jesus had not only proclaimed the imminent coming of the kingdom of God, but also distinguished the Twelve from among his disciples by associating them with his ministry. Loisy also believed that Jesus designated Peter as the one who stands first among the Twelve. But Loisy's primary thesis was not acceptable to the hierarchical Church of his time. On July 3, 1907, the Holy Office at Rome issued its decree *Lamentabili* wherein the fifty-second "Modernist" proposition condemned was: "That Jesus never intended to found the Church as a society which would endure on earth for a long series of centuries, because in the mind of Christ the Kingdom of Heaven was identified with an imminent end of the world."[104]

As Rahner noted, "it has taken the Catholic Church fully sixty or seventy years to deal to some extent with the ecclesiological problems...brought sharply into focus by the Modernist movement."[105] In light of what contemporary Catholic biblical studies and theology can say about Jesus, Rahner believes the essential question is not, "Did Jesus intend to found a Church?" but rather, "Why did the Church have to come from Jesus?" He explains that Jesus did not found the Church in the sense of bringing a society into being in a way that necessarily involved both a conscious and clear idea of its constitution and the will to establish it: "[I]t cannot be established as a matter of historical fact that the historical Jesus either willed or carried through the founding of the Church as understood here."[106] But Rahner declares that there has to be a "community" making present the Jesus in whose life, death, and resurrection we are called to share. There always has to be a community of believers, led by those who succeed to the task of the Twelve, proclaiming that Jesus is not dead but alive, and that he is present in his risen life through their community empowered by the Spirit.

Aquinas captured an important truth in his statement that the Church of Christ was formed *(fabricata)* through the sacraments which flowed from the side of Christ (John 19:34) hanging on the cross (*Summa Theologiae* 3, q. 64, a. 2, ad 3). As Vatican II (*Lumen gentium* 2–5) proposes, the Church emerged, not in a single moment, but through a dynamic process. It has an "extended establishment" that took place in stages involving the activity of both the earthly and exalted Jesus. The Church came especially from the death and resurrection of Jesus because the meaning of those events always had to be tangibly proclaimed in the world. The experiences called Easter and Pentecost provoked a new gathering into a community called to holiness, growth, service, and renewal (*Lumen gentium* 3–4). "The new community needed no express word of establishment."[107] The "foundation stones" from which it was built were Jesus' ministry, his meals, especially his last meal before his death, and the symbolic role of the Twelve. In that sense, the Church has its roots in and comes from what the earthly Jesus actualized. *"[T]he eschatological gathering of Israel, initiated by*

Jesus, was continued by the post-Easter community of disciples in faithfulness to Jesus," but it now proclaimed the new salvific possibility established through Jesus' death and resurrection.[108] There was continuity between the life of Jesus and the life of the church, but that continuity did not necessarily mean "more of the same." Instead, "The church begins where Jesus left off."[109]

Contemporary theology's perspectives on the relationship of the Church to Jesus admittedly go beyond the language of Vatican II's Constitution on the Church, promulgated in 1964. In discussing how Jesus "established" the Church and the episcopacy, *Lumen gentium* (18–22) did not fully incorporate the insights that would flow from a recognition of stages in the gospel tradition, endorsed by the Constitution on Revelation in 1965. Yet, as already noted, Vatican II did propose that the Church emerged not in a single moment but as a dynamic process (*Lumen gentium* 2–5). And its teaching that bishops have succeeded to the place of the apostles "by divine institution" (20) did not intend to deny the fact that the constitution of the primitive Palestinian and Pauline communities had been somewhat fluid. The promulgated text simply considers the episcopate as being "of divine right" and does not interpret the historical complexities of that statement or the meaning of "divine right."[110] There was an awareness of the historical issues, but the council did not engage in any full analysis or complete resolution. Because *Lumen gentium* did not fully apply the perspectives of the Constitution on Revelation to the question about Jesus founding the Church, that task has been taken up by post–Vatican II theology. As Kasper has put it, "A council presents the indispensable 'frame of reference.' The synthesis is then a matter for the theology that comes afterwards."[111]

Loisy's saying, "Jesus foretold the Kingdom, and it was the Church that came,"[112] has sometimes been interpreted as intimating that the Church would be something unexpected for Jesus. In that regard, one must make clear that the reign of God which Jesus proclaimed was not simply "otherworldly" but also "thisworldly," and that Jesus endowed the community gathered around him with an ongoing task. As already stated above, "It makes sense, within his aims..., to suppose that he envisaged his followers becoming in their turn Isaianic heralds, lights to the world."[113] Surely the Jesus who had been radically open to trust amid seeming failure would be open to the development of the Church "from him." The Jesus who ate and drank with sinners and tax collectors, and who considered the very human Twelve, with Simon called Peter, as his friends, could certainly accept the community of disciples in any century as "his" Church. We can be confident that, despite the deficiencies of its fully human community, the risen Jesus recognizes the Church we know as coming from him and his community of the unexpected. However imperfectly, he is made present by it and sends the Spirit to work in its midst.

Yet the emergence of the postresurrection community called Church was admittedly a development beyond the community of the unexpected that gathered around Jesus during his earthly ministry. That development paralleled the continuity *and* discontinuity between the deeds and words of the historical Jesus and what was later proclaimed and written about him in the light of resurrection faith. What was finally written in the Gospels often made explicit what had been implicit in Jesus' ministry. Similarly, the Church has its foundation in the earthly Jesus to the extent that his proclamation and action, in gathering the Twelve and a community of the unexpected, were clearly open to further development and interpretation.

Francis Schüssler Fiorenza has insightfully maintained that a hermeneutics of reception best explains the relationship between Jesus and the Church. The Church's continuity with Jesus was constituted by the very way it had to interpret him.[114] The early communities' practical decisions about how to implement his "way" in their particular time and place established their continuity with him. That continuity was actualized in the disciples' judgments about what was accidental and what was essential.

As Fiorenza writes, "The meaning and significance of Jesus has endured in history because of the Christian Church's faith in

Jesus and because of the gospel accounts expressing this faith."[115] The gospel grounds faith in Jesus, but the Church grounds faith in the gospel. Emerging from the Easter event, the community of disciples that was called Church retrospectively recapitulated the full meaning and significance of Jesus, which could be known only from the way the story of his entire life ended. Thereafter, the Church continually had to receive and interpret Jesus' meaning and significance in order to show what a disciple's vision and practice should be in new historical contexts. Such ecclesial reception constitutes the Church's relationship of continuity with the historical Jesus. As Augustine observed, the Church assures that we receive the true Christ from the scriptures (Epistle 93.23). At the same time, ecclesial reception also involves the "discontinuity" of what emerges out of the present moment of experience. The Church always has to interpret the meaning of Jesus in relation to the new needs of the "here and now."

Church as Ongoing Sacrament Flowing from Jesus

To reiterate, to say that Jesus did not institute a completely organized Church in no way excludes the affirmation that the present institutional Church is his community, namely, God's people led by those filled with the Spirit. The Church is the lasting presence of God's self-communication in Jesus. There always has to be a historical or sacramental community proclaiming the irreversible presence in the world of God's salvation through the death and resurrection of Jesus.[116] The Church had to come from Jesus because the unconditional love of God that he made irreversibly present always has to be proclaimed and tangibly effected in history. There always has to be a community of disciples proclaiming that Jesus is not dead but alive and present in his risen life through their community empowered by the Spirit.

The proximate origin of the Church was a process flowing from the dynamic of Jesus' behavior and teaching. For Luke, the process commenced in Israel among pious Jews like Simeon,

Anna, and John the Baptist.[117] It received new impetus through the events of Easter and Pentecost and ultimately culminated in an ongoing ingathering by which God rebuilds the true Israel, without excluding Gentiles (Acts 15:16–18). Such a view of the Church as process can also be legitimated by the future tense in Matthew 16:18: "[Y]ou are Rock *(Petros)*, and on this rock *(petra)* I *will* build my assembly *(ekklēsia)*." The question that remains is whether the risen Christ's work of building the Church ever becomes absolutely complete before the final consummation. Does building a house on a rock (Luke 6:47–49; Matt 7:24–27) so that it will survive every storm exclude God's intending that certain components could be remodeled in order better to meet the needs of its inhabitants in a third millennium and beyond?

We look to the past in order to decide for the future. In that framework, whatever emerges later—including structures such as the *mono-episkopos* or bishop of the second century and the unifying, petrine role of the bishop of the Church of Rome—is not less "of God." One might further ask whether anything more can still emerge and be "of God." If God intended that human creativity should contribute to the formation of the early Church, is that still a possibility for the Church of the future? Is everything now fixed and determined, until the end time, whenever that may be? What might be remodeled? Can something new be introduced and still be in continuity with Jesus? Might continuity with Jesus even require that something new be introduced, so that the good news coming from him will continue to find reception among persons living in a new situation?

The Gospel of Mark emphasized the earthly ministry of Jesus and awaited his imminent coming as savior and judge. Unlike Paul, it placed no great emphasis on the Church as medium of the salvific activity of the risen Christ, but simply saw Jesus' disciples as his *new* family (Mark 3:31–35, 10:29–30) who had to be open to suffering the way Jesus had been. In the last Gospel of John, we find a high Christology emphasizing Jesus' divinity combined with what we might term a low or "unhierarchical" egalitarian ecclesiology. By contrast, the later, traditional theories of Church that presupposed John's Christology were as a rule hierarchical. As Raymond Brown has shown, the high Christology of the community of the Fourth Gospel, in which the Word become flesh manifests his glory, allowed it to place less emphasis on leadership structures than the congregations reflected in other Gospels.[118] The community of the Beloved Disciple was united in the loving relationship of its members to a Jesus who served and who left a command of love (John 13:1–35): "[I]f I...have washed your feet, you also ought to wash one another's feet....[Y]ou also should do as I have done to you" (John 13:14–15). Jesus is the vine and his followers are the branches who live in him by their love (15:1–17). As already noted, even Peter's postresurrection role is linked to his love for Jesus (21:15–17). According to the Fourth Gospel, Jesus contemporized everything he received from the Father by proclaiming it to his disciples in their situation on earth. The Paraclete who dwells in the heart of each believer within the community receives everything from Jesus (14:26, 16:13–15), but will contemporize it in each period and in each place, thus enabling Christians to face the things to come.[119]

The Johannine vision was but one synthesis that developed. Other communities had differing viewpoints about the patterns that would best enable them to continue living the "way" of Jesus. Various ways of coming to terms with Jesus' message and of being disciples produced diverse modes of leadership. Matthew, Luke/Acts, and the later "deutero-Pauline" tradition (in the Epistles to Timothy and Titus) placed greater emphasis on diverse structures of authority and leadership, which produced communities more sociologically stable than those reflected by the Johannine Epistles. That gave them more impact on the long run of history, but never without the need for further development.

In the following chapters we shall consider the nature of the unity that bonded communities with different situations, theologies, and leadership patterns into a single communion of communities, a Church of Churches. Like the community of the unexpected gathered by the historical Jesus, they never completely gathered in one place and time but were *bonded in communion* by their openness to the presence and impact of the risen Jesus in their own situation. As time-conditioned actualizations of Jesus' continued presence, those local assemblies or churches actualized the one community, or Church of Christ. They proclaimed, and made tangible by their deeds and words in the Spirit, the self-giving and creative love of Jesus the Christ and of the *Abba* to whom Jesus entrusted himself.

In speaking of the Church as a sacrament or a sign and instrument of union with God and of the unity of humanity (*Lumen gentium* 1, 3, 5, 9, 48, 59; *Gaudium et spes* 45), Vatican II adopted a conceptualization that had emerged in nineteenth- and twentieth-century theology.[120] That perspective was particularly indebted to the "new theology" and the "return to the sources" *(ressourcemont)* that had emerged in France. In 1938, Henri de Lubac had written: "If Christ is the sacrament of God, the Church is for us the sacrament of Christ; she represents him, in the full and ancient meaning of the term, she really makes him present. She not only carries on his work, but she is his very continuation, in a sense far more real than that in which it can be said that any human institution is its founder's continuation."[121]

By the time of Vatican II, that idea, along with other important insights of the "new theology," had become part of the air that theology was breathing. Theology came to realize that the historically developed idea of the supernatural had to be rethought in relation to the destiny of all humans (de Lubac), that the Christian tradition and theological reflection were inseparable from historicity (Marie-Dominique Chenu), and that the Church, wherein God dwells in a community of people open to the world, could not be satisfied simply with past historical developments or divisions (Yves Congar). During the fifties and sixties, Otto Semmelroth, Rahner, and Schillebeeckx wrote their pivotal studies about Jesus as the sacrament of God's love and the Church as the sacrament of Christ.[122] In their perspective, the Church is the enduring presence of Jesus the Christ, continuing his work of actualizing God's merciful love within history.

More recently, Kasper and Leonardo Boff have argued that the Church should be called the sacrament of the Spirit—who founded the Church after Easter by inspiring the disciples to initiate a new universal community of Jews and Gentiles in the final time. Along with Joseph Ratzinger, these theologians maintain that the Spirit brought forth something new after Jesus' rejection within Israel and is therefore the means by which the now-living and risen Lord remains present in history.[123]

According to Boff, the historical Jesus "preformed" the Church "in its essential elements—its message, the Twelve, baptism, the Eucharist."[124] But its *concrete historical* form as an institution is based on a decision made by the apostles, as inspired by the Spirit, whereby they moved from eschatology and the end-times to the present situation of the Church. The apostles thereby translated the teachings about the kingdom into a doctrine about the Church, making it an instrument and sign for the realization of the kingdom in this world.[125] The Spirit, as the principle of unity within the Trinity and also as the source of union and reconciliation in creation, makes that Church "the Sacrament of intratrinitarian relationships."

In his concern to counter any notion of the Church as static and fixed, Boff insists that the boundaries of the Church must be coextensive with those of the risen *cosmic* Christ. He locates the Church's foundation in a decision of the apostles that always has to be renewed, and he emphasizes the Spirit's role within the Church as the presence of the pneumatic (risen) Christ. Because it is the sacrament of the Spirit, no particular incarnation of the Church can be considered exhaustive: "The founders of the Church kept in mind that it was not so important to look to the past and repeat what Christ said and did, but to look to the present and allow themselves to be inspired by the Holy Spirit and the risen Christ, making decisions that would best lend themselves to salvation and to the passing on of Christ's project."[126] The task faced by Paul and the writer of the Fourth Gospel, who translated Christ's message for the Greek world, must always be repeated.

Emphasizing the activity of the Spirit within the community that makes present the risen Christ (*Lumen gentium* 48), Boff argues that "[t]he Church as institution is not based on the incarnation of the Word but rather in the faith in the power of the apostles, inspired by the Holy Spirit."[127] In his view, the Spirit originally enlightened and then continually renews the apostles' historical decision that translated Jesus' teachings about the kingdom into a doctrine about the Church. But I would maintain that the dynamic openness of the Church as institution can also be grounded in an understanding of Church as the sacrament of Jesus—who emptied self and took on the form of a slave (Phil 2:6–8). It is a kenotic, flexible Church that is truly the persisting presence of the Incarnate Word in time and space. For if the humanity of Jesus was not a masquerade or disguise, but the self-disclosure of the Word in a full human freedom,[128] then it seems appropriate to affirm that the Word who "became" human has always been open to the need for change and adaptation within history. The Jesus of history was the mystery or sacrament of God's love (Eph 1:3–10) precisely by the time-conditioned way he was human.[129] The Church is likewise a sacrament in its humanity. Its limited and time-conditioned human ministry, open to the unexpected, continues the "way" of that Jesus who was an effective sign of God's love in the struggle of human life. Like Jesus, the Church is sacrament in and through history.

It is fitting that "the risen Christ, when he shows himself to his friends, takes on the countenance of all races and each hears him in his own tongue,"[130] since he is always recognized as the Jesus who once shared the particularity of our humanity. As the community which prolongs Jesus' human, embodied sacramentality, revealing God's merciful love through what it does and says within history, the Church can quite appropriately be called the sacrament of Jesus whom God made Lord and Christ through his death and resurrection (Acts 2:36; Phil 2:8–11). That does not require it *simply* to repeat what Jesus did and said. The Spirit, with whom Jesus was filled in his ministry (Luke 4:18–22), now enables the Church, immersed in the particularities of history, constantly to reincarnate Jesus' way of living with trust and openness toward a new future so that his "way" can be dynamically proclaimed and lived in every time and place.[131] True Catholicity need never be afraid to say that "every people in the Church sings to the Creator according to their culture."[132] "The Church is at home everywhere, and everyone should be able to feel at home in the Church" in every era.[133]

2
Shaping the Early Church: Human Decisions in the Spirit, Circa AD 30–110

In proclaiming God's reign, Jesus made known that God is unconditional Love, who considers everyone valuable and wants no one to be lost, who searches for the outcast and the sinner like a shepherd looking for one lost sheep or a woman sweeping her whole house looking for one lost coin (Luke 15:1–10). When those for whom God searches have been found, that invisible God so intimately united with Jesus rejoices and celebrates, like the woman who has found her lost coin, or the father who welcomes home his prodigal son returning from a self-imposed exile.

Jesus announced a human future open to renewal. By eating and drinking with outcasts and by healing those who suffered, he showed that tears, sorrow, and alienation could be transformed. In dying, Jesus lived out what he had proclaimed by entrusting himself to his *Abba*, who then had the last word about the injustice done to Jesus. Through the resurrection event, Jesus' followers realized that he himself, in his way of living and dying, was their source of hope, and they entrusted themselves to him. Since the new possibilities revealed by his resurrection did not exclude anyone, Jesus had to be proclaimed to everyone. Much was left for the postresurrection community to do.

In their efforts, the early followers of the risen Jesus did not depend solely upon their own ability and initiative. They themselves belonged to the risen Christ because the Spirit of God had come to dwell in them (Rom 8:9; 2 Cor 1:21). Filled with that

Spirit, who was the source of their joy (1 Thess 1:6) and of all the gifts by which the community was served (1 Cor 12), the disciples were enabled to proclaim Jesus in ways that were intelligible to all the cultures of their world (Acts 1:8, 2:1–12).[1] A small nucleus of disciples grew into a community of assemblies called Church.

Yet the Spirit's presence within the community of Jesus' followers did not eliminate debate and even disagreement over how to proceed, or the need for consensus in making decisions. In fashioning the early Church, God worked through the efforts of humans who remained limited and time-conditioned, even as they lived "the Way" of the Lord (Acts 9:2, 18:25–26, 22:4). In this chapter, we shall consider how the human decisions of the early disciples, made under the guidance of the Spirit, shaped the organization and the ways of proceeding of the community called Church. We will consider both how the Church actually developed and, as importantly, the concepts and ideals it fashioned for itself.

A Community of New Possibility

Since the beginning, persons were initiated into the community of the crucified but risen Jesus by baptism, which effected what it symbolized. Immersed under water and thereby buried with Christ, new disciples were baptized into his death, so that, just as Christ was raised from the dead by the glory of the Father, they, too, might live a new life (Rom 6:4). Going into the water was also understood as a return to the womb, in order to be born again into the reign of God (John 3:3–5). The new life of the baptized transformed the way they viewed the reality around them. As members of the community that followed Jesus, they now shared his vision of a renewable creation.

The impact of the crucified but risen Jesus bursts through the words of Paul: "[I]f anyone is in Christ, there is a new creation" (2 Cor 5:17). Made holy in Christ (1 Cor 1:2), or clothed with him through baptism (Gal 3:27), the adopted sons and daughters who call God "Abba" in the spirit of the Son (Gal 4:6) are no longer bound—in principle at least—by the distinctions or privileges of descent, social class, or gender. That is made clear in the baptismal formula quoted by Paul: "There is no longer Jew or Greek, there is no longer slave or free, there is no longer male and female; for all of you are one in Christ Jesus" (Gal 3:28). Such distinctions no longer matter; only the "new creation" has meaning (Gal 6:15).

All four Gospels say that women came to the tomb of Jesus and found it empty on "day one" (in a literal reading of the Greek text). This "day one" recalls the symbolic "day one" in the Priestly creation narrative of Genesis 1:3–5 on which God said, "Let there be light," and separated light from darkness. In the Gospels, the women's arrival at the tomb is linked with the new light that comes after the darkness of night (Mark 16:2; Matt 28:1; Luke 24:1), or with the darkness that could not overcome the light (John 1:5, 20:1). The tomb was empty and Jesus was not among the dead (Luke 24:5). His resurrection established the "day one" of a new creation, in which life and light had overcome death and darkness. Jesus was the new Adam (Rom 5:12–19) in whom creation had a new beginning. The disciples came to understand that through Jesus, the creative Word of God become human, one received the life that was the light of all humans (John 1:4). "Day one" or Sunday thus became the day on which they gathered to remember and celebrate his victory over sin and death. For them, Sunday marked the eighth day of creation, the day on which God's creation was renewed, or started over again in Jesus' resurrection. That Day of the Lord celebrated a new creation that offered the hope of new possibility to all women and men, a possibility that came to be expressed in the word *ekklēsia*, or church.

EKKLĒSIA: The Assembly of God

The Greek word *ekklēsia* literally means people gathered together, "an assembly."[2] The term appears most frequently in the letters of Paul, in Acts of the Apostles, and in Revelation. In the Gospels, it is found only in Matthew in two passages. There Jesus says he will build his *ekklēsia* or assembly on Peter or "Rock" (Matt 16:18), and then gives directives about how recalcitrant sinners should be excluded from a local *ekklēsia* (Matt 18:17). Since the two passages referring to *ekklēsia* or Church do not appear in any other Gospel, contemporary exegetical scholarship asks whether they were actually spoken by the historical Jesus. In particular, there is ongoing debate regarding the second clause of Jesus' statement about Peter being phrased in the future tense: "You are Rock *[Petros]*, and on this rock I *will* build my church *[ekklēsia]*." Some scholars offer significant arguments for the authenticity of the passage as a saying of the historical Jesus.[3] A number, however, believe the saying is a postresurrection faith proclamation, recognizing the post-Easter role of Peter and making clear its continuity with the ministry of Jesus.[4]

Even if one allows that the historical Jesus may not have explicitly spoken of "my assembly or Church," that does not preclude the assertion that Jesus gathered a distinctive community that would continue his vision and aims of a restored Israel. Matthew's Gospel was itself written within a community that considered Jesus to be its builder and director, and that saw itself continuing his earthly ministry by its distinctive, "Jewish" emphasis on the justice or holiness of doing God's will (Matt 5:20, 7:21, 12:50). Whatever position one assumes regarding the historicity of Jesus' declaration about the future foundational role of Simon, the Rock, it is clear that the author or authors of Matthew were intent upon proclaiming the continuity between Jesus' earthly ministry and Peter's postresurrection ministry—which included the faith and practice of the Spirit-filled Matthean *ekklēsia*.[5]

It is difficult to say when the postresurrection community first called itself *ekklēsia*, or to specify the precise meaning intended by the initial usage of that word. Whether it originally designated the Jewish Christian community of Jerusalem, and was only later extended to other Jewish Christian assemblies and finally to Gentile communities, is not absolutely clear. The earliest followers of the risen Jesus were Jews, who still participated in the cult of the temple in Jerusalem and of the synagogues elsewhere. Known as "the sect of the Nazarenes" within Judaism (Acts 24:5, 14; 28:22), they also gathered in homes for their own assemblies, in which other Jews who did not follow Jesus were not participants.

In the Septuagint, the Greek version of the Hebrew Scriptures from the third century BC, both *sunagōgē* and *ekklēsia* had been used to translate *qahal*, the Hebrew word for *assembly* or *community*. When Christianity was emerging, Jews living outside Palestine used the term *ekklēsia* for both their political and religious assemblies.[6] In the mindset of the time, such usage expressed a lived experience of dynamic unity. But *ekklēsia* had an even deeper connotation for Greek-speaking Jews since that word had also been used to denote the "community of Yahweh." The Septuagint had rendered *Qahal Yahweh* (the assembly of the people of God referred to in Deut 23:2, Judg 20:2, 1 Chr 28:8, Neh 13:1, and Mic 2:5) as *ekklēsia tou theou*, the assembly of God.

In the epistles of Paul, both the universal community of Christians and their local assemblies are called *ekklēsia tou theou* or sometimes *tou christou*. For Paul, the universal "assembly of God," or "of Christ," was not simply an aggregate of local assemblies. Rather, the local assemblies made God's one, universal people present and visible in a particular place. And as Stephen's discourse in Acts 7:38 indicates, the assembly of Jesus' followers saw itself related to the *ekklēsia* of Yahweh's people in the wilderness of Sinai, which was Israel as the *Qahal Yahweh* in the Hebrew Scriptures.

In calling their congregation an *ekklēsia*, the early followers of Jesus indicated their sense of continuity with God's chosen people. The Jewish disciples of Jesus considered themselves the vanguard of a renewed Israel in the time of fulfillment. This observation accords with a consensus among contemporary Catholic scholars that Jesus had not intended to found a religious community distinct from Israel. Unlike the Essenes, he did not separate his community from the totality of Israel.[7] Jesus never excluded anyone from God's reign, which would somehow break through the whole people of Israel.

The upshot is that an understanding of the Christian *ekklēsia* as a new people of God differentiated from Israel as

God's "old" people need not be attributed to the earliest disciples of the risen Jesus. Initially, it was hoped that many within Israel would accept the good news of a risen Christ. Gradually, it became clear that most Jews would not be gathered into the community of Jesus' people. In our moment of history, the Spirit of Jesus requires that we reconsider the polemical differentiations that were later made.

A Network of Grassroots Assemblies

Reconstructing the experience of the earliest communities called Church is a complex task. The scriptures simply do not provide us with a clear timeline or chronology of ecclesial developments during the decades of the first century. In the Acts of the Apostles, we find layers of interwoven memories or strands that must be carefully analyzed to determine which time period they might represent.[8] In some passages, we encounter the theology and structure of the earliest decades, while in others we find the perspectives of the eighties, the time when Acts was written. Furthermore, Acts has often idealized its descriptions of early Christian community life, thereby proclaiming a model for imitation. Such idealized portrayals must be tempered by less favorable memories found in other passages in Acts or in other sources, such as Paul.

What clearly emerges from an analysis of the Christian Scriptures is a portrait of small, close-knit, and yet diverse communities seeking to live the "way" of Jesus. As those early communities grew in number and cultural diversity, their lived faith generated a richness of theological reflection and of structures. The women and men who formed the communities had to resolve difficult questions about how to proceed in implementing a Christian lifestyle for their context, not entirely unlike the dilemmas we face in our own time. Their proclamations of Jesus had to reflect their diverse cultural life experiences, so that his meaning could truly be understood and lived.

The earliest *ekklēsia* gathered in homes. At Jerusalem it was probably Greek speaking or Hellenistic Jewish followers of Jesus who assembled for prayer in the house of Mary, the mother of John, also known as Mark (Acts 12:12). When Peter unexpectedly came there one night, Mary's maid, who had the Greek name Rhoda or Rose, ran to tell everyone inside (12:13–14). After requesting that "James and the believers [Greek text: *brothers*]" be notified of his liberation from prison, Peter left for another place (12:17), perhaps an assembly distinct from the Hellenists in Mary's house and from the Hebrews gathered around James.

At Corinth, Paul initially lodged in the home of Aquila and Priscilla, or Prisca, a Jewish couple who were themselves recent arrivals expelled from Rome by the Edict of Claudius (Acts 18:2). After he no longer felt welcome to preach in the local synagogue, Paul moved into the house of Titus Justus, a Gentile who was a Jewish proselyte. His home was next door to the synagogue (Acts 18:7). Elsewhere we are told that Gaius, whom Paul baptized (1 Cor 1:14), was host to the whole Church at Corinth (Rom 16:23).

Prisca and Aquila then traveled with Paul as far as Ephesus, where they instructed Apollos in God's "way" (Acts 18:18–26). In his first letter to the Corinthians, Paul extended greetings from the church that met in the couple's home at Ephesus (1 Cor 16:19). Later still, Paul sent greetings to the church assembled in the couple's home back in Rome again, referring to the couple as working with him in Christ Jesus (Rom 16:3–5). Paul likewise greeted groups that probably assembled in two other Roman homes (Rom 16:14–15).

At Colossae, a church gathered in the home of the well-to-do Philemon, whose hospitality Paul himself hoped to enjoy during a visit (Phlm 22). At Philippi, the "brothers" and evidently sisters gathered in the home of Lydia of Thyatira, a woman who was a merchant of purple cloth (Acts 16:14–15, 40). In the Epistle to the Colossians (4:15), greetings are sent to Nympha and to the church that meets in her house in Laodicea.

Acts describes Paul participating in an assembly at Troas on the coast of Asia Minor. Everyone had gathered for the breaking of bread on the first day of the week, assembling in a third-floor room lit by many lamps. Because Paul intended to leave the next day, he kept on talking until midnight. After Eutychus, who had dozed and fallen out the window, was declared alive, Paul broke bread and ate. Then he again spoke for a long while, until his departure at daybreak (Acts 20:7–12).

In editing his material, the author of Acts may have sometimes combined traditions that historically did not belong together, so there is some question whether the passage about Troas testifies to an actual celebration of Sunday by Paul or whether it describes the kind of celebration usual in the time when Acts was written.[9] In any case, the portrait of the community at Troas as attentive to an apostle's instruction, celebrating the breaking of bread and praying together, closely parallels the core elements in the Acts of the Apostles' depiction of the Jerusalem community. (The detail of Eutychus's falling asleep also alerts us that inattention to long-winded speakers is itself a very long-standing tradition, although the many lamps in the upstairs room did diminish the oxygen supply!)

The summaries found in Acts 2:42–47, 4:32–35, and 5:12–16 paint an idealized picture of a close-knit community at Jerusalem,[10] repeatedly emphasizing perseverance and unanimous accord.[11] We are told that everyone persevered in, or devoted themselves to, the teaching of the apostles, to fellowship or communal living *(koinōnia)*, to the breaking of bread, and to prayers (Acts 2:42). Being of one heart and spirit, they shared all things in common, providing for each other according to need (Acts 4:32–35, 2:44–45). All persevered in or were devoted to meeting together at the temple every day (Acts 2:46), mutually agreeing to gather at Solomon's Portico (5:12). They also gathered in homes for "the breaking of bread," sharing their food joyfully (2:44–46). Their joy at table seems to have anticipated the return of Jesus, the *Parousia* for which the earliest communities prayed, "*Maranatha*"—"Our Lord, come!" (1 Cor 16:22, cf. 11:26).

Unfolding Realization of Universal Mission

It seems well-founded that Jesus did not intend to found a completely new religious body distinct from Israel. His aim was to gather and renew the whole people of Israel for the "inbreaking" of God's kingdom. Jesus' proclamation of God's love was not, however, limited to a "holy remnant" of Israel, or even to Israel itself.[12] To be sure, his calling of the Twelve, whom he envisioned sitting on thrones judging the twelve tribes, symbolized the renewed Israel (Matt 19:28; Luke 22:30). Yet, in the parable of the great supper, those who refused an invitation to the banquet in the renewed Israel were replaced by guests brought in from the streets (Luke 14:21; Matt 22:10). Many from the east and west would sit at the table in the kingdom (Matt 8:11; Luke 13:29). What Jesus never specified was just how the Gentiles were to be brought in. This question accordingly became a matter of much dispute within the postresurrection Church.

The early postresurrection community thought that it was living in an end-time and still hoped to gather in Israel. The fact that the majority of Israel refused to follow Jesus ultimately reshaped the identity of the phenomenon called Church in a different direction. The Jesus movement would look outward toward the Gentiles in a new way. Significantly, it was at Antioch, where the *ekklēsia* was a mixture of Jews and Gentiles, that the disciples were first called Christians (Acts 11:26), a title suitable for the wider perspective of a multicultural community united by faith in Jesus the Christ.

The earliest disciples of the risen Jesus at Jerusalem were practicing Jews, who worshipped "the God of [their] ancestors" according to "the way" of those following Jesus (Acts 24:14; also 9:2, 18:25–26, 19:9–23, 22:4; Matt 7:13–14; 1 Cor 12:31; 2 Pet 2:2). Within Judaism they were known as "the sect of the

Nazarenes [or Nazoreans]" (Acts 24:5, 14; 28:22). Some spoke Hebrew or Aramaic, but others who had lived in various places around the Mediterranean spoke Greek. After the violent reaction sparked by Stephen's discourse before the Sanhedrin, and especially his comments about the temple (Acts 7:44–49), the Hellenists left Jerusalem and scattered throughout Judaea and Samaria (8:1), while the Semitic-speaking apostles remained. Some of the Hellenists traveled as far as Phoenicia, Cyprus, and finally Antioch, where, after first preaching to Jews, they began to announce the good news of Jesus to the Gentiles (Acts 11:19–20).

From Paul's Epistle to the Galatians and from Acts, we know that the mix of Jewish and Gentile Christians in the church at Antioch caused tensions. But each source provides a different version of how the problems developed. According to Galatians (2:1–10), Paul and Barnabas had gone to Jerusalem for a private conference with the acknowledged leaders or "pillars," James, Cephas (Peter), and John. They discussed Paul's preaching to the Gentiles and decided that those such as Titus, who had come with Paul, were not required to undergo circumcision. It was agreed that God had given Paul and Barnabas a mission to the Gentiles, who did not observe the law of circumcision, just as Peter and the others had been given one to Jews, who kept the law of circumcision. That accord was sealed by a handshake termed "the right hand of communion" (*koinōnias:* Gal 2:9). The only condition was that Paul should be mindful of the needs of the poor, which he was eager to do.

When Peter later came to Antioch (Gal 2:11–14), he at first ate with the Gentiles until a group sent by James arrived. Peter then pulled back and avoided the Gentiles, out of fear of those who advocated circumcision. Other Jewish Christians, who had previously been persuaded not to be bound by the Mosaic laws, now acted as if they were. Even Barnabas joined in this hypocrisy. Paul reacted by publicly confronting Peter. He asked how Peter, a Jew who was living like a Gentile, could compel Gentiles to live like Jews.

According to Acts (10:1–48), Peter was the first to baptize a Gentile, Cornelius in Caesarea, after having a vision in which he was told to eat unclean or nonkosher animals. He then had to defend what he did, because the circumcised followers of Jesus at Jerusalem objected to his entering the house of uncircumcised persons and eating with them (Acts 11:1–18). The Hellenistic Jewish disciples, dispersed from Jerusalem by the persecution of Stephen, then began to announce the good news to the Gentiles in Antioch (11:19f.). A great number believed and were converted, but they did not observe kosher dietary regulations or the law of circumcision. After some men from Judea arrived and began to teach them that, "[u]nless you are circumcised according to the custom of Moses, you cannot be saved" (15:1), the Antiochene church sent Paul, Barnabas, and others to consult the apostles and presbyters in Jerusalem about this question (Acts 15:2–3).

Acts says that the Antiochene delegation was welcomed by the entire church at Jerusalem. Since some believers who were Pharisees still demanded that Gentiles "be circumcised and ordered to keep the law of Moses," the apostles and elders convened a meeting of the whole assembly (Acts 15:4–29). Peter spoke about how God had selected him as the one from whom Gentiles would first hear the gospel message. Barnabas and Paul are said to have stated their case next, but what they said is strangely omitted. Finally, after referring to the speech of "Simeon," James, "the Lord's brother" (Gal 1:19), announced his judgment, which intended to relieve the Gentile converts of any difficulties. They were to be instructed "to abstain only from things polluted by idols and from fornication and from whatever [meat of an animal that] has been strangled and from blood" (Acts 15:20; cf. 15:29 and 21:25). Two prophets from the Jerusalem community, Judas, known as Barsabbas, and Silas accompanied Paul and Barnabas back to Antioch. There they delivered a letter from the Jerusalem church and explained the decision not to lay any burden on Gentile converts beyond the stated necessary essentials (Acts 15:22–32).

Trying to reconcile the different accounts is a difficult task. Paul J. Achtemeier has observed that the conference about preaching the gospel to the uncircumcised, which Paul describes in Galatians, best coincides with the agenda of the meeting at which Peter defended his baptizing of the Gentile Cornelius (Acts 11:1–18).[13] Achtemeier proposes that an initial, liberal decision for supporting a mission to the Gentiles, in which Peter had a key role, satisfied Paul but probably dissatisfied many Jewish Christians. In Achtemeier's hypothetical scenario, their discontent possibly gave rise to another meeting, described in Acts 15, which may have been presided over by James, perhaps after Peter had gone to Antioch. It produced a decree with more stipulations (Acts 15:22–35), prompting Achtemeier to suggest that some may have been trying to turn back the clock on a direction already initiated. That might explain the disruption reported in Galatians, if those who came from James brought such a decision to Antioch.

The author of Acts depended on incomplete and sometimes even conflicting historical memories, which he shaped and reworked to fit the theological purpose of his composition. Clearly, Acts knows about the strife at Antioch, but wants to portray the Church as developing in complete harmony from Jerusalem. So it presents Peter, Paul, and Barnabas as participants at the crucial meeting at which James announced his momentous decision. Yet it seems telling that what Paul and Barnabas said is not reported.

If the meeting in Acts 15 was convened to resolve the tension in Antioch, then Paul evidently learned to live with its compromise. But if, instead, it exacerbated the tension—the other possibility—then the early Church never really achieved the deep unity that Acts sought to portray. That might explain why there is no mention of Paul's collection for the poor (Gal 2:10; Rom 15:25–31) ever being accepted in Jerusalem (see Acts 24:17).[14] But no matter which scenario is correct, whether there was harmony or not, the Church had once and for all been opened to the Hellenistic world of the Gentiles, who would eventually outnumber Jewish

Christians. Paul's initiative may possibly have suffered a short-term setback, but a new direction had been established that would inevitably define the future of the Church.

The Gospel of Matthew was probably written at Antioch, decades after Paul confronted Peter there about the Jewish law and Gentiles. Reflecting a Jewish Christian community that had been joined by Gentiles, Matthew portrays Jesus as the new Moses, seated on a mount and teaching in a way that does not abolish but rather fulfills the law given to Moses on Mount Sinai (5:17).[15] Without any details about meetings and debates, as provided by Galatians and Acts, Matthew makes clear that the Gentile mission was a postresurrection development by attributing two *contrasting* "sayings" to Jesus. During his earthly ministry, Jesus instructs the Twelve not to go among Gentiles or into Samaritan towns, but rather to go to the lost sheep of the house of Israel (Matt 10:5–6). By contrast, after his death and resurrection, the risen Jesus instructs the Eleven gathered on the mountain in Galilee to "Go therefore and make disciples of all nations, baptizing them in the name of the Father and of the Son and of the Holy Spirit, and teaching them to obey [*tērein:* heed] everything that I have commanded you. And remember, I am with you always, to the end of the age" (Matt 28:19–20).

In Luke, Jesus appears to the Eleven and others with them in Jerusalem and tells them that "repentance and forgiveness of sins is to be proclaimed in his name to all nations, beginning from Jerusalem" (24:47). In Acts (1:8), Jesus instructs the apostles, "[Y]ou will receive power when the Holy Spirit has come upon you; and you will be my witnesses in Jerusalem, in all Judea and Samaria, and to the ends of the earth." In the longer ending later added to Mark's Gospel, Jesus instructs the Eleven, "Go into all the world and proclaim the good news to the whole creation" (16:15).

Such gospel texts contain the central core of an ecclesiology.[16] Reducing a complex process to its conclusions, they reflect an already-developed sense of universal mission on the part of the disciples assembled together as the *ekklēsia*. They omit any chronicle of the struggle, debate, and even conflict through which the disciples of the risen Jesus clarified their intuitive consciousness of a universal mission and their sense of how to implement it.

In sum, the four Gospels do proclaim the truth: the mandate or deputation to preach to the whole world and to baptize was grounded in the Easter event. Easter faith gave the disciples the confidence that the God who could overcome death had given them a creative potential not bounded by any geographic or temporal limitations.[17] Their experience of the risen Jesus ultimately brought them to the realization that there were no limits upon their sharing the message of good news. Yet God left their humanity intact. In determining how the gospel was to be preached to all nations, the earliest disciples were not spared the need to struggle and to debate in order to reconcile different understandings of the means to achieve that goal.

Communion as Shared Reception: A Foundation of Early Church Order

Whatever the sometimes-difficult facts in reality, the ideal put forth by the summary passages in Acts (2:42–47, 4:32–35) portrays the Jerusalem community as an ideal harmony in which everyone persevered in *koinōnia* or communion.[18] That communion was understood primarily to be a participatory unity in which all the disciples of the risen Jesus mutually shared a relationship with God, given gratis in and through Jesus. The mutual reception of God's gift of self in turn generated a spirit of community and generous sharing among the recipients themselves. Christians had a communion among themselves that flowed from their mutual communion with God. Such was the life to which they aspired. We return to it here in order to clarify the theoretical foundations of the early Church, the norms which it prescribed itself.

In Acts, *koinōnia* or communion is one of a set of concepts expressing the participatory unity or corporate spirit of the Jerusalem community. Those who lived the "way" of the risen

Jesus were further described as acting "in one accord" or "unanimously" (*homothumadon:* Acts 1:14, 2:46, 5:12) and as being "steadfast" or "persevering" (*proskartereō:* Acts 1:14, 2:46), especially in communion. Such motifs were also in the air of Judaism. The Essenes at Qumran claimed to be living the "way," like Israel in the wilderness (Is 40:3). The members of that community by the Dead Sea called themselves the *yahad* or "union" (1 Chr 12:17), which Philo of Alexandria translated into Greek as *koinōnia.* Earlier, the Septuagint had used *homothumadon* to translate *yahad.* But there were significant differences between the Essenes and the followers of Jesus. The latter never used *koinōnia* as a proper name in place of *ekklēsia.* Nor was the *koinōnia* or communal life of the early churches solidified through the separation and ritual cleanness that characterized the *yahad* of the Essenes.

Paul proclaimed that God called those who are the Church into *koinōnia* or communion with Jesus, the Son (1 Cor 1:2, 9). Christ now lives in them (Gal 2:20). In and through Christ, all were participants or sharers *(koinōnoi)* in both sufferings and encouragement or consolation (2 Cor 1:7; cf. Phil 3:10). Paul also prayed that "the communion of the Holy Spirit" be with them all (2 Cor 13:13). Their *communion* of spirit was to enable them to "be of the same mind, having the same love, being in full accord and of one mind" (Phil 2:1–2; cf. Acts 4:32a). "God has sent the Spirit of his Son into [their] hearts, crying, 'Abba! Father!'" (Gal 4:6). Having shared in receiving a gift from God, Christians rightly choose to have a communion in one another's hardships and suffering (Phil 4:14; see Heb 10:33; Rev 1:9) and to look upon the needs of the community as their own (*koinōnountes:* Rom 12:13). Mutually sharing in the reception of God's Spirit produces a communal spirit of participation and cooperation, wherein all share one another's needs and material goods. Such concern about the needs of others was a "koinonial" expression of love.

According to the first letter of John (1:3–7), the faith is proclaimed so that others may have communion with those who are already in communion with the Father and Son. *Koinōnia* thus has two distinctive dimensions. It is, first, a receptive participation in the Spirit of God's self-giving, whereby we become sharers *(koinōnoi)* of the divine nature (2 Pet 1:4). Such vertical or receptive communion generates, second, an active and practical community among all who share God's gift of self. They thus have a horizontal *koinōnia* with one another, which is grounded in their mutual communion in the divine nature. "[W]e declare to you what we have seen and heard so that you also may have fellowship *[koinōnian]* with us; and truly our fellowship *[koinōnia]* is with the Father and with his Son Jesus Christ" (1 John 1:3).

Paul spoke of a bond of communion or partnership among those who worked at sharing the faith with others (Gal 2:9; Phlm 17; 2 Cor 8:23), a task which was itself an exercise of *koinōnia* (Phlm 6 and 17). Sharing material goods with the teacher who instructed one in the faith was likewise an act expressing *koinōnia* (Phil 4:14–15; Gal 6:6). It was a communion or sharing in the gospel or evangelization (Phil 1:5).

Ideally, sharing in receiving God's generosity was inseparable from the generosity of sharing with other believers. The generous contributions which the Macedonians and Achaians collected for the needy of the Jerusalem community were thus called a *koinōnia* (Rom 15:26; 2 Cor 9:13). Although those offerings were freely made, Paul believed that the contributors were indebted to the recipients. Like a grafted branch in communion with the root of a most productive olive tree, Gentile Christians owed much to the Jewish Christians of Jerusalem (Rom 11:17), with whom they were now God's beloved people (Rom 9:25–26). "[F]or if the Gentiles have come to share in *[ekoinōnesan]* their spiritual blessings, they ought also to be of service to them in material things" (Rom 15:27). Such material contributions were a communion of service, a *diakonia* (2 Cor 8:4).

In Acts (2:44–45, 4:32–35), the disciples who persevered in *koinōnia* are said to have shared all things in common. Even so, those called the "saints," or a people called to holiness,[19] did not always live in complete unanimity. At Jerusalem, those who spoke

Greek complained that their widows were being neglected in the daily distribution of food, as compared with the Semitic-speaking widows (Acts 6:1). From Paul, we learn that the Philippians were the only church in Macedonia that shared with him, by giving him something for what they had received (Phil 4:15). And he rebuked the Corinthian community (1 Cor 11:17–20) for being divided when assembled for the Lord's supper or Eucharist: "one goes hungry and another becomes drunk" (1 Cor 11:21).

Apparently, the more prosperous Corinthian Christians brought their own private stock of food and drink and, in eating, each one went ahead with his or her own supper (1 Cor 11:21). They were quite likely following the widespread Greco-Roman practice of meals at which the host and a few select guests enjoyed elegant dishes and fine wine while guests of lower social status ate and drank cheap and paltry food and wine, a custom criticized by Pliny the Younger, Martial, and Juvenal.[20] Paul would not stand for such discrimination during the Lord's Supper. "Do you not have homes to eat and drink in? Or do you show contempt for the church of God and humiliate those who have nothing?" (1 Cor 11:22).

In keeping with the baptismal formula of Galatians 3:28, the communion which Christians had with one another was supposed to transcend every boundary of class and stratification. The poor, servants, and even slaves were not to be treated as lesser members in Christian assemblies. Failing to share was unthinkable for those who had come to eat "the Lord's supper" (1 Cor 11:20). To be a genuine expression of *koinōnia*, the meal for which Christians assembled truly had to be a sharing in common. It became a principle that all who shared an imperishable gift together were expected to share perishable things with one another (*Didache* 4.8; *Ep. of Barnabas* 19.8).

Koinōnia was inherently ecclesial. Its focal point was the "table of the Lord" around which the *ekklēsia* in a particular locale gathered (1 Cor 10:21). The cup that was blessed was a *communion* in the Blood of Christ, and the bread that was broken was a *communion* in the Body of Christ (1 Cor 10:16). A unique oneness was thereby actualized among all who participated. "Because there is one [loaf of] bread, we who are many are one body, for we all partake of the one bread" (1 Cor 10:17). Those assembled as an *ekklēsia* did not unite themselves. They were made into one body by their mutual *koinōnia* or participation in the bread and the cup become Christ's body and blood.

Thus understood, the Eucharist symbolized and effected an ecclesial communion. Unfortunately, there could be a negative side to such communion. At Antioch, the influx of Gentiles gave rise to an internal crisis of *koinōnia.* When the Jewish Christians stopped eating with Gentile Christians (Gal 2:12–13), that church no longer shared one loaf at a common Eucharist. *Koinōnia* had disintegrated, and the oneness of the Antiochene *ekklēsia* was broken. Christians were encouraged to be loving and to offer hospitality (Rom 12:13, 14:1; 1 Pet 4:8–9; Heb 13:1–2), but they were also instructed not to welcome into their homes anyone who brought a false teaching (2 John 10–11). Hospitality was to be denied, "for to welcome is to participate *[koinōnei]* in the evil deeds of such a person." Only those who walk in light have *koinōnia* with God and with one another (1 John 1:6–7).

Paul excoriated the Corinthians for allowing a man living in an incestuous relationship to remain in their community (1 Cor 5:1–8). He instructed them not to associate with any "brother" Christian if he is sexually immoral, greedy, an idolater, an abusive speaker, a drunkard, or a robber, and not even to eat with such a person (1 Cor 5:9–11). Evil persons inside the community had to be judged and expelled (1 Cor 5:12–13). The unacceptable behavior of some "Christians" led to the establishment of criteria for exclusion.[21]

Jesus' meal fellowship with "sinners and outcasts" proclaimed the reign of the God of unconditional love, but it caused some to reject him as "a glutton and a drunkard, a friend of tax collectors and sinners" (Matt 11:19). In the postresurrection assemblies, communion in the bread become the body and in the cup become the blood effected a unique bond between Jesus and the members of his community. But it likewise separated Jesus' followers from persistent sinners who were purposefully excluded. In a passage found in no other Gospel and cited already, the Matthean Jewish Christian community was directed first to warn a brother in sin, then to report him to the *ekklēsia*, and finally, if there still was no change of heart, to treat him, ironically, as a Gentile or tax collector (Matt 18:15–17).

The policy of shunning grievous sinners paralleled the practice called *herem* in Judaism. Certain Christians were declared *akoinōnetos*, cut off from the communion, or excommunicated. As Paul exclaimed in 1 Cor (16:22), "Let anyone be accursed *[anathema]* who has no love for the Lord." Yet the goal, it should be emphasized, was not to permanently exclude the person, but to shame the one excluded into correcting his or her behavior (2 Thes 3:14–15). In Matthew, the passage about excluding a person from the assembly or church is thus carefully located between the parable about searching for one lost sheep (18:10–14) and instructions about forgiving not seven but seventy-seven times, followed by the parable about the unforgiving servant, which reminds all followers of Jesus that they must forgive small debts because their own great debts have been forgiven (18:21–35).

The internal communion of the early Jewish Christians also demarcated a growing separation from other Jews who chose not to believe in the risen Jesus.[22] The Pharisees, who assumed primary leadership within Judaism after the destruction of Jerusalem and the temple, did not accept the risen Christ and apparently dissuaded other Jews from following him by making his disciples feel unwelcome in the synagogues (Matt 23:13; John 9:22, 12:42, 16:2). As more and more Gentiles came from east and west and took their place at the table (Luke 13:29; Matt 8:11), no longer having to settle for "the children's crumbs" from the table (Mark 7:24–30; Matt 15:21–28), the relationship between church and synagogue deteriorated.

The *koinōnia* that Christians had with one other was thus both inclusive and exclusive, in response to internal problems and external divisions. Those united with Jesus were bonded to one another, but at the same time their communion excluded recalcitrant sinners and increasingly denoted their separation both from other "Christians" whose faith or behavior was problematic and from Jews who did not become disciples of Jesus. Material support and hospitality were extended to fellow believers, but denied to those not in the unity of faith. The deep unity that Christians enjoyed among themselves intensified their disunity from others. The "holy kiss" of peace which they shared with one another was not given to those who were "anathema," nor, as later tradition testifies, to those not yet fully initiated into the assembly.[23]

A Cosmic Body of Christ: Corporate Historical Sacrament

Although the Church is never called the Body of Christ in Paul's letters to the Corinthians or Romans, a relationship is suggested in passages dealing with the Eucharist. It is the *ekklēsia* that assembles for the Lord's Supper (1 Cor 11:18). And it is by their *koinōnia* in Christ's body and blood that those assembled are united into the Body of Christ (1 Cor 10:14–21). Paul's imagery is very concrete and simple. One loaf (of *leavened* bread in the early Church) is broken and shared by the many; so the many are one body, in and through their communion in the Body of Christ. Accordingly, we turn now to the theme of the Body of Christ in order to understand more deeply the communal character of the Church.

In Corinthians and Romans, we find the idea that through baptism a person is identified with the Body of Christ who died and was raised up (1 Cor 15:2–29; Rom 6:4–13). In one Spirit, all of us, whether Jew or Greek, slave or free, were baptized into one body (1 Cor 12:13). Having died to the law through the Body of Christ, we belong to the one who was raised from the dead (Rom 7:4). Having become one spirit with Christ (1 Cor 6:17), we share his life and will be united in his resurrection (Rom 6:5; 1 Cor 6:14). Or, as Galatians (3:27) proclaims, "As many of you as were baptized into Christ have clothed yourselves with Christ."

For Paul, our bodies are members of Christ (1 Cor 6:15). Just like a hand, foot, eye, or ear, we are the many members of one body (1 Cor 12:12–31; Rom 12:4–8). And so, despite our diversity and our different gifts, as apostles, prophets, teachers, workers of mighty deeds or miracles, healers, assistants, administrators, speakers in tongues, and interpreters, we need one another and must care for one another. The diversity or variety of our gifts must work together for the unity of the whole Body of Christ.

Only in Colossians and Ephesians, which a number of contemporary scholars consider deutero- or post-Pauline, is the Church called the Body of Christ.[24] It is described as a living, universal, corporate reality in Christ, and related to a kingdom into which one can be brought (Col 1:13). Expanded to cosmic proportions, the Church is associated with the fulfillment of God's plan, the "mystery" revealed in the fullness of times, to unite ("recapitulate") everything in the heavens and on earth in Christ as head (Col 1:26–27; Eph 1:3–10). Colossians (2:9) sees the "fullness" of the deity dwelling in bodily form in Christ. "He is the image of the invisible God, the firstborn of all creation" in whom everything was created. As the fullness who reconciled everything, "making peace through the blood of his cross," Christ is the head of the body, the church (Col 1:15–20, 24–25). His peace must reign in the hearts of the members called into one body (Col 3:15).

Ephesians declares that God has made the exalted Christ, with all things beneath his feet, the head of the church, which is his body. The Church itself is "the fullness of him who fills all in all" (1:22–23). Gentiles and Jews are now members of the same body, heirs and partners together in the promise in Christ (Eph 3:6). All are called to live with humility, gentleness, and patience, and to bear with one another in love. They must make every effort "to maintain the unity of the Spirit in the bond of peace. There is one body and one Spirit" (Eph 4:2–4).

The whole body must remain connected with its head, Christ, who is the source of its growth (Col 2:19). By truly acting in love, we grow into Christ who is the head—"from whom the whole body, joined and knit together by every ligament with which it is equipped, as each part is working properly, promotes the body's growth in building itself up in love" (Eph 4:15–16). Christ is both head and savior of his body the Church: he "loved the Church and gave himself up for her" (Eph 5:25). Ephesians (5:22–31) presented that love of Christ for his Church as a model for the husband's relationship to his wife: "[H]usbands should love their wives as they do their own bodies." But that insight was expressed in a time-conditioned manner that unfortunately also seemed to enshrine the hierarchical subordination found within the first century's patriarchal family structure of husband, wife, children, and servants or slaves.

According to Ephesians, the goal of Christ's salvific activity is to establish the Church in its holiness: "[He] gave himself up for her, in order to make her holy by cleansing her with the washing of water by the word, so as to present the church to himself in splendor, without a spot or wrinkle or anything of the kind—yes, so that she may be holy and without blemish" (Eph 5:25–27). Yet, as Raymond Brown has noted, that perspective differs from the emphasis of 2 Corinthians 5:14 and Romans 5, where Christ died for all, including the unrighteous and sinners.[25] In Colossians, Paul is now called a servant of the Church (Col 1:24–25), and the ministries of apostles, prophets, evangelists, pastors, and teachers serve to build up the Body of Christ (Eph 4:12). The Church is now more of an end in itself. The great *mysterion*, or God's hidden plan that has been revealed, is Christ and the Church (Eph 5:32).

The vision of the Church as Christ's holy and spotless body, or a cosmic fullness, should be tempered by a certain reserve. The Church is the Body of Christ, and it does mediate holiness; but Christ is more than the Church, and there are times when those who are the earthly Church may not mediate his presence by what they do and say. Just as Jesus was the image of the invisible God (Col 1:15) by the way he was human, so the Church is the image of the now invisible Christ by the way it is human. It is a transformed community that leads others to look beyond themselves, and indeed itself, to God's love and mercy. Jesus did not proclaim his own goodness but that of his *Abba* (Mark 10:17–18). That must be kept in mind lest an emphasis on the Church's perfection seem unwelcoming to those living in imperfection and sin.

A further point to keep in mind is that a cosmic vision of the Church, in which earthly believers are joined to heavenly "saints in the light" (Col 1:12), should not be disengaged from the perspective of First Corinthians (10:16–17), where the many become one body in Christ through their communion in the Eucharist. Our primary experience of the Church as Body of Christ comes through a local assembly of ordinary people united through, with, and in Jesus (Matt 18:20). He is "God with us" (Matt 1:23) who once gathered sinners and outcasts around him (Matt 11:16–19) and who as the risen Christ will always be with us, "to the end of the age" (Matt 28:20). Nevertheless, the cosmic vision of Church rightly proclaims that our communion with Christ and one another is not limited to history. As our love relationship with another person does not die when she or he dies, our communion as a resurrection people transcends time and space. In and through Christ, there is a deeper communion of saints.

Wherever two or three are gathered in his name, Jesus is in their midst (Matt 18:20). And those in whom he continues to be present in history do to him (Matt 25:34–40) what they do for the hungry, the thirsty, the stranger, the naked, and the imprisoned. Ordinary things done by ordinary people do have cosmic implications. As a community celebrating with the elements of life—such as water, bread, wine, oil, and the touch of a hand, transforming them by the word of faith—the Church continues to make present the mystery or sacrament of Jesus who made tangible the love of the invisible God by what he did and said. As Body of Christ, the Church effects what it symbolizes in history. It actualizes a mystery or sacrament of cosmic proportions: the union of God and humanity, and a unity among humans. That is the mystery revealed or actualized by Jesus, and by the community called Church that embodies and continues his presence within history (Eph 1:3–23).

The Pluriformity of Early Leadership Patterns

The image of the Church as the Body of Christ, with Christ as its head, is significant in two regards: cosmically, inasmuch as our communion with one another is radiated through Christ, and pragmatically, inasmuch as that image indicates the critical role believers have to play in realizing Christ's plan. Just as a body must have organs in order to function, so must the Body of Christ have organizational structures, at once dependent on, yet essential for, the mission of proclaiming his good news.

A number of patterns were available as models that the early Christian assemblies could imitate.[26] In Judaism, there were the "elders" *(zeqenim)* in the synagogues, and the "overseer" *(mebaqqer or paqid)* in the Essene Community at Qumran (1 QS 6:12; CD 14:9). In the Greco-Roman society of the Mediterranean basin, there were the private associations or clubs for religious and social purposes, and the patriarchal family structure of a father ruling over his obedient "household" of wife, children, and slaves. The churches of the first century reflected all of these models to some degree. In this section we will consider the manifold leadership patterns or roles operative in the earliest decades.

The Twelve

Jesus himself chose the group called "the Twelve."[27] The fact that they became known as "the Eleven" after Judas Iscariot's departure corroborates their existence during Jesus' earthly ministry. In an authentic saying preserved in Q (Matt 19:28; Luke 22:29–30), Jesus tells the Twelve that they will sit on twelve thrones judging the twelve tribes of Israel. That was the role Jesus seems to have envisioned for them within a renewed Israel.

In the previous chapter, we considered how the faith of the Eleven was foundational for the emergence of the postresurrection Church. Describing the election of Matthias to replace Judas, Acts 1:15–26 defines the Twelve as official witnesses to the resurrection, who had been with Jesus throughout his entire ministry, from his baptism by John until the day that he was taken up. The Book of Revelation (21:14) describes the wall of the heavenly Jerusalem as having twelve foundations engraved with "the twelve names of the twelve apostles of the Lamb."

Mark (3:14–15) interpreted the role of the Twelve by saying that Jesus named them as his companions whom he would send to preach the good news, with authority to expel demons. We are told that they were sent out two by two, instructed to carry nothing for their journey, but to depend on those who received them (Mark 6:7–13). In Matthew (10:5–8), the earthly Jesus sends them to the lost sheep of Israel to proclaim the kingdom and to heal. The risen Jesus gives them a universal mission (28:16–20). In Luke (24:45–49), the risen Jesus opens their minds to the understanding of the scriptures and tells them that penance for the forgiveness of sins is to be preached to all nations, beginning from Jerusalem. They are to be witnesses. In Acts (10:39, 42), they are witnesses to all that Jesus did during his ministry, commissioned by the risen Jesus "to preach to the people and to testify that he is the one ordained by God as judge of the living and the dead." Both Luke 24:23 and Acts 1:14 say that others were with the Eleven gathered together. They are not apart from a wider community of disciples.

The New Testament provides no evidence of the Twelve working outside Palestine, except for Peter at Antioch (Gal 2:11) and perhaps at Corinth (1 Cor 1:12). According to Acts, they concentrated not on administration but on prayer and the ministry of the word (6:2–4). Yet only Peter and John are actually portrayed as actively preaching in Jerusalem (1:15, 2:14, 3:1, and 4:13) and Samaria (8:14). Whatever collective role the Twelve had in decision making at Jerusalem (Acts 6:2; 15:6), we shall see that it was never isolated from other leadership structures. The notion that the Twelve were the first bishops emerges later.

Simon the "Rock"

Four of the Twelve—Peter and Andrew, James and John—are mentioned more frequently than the others. Of all the Twelve,

Simon called "Rock," *Cephas* or *Petros,* is the most prominent. In Galatians (1:18), Paul says he visited with Peter in Jerusalem for fifteen days. Peter is also a participant in the meeting about the Gentile mission (2:9) and is the person whom Paul confronts during the crisis at Antioch (2:11). There are four references to Peter in 1 Corinthians (1:12, 3:22, 9:5, and 15:5), where Paul presents him as the first witness of the resurrection (15:5). In Acts 1:15—11:17, Peter stands in the middle of the brothers before they receive the Spirit (1:15) and then becomes their primary preacher in the Spirit (2:14). He is the first to baptize a Gentile (10:48) and is a proponent of the Gentile mission in Acts 15.

In the Gospels, Simon Peter always appears first in the lists of the Twelve (Mark 3:16–19; Matt 10:2–4; Luke 6:14–16; cf. Acts 1:13), and he has the most active role among them. In the Fourth Gospel, Simon Peter is even mentioned more than the "disciple whom Jesus loved," the founder of the Johannine community (19:35, 21:24). We have already discussed Simon Peter's confession of Jesus as Messiah in Mark 8 (Matt 16; Luke 9) and his denial of Jesus in Mark 14 (Matt 26; Luke 22; John 18). We also noted Simon's pivotal role in the emergence of resurrection faith among the Twelve. He is portrayed as the first male disciple to have experienced the risen Jesus; Matthew and John describe appearances to women first.

In 1 Corinthians 15:5, Paul says that Jesus appeared to Cephas and then to the Twelve. The resurrection accounts in Mark, Luke, and John also explicitly refer to Simon Peter. In Mark (16:7), the women at the tomb are instructed to tell the disciples, and specifically Peter, that Jesus has risen. In Luke (24:12) and in John (20:6), Peter goes to the tomb to see that it is empty. In Luke's account of the Last Supper (22:32), Jesus prays that Simon's faith might not fail so that he may turn back and strengthen his brothers. Simon is then in the midst of the Eleven as they come to understand that Jesus had been raised from the dead: "The Lord has risen indeed, and he has appeared to Simon!" (Luke 24:34). Matthew's account of the resurrection makes no explicit reference to Simon, but only in that Gospel does Jesus previously tell Simon that he is the Rock *(Petros)* on which the Church *will* be built (Matt 16:18). As indicated above, in that passage, Simon Peter's central role in the emergence of the Church—through the resurrection experience and the coming of the Spirit—is explicitly, but perhaps retroactively, grounded in the earthly ministry of Jesus, thereby making clear the continuity between Jesus and the Church built upon Peter's resurrection faith.[28]

In Mark (1:17) and Matthew (4:19), Simon and Andrew are called to be fishers of men.[29] Luke (5:1–11) tells of a miraculous catch after which Jesus instructs Simon: "Do not be afraid; from now on you will be catching people." In the appendix to the Fourth Gospel, written after Peter's crucifixion (21:18–19), the risen Jesus facilitates a remarkable catch of fish and then asks Peter to state his love for him three times, while telling him to feed his lambs, to tend his sheep, and to feed his sheep (21:1–17). In the Gospel that comes from the community of "the disciple whom Jesus loved," Peter was appointed shepherd because of his love for Jesus, elicited three times to offset his earlier denial.

The role of shepherd brought ministerial obligations. Like Jesus the good shepherd, Peter would have to know his sheep, lead them to pasture, and lay down his life for them. Those whom he calls by name will follow him because they "know his voice" (John 10:1–18). The Fourth Gospel also makes clear that Peter's unique role could not involve domination. After washing the feet of the disciples, including those of the protesting Peter, the Jesus who acted like a servant reminds everyone: "Very truly, I tell you, servants are not greater than their master, nor are messengers [in Greek: *apostolos*] greater than the one who sent them" (John 13:16). That saying is extraordinary in a Gospel that otherwise does not speak of apostles, but of disciples.

Peter's role was never isolated from that of all the other disciples.[30] To reiterate, in Acts 11:1–18, he has to defend his baptism of the household of the Gentile Cornelius; and later he is also confronted by Paul (Gal 2:11–14). Peter is entrusted with the keys of the kingdom and given the authority to bind and loose in the context of the universal *ekklēsia* (Matt 16:19); but all disciples, in whose midst Christ is present (Matt 18:20), seem to be given the power to bind and loose in the context of a local *ekklēsia* (Matt 18:18). While Peter is appointed shepherd in John 21, all the disciples (Thomas being absent) receive the Spirit and are sent to forgive or to retain sins in 20:21–23.

The Seven

In Acts 6:1–6, the Twelve mediate a dispute between Semitic-speaking Jewish Christians and Greek-speaking or Hellenist Jewish Christians. The controversy arose because Hellenist widows were being overlooked in the daily distribution of food. The deeper theological differences between the two groups, such as the Hellenists' perspectives on the temple (Acts 6:13–14, 7:48), go unmentioned in this context. To resolve the problem, the Twelve are said to instruct the Hellenists to choose seven men with good reputations, "full of the Spirit and of wisdom," whom the Twelve then appoint to the task of serving at tables by praying over them and laying hands on them.

The Seven are said to have been chosen so the Twelve could concentrate on prayer and the ministry of the word of God, without having to wait on tables *(diakonein)*. But the Seven do not seem to be "deacons."[31] They are never portrayed as waiting on table; instead they carry on the same ministry as the Twelve. Two of the Seven, Stephen and Philip, preach and baptize (Acts 6:8—8:40). In considering the roles of the Twelve and the Seven, one might recall the narrative about Jesus feeding "five thousand" on the Jewish side of the Sea of Galilee, in which there were *twelve* baskets of leftovers (Mark 6:35–44; Matt 14:15–21). In a second story about Jesus feeding "four thousand" on the Gentile side of the lake, there were *seven* baskets of leftovers (Mark 8:1–9; Matt 15:32–38). What the Twelve were among Hebrew or Aramaic-speaking Jewish Christians, the Seven were among Hellenist Jewish Christians. During the turmoil following the martyrdom of Stephen, the remaining six had to leave Jerusalem, while the Semitic apostles remained (Acts 8:1).

James, Brother of the Lord and Pillar of the Church

In 1 Corinthians 15:5 and 7, we read that Jesus appeared to Cephas and the Twelve, after that to five hundred brothers, and next to James—who is thus distinguished from the Twelve, then to all the apostles, and finally to Paul. Both the Epistle to the Galatians and Acts of the Apostles present James as a person of obvious importance in Jerusalem. Other "brothers" (or relatives) of Jesus were active in the Jerusalem community (Acts 1:14; cf. Mark 6:3; Matt 13:55), but James's leadership role brought him particular recognition and prominence. As previously noted, Peter is said to have requested that James be informed about his liberation from prison (Acts 12:17). During Paul's first visit to Jerusalem, three years after his conversion, he stays with Cephas or Peter and sees no other apostle, but only James, whom he identifies as "the Lord's brother" (Gal 1:19). Paul also tells us that his mission to the Gentiles was approved at a later meeting with the acknowledged "pillars" in Jerusalem, who were James, Cephas, and John (Gal 2:9). And, as we have also seen in Acts (15:13-21, 21:25), James is portrayed having a central role in the meeting about the debate over circumcision and Jewish practice in Antioch.

Although Paul's reference in First Corinthians (9:5) seems to presume that "the brothers of the Lord" were known to the Corinthians, there is no evidence that James ever left Jerusalem. During Paul's last visit to that city, James was still there, presiding over a group of "elders" gathered around him (Acts 21:18). Yet, although he did not personally found new churches, James clearly made his influence felt beyond Jerusalem. The group who came from him caused the problem in Antioch (Gal 2:12), even influencing Peter's behavior, to which Paul strongly reacted. James was evidently someone with whom one had to reckon. But, like Peter, the Twelve, and the Seven, James shared the mission of proclaiming the message of the risen Jesus with many others.

Apostles, Prophets, and Teachers

Jesus was an itinerant teacher moving through Galilee and Judaea. According to Mark (6:7; also see Luke 9:1ff. and Matt 10:1ff.), he sent the Twelve out *two by two.* There is evidence, however, that many more than the Twelve continued his style of ministry in Palestine and its surrounding regions. Pairs of itinerant preachers populate the Gospel of Luke and Acts. In Luke (10:1–16), seventy-two (or seventy in some manuscripts) are said to have been sent out to preach *two by two*, taking no provisions with them. As they moved from town to town, they depended on those who accepted their preaching to give them food and lodging. Luke (24:1–8) has *two* men in dazzling garments ask the women at the empty tomb, "Why do you look for the living among the dead?" *Two* are on the road to Emmaus and then return to the Eleven in Jerusalem after they realize that they have encountered Jesus (Luke 24:13–35). And *two* men in white suddenly stand next to the apostles after Jesus' ascension in Acts 1:10. Such passages reflect the fact that the prophets and teachers who proclaimed the message of the risen Jesus were sent out in pairs, as was the case with Barnabas and Paul in Acts 13:1–3.

Looking back, Ephesians (2:20) will say that the "apostles and prophets" are the foundation on which the Church was built. But this verse requires some interpretation. Throughout Acts, the term "apostle" (an envoy, or one "sent") usually designated the "Twelve," who had been with Jesus during his earthly ministry, had witnessed his resurrection (1:21–22), and were later filled with the Spirit (2:4). Beyond the Twelve, Acts extended the term "apostle" only to Barnabas and Paul (14:4, 14). Filled with the Spirit (Acts 9:17) after his conversion by the risen Jesus, Paul clearly identified himself as an apostle (1 Cor 9:1, 15:9; Rom 1:1). For him, though, the Twelve were distinguished from a larger group of apostles (1 Cor 15:5–7) who worked as missionaries and who were also called prophets and teachers.

According to Acts 13:1–3, certain prophets and teachers at Antioch—namely Barnabas, Simeon known as Niger, Lucius of

Cyrene, Manaen, and Saul—were worshiping the Lord and fasting when the Holy Spirit spoke to them, "Set apart for me Barnabas and Saul for the work to which I have called them." After fasting and praying the group imposed hands on these two and sent them off. Thus "sent out by the Holy Spirit," they embarked on what later became known as Paul's first missionary journey (Acts 13:4—14:28).

Barnabas had earlier been sent to Antioch from Jerusalem (Acts 11:22). Other prophets from Jerusalem followed. One was Agabus, who subsequently moved to Caesarea (Acts 11:27–30, 12:25, 21:10). The Jerusalem church later commissioned Judas Barsabbas and Silas, two leading men of the community (Acts 15:22, 27) and prophets (15:32), to carry the crucial letter to Antioch after the meeting about Jewish law and practice.

Acknowledging all who were apostolic in the early Church is an impossible task, but it is important that we realize it was not just Peter, Paul, and a few others. A multitude of prophetic apostles was at work in the early decades. Barnabas certainly continued his efforts after his split with Paul (Acts 15:39). Paul later presumes that he was known to the Corinthians (1 Cor 9:6). John Mark, whom Acts blames for the separation of Paul and Barnabas, likewise remained active (Phlm 24; Col 4:10; 2 Tim 4:11). In Romans (16:7), Paul greeted Andronicus and Junia, a man and woman, as prominent apostles. Paul's reference to "apostles of the churches" may indicate a group of persons appointed for a specific task (2 Cor 8:23). The Gospel of Matthew speaks of welcoming Christian prophets (10:41) and of scribes who are learned about the reign of God (13:52). It also gives a warning about false prophets (7:15–23). Clearly, the Church we know emerged out of the labor of many whom our sources have left anonymous.

The church order document called the *Didache* or "Teaching of the Apostles" indicates that some communities long retained and valued the Antiochene structure of prophets-teachers. Dated around 90 to 100 in its final form and probably composed in a rural, breadbasket region of Syria where grain grew on the mountainsides

(9:4), the *Didache* reflects a time of structural transition. Its communities so honored the itinerant prophets and teachers that they had to be exhorted not to look down upon the more recently appointed, resident leadership structure of overseers *(episkopoi)* and deacons (15:1–2).

Using the terms *teachers*, *apostles*, and *prophets* interchangeably, the *Didache* (10:7) says that prophets should be allowed to give thanks or "eucharisticize" *(eucharistein)* as they wish. It also provides criteria for distinguishing true teachers-apostles-prophets from false ones (ch. 11). True "apostles and prophets" never stay in a place more than two days. They never ask for money and receive only enough bread for the journey to their next destination. They never eat anything at a meal they ordered in the Spirit, and the truth of what they teach is recognized by the way they live. Constantly on the move, the apostles and prophets of the *Didache*'s milieu do not seem to be traveling the long distances between cities of the ancient world. Their lifestyle is suited to the proximity of small towns and villages in rural areas, which may have preserved the pattern of self-authenticating prophetic ministry longer than urban churches.[32]

Paul, an Urban Apostle

According to Acts, after his conversion Saul or Paul began his ecclesial ministry as a Spirit-filled prophet sent out from Antioch with Barnabas on a mission to Asia Minor. As an itinerant apostle founding new churches, Paul later traveled from city to city throughout the Mediterranean, which would have required some strategic planning and organization. Unlike prophetic apostles who depended on others for their support, Paul generally chose not to make his living by the gospel (1 Thess 2:9; 1 Cor 9:1–18), perhaps for strategic reasons. It seems that some interpreted this decision as indicating a lack of trust, since we find Paul defending himself, and the fact that he accepted nothing from the Corinthians, against Hebrew Israelite "super-apostles" of Christ

(2 Cor 11:5–23, 12:11–17) who may also have preached a different Christology to the Corinthians (2 Cor 11:4).

The mission of apostles like the Twelve and Paul was grounded in their personal experience of the resurrection. Paul declares that the risen Jesus was seen by Cephas and the Twelve, by five hundred brothers at once, by James, then by all the apostles, and last of all by himself, "the least of the apostles" (1 Cor 15:5–9). He insists that he did not receive his mission from any apostle at Jerusalem but directly from God (Gal 1:15–20). Paul's apostolic perspective was universalist or catholic. He showed continuous concern for all his churches (2 Cor 11:28; 1 Cor 4:14–21), intervening from afar when necessary (1 Cor 4:14), giving directives (1 Cor 7:17), and warning against factions when conflicts developed between his converts and those of another (1 Cor 1:10–17, 3:4–6; see 16:12). But it seems that he also never left his churches without some kind of local leadership. As early as First Thessalonians (5:12–13), Paul urged his readers "to respect those who labor among you, and have charge of you in the Lord and admonish you; esteem them very highly in love because of their work."

Paul never worked alone. His ministry was facilitated by a whole array of persons, like the many men and women whose help he acknowledges in Romans 16:1–15. He was even more closely assisted by his "coworkers," such as Timothy, whom he sent to represent him in the cities of Thessalonica, Philippi, and Corinth (1 Thess 1:1, 3:1–5; Phil 2:19–23; 1 Cor 4:17; Rom 16:21; Acts 16:1—17:15), Titus whom he sent to Corinth (2 Cor 8:16–23, 12:18), and Silas or Silvanus (1 Thess 1:1; 2 Thess 1:1; 2 Cor 1:19; Acts 15:40—17:14). In Paul's words, Timothy's task was to remind the Corinthians "of my ways in Christ Jesus, as I teach them everywhere in every church" (1 Cor 4:17).

Paul also had coworkers who were sent to him by a church. Epaphroditus was sent by the Philippians (Phil 2:25–29; 4:18). The unidentified "brother" who accompanied Titus to Corinth, to assist in auditing the collection for the saints at Jerusalem, had been appointed Paul's traveling companion "by the churches"

(2 Cor 8:18–21). The reference to "brothers" who are "apostles of the churches" may indicate a special category of persons, as earlier mentioned, appointed and sent as messengers for a specific task (2 Cor 8:23).

A collegial model seems to have prevailed throughout the original Christian mission.[33] There is evidence that the Pauline mission always involved a team effort in which Paul played a dominant, central place (1 Thess 1:1; Phil 1:1; 1 Cor 1:1). Some members of the team, whom Paul called "our brother" or "our sister" (Rom 16:1), had leadership and service roles that were both local and more than local in their scope. Titus, Paul's coworker for the Corinthians, and other team members simply called "brothers," assumed a temporary function within that urban community of believers. But Titus and the unnamed "brother appointed by the churches" as Paul's traveling companion also looked beyond the local church of Corinth to the many other communities in which they preached (2 Cor 8:16–23). Moreover, alongside Paul's team of coworkers, an even wider group "worked for the churches" as teachers, leaders (male or female) of house communities, evangelists, prophets, and deacons. About eighty such persons are named in Paul's authentic letters.

Charismatic Ministries

Apart from Paul's general oversight, the local leadership structures in his communities seem to have differed from church to church. In his epistles to the Corinthians (1 Cor 12:4–11, 27–31) and to the Romans (12:6–8), Paul recognizes a multiplicity of charisms or gifts and ministries. According to First Corinthians (12:28–31), God has set up in the church first apostles, second prophets, third teachers, then workers of mighty deeds, healers, assistants, administrators, those who speak in tongues, and interpreters. All do not have the same gifts, and should strive for the greater gifts. Paul likewise advocated good order (1 Cor 14:26–32): each should use his or her gift in the Spirit and then step back to allow another to exercise that same gift or another. In that way, the charismatic ministry of Corinth was to be validated by the way it operated: the gifts of the total community acted as a control over the gift of each individual. Genuine prophets or Spirit-filled persons would know that Paul's directives for good order were from the Lord (1 Cor 14:37–40).

Overseers and Deacons

Paul's epistle to the Philippians (1:1) is addressed to the holy ones or saints "with the overseers *[episkopois]* and deacons." Apparently those two collegial groups provided local leadership and service for the community at Philippi, although we are not told what either group specifically did. *Episkopos* was the term for a financial administrator in the private associations and clubs of the Greco-Roman world. Unlike the Essenes at Qumran where a single Overseer presided over a group, such organizations had collegial leadership patterns, which may have provided the model for the leadership structure at Philippi.

In his Epistle to the Romans (16:1–2), Paul commends "our sister Phoebe, a deacon *[diakonon]* of the church of Cenchreae." She was a benefactor or patron to many, including Paul. He also singles out the household of Stephanas, which was devoted to the service *(diakonian)* of "the saints" at Corinth, and urges the Corinthians to put themselves at the service of such persons and to everyone who cooperates and toils with them (1 Cor 16:15–16).

Elders

The structure called *presbyteroi*, or elders, does not appear in the epistles undisputedly attributed to Paul. By contrast, Acts (14:23) says that Barnabas and Paul installed presbyters, and commended them to the Lord with prayer and fasting, in every church they founded during their first missionary journey through the cities of Asia Minor. Schillebeeckx has suggested that Barnabas, the senior leader of that mission, introduced a structure he knew from Jerusalem.[34] Brown instead believes Acts anachronistically projected back a structure prevalent only at the time of its composition.[35] He points out that some churches of the Pauline mission still did not have presbyters in the eighties, since Titus is admonished to accomplish what had been left undone, especially to appoint elders in every town in Crete (Titus 1:5).

Acts refers to both Jewish (4:5, 8, 23) and Christian "elders" or presbyters at Jerusalem. At some point the sect of the Nazarenes adopted that collegial Jewish leadership model for its own assembly or "synagogue" (*synagōgēn;* James 2:2). We are told that Barnabas and Saul delivered the Antiochene church's collection for the relief of the Judaean Church to the elders at Jerusalem (Acts 11:30; cf. 12:25). The meeting about the necessity of circumcision and dietary laws is said to have been convened by "the apostles and the elders" at Jerusalem (Acts 15:2, 4, 6, 22–23). And the elders, gathered around James, greet Paul on his last visit to Jerusalem (Acts 21:18). Besides their administrative function of receiving monies, they are portrayed as sharing authority in regard to teaching and decision making. No liturgical function is mentioned in Acts. The Epistle of James (5:14) says that the elders of the *ekklēsia* are to be asked to pray over and anoint the sick.

In sum, a collegial group of elders was definitely operative within the Jerusalem *ekklēsia* when Acts was written, but it is difficult to determine how long that leadership structure had previously been in existence. The references to elders at the meeting about Jewish law (Acts 15:2, 4, 6, 22–23) may reflect the author's presupposition that the leadership pattern functioning in Jerusalem at the time of composition also had a role in that earlier event.

A Community of Disciples United by Love

A survey of the diverse leadership and service structures in the earliest churches reveals, besides these multiple leadership positions, that some assemblies were more structured than others. The Johannine communities initially had the simplest order of all. In the communities of "the disciple whom Jesus loved," all were equally disciples, united by their love for Jesus and one another (John 15:8–17). Like the branches on a vine (John 15:1–17), they were bonded to Jesus, who had not left them orphaned, but guaranteed their unity and their witness through the Paraclete or Advocate Spirit sent by him (John 14:15–31; 16:4–16). No institution or structure could substitute for the living presence of Jesus in the Spirit.[36] Within the community of the beloved disciple, even the recognition of Simon Peter's role as shepherd had to be grounded in his love for Jesus (John 21:15–17) and in his imitation of Jesus as servant (13:1–16).

After the death of "the beloved disciple," elders may have tried to carry on the tradition of a church order based on love, despite the difficulties posed by unacceptable teachers and by divisions within the communities (1 John 2:19–23; 2 John 1, 9–11; 3 John 1). The ongoing attempts simply to live in love were ultimately supplanted by stronger patterns of supervisory authority better able to cope with the threats to unity. The role of Diotrephes in 3 John 9–10 may mark the beginning of that development.[37] According to the elder (2 John 1 and 3 John 1) who opposed Diotrephes as one "who likes to put himself first" (3 John 9), the Spirit enables the community to discern what is false; there is no need of teachers for that purpose (1 John 2:27). Holding onto the original perspective of the Johannine churches, the elder rejected Diotrephes's claim that his stricter supervision was needed to counter false teachings within his local Johannine church. Diotrephes apparently considered the earlier emphasis to be inadequate.

Service for Unity, Not Power

Despite the diversity of structures in the earliest decades, they are united in one significant aspect: they were not related to power over the Eucharist or over persons, but were understood as ministries for building up the community of believers. They served the unity of all who believed that Jesus was Lord, in all the local churches within the one *ekklēsia.*

In the Synoptics, the passages wherein Jesus institutes the Eucharist are addressed to the Twelve (Mark 14:17; Matt 26:20) or the apostles (Luke 22:14). (The slight variations in wording reflect the fact that the memory of Jesus' words had become intertwined with liturgical usage and theological development within the various postresurrection communities.) Only Paul (1 Cor 11:24–5) and Luke (22:19) report that Jesus said, "Do this in remembrance [memory] of me." But the New Testament does not directly tell us that one of the Twelve, or anyone else, presided at the Eucharist. Neither does it tell us who should preside.[38] The Greek text of Acts 13:2 literally says that the prophets at Antioch were "engaged in liturgy *[leitourgountōn]* to the Lord," but precisely what that involved is not clear. The *Didache* (10:7) says that the prophets should be allowed to "eucharisticize" as they will.

The first text giving clear guidelines for "ordination," thereby distinguishing those who lead and serve from the rest of the community, is the *Apostolic Tradition* of the third century. During the previous two centuries, attention was focused on the concrete realization of unity by the total community, and not on the person or persons who presided at the Eucharist (1 Cor 10–11). As Alexandre Faivre has shown, the *kleros* or "clergy" (1 Pet 5:3) of the early church included all believers.[39] There was a distribution of roles, not a distinction of powers, in that participatory, priestly (1 Pet 2:9) community in which Jesus was still the only high priest (Heb 3:1, 4:14—5:10, 9:11, 10:21).

Transitional Leadership for Another Generation

When the foundational leaders of the first generation, such as Peter and Paul, died during the sixties, there was no shortage of personnel in the churches, but none enjoyed their personal authority and universal stature. And since Christianity had grown, so had its problems. A defensive concern for the continuity of churches now threatened by enemies of sound teaching led to the development of a new nucleus or framework of leadership. That is the situation behind the Pastoral Epistles, probably written in the eighties, and First Peter, written in the sixties if it is considered authentic, or in the eighties, possibly by Sylvanus at Rome (5:12), if it is judged to be pseudonymous.

The New Testament provides no absolutely clear evidence about whether or how the Twelve appointed successors. After Paul's death, those who tried to assume and carry on his kind of personal authority and leadership may have met with resistance. That is probably why First and Second Timothy and Titus were written in Paul's name. As Brown observes, the author of the Pastorals may be trying to deal with the resistance by saying to his times what he thinks Paul would have said were he alive.[40] Pseudonymity was a way of making Paul present, in order to have him facilitate the response to a new situation.[41] According to Second Timothy (4:6), a Paul who is nearing the end of his life names Timothy and Titus as his delegates, thereby empowering them to substitute for him in his absence. Timothy is told not to let anyone disdain him because of his youth (1 Tim 4:12) and to rekindle the charism or gift of God that was in him through Paul's laying on of hands (2 Tim 1:6). But Paul and the Twelve were not the only apostles who had to be replaced. A whole new generation of leaders had to succeed the many apostles of the early church. Those who went before had laid the groundwork by preparing their younger coworkers. Those delegates provided some continuity to the kind of ministry that Paul had exercised, but at the same time something new had to be built from the ground up.

Titus (1:5) is told to appoint presbyters in every town in Crete, a task which Paul seems to have left undone during his lifetime. That would indicate that many Pauline churches still did not have elders in the eighties. The Pastoral Epistles also reflect a further development in which the collegial structure of presbyters or elders (adopted from the Pharisaic synagogue) is now connected to, and eventually made interchangeable with, the office of overseer or supervisor, as found among the Essenes at Qumran. When Titus is given directives (1:6–9) about the qualities required for the selection of elders, the term *episkopos* or overseer suddenly appears in the singular (1:7). Similarly, First Timothy (3:1–7) lists the qualifications for an *episkopos* or overseer, and later (5:17) says that presbyters who preside well deserve to be paid double (literally, double honor), which may indicate that perhaps only one or some of the elders acted as overseers.[42]

In short, elders and overseers (*presbyteroi* and *episkopoi*) initially designated diverse collegial leadership groups in different churches, but at some point the terms became interchangeable. If the structure reflected in 1 Peter 5:1–2 should include the reference to "overseeing" *(episkopountes)*, not found in all ancient manuscripts, there is reason to argue for a date in the eighties. Peter is presented here as a fellow-elder instructing elders *(presbyterous)* to "shepherd" God's flock, "overseeing" *(episkopountes)* it not through coercion but by free persuasion. Such a presentation coincides with the pattern in Acts where Paul is portrayed summoning the presbyters or elders of Ephesus (20:17). In a subsequent verse, those same "elders" are instructed to keep watch over the whole flock of which the Holy Spirit has appointed them "overseers" *(episkopous)*, to shepherd or tend the Church of God (20:28).

The Pastorals do not directly tell us what a presbyter-overseer did. We can only surmise the tasks from the qualifications required. According to Titus 1:6–9, the candidate must be married only once, with upright children who are believers. He should be an exemplary, blameless person of self-control and holiness, not greedy for money, hospitable, and a teacher of sound doctrine. In 1 Timothy 3:1–7, we are told further that he must manage his own family well, "for if someone does not know how to manage his own household, how can he take care of God's church?" In addition, he cannot be a recent convert and must have a good reputation outside the church. In other words, the elder/overseer had to deal with people, teach, manage an organization, and administer funds.

Since individuals enjoy different gifts or skills, it is possible that diverse tasks were distributed among the members of the collegial group of elders/overseers, much as the exercise of gifts was shared in the charismatic structure of Corinth. Such a situation is indicated in *The Shepherd of Hermas*, a document written at Rome, probably in installments between about 90 and 150. Hermas is instructed to write an account of his visions and to give one copy to Clement, who has the responsibility of instructing the foreign cities, and another to Grapte, who shall instruct the widows and orphans (Vision 2, 4:2–3 [8]). Clement and Grapte appear to have been members of a collegial group of elders/overseers administering the church at Rome who had been assigned special functions (Visions 2:4 [8], 3:5 [13]; Parable 9, 27 [104]). In that regard, they are reminiscent of the presbyters who deserve to be paid double (a "double honorarium") in 1 Timothy 5:17.

In the Pastoral Epistles, the qualifications for elders/overseers and the criteria for deacons (in 1 Tim 3:8–13) reflect the influence of a household model.[43] Although the responsibilities of deacons are not specified, the title itself indicates a service function. The way that guidelines for women suddenly appear in 1 Timothy 3:11 might suggest that some deacons were women. In that regard, one should *not* presume that women deacons, like Phoebe mentioned in Romans 16:1, simply had the limited functions of the "deaconesses" of later centuries.

Some believe that the term *neoteroi* or young men (who are instructed to accept the authority of the elders) in 1 Peter 5:5 may be another designation for deacons. There is also some speculation whether the parallels between male and female "elders" and male and female "youngers" *(neoterous/as)* in 1 Timothy 5:1–2 might indicate that there were also women "elders" in this phase of the Church's development.[44] If that were so, it would give a different coloration to the passage in 1 Timothy 2:12 about not permitting a woman to teach or to have authority over a man. This text might refer to women elders being excluded from the role of overseer within the group of elders.

Without resolving the questions about terminology, diversity of internal roles, and the issue of women's inclusion, we may conclude that two collegial structures, elders/overseers and deacons, became ever more universal from the eighties onward. For example, the *Letter to the Corinthians*, also known as *First Clement*, written from the Church at Rome about the year 96, just after the Domitian persecution, interchangeably refers to elders/overseers at Corinth, always in the plural, and also to deacons (1:3, 21:6, 42:4, 44, 47:6, 54:2, 57:1). Those structures have evidently supplanted the charismatic pattern earlier found at Corinth; but there is no evidence about when they came into existence at Corinth.

The Roman Church's letter sought to heal a feud in the Corinthian Church, in which a rebellious group had ousted all the elders/overseers (47:6, 57:1). The way that Rahab, Judith, and Esther are invoked as models (12, 55:3–6) suggests that women were involved in the difficulties.[45] Stressing order, obedience, peace, and the harmony or concord exemplified by the order of the universe and the succession of days and seasons (chs. 15, 19–20, 30, 61, 65), the letter asks that the deposed leaders be restored.

First Clement maintains that overseers/elders and deacons were appointed by the apostles. According to chapter 42, the apostles were made evangelizers by Jesus Christ, who was sent by God. Filled with confidence through the resurrection of Jesus and confirmed by the word of God, they went out with the full assurance of the Holy Spirit to announce the coming of the reign of God. Preaching throughout rural regions and towns, they appointed their first-fruits as overseers and deacons of those who would come to faith. As further proof that such order had been preordained by God, the letter cites Isaiah 60:17 and Numbers 17, tailored to suit its conclusions.

The epistle presents the collegial leadership structure of elders/overseers as an apostolic creation for good order. Chapter 44 claims that the apostles had foreknowledge, through Jesus, that disputes would arise about overseers. That is why the apostles appointed them and afterward established a succession, so that when these overseers died other proven men might continue their ministry. "Those, therefore, who were appointed by them or, later on, by other reputable men with the consent of the whole church"[46] continue the preaching and ministry of the apostles, as well as a liturgical service of offering gifts (44:4).

In First Clement, structure and order are given a sacral and immutable character. Exhorting the Corinthian Christians not to disturb the existing order, the letter invokes the hierarchical pattern of offices in the Roman empire (ch. 37) and in the temple worship of Judaism (chs. 40–41) as models. Like soldiers, Christians should obey the rulers to whom God has given power in the Roman empire (chs. 37, 60–61). The rebels at Corinth should submit to the elders in obedience and do penance, "bending the knees of their hearts" (57:1). The letter sees the deposition of the Corinthian overseers/elders as no small sin, since they were removed from their liturgical ministry (44:4, 6) that they had honorably and blamelessly performed.

In drawing an analogy from the Hebrew Scriptures, the letter nevertheless recognizes that *everyone* has a distinctive role in the Church.[47] It points out that, in the offerings and liturgies of Judaism commanded by God, the high priest was given his own proper services (liturgies), the priests were assigned their own place, the Levites had the responsibility of service *(diakonia)*, and lay persons were bound by lay precepts (40:5). Moreover, despite the reference to the high priest in Judaism, there is no indication that one individual presided over the elders at Corinth, or at Rome. The letter from Rome was not attributed to or sent over the signature of any one person, nor was any one person singled out as presiding at Corinth. Yet the tripartite model of high priest, priests, and Levitical servants remained a portent of things to come.

Toward the end of the first century, the structures of elders/overseers and deacons seem gradually to have permeated more and more churches. The *Didache* (ch. 15) gives the directive "to elect overseers and deacons worthy of the Lord, who are gentle and not lovers of money, truthful and proven; for they will perform *[leitourgousi]* for you the ministry or service *[leitourgian]* of the prophets and teachers." But the new, resident leadership of overseers/elders and deacons, patterned on the household model, did not yet enjoy the prestige of the itinerant, charismatic prophets. The *Didache* has to add: "Do not disdain them, for they are your honored men, along with the prophets and teachers." The displacement of the wandering apostolic prophets and teachers apparently met with resistance during the time of transition.

Mono-Episcopacy: The Personification of Ecclesial Unity

Because they were assemblies of humans like ourselves, the early churches were not pristine, trouble-free communities. We have already alluded to the disputes at Jerusalem, Antioch, and Corinth. *The Shepherd of Hermas*, written at Rome between about 90 and 150, and the seven epistles of Ignatius of Antioch, written about 110, reveal that the churches at Rome and Antioch had to cope with internal tensions into the second century. The concern for preserving ecclesial unity culminated in the leadership structure we know as the bishop.

As a prophet given authority to teach the saints at Rome by virtue of his visions (Vision 3, 1:1–2 [9]; 3, 3:4 [11]; 3, 8:9–11 [16]), Hermas recounts how the Church appeared to him, initially in the form of an old woman created the first of all things, for whom the cosmos was ordered or formed (Vis. 2, 4:1 [8]). This notion of the Church as the first creation was a theological development beyond Colossians and Ephesians, yet an idea current beyond Rome. A Corinthian homily from the same period, known as Second Clement (14:1), also speaks of the church as created at the beginning, before the sun and moon. In Hermas, the old woman who is the Church grows ever younger and more beautiful with each passing appearance. She is rejuvenated by the penance and purification of her members (Vis. 3, 10–13 [18–21]).

In her final appearance to Hermas, a young and beautiful Church shows him a tower being built on top of water, which is the Church rising from the water of baptism. Stones taken from the water are the newly baptized, who easily fit into the tower. Other stones taken from land have to be examined, and some are rejected. These symbolize the baptized who had sinned. Those rejected have to be further purified by penance before being readmitted into the Church (Vis. 3, 2–7 [10–15]). Separated from the Church, the baptized who sinned are grouped according to the degree or stage of their repentance. Like branches lopped off a willow, some are alive and green. Because of their repentance they are again filled with the life they received through the waters of baptism, and can be readmitted into the Church. Others, still dried up and withered from a lack of penance, are denied reentry (Parable or Similitude 8, 1–11 [67–77]). In the process of building the tower, some square, white, perfectly shaped stones are placed into it. These are identified as "the apostles, overseers *[episkopoi]*, teachers, and deacons, both living and dead, who have walked in the holiness of God, 'overseeing,' teaching, and serving the elect of God in a pure and holy manner." They were always in harmony, had peace among themselves, and listened to one another, which is why they fit so harmoniously into the tower being built (Vis. 3,5 [13]).

Apostles and teachers are said to have preached and taught in the whole world (Par. 9, 25 [102]). Overseers and deacons ministered to the local church. The overseers *(episkopoi)* offered generous hospitality to the servants of God and sheltered the poor and widows (Par. 9, 27 [104]). Overseers and elders appear here to remain interchangeable terms, for elsewhere the aged woman who is the Church asks Hermas if he gave his revelation to the elders who preside. He is told to give one copy to Clement, who will send it to other cities, and another to Grapte, who will advise the widows and orphans (Vis. 2, 4:2–3 [8]). As already noted, they appear to have been elders/overseers with a distinctive function. As in 1 Peter 5:2–3, shepherds are held responsible for their flocks (Par. 9, 31:5 [108]).

Elders, confessors who had witnessed to the faith by suffering, and visionary prophets each had their assigned places (Vis. 3,

1–2 [9–10]; Mandate 11 [43]) among the seats of honor in the assembly (Vis. 3, 9 [17]). As a charismatic, visionary teacher, Hermas found it difficult to get the recognition connected with sitting in the teacher's place, which was among those front benches in the assembly. A rivalry over precedence had developed among unworthy leaders and false prophets, causing tension among teachers in the church (Vis. 3, 9 [17]; Mand. 11 [43]). Although the Church was just beginning its second century, the quest for prestige by unworthy leaders had already blurred a genuine concern for the charisms of teaching and service.

In calling all the baptized to one last repentance before the end comes (Vis. 2, 2 [6]; Mand. 4, 1–3 [29–31]; Par. 9, 26:6 [103]), Hermas accordingly feels the need to include the leaders who sit in the front seats. They are overly concerned with precedence and foment rivalry in their ranks (Vis. 2, 2:6 [6]; 3, 9:7–10 [17]). Some deacons have embezzled the funds for widows and orphans (Parable 9, 26:2 [103]). False prophets are vying for a seat of honor and demanding money (Mand. 11, 1–12 [43]). Hermas points out that the first apostles and prophets were not guilty of such greed (Par. 9, 25:2 [102]). Nor, significantly, are hospitable overseers (Par. 9, 27 [104]).

It must not have been easy to maintain good order in a church where true and false charismatic, visionary prophets operated alongside a college of overseers/elders. That situation would have been particularly complicated by the added ingredients of a more liberal group espousing an exaggerated Pauline theology and a more conservative party emphasizing Jewish perspectives beyond those of James, the brother of the Lord. Brown proposes that such a situation may have been the Roman background for the Second Epistle of Peter, written in the early second century.[48] That epistle invoked the long dead Peter as an authority who could mediate between those who misread Paul on the *Parousia* (2 Pet 3:15–16) and those who listened to the false prophets (2 Pet 2:1–22). Such false prophets were also opposed in the Epistle of Jude (verses 4–13), whose author is identified as the "brother of

James" (Jude 1). Second Peter (3:2) counsels its readers to "remember the words spoken in the past by the holy prophets, and the commandment of the Lord and Savior spoken through your apostles."

A very similar situation may have been prevalent at Antioch when the Gospel of Matthew was written during the eighties. Peter was declared the rock upon which the Church was built, in a community that valued the work of prophets and teachers, because his stature could mediate the long-existing internal tensions between those with Pauline perspectives and those of the party of James.[49] It is from that same community at Antioch that a vocal proponent of one *episkopos* presiding over a college of elders and deacons suddenly emerged.

About the year 110, Ignatius of Antioch was on his way to Rome for trial and probable martyrdom. During his journey he wrote seven letters in which he strongly advocated that one *episkopos* preside over each church or eucharistic assembly, as if that were normative. In his Epistle to the Trallians (3, 1), he maintains that no church can be recognized if it does not have deacons, reverenced like Jesus Christ, an *episkopos*, who is the type of the Father, and elders, who are like the council of God and college of apostles.

Although Ignatius presumes that the entire *ekklēsia* celebrates the Eucharist, he insists that a valid Eucharist is one presided at by the *episkopos* or one to whom he entrusts it. No one should do anything that pertains to an *ekklēsia* apart from its *episkopos*, which we can from this point translate as *bishop*. Without the bishop, it is not permissible to baptize or to celebrate the *agape* or love-feast (Smyrnaeans 8:1–2). In regard to the care of widows, which also involved the administration of funds, Ignatius tells Polycarp, the *episkopos* of Smyrna, to let nothing take place without his approval (Polycarp 4:1) Finally, when a man and woman planned to marry, they, too, were to seek the bishop's approval (Pol 5:2).

Ignatius's Epistle to the Smyrnaeans is also the first document to use the term "Catholic Church." In its perspective, each local church, organically united under its bishop,[50] makes present the whole, universal Church united under Christ: "Wherever the bishop appears, there the multitude of people should be, just as wherever Jesus is, there is the universal assembly" (*katholike ekklēsia;* Smyr 8:2). Ignatius also says in his Epistle to the Ephesians that all the members of an undivided local church are commingled or united with their bishop, as the whole Church is with Jesus Christ (5:1).

As is evident, Ignatius's emphasis on the bishop is tied to a concern about unity and harmony in each church (Eph 4:1–2, 5:1, 13:1; Magnesians 6, 7; Tral 7, 12:2; Philadelphians Intro, 2:2, 3:2, 8:1). The bishop serves as the guarantor of orthodox beliefs and unity, particularly against the divisions being caused by the Judaizers and the Docetists, who denied the full human bodiliness and suffering of Jesus.[51] To counter the separatist assemblies of the Docetists and Judaizers, Ignatius admonishes everyone to "use" or celebrate one Eucharist, for there is one flesh of our Lord Jesus Christ, and one cup for union in his blood, one altar, just as there is one *episkopos* with the presbyterate and the deacons, his fellow servants (Philad 4:1). If the prayer of one or two is so powerful, how much more that of the bishop and the whole church (Eph 5:2), who together break one bread (Eph 20:2).

Obedience to the bishop is so important to Ignatius that he virtually defines being Christian in terms of it (Eph 5:3, 20:2; Magn 4:1, 13:2; Tral 2:1, 7:2).[52] For him, a church of unity and concord is attuned to its bishop like a chorus singing harmony with stringed instruments (Eph 4:1–2). Yet, from the way Ignatius defends himself (Philad 6:3), some wonder if he may have pushed his views too far for some (Magn 4). Might he, like Diotrephes in 3 John 9, have been claiming and advocating a degree of authority and power that exceeded even what other bishops currently exercised, demanding more control than even some incumbent bishops deemed necessary (Philad 7:2)? The intensity of Ignatius's lobbying seems to indicate that the role of bishop was emerging and not yet fully defined.

We do not know when mono-episcopacy first appeared in Antioch and in Asia Minor. It is not absolutely clear whether the Book of Revelation, probably written during the nineties, provides evidence of such development when it addresses letters to the angels of the seven churches in the province of Asia (1:4—3:22). Clearly mono-episcopacy was not a universally diffused structure in Ignatius's time.[53] His own Letter to the Romans does not single out any individual leader, which he certainly would have done if that church had a *mono-episkopos* or bishop. When Polycarp, the bishop of Smyrna and Ignatius's friend, later wrote his Epistle to the Philippians, he referred only to deacons and elders, urging them to be compassionate and not lovers of money in their work with the infirm, widows, orphans, and poor (Philad 5–6, 11). The collegial leadership group called overseers *(episkopoi)* in Paul's epistle to the Philippians (1:1) was apparently still functioning, but Polycarp calls its members "elders." He refrained from using the term *episkopoi* because he reserved the term *episkopos*, in the singular, for the office of bishop, which apparently did not yet exist at Philippi.

It should also be noted that, although Ignatius supported a strong role for the bishop, he did not advocate unbridled power. He repeatedly referred to the gentleness of a bishop, seeing that as a power which even nonbelievers respected (Tral 3:2; Philad 1; Pol 2:1). His desire for information about his own church at Antioch reveals a genuinely pastoral concern. He is thankful to hear that the community, which he will never see again, is at peace (Philad 10:1; Smyr 11:2; Pol 7:1).

The ministry of the *mono-episkopos* was still genuinely collegial. Ignatius himself says one should do nothing without the bishop *and* the elders and deacons (Mag 7:1; Tral 7:2).[54] The bishop was the primary liturgist; but as later sources tell us, the elders—his advisors for administration—probably sat beside him when he presided, concelebrating the one Eucharist with him or the one whom he appointed.[55] In those assemblies, the Eucharist was not something "confected" and then administered by the ordained to the nonordained, but a concelebration of the entire church. The literature of the early centuries never spoke of the bishop as "saying" the Eucharist, while the congregation "heard" it. Rather, the whole community "did" the Eucharist, in which Christ's presence, through the bread and wine become his body and blood, effected a unity of the entire community with Jesus and among themselves. In congregations that were smaller than most of our modern city or suburban parishes, all members participated in the concelebration according to their own function (Philad 4; Smyr 8:2). The upshot is that, as W. R. Schoedel writes, "The threefold ministry promoted by Ignatius is still more remarkable for its sense of solidarity with the community than for its emergence as a distinct segment of the group."[56]

3
The Jesus Movement as a Communion of Churches, AD 110–600

Ignatius of Antioch advocated frequent Eucharists (Eph 13:1) and frequent assemblies where the bishop could greet everyone by name (Pol 4:2). Those practices actualized and nurtured the unity of a particular or local church. But such internal unity also opened each church outward. To celebrate the restoration of unity in his own church at Antioch, Ignatius urged that delegates should be sent from Philadelphia (Phil 10:1–2) and Smyrna (Smyr 11:2; Pol 7:2), who would join those sent from neighboring churches, to rejoice with the Antiochene community when it assembled. By their presence, such delegates symbolized how the unity of the local church reflected the catholic or universal assembly of Christ. In its internal unity, each local church was also united with every other assembly in the world. The catholic or universal Church was made present in every place through each church united in communion or *koinōnia* with every other church.

One, Holy, Catholic, and Apostolic "Episcopal" Church

A baptismal creed used at Rome from about 340, which Rufinus of Aquileia later attributed to the apostles, expressed belief in "the holy Church." Another creed promulgated by the bishops at the Council of Nicaea in 325 anathematized the Arians in the name of "the Catholic and Apostolic Church." The

Nicene-Constantinopolitan Creed, approved at the Council of Chalcedon in 451 and then gradually introduced into the liturgy, professed faith in "one holy Catholic and Apostolic Church."[1] Those few adjectives presupposed a complex set of developments within the community that came from Jesus.

As the Church lived through the second, third, and fourth centuries, it was confronted by opportunities and threats, both external and internal. The number of believers increased so that by the third century the "Great Church" began to take shape. This expansion occurred despite the fact that Christians were persecuted. After the great persecution organized by Emperor Domitian during the nineties, local police regulation became the method employed. Another centralized attempt to rid the empire of Christians would be initiated by Emperor Decius in the mid-third century.

Writing between 155 and 165, the Christian apologist Justin Martyr sought to overcome the misunderstandings and fears that Christianity had engendered in the Greco-Roman world. Defending Christians against the charge of atheism, because they refused to worship the gods of the empire, Justin explains that they believe in God as Father, only begotten Word or Son, and Spirit. They worship the Creator of the universe, who does not need bloody sacrifices, with prayer and "thanksgiving" (1 *Apology* 5–13).

Justin described what happens in baptism and at the assembly for the Eucharist on Sunday, the first day, on which God transformed darkness and ordered the matter of the universe, and on which Jesus rose from the dead (1 *Apology* 61–67). During the Sunday assembly, the memoirs of the Apostles or the writings of the Prophets were read, as much as time allowed. After an exhortation by the one presiding, the members of the assembly then greeted one another with a kiss. Bread, wine, and water were presented, and the one who presided offered prayers and thanksgiving, which the people approved by saying "Amen." Justin explained that, through the word of God, the bread and wine became the flesh and blood of that Jesus who was made flesh. They were then shared by those present and, through the deacons, sent to those who were absent.

Those who were well-off gave what they wished during the assembly. The one presiding used the funds to care for orphans, widows, the sick, the needy, the imprisoned, and traveling strangers staying with the community.

As a philosopher who had become a believer, Justin remained in dialogue with the world beyond the Church and critically accepted the positive insights he found. In his view, all truth (which, for Justin, especially included Platonism) reflected a participation in the creative divine Word or *Logos*, which had seminally permeated the created universe as the source of all life and rationality (2 *Apology* 13) and then became incarnate in Jesus (John 1:1, 14). Justin's openness and his efforts to explain Christian faith in ways that were intelligible and attractive to the nonbelieving intellectuals of his time initiated a further Hellenization of the Jesus movement, beyond its original opening to the Gentile world. His irenic worldview was also open to an ongoing exchange with Judaism, reflected in his *Dialogue with Trypho*. Justin was open to every expression of truth in his search for it.

The problematic issue was how to deal with Christians who held positions that were considered unacceptable. As noted above, Paul instructed the Corinthians not to associate with a fellow Christian living with his father's wife (1 Cor 5:1–11). Ignatius of Antioch insisted that one should not associate with, but only pray for, the docetists, who maintained that Jesus only *seemed* to have a body (Smyr 4.1), emphasizing Jesus' divinity at the expense of his humanity. Justin Martyr likewise presumed that sectarians with unacceptable beliefs were to be excluded from *koinōnia:* "we will communicate with none" who are called Marcionites, Valentinians, Basilidians, Satornilians, and others (*Dialogue with Trypho* 35:5–6). But Justin's criteria for breaking off communion were nuanced enough to allow for internal diversity. For example, Christians who adhered to Jewish law without forcing others to do so were considered true believers with whom one should share in *koinōnia* (*Dialogue* 47:2–3).

Writing about 180–90, Irenaeus of Lyons approvingly noted that the apostles and their disciples, such as Polycarp of Smyrna, would not even verbally communicate with Marcion or others who had corrupted the faith (*Against the Heresies* 3.3, 4). Irenaeus was himself vigorously engaged in defending the faith of the Church against the teachings of those known as Gnostics. In its many forms and varieties, Gnosticism distinguished the Creator of the Hebrew Scriptures from the good God proclaimed by Jesus of Nazareth. Considering creation to be the result of some cosmic catastrophe, the Gnostics had a negative understanding of matter and the human body, viewing the body as the prison of a spiritual light that dozes within each of us. Gnostics taught that Jesus was sent to reawaken that hidden spark of light within us by his teaching or enlightenment. But they denied the fullness of the incarnation, or that Jesus bodily suffered and was resurrected. It was the *gnosis* or knowledge that he imparted that freed our spiritual essence from our bodies, allowing it to be reunited with the previously unknown God whom Jesus proclaimed.

Gnosticism's devaluation of the body engendered the possibility of androgynous equality between men and women, in a time when the Church's organization had become ever more patriarchal. If the inner spirit and not the body mattered, women could not be excluded from a prominent role, such as was attributed to Mary Magdalene who rivaled Peter in Gnostic literature.[2] The perfect ones who abstained from sexual relations were all equal in their inner spark of light, whether male or female. Our own sociocultural setting might be favorable toward Gnosticism's recognition of equality for women, but the movement's negativism about material creation and the human body was not, and is not, compatible with a Christian faith understanding of creation and the incarnation. A genuine understanding of gender equality cannot be grounded in a devaluation of the body.

To counter the teachings of the Gnostics, Irenaeus emphasized the Church's unity of faith on a universal scale: the whole Church, spread throughout a world speaking many different languages, believes and teaches as if having one heart and soul because it has received the faith from the apostles and their disciples. Despite the many different languages, the meaning of the Church's tradition is said to be one and the same. Irenaeus affirms that churches in Germany essentially have the same beliefs or traditions as those in Spain, among the Celts, in the East, in Egypt or Libya, or those at the center of the earth (*Against the Heresies* 1.10.2). Unlike the Gnostics, the Church teaches and preaches the same beliefs everywhere, just as the same sun shines throughout the world.

According to Irenaeus, we receive our faith from the Church and preserve it ever-rejuvenated by the Spirit who worked through apostles, prophets, and teachers (1 Cor 12:28). The Spirit is found where the Church is, and the Church is found where the Spirit is. Those who do not unite themselves to the Church do not, therefore, share in the Spirit who is truth (*Against the Heresies* 3.24.1). That truth is said to be found in the Catholic Church but not among the Gnostics. To see it, one should look to the tradition of the apostles manifested in every church in the whole world (3.3.1–2). What the apostles once taught is preserved through the succession of bishops, to whom the apostles gave the care of the church in each place (4.33.8). Therefore, the presbyters who have their succession from the apostles should be listened to, since they have received the gift of truth through their succession in the episcopate (4.26.2).

The letter from Rome to Corinth, later attributed to Clement of Rome, had spoken of apostolic succession but not of mono-episcopacy or the bishop. Ignatius of Antioch emphasized the role of the *mono-episkopos* or bishop but never referred to him as a successor of the apostles. Irenaeus brought together the two concepts, arguing that bishops in apostolic succession defended and guaranteed the faith of the churches against the Gnostics.[3] Stating that he could produce lists of the bishops appointed by the apostles and their successors, Irenaeus observes that none of them taught the absurd "mysteries" that the Gnostics imparted to the "mature." Certainly, if the apostles had known such secrets they would have told those whom they entrusted with the care of the churches (*Against the Heresies.* 3.3.1). To avoid boring his readers with lists for all the churches, Irenaeus focuses on the tradition of the church he calls the greatest and most ancient, the one known to all, founded and established at Rome by Peter and Paul (3.3.2). But in so doing he has no intention of diminishing the importance of other bishops, such as Polycarp of Smyrna, who likewise taught what he learned from the apostles, in particular from John (3.3.4).

The themes of apostolic succession and unity in faith had earlier been stressed in the now-lost works of Hegesippus. Writing shortly before Irenaeus, Hegesippus declared that all the bishops he met in his travels taught the same doctrine. Presupposing that the mono-episcopacy of his time had existed since the very beginning, Hegesippus also compiled lists tracing the succession of bishops, including one which named the bishops of Rome down to Anicetus. Hegesippus's list may well have been the source of the list provided by Irenaeus.[4]

Writing from Carthage at the turn of the century, Tertullian said that the apostles, or those who continued their work, founded churches in every city from which other churches borrowed the "shoot" of faith and the seeds of doctrine. Because apostolic churches begot all the other churches, all the churches united to one another have the same primeval roots and are apostolic (*On the Prescription of Heretics* 20, 4–9). Like Irenaeus, the earlier, still-Catholic Tertullian regarded the succession of bishops to be a guarantee of the true faith received from the apostles. He challenged heretics to unroll their list of bishops in succession to one of the apostles or to the apostolic men who persevered with them. Only the communion of churches with an apostolic foundation had the rule of faith that was preserved by episcopal succession (*Prescription* 20–21; 32; 36–37). Tertullian observed that doctrinal agreement grounded a communion of peace between apostolic churches. That communion was expressed through a mutual bond of hospitality, which heretics were not allowed to share (*Prescription* 20, 4–9; 32, 8; 21, 7).

Later, having joined the ultrarigorous Montanist sect, Tertullian differentiated the Church of bishops from a prophetic Spirit-filled Church. Proclaiming a discipline of ethical purity in which serious sins committed after baptism could not be forgiven, the Montanists saw no need for a network of bishops acting as organs of the Spirit for discipline or doctrine. In their view, the Spirit directly guaranteed holiness and unity, and not lenient bishops who forgave sinners (*On Modesty* 21, 16–17). But, ironically, the Montanists actually helped to consolidate the power of bishops. Their excessive claims contributed to a marginalization of "prophetic" persons in the mainstream Church. The prophetic function would be evaluated and authenticated by bishops. Orderly and predictable structures supplanted the wandering prophets-teachers-apostles of the earlier churches.[5]

In his advocacy for the role of the *mono-episkopos* or bishop, Ignatius of Antioch never specified how new bishops, or elders and deacons, were appointed. Whether the earlier references to an imposition of hands (1 Tim 4:14 and 2 Tim 1:6; cf. Acts 13:3 and 14:23) provide evidence that a systematic practice of ordination already existed is a matter of debate.[6] The first clear description of "ordination" through the imposition of hands is provided by the *Apostolic Tradition*, a church order document from the early third century, traditionally attributed to Hippolytus of Rome.[7] It directs that a new bishop was to be chosen by all the people (*Apostolic Tradition* 1). After a candidate acceptable to all had been named, the people were to assemble on a Sunday and bishops from neighboring churches were to lay hands on him, while the elders watched (*Ap. Tr.* 2). One bishop then imposed a hand and prayed that the Spirit would descend upon the new *episkopos* (*Ap. Tr.* 3).

For Cyprian of Carthage, the Church is one and holy in its bishops. He concluded that bishops had to be the essential organs of the Church's unity and the bearers of her holiness because many Christians had failed to witness to their faith during the Decian persecution of 250.[8] Like Ignatius of Antioch, Cyprian considered the unity of the local church to be grounded in the

Eucharist presided over by a legitimate bishop (*Epistles* 63:13, 69:5). He therefore insisted that only the bishop could restore persons back into ecclesial communion. Those who had abandoned the unity of the church at Carthage by their infidelity during the persecution could be readmitted only through the imposition of their bishop's hand, after they had undergone penance (*Ep.* 16:2).

Cyprian portrays the Church as a sacrament of unity (*Epistles* 59:2, 69:6, 73:11, 75:14). Each bishop, presiding over a eucharistic assembly, personifies the unity of his local church, which is built on him, the elders and deacons around him, and all those who remain faithful (*Ep.* 33:1). The unity of all the bishops, each inseparably united to the people of a particular Church, is what guarantees the communion of all the churches within the one catholic or universal Church founded on Christ. For Cyprian, "the bishop is in the Church and the Church is in the bishop." Anyone not with the bishop is not in the Church. Bishops are the glue, bonding themselves and the churches united to them into one universal Church (*Ep.* 66:8). In Cyprian's view, there is no salvation outside such a church of bishops, even for one who is martyred (*Ep.* 73:10, 21).

In Cyprian's perspective, Church and bishop have become almost synonymous terms (*Ep.* 66:8, 55:21, 43:5). The catholic or universal Church is a communion of churches united by a communion of bishops. Just as the Church of Christ is a single body with many members, so there is one episcopacy harmoniously shared by many bishops throughout the world (*Ep.* 55:24). Acting together, those bishops have never fallen into errors of faith (*Ep.* 67:8). They listen and learn from one another through dialogue, following the example of Peter, who did not invoke primacy and simply demand obedience when Paul disagreed with him at Antioch (*Ep.* 71:3).

Cyprian's focus on the bishop did not exclude a collegial and participatory role for others. Both the ordained and the faithful participated in the election of a new bishop, who was then approved and ordained by neighboring bishops (*Ep.* 55:8, 59:5–6, 67:3–5, 68:2, 43:4). Cyprian and the Roman Church also agreed that members of the baptized "faithful" were to be present and consulted at the common councils where important decisions were made (*Ep.* 17:1, 19:2, 30:5, 31:6). Their presence for the election of a new bishop was particularly crucial since they knew the life and actions of the candidates (*Ep.* 67:5). They had the power to elect worthy bishops or to refuse unworthy ones (*Ep.* 67:3). As Origen earlier emphasized, the bishop was not to be just an administrator (*Homily on Numbers* 12:2) but a spiritual guide whose life reflected what he taught others.[9] He was to be the incarnation of the true Christian.[10]

During the second century, bishops claiming apostolic succession became the supervisors and guarantors of the Church's communion (Irenaeus, *Against the Heresies* 1.10, 1–2; 3.2, 2 and 3, 1–3; Tertullian, *Prescription* 32:1–7, 36:1–8). The disputes of the third century, particularly the debates about who could reconcile sinners and about the validity of baptism by sectarians, further consolidated that prerogative. As the personal symbol of the unity of a particular church, the bishop determined who was to be included in, excluded from, or readmitted to the table of the Eucharist, and thus admitted to or excluded from the *koinōnia* or communion of the *ekklēsia.* But Irenaeus himself recognized that a bishop had to take care in discerning what constituted a real threat to faith and communion. He later admonished Victor, the bishop of Rome, for breaking communion with the churches of Asia Minor simply because they celebrated Easter according to a different calendar (Eusebius, *Church History* 5.24, 9–18).

To combat the growing problem of sectarianism, bishops who were *orthodox,* or who taught "right belief," developed and administered an institutionalized interecclesial structure or system of communion among themselves and their churches. Ludwig Hertling defined that *koinōnia,* which was both intra- and interecclesial, as "the bond that united the bishops and the faithful, the bishops among themselves, and the faithful among themselves, a bond that was effected and at the same time made manifest by eucharistic communion."[11] It was nurtured and expressed by means of synods or meetings, at which the bishops of a region resolved the problems they faced in common by the exchange of letters and by their shared celebration of the Eucharist.

By Augustine's time, communion referred to the unity of churches that were not sectarian in their doctrine or discipline (*Ep.* 61.1–2, 92.23). That ecclesial communion was mediated through the relationship of bishops who presided at the Eucharists of local churches or assemblies. One particular church was recognized as being the center of the *communion.* As Optatus of Milevis observed, a church in communion with Rome was considered to be in communion with the whole Catholic Church (*On the Donatist Schism against Parmenian* 2.3). The communion among bishops and their churches did not stem from friendship, nor simply from a unity of interests against sectarians. It arose from their mutual communion in Christ, effectively symbolized in the celebration of the Eucharist.

In the course of the early centuries, firm and narrow lines were gradually established as the boundaries of communion. Werner Elert has pointed to a developing confessional isolation through growing loyalty to formulas of faith.[12] In our time a rather fractured Christianity seeks to rekindle the shared gift of relationship and active partnership called *koinōnia.* We strive to look for what unites us, and not just what divides us. We speak of ecumenism, of Jewish-Christian relations and, internally, of ministry to the divorced and marginalized. As in the early Church, certain situations (such as marriage after divorce, etc.) cause persons to be excluded from active communion, which leads some to accuse the Church of a lack of compassion. In its concern to preserve the faith and to nurture ethical values and good order, the *ekklēsia* must always ask whether its practices are truly in continuity with what Jesus did and said. On its pilgrimage through history the Church can never forget the eschatological dimension of *koinōnia,* which looks to the future for completion and fulfillment. Everyone within the earthly communion of the Church must ever acknowledge his or her own need of God's mercy. For every Christian remains as one who ever hopes to become a participant *(sygkoinōnos)* in the gospel (1 Cor 9:23) and a sharer *(koinōnos)* in the glory that is to be revealed (1 Pet 5:1).

Synods and Councils as Expressions of Ecclesial Communion

Episcopal unity was vividly symbolized when a local bishop shared the eucharistic celebration with a bishop from another church. The *Didascalia*, a Syrian church order document of the third century, instructed that a visiting bishop should be invited to give the homily or to say the words of the Eucharist at least over the cup (2, 58, 2–3).[13] But such face-to-face communion was not always possible in a rapidly expanding Church. Other modes of expressing communion were essential. Problems extending beyond a local Church were resolved by letters of communion in which both the sender and the addressee had to be validly elected bishops who were teachers of orthodox doctrine and whose names therefore appeared on the lists, or diptychs, maintained especially by the principal churches. Bishops also exchanged letters of peace and commendation as credentials for traveling ministers and members of their churches.[14]

During the second and third centuries, provincial and regional synods of bishops were convened to resolve the controversies concerning the date of Easter and the problems posed by Montanism.[15] Letters explaining the decisions of such meetings were then sent to bishops in other areas. By the fourth and fifth centuries, the *koinōnia* or communion of the universal Church had come to mean the unity of churches that were not sectarian in their doctrine or discipline. The universal communion of such churches was mediated via the communion of their bishops, who now also assembled for general or ecumenical councils, convoked by the Christian emperors, to respond to serious threats to the unity of the faith and of the newly Christian empire.

As already noted, Cyprian and the Church of Rome agreed that the baptized "people" were to be present and consulted at synods. That practice persisted in the West. Canon 13 of the synod of Tarragona in Spain (516) still instructed bishops to bring not only the priests of their cathedral but also rural priests and some laymen. Canon 4 of the Fourth Council of Toledo (633) gave instructions about seating representatives from the laity. The problem is that emperors, kings, and wealthy nobles had become foremost among those attending. Policies affecting local churches were more and more decided at meetings of bishops away from their own assemblies, with diminishing participation by the rank and file who would be affected. Initially, bishops represented their churches at the synods, but eventually they came to represent the decisions of the synods to their churches.

The Church had to give a unified response to heresies that denied the full divinity and humanity of Jesus. As Vincent of Lerins observed in 434, the decrees of a universal council were to be preferred to the ignorance of a few (*Commonitory* 3; also cf. 27). Experience had also shown that the authority of the scriptures had to be supplemented by norms for distinguishing erroneous interpretations from the acceptable ecclesial, catholic understanding. To counter the vagaries of the heretics, Vincent invoked a "catholic" or universal tradition. He insisted that within the Catholic Church there was great care "to hold that which has been believed everywhere, always, and by all" (*Comm.* 2). The "deposit of faith" entrusted to that Church was a public tradition that did not exclude development or progress, as long as it was not an alteration. New doctrines could not be declared, but old ones could be taught in a new way (*Comm.* 22–23).

The ecumenical or general councils recognized the continuing need for intermediate ecclesial structures between the local and universal levels. Canon 5 of the Council of Nicaea in 325 (and canon 19 of Chalcedon in 451) directed that provincial synods should meet biannually. Lacking such subdivisions, the bishops of central and southern Italy and northern Africa gathered for numerous synods in

Rome and Carthage. The Council of Nicaea likewise recognized the wider regional authority of Rome, Alexandria, and Antioch, and assigned a position of honor to Jerusalem (canons 6 and 7). Later, canon 2 of the First Council of Constantinople (381) organized the groups of churches that formed provinces into still larger structures called dioceses, thereby conforming to the vast civil districts established by the Emperor Diocletian in 294. (Such historical developments long preceded the establishment of episcopal conferences according to national groups after Vatican II.) Finally, canon 28 of the Council of Chalcedon (451) proposed a structure of five major churches within the Empire: Rome, Constantinople, Alexandria, Antioch, and Jerusalem, which became known as the patriarchates. Rome, however, refused to recognize the patriarchal claims of the newly founded capital at Constantinople until the Fourth Council of Constantinople (869–70).[16]

The Church of Rome as the Center of Unity

We have noted that the Gospel attributed to Matthew omitted any mention of Simon Peter in its resurrection account, but earlier had Jesus tell him, "You are 'Rock,' and on this rock I will build my *ekklēsia*." Matthew thereby had Jesus proclaim the central role of Peter as it had come to be understood by the Matthean community after it "had been instructed by the events of Christ's risen life and taught by the light of the Spirit of truth" (Vat. II, *Dei verbum* 19). As Raymond Brown has observed, for Matthew, there is no time of the church separated from the time of Jesus. "Matthew has interwoven his understanding of the postresurrection era [and of Peter's crucial position in the postresurrection *ekklēsia*] into the account of Jesus' public ministry, writing, as it were, his Acts of the Apostles in and through the gospel."[17]

In Luke's Gospel, it is in Jerusalem that the infant Jesus is first recognized as savior and that the young Jesus teaching in the temple foreshadows his later ministry (2:22–50). It is likewise in Jerusalem and its environs that the risen Jesus appears to his disciples (Luke

24). In Luke's Acts of the Apostles, it is in Jerusalem that the Church begins. There, "Peter, standing with the Eleven," first proclaims the risen Jesus, after all had been filled with the Spirit (Acts 2:4–14). Having emphasized the role of Peter and the importance of Jerusalem, Acts proceeds to tell how the Church's proclamation of Jesus was carried throughout the Mediterranean region until it was brought to Rome. In that regard, it introduces Paul, describing his conversion and telling of his baptism within another influential community already existing at Damascus (Acts 9:1–20). Paul himself insists that three years passed before he finally went to Jerusalem, to come to know Cephas and to meet James (Gal 1:17–19). After moving to Syria and Cilicia, another fourteen years passed before Paul again visited Jerusalem, to confer with Peter, James, and John about his ministry to the Gentiles (Gal 2:1–10). On a final visit, he brought his collection for the needy of the Jerusalem community (Acts 21:17, 24:17).

Since Rome was the center of the Mediterranean world, it was inevitable that the leaders of the Church's expansion would eventually be drawn to that imperial capital. Acts of the Apostles (28:16) describes Paul's arrival there. In regard to Peter, the scriptures only tell us that he traveled to Antioch (Gal 2:11) and perhaps to Corinth (1 Cor 1:12). The letter known as *First Clement*—sent by the church at Rome to the church at Corinth about the year 96—makes reference to the persecution and death of the "pillars," and the hardships that Peter and Paul endured before their deaths, but it does not directly say that they were martyred at Rome (ch. 5). Neither does Ignatius of Antioch's epistle, written about fourteen years later "to the church which presides in the place of the district of the Romans" and "over love." Asking that nothing be done to prevent his martyrdom, Ignatius simply adds, "I do not command you as Peter and Paul did" (ch. 4). That Peter eventually went to Rome and was martyred there is explicitly attested by later tradition and by the archeological evidence uncovered in our century. Excavations two levels beneath the present altar have verified that Constantine's engineers built the first

St. Peter's Basilica over a grave that was the focus of Christian devotion to Peter in the earliest centuries.[18]

When the Roman church felt obliged to intervene in the internal crisis faced by the Corinthians (*1 Clement* 1.1), it demanded obedience in the name of Jesus (59.1). But, since Rome's letter seems to allow the possibility of mutual admonition (56.2), its intervention beyond the peninsula of Italy may have been an expression of interecclesial responsibility for a sister church, and not a protoprimatial claim. Rome's primatial claims required more time to solidify.

Countering the Gnostics, toward the end of the second century, Irenaeus of Lyons declares that "because of the Roman church's more powerful leadership, it is necessary for every church, that is the faithful everywhere, to agree with [or come to] that church; for in her, those from everywhere have always preserved what comes from the apostolic tradition" (*Against the Heresies* 3.3.2). Tracing the foundation of the Church at Rome to Peter and Paul and simply presupposing that the mono-episcopacy of his time had existed from the beginning, Irenaeus lists those who succeeded the blessed apostles at Rome: Linus, Anacletus, Clement, Euarestus, Sixtus, Telesphorus, Hyginus, Pius, Anicetus, Soter, and the incumbent Eleutherus (174/5–189), twelfth from the apostles. As Irenaeus sees it, "By this order and succession, the apostolic teaching came down to us in the Church's tradition and preaching of truth" (3.3.3). In his perspective, the bishop of Rome taught in a way that reflected the genuine apostolic faith of all the churches, because his church gathered together or was in dialogue with persons from many different parts of the world. Thus, by listening to Rome, one heard the faith of the entire Church. Among all the churches, the church of Rome and its bishop effectively symbolized the unity of all churches.

While Irenaeus maintained that everyone should come to Rome to know the true faith, he did not hesitate to voice his opposition if he thought the bishop of that city had overstepped his authority. As noted above, when Victor of Rome broke communion with the churches of Asia Minor because they followed a different calendar for Easter, Irenaeus reminded him that his predecessors at Rome had respected such diversity and variations. Victor was to work for peace and unity rather than to break communion with other churches over such a matter (Eusebius, *Ecclesiastical History* 5.24).

At the dawn of the third century, Tertullian reports that the Romans claimed that Clement was appointed or "set in order" by Peter, and that the church of the Smyrnaeans asserted that Polycarp was placed over it by John (*Prescription* 32). Among all the apostolic churches, "where the very chairs *[cathedrae]* of the apostles still presided in their stead," Rome is fortunate to be the place where Peter and Paul poured out their teaching and their blood through crucifixion and beheading (*Prescription* 36). Even after he has become a Montanist, Tertullian still acknowledges the special significance of communion with Rome (*Against Praxeas* 1, 4–6).

In the middle of the third century, Cyprian of Carthage refers to the Roman Church as "the source and root of the universal Church" (*Ep.* 48.3) or "the principal church from which episcopal unity arose" (*Ep.* 59.14). He considers communion with the bishop of Rome to be synonymous with the unity and charity of the universal Church (*Ep.* 48.3 and 55.1). In chapter four of the first draft of his treatise *On the Unity of the Catholic Church*, he cites Matthew 16:18–19 and John 21:17 and concludes on this basis that the Lord built the Church on Peter and entrusted the feeding of the sheep to him. Cyprian explains that all the apostles were given equal power, but Christ established only one Chair as the origin and hallmark of unity: "The other apostles were what Peter was, but primacy [in the sense of priority or seniority[19]] is given to Peter to demonstrate that there is but one Church and one Chair. They are all shepherds, but there is shown to be one flock which is fed by all the apostles in unanimous agreement." For Cyprian, all who hold the faith have to hold to the unity of Peter; whoever deserts the Chair of Peter is not in the unity of the Church.

Cyprian himself later disagreed with Stephen of Rome's opposition to the North African practice of rebaptizing heretics and sectarians. Stephen seems to have claimed a "primacy" entitling him to the obedience of other bishops on that matter,[20] but Cyprian did not comply. That appears to be the reason why he revised chapter four of *On the Unity of the Catholic Church*, omitting any reference to "primacy."[21] Yet, as in the first edition, Cyprian's second draft still interpreted Matthew 16:18–19 to mean that the Church is one because it was first built on one person. The Church thus had unity in its very beginning. Peter alone was the originating source of the Church's oneness, but all bishops who preside in the Church must sustain its unity, thereby proving that the episcopate itself is also one and undivided.

Neither draft of Cyprian's *On the Unity of the Catholic Church* advocates the kind of Roman administrative centralization that would emerge in the medieval period, or the primacy of universal, full, and supreme jurisdiction proclaimed by Vatican I.[22] Both drafts say the Church is one because it had its start in Peter alone, but both also say that all the apostles had equal power. Cyprian understood the episcopate as "one whole, which individual bishops, each responsible for their own churches, share in a way that makes them also responsible, with one another, for the entire Church" (*On the Unity* 5). His emphasis on the role of Peter always sought to support the apostolic authority of all bishops viewed as a college (*Ep.* 33.1). For Cyprian, the universal communion called Church is like the many rays coming from one sun, the many branches on a tree with one root, or the many streams flowing from one spring. All such multiplicity starts in oneness and must remain in union. A branch broken off the tree dies, and a stream cut off from its source dries up (*On the Unity* 5). Thus bishops, as a collegial group, were to bear with one another in love, making every effort to preserve the unity of the Spirit in the bond of peace (*Ep.* 55.24; cf. Eph 4:2–3).

Cyprian's views persisted in the Catholic churches of North Africa. During the fourth century, Optatus of Milevis argued, against the Donatists, that the Catholic Church is holy because it possesses, among other elements, the first episcopal chair on which Peter, the head of all the Apostles, sits (*Donatist Schism* 2, 2). But, like Cyprian, Optatus understood the saying that "Peter alone accepted the keys" to mean that he was the first to receive the episcopal commission in which all the other apostles and their successors equally participated (*Donatist Schism* 1, 10).

Augustine followed Optatus in maintaining that the Catholic churches of North Africa were distinguished by their bonds of peace and communion with apostolic churches throughout the world and with the bishops who succeeded to the apostles in those churches.[23] He reminded the sectarian, Donatist communities that they could not claim such communion or universality (*Ep.* 49.3, 93.23).

Communion with the Church of Rome had special importance for Augustine. Recognizing the primacy *(principatus)* of the apostolic Chair at Rome, Augustine observes how bishops could invoke their communion with that Church, expressed by means of letters, to counter local pressure from the Donatists (*Ep.* 43.7). But in that context, Augustine likewise recalls Cyprian's remark (*Ep.* 71.3) that Peter did not arrogantly invoke his primacy to silence Paul at Antioch; he was willing to learn through dialogue and to change (*On Baptism* 2.1.2).

Like Cyprian, Augustine considered Peter to be the representative or symbol of the unity of the whole Church and of all the apostles. He believed that Matthew 16:18–19, which referred to Peter, was really addressed to the entire Church, which was personally represented by Peter on account of his primacy among disciples. Peter was a type of the Church, just as Judas was in some way a type of all the enemies of Christ.[24] In Peter, the whole Church confessed that Jesus was the Christ (*Retractions* 1.21.1). Accordingly, the keys of the kingdom were accepted not just by one man but by the entire Church, whose universality and unity Peter represented (*Sermon* 149.7, 295.2). The Church founded in and on Christ received the keys in the person of Peter (*On John* 118.4, 124.5).

Augustine found evidence for his interpretation that Peter was the type of the whole Church in the fact that all the Apostles received the Spirit from the Lord and that all were to forgive or bind sins (John 20:22–23). Likewise, according to Matthew 18:15–18, the whole Church built on the rock could bind and loose sinners in its midst (*Sermon* 295.2). Acknowledging that Ambrose had earlier considered Peter the rock on which the Church was built, Augustine believed that Matthew 16:18 could also be interpreted as meaning that Christ was the rock on which Peter and the Church that he personified were built.[25]

Augustine declared that one of the things that kept him "in the lap of the Church" was the succession of bishops from the Chair of Peter, to whom the risen Lord had entrusted the feeding of his sheep.[26] Yet, while he recognized the greater responsibility of the bishop of Rome, Augustine's predominant emphasis was the coresponsibility of all bishops (*Against Two Epistles of the Pelagians* 1.1.1–2). He metaphorically described himself as a trickle compared to the abundant stream of the bishop of Rome, but quickly added that they both flowed from the same fountain (*Ep.* 177.19). The bishop of Rome together with all the other bishops cared for the *one* flock of the Shepherd of shepherds, Christ, who assisted them in doing *his* work (*Against Two Epistles* 4.12.34).

Augustine observes that, although there were many apostles, Christ told only Peter to feed his sheep (John 21:17) because all good shepherds are not divided into many, but are united in one shepherd. He buttresses that position with a number of metaphors. When good shepherds feed the sheep, Christ feeds. His voice and his love are in them. Christ made Peter, who loved him (John 21:15), one with him, and gave the care of his sheep to him so that he should be the head and type of the body, the Church. Like husband and wife, Peter and the Church were two in one flesh. Since there is thus only one flock and one shepherd (John 10:16), all the good shepherds speak with the voice of one shepherd (*Sermon* 46.30; see 295.4). They are all united with Peter who is one with Christ, and with the bishop of Rome who succeeded Peter (*Ep.* 53.2).

For Augustine, the bishop of Rome represented the unity of the Church as a whole, as Peter had. Peter's successors taught what the Roman Church had always held in harmony with the faith of all the other churches, whether Latin or Greek, in the one truly catholic or universal Church (*Against Julian of Eclanum* 1.4.13). When problems could not be adequately resolved locally, among North Africans, Augustine did not oppose an appeal to Rome (*Ep.* 209.9).

The Solidification of Papal Claims

In the long run, the theory and claims of Roman primacy were especially solidified by the bishops of that city, called popes (*papa:* father) since the third century. Damasus of Rome (366–84) refused to recognize the First Council of Constantinople, held in 381, because it had been convened by the emperor and no legates from Rome participated. He particularly objected to the third canon promulgated by the council, which both granted a primacy of honor to the bishop of Constantinople and ranked that "new Rome" second after Rome. That ranking modified the previous order of Rome, Alexandria, Antioch, and Jerusalem, established by canons 6 and 7 of the Council of Nicaea. In a decree that was probably formulated at a synod convened by Damasus in his "apostolic church" in 382, Rome claimed precedence over all other churches and based that claim on the Roman church's foundation by the apostle to whom Jesus said, "You are Peter and on this rock I will build my Church."[27]

Such insistence on the prerogatives of the bishop of Rome did not lack encouragement from others. Jerome had previously written to Damasus in 376, urging him to take a stand in a christological controversy. Professing his communion with the chair of Peter, the rock on which the Church is built, Jerome observed how those not aboard "Noah's Ark," the Church built on Peter, would perish when the flood comes (*Ep.* 15.1.2).

Siricius (384–99), who succeeded Damasus as bishop of Rome, considered himself an "heir" to Peter, which in Roman law meant that he had assumed Peter's legal status and responsibilities. Siricius believed that in his "persona" Peter himself carried the burdens of all who were weighed down (*Ep.* 1. *praef.* <1>).[28] Invoking Paul's solicitude for all the churches, as expressed in 2 Corinthians 11:28, and adopting the style of the Roman emperors, Siricius also initiated the practice whereby Roman bishops issued decrees in response to questions about ecclesial problems (*Ep.* 1.7). He made it clear that those who brought their questions to the Roman church had come to "the head of the body," and that no bishop was free to be ignorant of the statutes of that Apostolic See or of canonical definitions (*Ep.* 1.15). Rome's rules about baptism were to be observed by all bishops who were unwilling to separate themselves from the solidity of the apostolic rock upon which Christ had built the universal Church (*Ep.* 1:2). Such claims were effective, for papal decretals subsequently built up into a body of law.

Pope Innocent (402–17), who assumed the formidable task of protecting Rome from invasion by the Goths, sought to impose disciplinary and liturgical uniformity on the churches of the West. He asserted that no church had ever been founded in all of Italy, Gaul, Spain, Africa, Sicily, or any of the islands unless Peter or his successors appointed bishops for it, since no other apostle was ever mentioned as having taught in those places. Innocent concluded that all Western churches must therefore follow the practice of the Roman Church from which he presumed they had begun (*Ep.* 25.2.1–3).[29] Like Damasus and Siricius before him, Innocent also tried to extend his influence over Illyricum, or the Balkans, in the East (*Ep.* 1: to Anysius; *Ep.* 17: to Rufus and others). This effort brought him and later popes into conflict with the bishop of Constantinople.

In his numerous letters to bishops seeking advice, Innocent simply presupposed that major disputes had to be brought to the apostolic seat of Rome for resolution (*Ep.* 2.3 <6>). He compared his authority to that of Moses, who set up judges over Israel (Exod 18:13–26) but reserved more important decisions to himself (*Ep.* 13.1 and 3). But, above all, Innocent claimed the assistance of Peter, in whom apostolicity and the episcopacy had their beginning from Christ (*Ep.* 2.2). The bishops of the Roman See succeeded that apostle from whom the episcopacy and all its authority arose (*Ep.* 29.1). When other bishops came to Rome with their questions, they came to Peter, the author of their name and honor. And, by consulting the Apostolic See, which exercised a "solicitude for all churches" (2 Cor 11:28), they benefited the unity of all churches (*Ep.* 30.2).

In a letter to the bishops of Africa, Pope Zosimus (417–18), Innocent's successor, claimed that Rome's authority was so great that no one could review or dispute a decision made by its bishop. Because Peter is the "head" or source of such great authority, the bishops who inherited his See with his consent have been given his power to bind and loose. Peter's care for all the churches, and for the Roman See where he sat, has been given them to defend (*Ep.* 12.1).[30] Later, Pope Boniface (418–22) insisted that the very institution of the emerging universal Church had its beginning from the honor of Peter and his leadership. For that reason, the Roman Church was a font of ecclesial discipline and acted as the head of its members, namely, all the Churches spread throughout the world (*Ep.* 14.1).[31] Because of such principality *(principatum)*, the Apostolic See of Rome could accept all legitimate complaints (*Ep.* 14.4). Moreover, its judgments could not be revised (*Ep.* 15.5).

Despite the assertions of Zosimus and Boniface, other bishops did not hesitate to protest what they considered undue interference with their own authority when Rome intervened to resolve internal matters in their churches. Writing to Pope Celestine (422–32), Aurelius and the other bishops of North Africa, assembled in a synod at Carthage, asked how God could give one person across the Mediterranean, without access to key witnesses, the ability to render just decisions, and deny it to a large number of bishops gathered in a local council. Invoking the canons of the Council of Nicaea, the bishops insisted that matters "should be settled in the place where they arose."[32] But Rome's bishops continued to affirm their authority to intervene. Pope Sixtus III (432–40) would insist that bishops have to be in agreement with Peter's successors, for they handed down the teaching he received from Jesus himself (*Ep.* 6.5).[33]

Calling himself an "unworthy heir" of Peter, upon whom Jesus had bestowed a personal primacy for governing the Church after his confession of faith at Caesarea Philippi, Pope Leo the Great (440–61) claimed a unique position, distinct from that of all other bishops. He declared that the whole world came to Peter's See, and that the care of its bishop extended over the universal Church (*Sermon* 3.4, 4.2–3, 5.2; *Ep.* 5.2).[34] In Leo's view, all bishops were equal in dignity but not in rank. Accepting the structural system of metropolitan sees, or the incipient patriarchates, recognized at the Council of Nicaea (canons 4 and 6), Leo carefully positioned Rome as the "head" of that ecclesial system: one bishop in each province, and the bishops of particular larger cities had precedence over others. But through them, care of the universal Church converged in the one Chair of Peter (*Ep.* 14.11). The one who presided at Peter's See at Rome was also primate of all bishops (*Sermon* 3.4) and "head" of the universal Church (*Ep.* 103). The principality that Christ gave Peter over all the other apostles remained in the Roman Church (*Ep.* 9, pref.).

Leo grounded his claim to a power distinct from that of all other bishops upon a difference he saw in the power of the apostles. Christ had given authority, or the principality *(principatum)* that remains in the Roman Church, to Peter first and through him to the other apostles (*Ep.* 9 pref., 10.1–2, 14.11). For example, teaching the truth was a task Christ gave all the apostles, but it flowed down from Peter as from a head into a body (*Ep.* 10.1) Similarly, Peter's right of power to bind and loose (Matt 16:19) passed over to the others, who were his equals in honor but not in power. Peter's privileged position remained (*Sermon* 4.3, 83.2). Participating in the power of Christ with whom he was united,

Peter also became the first bishop of Rome, and he still governs and teaches the Church through each succeeding bishop of that city (*Ep.* 10.1; *Sermon* 3.2–4, 5.4, 83.1). The Peter who enjoys apostolic and episcopal dignity has not ceased to preside over his See (*Sermon* 5.4). For Leo, Peter still presides in the *sacramental persona* of his heir.

Leo claimed to act both as heir and *vicar* of Peter, whose faith and authority lives on in the Roman See. Precisely because he shared in the power and responsibility to bind and loose that Peter received as the "foundation" and "doorkeeper of the kingdom of heaven," Leo considered his authority to be above that of all other bishops (*Sermon* 3.2–4; *Ep.* 103). Leo thus believed that only he as bishop of Rome had principally, by divine institution, received care over all the churches, for their mutual concord. He could appoint delegates who would refer major cases to him for his decision, since they shared part of his solicitude, but not the fullness of his power *(plenitudinem potestatis)* for the unity of all churches (*Ep.* 14.1). Many shepherds cared for the sheep, but only one, Peter, through his heirs and vicars at Rome, cared for the whole flock (*Sermon* 3.2 and 4).

Bishop Hilary of Arles, who was allegedly using even armed soldiers to extend his authority over the churches of Gaul, was ordered not to interfere in the province of Vienne; he was not to be present at the ordination of any bishop or to ordain anyone there. For Leo, such actions were contrary to the primacy of Peter, who had been given the authority to bind and loose, and entrusted with the special care of feeding the sheep *before* any of the other apostles. But Leo did not reserve ordinations in the province of Vienne to himself, as Hilary falsely alleged. Rather, he recognized the privilege or right of local bishops to preserve discipline in their own province (*Ep.* 10.2–9) and reiterated the tradition whereby a new bishop was elected with the consent of the clergy and people (*Ep.* 14.5). However, no one was to be consecrated bishop in the churches of Illyricum, where Rome's claims were contested by Constantinople, without consulting Leo's delegate for that region (*Ep.* 6.1).

Leo insisted on the priority and fullness of the bishop of Rome's power but never suggested that it could displace the authority of other bishops.[35] Rather, his solicitude for all churches was to be shared by his "brothers and cobishops" (*Ep.* 10.9, 14:1, 114.1) with whom he was joined in a "college of charity" (*Ep.* 5.2). Leo's stated intention was to preserve harmony among bishops and to urge them to unity in the bond of charity (*Ep.* 10.9). His cobishops were supposed to accept his exhortations and not to act out of rivalry (*Ep.* 12.9). But he also respected their authority. A bishop who wrote to Leo about a matter of general observance among all bishops was gently reminded that the metropolitan should have been consulted first (*Ep.* 108.1). Strongly supporting both local and regional synods of bishops, Leo believed that most problems could be avoided by close and frequent association among bishops.[36] Only major issues would have to be brought to him for resolution (*Ep.* 6.5, 15.17).

For their part, the bishops of the province of Arles acknowledged that, through Peter, who was first among the apostles, Rome had the first place *(principatus)* over all the churches of the world. But they still asked that Arles be restored to its place over the churches of Gaul (*Ep.* 65.2). Leo's understanding of Roman primacy, however, would not allow any such incipient patriarchates to take root among the Western churches.

In the sermons that Leo preached on his episcopal anniversary, his juridical emphasis on a Petrine, Roman primacy of power and rule is intertwined with mystical and sacramental perspectives.[37] For Leo, the solidity of Peter's faith is perpetuated in the bishops of Rome. What Peter believed in Christ and what Christ built on Peter (Matt 16:16–19) permanently endure in Rome's bishops (*Sermon* 3.2). Peter is still made present through his See, and he receives the love shown to his heirs (*Sermon* 2.2). His power and authority live on in his See, where he still daily confesses that Jesus is "the Christ, the Son of the living God," through the bishops of Rome, because every tongue that confesses the Lord is imbued with that master's voice (3.3). Likewise, Peter's solidarity with Christ has passed to his heirs, so that it is Christ who acts through the bishops of Rome (5.4). Christ, the omnipotent and perpetual Priest, thus continually provides his Church with the protection of apostolic strength (3.2) because of Peter's enduring presence and role in the bishops of Rome.

As we have seen, Augustine had presented Peter as a type or figure representing the faith of all believers. Leo declares that Christ has built an eternal temple, the loftiness of his Church rising into heaven, upon Peter and the firmness of his faith (*Sermon* 4.2, 83.2). He envisions the bishop of Rome as a sacramental figure who symbolically represents not only the unity in faith of the entire Church built on Peter's faith, but also its unity in one priesthood. Despite the diverse gradation of bishops and baptized within the Body of Christ, Leo emphasizes that all who have Christ as their head are one in Christ (Gal 3:28; 1 Cor 12:13). United in faith and baptism, all the members of Christ's Body have been consecrated by the anointing of the Spirit and so share in one royal priesthood (1 Pet 2:9).

As the heir of Peter, Leo understands himself to be the symbol representing that common priestly participation of all believers in Christ. Consistent with this understanding, he proposes that his anniversary as bishop of Rome be the occasion to celebrate "a single sacramental mystery of high-priesthood" shared by the whole body of the Church (*Sermon* 4.1). The community would thereby also venerate Peter, whom Leo rather excessively described as the one "who alone received so much from Christ, the source of all graces, that nothing passes to others without his participation" (4.2).

For Leo, the Incarnate Word dwelling among us was an effective sacrament through which both the unity of his Deity and the Trinity operated. He believed that Peter was uniquely made a partner of that sacramental, incarnate, divine power. "From all the world, one Peter was chosen and placed over the call of all nations, all apostles, and all Fathers of the Church, so that, although there are many priests and pastors in the People of God, Peter properly rules all whom Christ principally rules" (*Sermon* 4.2). Because he was first in confessing the Lord, and therefore in apostolic dignity, Peter was declared the rock on which the Church will be built. Christ remains the inviolable rock, the corner stone and foundation, but Peter is also rock because he participates in Christ's power and through him Christ rules (4.2, 83.1). Because of his special association with Christ, those who acknowledge Peter and his role come to know the mysteries of Christ (3.3). For Leo, such great power was given to him whom Christ made the first leader *(principem)* of the whole Church (4.4).

Leo maintained that the bishop of Rome's authority extends over all other bishops because he perpetuates the only apostle whom Christ vested with a plenary power over all the other apostles. Other bishops, however, did not accept all of his claims. At the second session of the Council of Chalcedon in 451, the assembled bishops shouted "Peter has spoken through Leo" when his Tome or letter concerning the Monophysite heresy was read. But, to Leo's dismay, the same Council proposed that Constantinople's civil status should make its church equal to Rome (canons 17 and 28).[38] He retorted that imperial power could not make an apostolic see; it had to be constructed on the Rock that the Lord had made a foundation (*Ep.* 104.3).

Since the emperors had left old Rome defenseless, only Leo's intervention prevented the destruction of that city during its looting by the Vandals in 455. Preaching soon after that painful experience of Rome's new powerlessness, Leo articulated a new vision of spiritual destiny for his city. Peter, the principal apostle, had been destined to come to Rome after he had "founded" the church at Antioch. By divine providence, Rome had already united many different peoples in preparation for the Church, and Christian peace would now bring it more subjects than Roman warfare could ever win. Peter's episcopal See made that priestly and kingly city "head of the world." The city that once embraced so many falsehoods had become the head from which the light of truth revealing salvation can flow into the body of the whole world, since the citizens of every nation come to and learn from Rome (*Sermon* 82.1–5).

The articulation of papal power during the early centuries culminated with Pope Gelasius I (492–96) who countered two threats to his authority as bishop of Rome: the interference in religious matters by Christian emperors and the expansionism of the bishops of the new imperial capital at Constantinople, who had now assumed the title of "ecumenical patriarchs." Within an empire become Christian, Roman emperors no longer claimed the kind of religious function their predecessors had enjoyed under paganism; Gratian (375–83) even renounced the imperial title of *Pontifex Maximus.* That designation, originally applied to the pagan Roman high priest, was now adopted by Pope Leo and other bishops. (Only centuries later would it be reserved just for the popes.) But despite their surrender of the title *Pontifex Maximus*, the Christian emperors carved out a distinctive religious role for themselves. It was they who convened all the early ecumenical councils in the East.

In response to the imperial presumptions, Gelasius distinguished two kinds of rule over this world, the sacred authority of bishops and the power of kings. He insisted that priestly authority involved greater responsibility, since God would hold bishops accountable even for the actions of kings. Therefore, the emperor who presided over the human race had to submit, like all the faithful, to the judgment of those who oversee divine matters, and especially to the one who presides at the See that God has placed over all other bishops.[39] The powers of this world had to learn about divine things from the bishops and especially from the vicar of blessed Peter because, according to the canons, the highest judgment in religious matters came from the Apostolic See.[40] The Roman Synod held under Gelasius in 495 again declared Rome's "principality" over the whole Church, since Christ had given Peter the power to bind and loose *everything*, without any exception.[41]

In a letter that he had earlier drafted for Pope Felix III, Gelasius made it quite clear that the Emperor was a son of and not a presider over the Church; in religious matters he was not to teach but to learn from the priests.[42] Later, as Pope, Gelasius declared that Christ had distinguished between the duties of priests and kings, and he further insisted that the emperor could not judge bishops, since an inferior could not absolve a superior.[43] Only Rome, the first See, could receive appeals and make judgments for the whole Church. The judgments of the Roman Church could not be reviewed, appealed, or dissolved, but only implemented.[44] Popes of later centuries would seek all the more to implement the full implications of such Gelasian claims.

Rome's authority continued to expand in the West, but the majority of the Eastern Churches recognized its primacy as one of honor, without jurisdiction over metropolitan bishops and provinces outside its Western sphere or patriarchate.[45] Unfortunately, those differences in vision were never resolved by a debate within the unity of ecclesial communion, since political, theological, and cultural differences ultimately divided the Latin West and the Greek East. Only since the Second Vatican Council, within the cultural pluralism of a Church spread over many continents, is the papacy again being given the opportunity—or the challenge—to renew its role for "unity in diversity." In that regard, the present moment reflects the situation of the early Church more than that of the rather "monolithically European" Church of later centuries.

A Church of Visible Sacraments and Invisible Holiness

The complex organizational development of the early Church did not displace the basic notion that the Church was the Body of Christ enlivened by the Spirit. That idea continued to be the emphasis of Augustine in the West and of John Chrysostom, and later of Cyril of Alexandria, in the East. For Augustine, Christ as head is so united with his members in the Church that together they are "one person."[46] Such unity was maintained by the Spirit, the soul of the Church. It was manifested in love and nourished through the Eucharist.[47] As Chrysostom explained in his *Homily on 1 Corinthians* (24.2), *koinōnia* meant that all shared one and the same body that made all one and the same body. Those united with one another and with Christ were to show the same love or be "of one heart and soul" (Acts 4:32). In Augustine's words, "In that bread you are taught how you should love unity" (*Sermon* 227). The structures had emerged to serve such communion.

Augustine maintained that "no religion, whether true or false, can unite humans unless they are brought together by participation in visible signs or sacraments" (*Against Faustus the Manichean* 19.11). That perspective permeated his theology of Church, which was also shaped by his debates with the Donatists and the Pelagians and by his Neo-Platonism. Especially after 412, he more and more emphasized the Church as a communion of sacraments that effected a unity in the Spirit. Baptism and the Eucharist were the means through which salvific grace was given, but only within the Catholic Church. Because a more institutionalized form of Augustine's theology formed the core of Western medieval perspectives on Church, his perspectives merit some further consideration.

The Donatists had separated themselves from the mainstream Church in North Africa after Diocletian's persecution. They claimed that they thereby avoided "contamination" by "unworthy" bishops who had handed over unneeded books to avoid persecution. Considering themselves the pure church, and invoking Cyprian as their authority, the Donatists also maintained that persons who left their community retained their own baptism but lost the right of baptizing others. Augustine disagreed and argued that even a lack of faith or holiness in the minister did not invalidate a baptism (or an ordination) given in the name of the Lord.[48]

For Augustine, persons baptized by the schismatic Donatists, or even by heretics, were like soldiers who had become deserters from the Roman army. They were still marked with a brand (*Ep.* 317.5) or character that made Jesus search for them.[49] The external sign of their baptism, which Augustine called the Lord's character, would never have to be repeated, but its full effects, the reception of the Spirit and love, were lacking.[50] Augustine maintained that a baptism received among schismatics or heretics, even one of blood through martyrdom, effected salvation only if those marked with the Lord's character became united with the universal Church,[51] for one could have the Holy Spirit only when one was within the unity of the Church that speaks all languages (*Sermon* 268, 2).

Some have accused Augustine of mechanizing and depersonalizing the sacraments, treating them like checks on which payment was stopped as long as the one who received them remained outside the Catholic Church.[52] But Augustine's intention was quite different. He never presumed that the sacraments automatically eliminated the need to strive for spiritual growth.[53] The person who was baptized had to have faith in order to *accept* the remission of sins effected by the sacrament (*On Baptism* 4.11.17). But the effectiveness of the sacrament did not flow from what the human recipient or minister did; it came from what Christ did (*Against the Letters of Petilian* 3.49.59). The holiness and orthodoxy of those who baptized were secondary precisely because they were exercising a ministry and not a power.[54] If those who baptized acted in the name of Christ, it was Christ who baptized.[55] For Augustine, the point was that union with Christ was impossible if one was not united into his body, the one universal communion.

The Donatists lacked "the charity of Christ" because they did not embrace his unity in the Catholic Church (*Ep.* 61.1–2). With no claim to universality, they were not the genuine Church, which had to be Catholic, a communion of all nations.[56] Only in that Church, born and strengthened by the labors of the apostles, was God's Spirit at work, gathering all into one.[57] Only within that Church, which is Christ, could one find the unique love that unites all the members into one (*Epistle to Catholics "On Unity"* 4.7). Only within that communion could sacraments guarantee true charity: a love that has feet which carry us to church, hands which reach out to the poor, and eyes which look to the needy (*On the Epistle of John* 7.10).

In contrast to the static and defensive insularity of the Donatists, who described the Church as a hermetically sealed Noah's Ark (*Epistle to Catholics* 5.9), Augustine's vision embraced a sense of the Church's dynamic and expanding destiny, which humans could not thwart.[58] The Church, which at Pentecost had already united all the languages divided at the Tower of Babel, was to be a "microcosm of the reestablished unity of the human race."[59] Its task was to restore the unity of all humans disrupted by the sin of Adam.[60] To accomplish that end, "Mother Church" would teach wives to be subject to their husbands, slaves to be loyal, masters to persuade rather than punish, people to be obedient to kings, and kings to rule for their people's benefit. Tempering the existing order of the world, rather than remaking it, the Church of Augustine's vision would unite all humans and nations by bonds that were rooted in the first parents common to all (*On the Mores of the Catholic Church* 1.30.63).

Christians were made holy within the universal Church in order to be like the grain among the weeds. They would continue to live among sinners, both within the world and the Church, in order to transform them in some way.[61] Because holiness was not always clearly visible, Augustine believed that only God, who had predestined a fixed number of saints before the creation of the world, knew which of the baptized in the Church were truly holy or just, and which of the sinners now outside the Church would ultimately be saved. Some who seemed to be *within* were really *outside*.[62]

Augustine attributed the holiness of the visible Church, which included both holy and sinful members, not to the holiness of its baptized or its ministers (*Ep.* 208.4 and 6), but to the efficacy of its visible sacraments guaranteed by Christ and the Spirit.[63] As the reflection or shadow of the heavenly City of Jerusalem (*Against the Epistles of Parmenian* 2.4.9), the Catholic Church was holy because it participated in the holiness of Christ (*Ep.* 261.2). Only within that Church, where one also found the authority of many talented and learned persons and a universally preserved oral tradition, could one share the life of Christ and the Spirit and receive the revelation of Christ.[64] Augustine thereby articulated what Yves Congar has termed an ecclesiological monopoly: "Outside the Catholic Church everything is possible except salvation."[65] Adding his own nuance to a position earlier articulated by Origen and Cyprian,[66] Augustine maintained that there could be sacraments outside the Church, but sacraments became "useful" or effective of a salvific relationship with God only if and when the recipient was united with the communion of the Catholic Church. That perspective endured for centuries, until ecumenical and interreligious dialogues required a nuanced reconsideration.

Augustine's perspectives on the Church were also shaped by his debates with the Pelagians, who taught that humans could avoid sin and do good if they really willed to do so. Augustine countered that grace was necessary for a person to be able not to sin.[67] In his later writings, God's will that all be saved is further distinguished from God's decision to give the grace of perseverance toward final salvation only to a few.[68] The older Augustine came to believe that only a few, even among the baptized within the Church, were given such final perseverance. His debates about the necessity of grace and his pastoral experience had led him to conclude that many within the Church do not have the Spirit and are not holy.[69]

Finally, Augustine also viewed the Church as the City of God in which love, rather than power, reigned.[70] Reflecting Neo-Platonic perspectives, he believed that the perfect "form" of Church had existed among the angels before the creation of the world and humans (*Literal Commentary on Genesis* 5.9) and would again exist at the end. With its mixture of saints and sinners, whose true qualities were often hidden or invisible, the earthly or pilgrim Church looked for its heavenly homeland, that more blessed, primordial City of God in which angels were the original citizens.[71] At the end, the saints who were the City of God on earth, an invisible community within the visible Church, would be united with the angels who never fell into sin (*City of God* 14:28). Those few humans, saved by means of the earthly Church and its sacraments, would replace the fallen angels who once populated the primordial heavenly Church, thereby fulfilling the number of citizens God had predetermined for the heavenly City before the beginning.[72] By giving the gift of perseverance to the saints within history, God is gathering a City of God that travels like a stranger on earth, waiting to be united into that heavenly City of angels (*Enchiridion* 66).

Although many of Augustine's perspectives deeply influenced later Western theology, it is significant that the Second Synod of Orange in 529 simply taught that to love God is a gift given by God, who loves even if unloved (canon 25). The official summary of the synod's conclusions (Denzinger, Hünermann 397 [cf. n104, ch. 1; hereafter cited as DH]) says nothing about predestination beyond condemning the idea that God predestines some humans to evil.

A modified and institutionalized version of Augustine's theology of Church as a communion of sacraments will ground the paradigm that emerges in medieval Western tradition. The Church will be viewed as a kind of divine franchise in which those empowered by ordination administer a system of sacraments, through which God distributes salvation by means of grace, sometimes misunderstood almost as if it were a thing rather than a transforming relationship. Instead of emphasizing communal concelebration and divine indwelling or participation in the divine life, the medieval focus will shift to the more individualistic categories of administering and receiving sacraments, with grace viewed as something that can be received, lost, and regained, given to some and withheld from others.[73]

Toward a Stratified, Hierarchical Church

There had always been *episkopē* or supervision in the community called Church, just as there had always been those who served. Gradually, function became linked to "order," and the office of bishop was seen as a continuation of the "apostolic" office. As noted above, both the *Apostolic Tradition* and Cyprian of Carthage directed that a new bishop was to be chosen by all the people. After a candidate acceptable to all had been named, the people were to assemble on a Sunday and bishops from neighboring churches were to lay hands on him, while the elders watched (*Ap. Tr.* 2). One bishop then imposed a hand and prayed that the Spirit would descend upon the new *episkopos* (*Ap. Tr.* 3). In the case of a new elder, the bishop and all the elders of a church imposed hands (*Ap. Tr.* 7). That imposition was omitted for an elder who had suffered in a persecution, but never for a new bishop (*Ap. Tr.* 9). Only the bishop imposed hands on new deacons, since they acted as "the hands" of the bishop in serving the needs of the community (*Ap. Tr.* 8).

The *Apostolic Tradition* further instructs that widows, readers, virgins, and subdeacons are not ordained by an imposition of hands, but are only appointed (chs. 10–13). That directive indicates a growing distinction between the ordained and the nonordained.[74] It is noteworthy, however, that the eucharistic prayer preserved in the *Apostolic Tradition* did not yet include a special petition for the bishop and "clergy."

In the time of persecution, the decision to become a Christian involved great personal risk. According to the *Apostolic Tradition*, a process of initiation—usually three years in duration—tested one's commitment and gradually actualized one's experience of the Church as a faith community. Candidates were instructed and had to prove themselves by a life of self-control and good works. The process culminated on the night before Easter. In places like Jerusalem and Milan, catechumens symbolically faced the west, where sunset marked the beginning of darkness, and definitively renounced Satan and evil.[75] At the hour of cockcrow, when a slightly brightening eastern sky signaled an approaching sunrise, they began to be immersed or buried with the crucified Christ in the water of baptism, while professing their faith in the Father, Son, and Spirit. Having risen from the water to a new life in Christ, they came before the bishop who prayed that they would be filled with the Spirit. Imposing his hand, he anointed them with oil, sealed them with the sign of the cross. and gave them the kiss of peace for the first time. Joined to the assembly or *ekklēsia,* they now could join in celebrating and receiving the Eucharist for the first time.

During the third century, the Christian communities in some cities grew so large that they had to be subdivided. There could no longer be just one Eucharist concelebrated by the bishop with the elders, deacons, and the entire community. Instead, elders began to preside at subassemblies, as representatives of the bishop. In the middle of the fourth century, this new liturgical role of the elders was recognized by a new title, "priest" (*hieros* or *sacerdos*).[76] The new situation likewise changed the role of the deacons. During the second and third centuries, they had been a small group (often seven) who acted as the bishop's staff for service to the community. By the late fourth century, their collegial group had dispersed and individual deacons now acted as liturgical and pastoral assistants for the elders/priests presiding over subassemblies within the larger Church now "administered" by the bishop. Since the *ekklēsia* in a city was no longer one concrete assembly gathered around the bishop, rituals were created to preserve a symbolic experience of being one community united with and under the bishop. At Rome, representatives from the various districts participated in the bishop's "stational" liturgy, celebrated earlier. They then carried a piece of the eucharistic loaf back to their own assemblies, where it was put into the cup to symbolize the unity of their Eucharist and community with the bishop and the entire church of Rome. A remnant of that ceremony of the *fermentum* still endures during the breaking of the host after the Lord's Prayer.

When Theodosius made Christianity the "official religion" of the Roman empire in 380, the number of Christians increased even more. Participation in the Eucharist effectively became a duty for loyal citizens, who were to pray for the well-being of the empire. But it stands to reason that such mandatory participation may have diminished the overall quality of Christians. Augustine will complain of "crowds that fill the churches on Christian feast days and then the theatres on the pagan ritual days" (*On Catechizing the Uninstructed* 25.48). The new official status of Christianity also transformed those who presided at the Eucharist into administrative and cultic functionaries. Since the time of Constantine, bishops, priests, and deacons "had their place in the strictly hierarchic gradations of Lower-Empire officialdom."[77] They now enjoyed titles such as "most distinguished" *(clarissime)*, "illustrious," and "most glorious" and wore the accompanying insignia.

The Roman Empire functioned through a hierarchical system of order or "concord." The "people," who were expected to live in accordance with all the laws, were differentiated from the governing "orders," likewise distinguished by rank. The "senatorial order," which governed the most important provinces, was above the "equestrian order," which controlled the lesser provinces. Within the imperial civil service bureaucracy, administrators worked their way up through a "course of honors" or successive grades of "dignity." One began as a *quaestor* and then moved up the ranks to the position of *consul.* The fourth century was an especially golden age for such imperial administration and bureaucracy. Functionaries, privileges, exemptions, and other categories flourished. As they were now considered a part of the imperial officialdom, the households of clerics enjoyed exemptions from taxes and military service, which made the clerical state very attractive. To avoid an excessive loss of tax revenues, imperial law specifically forbade the recruitment of clerics from the wealthy class of decurions.[78]

Facing the need to organize a growing abundance of clerics, the Church adapted the patterns of the empire. It began to differentiate the "people" from the "clergy" and to emphasize a gradation of rank among those who had been "admitted into" the diverse "orders" or collegial bodies of bishops, elders, and deacons. Bishops were called priests of the first order, and elders priests of the second order.[79] Invoking a system of seniority that required clerics to pass through all the lower ranks before becoming bishops,[80] the ecclesial legislation of the fourth century was reminiscent of imperial patterns. An internal hierarchy of the Christian community was becoming institutionally established. In the fifth century, Leo the Great ranked "episcopal excellency" above "presbyteral honor" and refers to subdeacons as "fourth from the head" (*Ep.* 14.4).

Arguably, however, in developing its own "course of honors," the Church lost something valuable. It eventually made the various orders into a series of promotions, in which deacons ranked below elders, like a stage on the way up a ladder. This arrangement would destroy the earlier idea of a permanent diversity of functions or ministries that were not interchangeable but organically united within a local Church. During the third century, the term "laity" or people had still designated all who were ministers by their baptism. The laity were included among those who ministered, along with the bishop, elders, and deacons, like the spokes on one wheel. By the fifth century, a professional clerical ladder had been erected in the midst of the laity, and even its bottom rung was considered a step above lay men and lay women. Laicization was the worst possible punishment for clerics, who became visibly distinguished by their tonsure in the sixth century. The "clericalization" so characteristic of later centuries had begun.

To reiterate, in the Western Church of the third century, one was made a bishop by election from within a local church community followed by "the laying on of hands" by bishops from neighboring churches. Espoused to one church, each bishop personified the unity of a community that he served for life. In Roman terms, the bishop was like the "tribune" of the *plebs* or people. The bishop interceded for them and protected them, except that a bishop was to temper justice with love. During the fourth and fifth centuries, new bishops were more and more chosen by neighboring bishops, headed by the metropolitan bishop of the province, or sometimes even by the bishop who preceded them, but they were still supposed to be approved by the people.[81] The Synods of Ancyra (314) and Antioch (341), in their 18th canons, simply presumed that a church could refuse to accept an appointed bishop. But, during the fifth century, the *Apostolic Canons* imposed sanctions on the clerics of churches that did not accept the bishop appointed for them (canon 36/37).

In the Western Churches, the "people's" participation in the process of selecting a new bishop continued until the eleventh century. But in the Eastern Churches, their role gradually began to erode. A synod at Laodicea in Phrygia (343/81) explicitly said that the multitude was not to decide the election of new "priests" (canon 13). Such an exclusion was not unrelated to a new problem faced by the Churches of the Eastern empire. During the fifth century, the *Apostolic Canons* instructed that any bishop elected through the influence of secular authorities should be deposed (c. 31). Interference by secular rulers obviously continued, since canon 3 of the Second Council of Nicaea in 787 had to repeat the same directive. So did canon 22 of the ecumenical Fourth Council of Constantinople (869–70), which added that only bishops could elect new bishops.

Ordination was still primarily bound to an office for serving the needs of a community and not to bestowing powers on an individual. Canon 6 of the Council of Chalcedon (451) insisted that no one was to be ordained without being appointed to a specific church. However, despite repeated efforts to halt the practice,[82] some Eastern bishops of the late fourth and fifth centuries began to transfer from smaller churches in towns to larger ones in cities. A clerical careerism was emerging in which bishops would act like mobile chief executive officers, administering churches now identified more with territories than with communities.

During the fourth century, bishops had been given imperial jurisdiction for settling certain civil disputes (*Code of Theodosius* 1, 27, 1). When secular government collapsed in the West, bishops, who managed the ever-increasing landholdings and wealth of their churches, also assumed responsibility for the needs of the poor and sick. Providing such social services brought a new civil leadership role. And just as imperial power had been considered to come from God, so now Christian authority, with its new role in society, would more and more claim divine origin.

Theory often confirms practice, and that was the case regarding certain views on episcopacy articulated at the end of the fourth century. To counter certain Roman deacons who claimed that they ranked above rather than below the elders, an anonymous Roman writer, later called Ambrosiaster, invoked the differences between lower officials and prefects in the Roman civil service, and those between servants and masters.[83] Blending memories of the past into a constitutional order for his own time, he further maintained that bishops and elders were really the same order, although they differed in rank. As noted above, presbyters or elders were now exercising a liturgical role and had assumed the title of priest, both of which had previously been reserved to the bishop.

From the interchangeability of the terms elder and overseer (*presbyteros* and *episkopos*) in First Timothy, "Ambrosiaster" concluded that the term *episkopos* or "bishop" originally indicated the chief presbyter, whom he called the "highest priest."[84] For him, every *episkopos* was an elder but not every elder was an *episkopos*, who was simply the first or the senior among the presbyters. It was because no one outranked Timothy as an elder that he was also an *episkopos*, who alone could ordain another *episkopos*, for no one bestows what one has not accepted. Ambrosiaster therefore insisted that both the *episkopos* and the presbyters were "priests," but the bishop was "first."[85]

In reviewing the diversity of ministries within the Church, Ambrosiaster says that all "orders" are in the bishop, who is the "first priest," the head *(princeps)* of the priests, and also prophet, evangelist, and other such ministries. Although he insists that all the apostles were bishops,[86] Ambrosiaster does recognize that the structures of the Church developed. At first, he says, all Christians could teach and baptize, but once the Church spread throughout the world rectors and offices emerged, so that no cleric would dare to presume an office to which he was not ordained. He observes that it would be irrational if everyone could still do everything. He also claims that the way in which bishops were chosen had changed. Because the first elder in rank had sometimes proven to be unworthy, merit rather than seniority now determined who would be appointed bishop "by the judgment of many priests."[87] The impact of such perspectives was enhanced by the fact that subsequent centuries attributed the writings of the anonymous Roman to Ambrose and Augustine. And "Ambrosiaster's" ideas also appear to have influenced Jerome in his opposition to the claims of the Roman deacons.

Tracing the authority of all elders and bishops—"by whose prayers the body and blood of Christ is confected"—back to the apostles, Jerome argued that the practice of choosing one elder to serve as bishop had emerged simply as a remedy for schism. Noting that certain New Testament epistles interchangeably used *episkopoi* and *presbyteroi* for one and the same collegial leadership group, and claiming that hands were not imposed on elders who were made bishops at Alexandria, Jerome concluded that elders could do everything a bishop did, except for ordination.[88] He considered the episcopal role for unity, wherein bishops were superior to priests in their authority to rule *(regimen)*, to be based on a custom of the Church and not on any disposition of the Lord.[89] For Jerome, the term "bishop" simply referred to "rank." He considered bishops, priests, and deacons in the Church to be parallel to Aaron, his sons, and the Levites in the temple (*Ep.* 146).

Jerome's position would become foundational for the Western, medieval distinction of the power of jurisdiction—said to held by bishops—from the power of orders—said to be shared equally by bishops and priests. Under the influence of "Ambrosiaster" and Jerome, medieval theologians would view episcopacy as only a different grade within one order of "priesthood." Although John Chrysostom expressed ideas similar to

Jerome's,[90] the Eastern Churches generally preserved the perspectives found in earlier Western sources, such as the *Apostolic Tradition* and Cyprian.

Toward a Church of Stratified, Hierarchical Holiness

After the persecutions had ended and the possibility of martyrdom had faded, the desire for a more intense Christian lifestyle led some to move beyond the practices and cult of a Church that now seemed too established. Leaving the churches in the cities and towns, individuals such as Paul and Antony went out into the deserts of Egypt to battle the evil spirits thought to inhabit that wilderness.[91] Those hermits or desert dwellers sought a more perfect holiness as anchorites or recluses from society. By *ascesis* or the exercise of self-denial, they made their bodies die the spiritual martyrdom of mortification.

The desert dwellers were initially "monks," living alone *(monos)*, but as their numbers increased they assembled into communities under the leadership of persons such as Pachomius. Now called "cenobites," because they shared a common life *(koinos bios)*, such ascetics came to be considered the ideal Christians, in contrast to those ordinary people who did not completely abstain from sex and who were burdened with the cares of their families and the world. The male cenobites' way of life, which soon spread beyond the Egyptian desert, was paralleled by the growth of female communities of virgins and widows within the Churches. One dimension of the "more perfect holiness" of those men and women also began to be demanded of major ministers in the Church.

From its beginnings, the Jesus tradition had valued and nurtured an ethical radicalism of surrendering family, property, and home. In the vision of the earliest Gospel, believers formed a new kind of family with Jesus: "Whoever does the will of God is my brother and sister and mother" (Mark 3:35). But how does everyone live the way of a Jesus who could say, "Foxes have holes, and birds of the air have nests; but the Son of Man has nowhere to lay his head," and who is presented as demanding the kind of commitment in which a disciple would leave the burial of his or her father to the dead (Matt 8:20–22; Luke 9:58–60)? Actualizing that vision has never been without its tensions. We should be cautioned by the fact that Mark (7:8–13) and Matthew (15:3–7) also present Jesus criticizing those who circumvented the responsibility of caring for their parents in need.

Celibacy had existed as a freely chosen option since the beginning of the Church (1 Cor 7:25–35), but disciplinary laws began to impose it on ecclesial ministers during the fourth century. Although some dispute its authenticity, canon 33 of the Council of Elvira (about 306) is usually cited as the first known prohibition demanding that bishops, elders, and deacons, or more generally all clerics, abstain from sexual relations with their wives and not generate children, under pain of deposition. Canon 10 of the Council of Ancyra (314) limited the possibility of marriage for a deacon, making him state that intention before his ordination. Canon 1 of the Council of Neocaesarea (between 314–25) excluded from the ranks of the clergy a presbyter who married after ordination. The decretals of Pope Siricius (384–99) imposed continence on all married bishops, priests, and deacons. Canon 2 of the Synod of Carthage in 390 concluded that such discipline was "what the Apostles taught and what antiquity preserved."[92]

The reasons for imposing continence and celibacy were complex. Because they presided at the Eucharist, Christian "priests" were beginning to be described as the bearers of tremendously awesome sacral powers.[93] Appropriating the Levitical rules of cultic purity for those who offered sacrifices within Judaism, Ambrose of Milan (339–97) demanded that priests not be "violated" by any intercourse with their wives (*On the Duties of Ministers* 1.50). Although ritual purity or cultic abstinence for those who dealt with the Eucharist were also factors in his decretals, Pope Siricius primarily emphasized virginity or continence as the characteristic that distinguished holiness in "New Testament" times from holiness in the "Old Testament." Major ministers within churches where many men and women had consecrated their virginity to God were to embody the virtues they recommended to others.[94]

"Ambrosiaster" said that priests abstained from their wives permanently because the Christian altar was holier than that of the "Old Dispensation" (*Commentary on 1 Cor* 7.9). Pope Innocent I (402–17) argued that priests and deacons had to relinquish marital relations permanently because, unlike the ministry of Jewish priests who abstained only during the time of their service in the temple, Christian ministry was exercised every day and was also not hereditary.[95] He further believed that such continence was "a discipline of divine law."[96]

Pope Leo the Great (440–61) insisted that a spiritual marriage should evolve from a carnal one for all ministers of the altar: "they should not put away their wives, but they should have them as if they did not have them. While the love of those united in marriage endures, the nuptial acts are to cease."[97] Local councils, at Turin in either 398 or 401 (canon 8), at Orange in 441 (canons 21–23), and at Arles circa 443 (canons 2, 3, 43–44), likewise demanded such continence. With continence as the hallmark of the really committed, two strata now became ever more defined within the Western Church. Those living "a more perfect holiness" were more and more distinguished from the rest of the baptized, the people or laypersons, who in Leo's view could licitly procreate children. At Rome, the nuptial abstinence of the nonordained was, at first, limited to the night before they joined in worship (Jerome, *Ep.* 49.15).

The Eastern Churches would ultimately take a somewhat different stance. The *Apostolic Constitutions* (6.17), dated about 400, directed that persons ordained as bishops, priests, or deacons could have been married only once and were not to enter a second marriage if their spouse died after ordination. Those who had never been married were likewise not allowed to marry after ordination. Acknowledging that the Roman Church imposed continence, the

Second (or Quinisext) Synod in Trullo of 692 invoked the *Apostolic Canons* (no. 5/6: in *Apostolic Constitutions* 8.47) and allowed deacons and priests in the Eastern Churches to continue fully in their marriages. They were to abstain from sexual relations at the times when they had to celebrate the divine services (canons 13 and 30). By contrast, the synod required the wife of a bishop to enter a "distant" convent after her husband's ordination, since both would have previously agreed to separate by common consent (canon 48). Any bishops still living with their wives, as was the case in Africa, Libya, and elsewhere, were to be deposed (canon 12). Paul's reference to Cephas, or Peter, and the rest of the apostles traveling with a Christian wife (1 Cor 9:5) was being forgotten. So was the injunction about choosing an overseer who nurtured his family well (1 Tim 3:4; Titus 1:6).

Even in the Western Churches of the fifth and sixth centuries, there were still many bishops who had previously raised families. Two of the more prominent were Pope Felix III (483–92), who was the great grandfather of Pope St. Gregory the Great, and Pope Hormisdas (514–23), who was the father of Pope Silverius (536–38).[98] But married persons gradually became the "silent majority" in a Church that now may have numbered as many as five million believers. Peter Brown has noted that most of the bishops and clerics who were the writers of the third and fourth centuries were simply not interested in rethinking the issue of the sanctification of the married. "Their slogan was virginity."[99] Leadership positions within the Church were more and more being assumed by men who had enjoyed power and wealth, and who even led armies into battle. They were expected to be free of at least one of the "stains" of worldly life: "the stain of intercourse." What emerged was a hierarchical notion of holiness.[100]

During the second century, Irenaeus had refused to accept the distinction of "perfect" from simple Christians advocated by the Gnostic Valentinus.[101] But the institutionalization of the Church ultimately did lead to comparable distinctions. Comparing the bishop to the "high priest" and the elders and deacons to the "priests and Levites" of Judaism (2.26), the third century Syrian church order document called *Didascalia* instructed the laity to love and fear the bishop as a father, king, and lord, and to honor him as God (2.20 and 34). The bishop, in turn, was to love the laity as his children, keeping them warm "like eggs from which young birds will come" (2.20). The role of the laity, a term now seemingly reserved for males with economic status, was to support widows and orphans and to honor the deacons, elders, and bishop with gifts and presents (2.28). Their "honoraria" financially supported the bishop's work and his care for the needy and strangers (2.24–36).

According to the *Didascalia*, the strength through which the laity could love God (Mark 12:30; Luke 10:27; Deut 6:5) was their worldly possessions (2.36). They were commanded to give and never to require any account from the bishop or to judge him. The bishop was responsible for distributing their contributions (2.34–36). He was instructed to make room for any poor or elderly man or woman who came to the assembly, even if he himself had to sit on the ground (2.58).

In the Epistles to Titus and Timothy, the good father of a family had been the model for an *episkopos* or overseer. At the turn of the second century, Clement of Alexandria still paid tribute to married persons who were inseparable from God amid all their familial cares and contrasted these persons to those who were free from temptations because they only had to care for themselves (*Miscellanies* 7, 12). The *Didascalia* marks the beginnings of a reversed emphasis. It makes the bishop the model for the father of a family, saying that the bishop has to care for everyone while the layman has to care only for himself (2.18).[102]

The internal stratification of the Church and the marginalization of the "laity" especially hardened during the fourth and fifth centuries. For many bishops, "[h]ierarchy, and not community, had become the order of the day." Ambrose of Milan, who had once been an imperial official, and Pope Siricius asserted the existence of distinct grades of perfection in the Christian life. Both believed that these distinctions could be measured in terms of the degree of a person's withdrawal from sexual activity: virgins came first, widows came second, and married persons third.[103] In Augustine's view, the Christian married couple "was to descend with a certain sadness" to the task of begetting children, for in that act their very bodies spoke to them of Adam's fall (*Sermon* 51.15, 25). They were to feel a "sexual shame."[104]

Augustine himself still insisted that all Christians are priests because they are members of the one priest, Christ (*City of God* 20.10), whom Augustine considered the only mediator between God and humans.[105] But the vision of the *entire* community of the baptized as a priestly people would eventually fade in the face of the growing emphasis on a hierarchy of holiness. By the mid-fifth century there was a distinct and privileged class of Christian monks and nuns, living a continent life, unencumbered by property and the weight of the social expectations that came with wealth.[106] By the late sixth century, when wives had more and more disappeared from the households of the clergy and the majority of bishops came from the monastery, the kind of clerical celibacy associated with the Western Middle Ages had begun, a world of celibate priests, monks, and nuns.[107]

Augustine pessimistically viewed the majority of humans as a "damned mass" destined for condemnation, from which only baptism into the full unity of the Catholic Church might save them.[108] Even unbaptized infants would be eternally separated from God because of "original sin," although their "damnation" would be mitigated by the fact that they had not been guilty of personal sin.[109] As a result, infant baptism became the norm, and a personal decision of self-sacrificing commitment to Christ was expressed by entry into an ascetic lifestyle, rather than by initiation into the Church itself. It was the decision to live a celibate life that was now identified with "conversion" or "religious" life.[110] During the sixth century, the baptismal commitment was further devalued by Justinian's imperial edict that all pagans report for baptismal instruction or suffer exile and the confiscation of their property (*Codex* 1, 2). This motivation was certainly not that envisaged by First Peter (2:9–10) when it described God's people as "a chosen race, a royal priesthood" called from darkness into a marvelous light.

The hierarchical developments of the fourth and fifth centuries were especially canonized by a work entitled *The Ecclesiastical Hierarchy*, written in the Eastern Church during the late fifth or early sixth centuries, under the pseudonym of Dionysius the Areopagite (Acts 17:34). In his other writings, *On Divine Names* and *The Heavenly Hierarchy*, Pseudo-Dionysius described creation as a stream of illuminating light pouring down, through the uncreated Word, from a God who is Goodness, Love, Beauty, Boundless Power, and Light. The creative cascade of light flowed down a hierarchical chain or ladder, consisting of different steps and degrees of being and understanding or "illumination": it descended from angels, through humans, to animals, plants, and rocks—the "faintest echo" of being.[111] Presupposing hierarchy to be the order of all sacred things,[112] Pseudo-Dionysius portrayed the earthly Church as a reflection of a Heavenly Hierarchy, in which three triads of angels were ranked in descending order beneath the Triune God. Like that Heavenly Hierarchy, the Church on earth was ordered into hierarchical triads.[113]

Just below the angels, on the higher rungs of the ladder leading down from and back to God, is the Ecclesiastical Hierarchy of the "Initiators." They form a hierarchic triad that includes, in descending order:[114]

- the "godlike" hierarch or bishop who has the power to perfect and consecrate (he is infused with the knowledge of God, symbolized by the Bible laid on his head at ordination)[115]
- the priests or "mystagogues" who provide illuminating instruction to initiates, and
- the deacons, called ministers *(leitourgoi)* or enlighteners, who purify those who approach the ceremonies of the priests

These Initiators together celebrate the mysteries or sacraments, especially the triad of baptismal initiation, Eucharist, and the consecration of oil, thereby actualizing the heavenly in the midst of the world.[116] Like the Initiators, the sacramental triad is likewise hierarchical in the way it leads to God: first, baptism effects a cleansing and an enlightening "illumination"; then, the mysteries of Eucharist and the holy oil perfect one's knowledge and understanding.

Below the Initiators is the triad of the "Initiated,"[117] comprising, in descending order:

- the consecrated monks
- the baptized "holy people," and
- the orders of purification: penitents and catechumens

Finally, all humans are being drawn up, toward the God of Light who has diffused Self in creation, through a hierarchic triad of ascending spirituality:[118]

- union with the light that is God (the highest rung)
- contemplation or illumination (the way toward union), and
- purification or purgation of bodily desires (the beginning of growth toward perfection).

Delineating the Church in terms of such hierarchical categories proved to be foundational for medieval thought and practice, which generally accepted the works of Pseudo-Dionysius as authentic writings of the Areopagite. For the ordinary baptized person, the Church was effectively becoming less a "we" and more a "they." Nonordained or nonmonastic baptized persons now formed an ecclesial version of the *"am-ha-aretz,"* the ordinary "people of the land" whose less-intense spirituality had been looked down upon by the "religious elite" of Jesus' time. Yet Jesus and his earliest followers had themselves come from such common folk.

"Neither Slave Nor Free...."— Unfinished Trajectories from Jesus

Continuity with Jesus is always expressed in and through particular cultures. As the eternal Word become fully human, Jesus had himself been subject to the contingencies of history. The faith proclaimed by those who "followed after him" was likewise inculturated. It was always mediated through categories that made sense in the particular time and setting of believing communities, which thereby also reshaped their own culture. Trajectories arising from the event of Jesus thus moved into the future by a dynamic, ever-repeated process, along paths requiring occasional adjustment.[119]

Early Christianity was a multihued phenomenon. Semitic-Jewish, Hellenistic-Jewish, and Gentile Christians developed distinctive interpretations of Jesus. Those varied expressions, reflecting diverse life situations, then became the strands woven together in the Christian Scriptures, mirroring the unity in diversity of all believers. The perspectives of Paul, a Roman citizen by birth (Acts 22:28) and a citizen of the influential Hellenistic city of Tarsus in Cilicia (Acts 21:39), were not exactly the same as those of Aramaic-speaking Jewish Christians in Galilee or Judaea. As the Hellenistic Jewish Christian mission brought more and more Gentiles into the community of the risen Jesus, the *ekklēsia* had to cope with ever-greater cultural and theological diversity. One could not proclaim the "good news" to those living in Macedonia, Achaia, or Rome by simply repeating the words of Jewish Christians steeped in the culture and expectations of Judaism and the Hebrew Scriptures. The Gentile mission had to translate the faith into shapes meaningful to the Greco-Roman world of the first century, thereby bridging two world views. That transition marked the beginning of a new epoch in the faith.[120] Unity amid diversity was its hallmark.

The baptismal formula in Galatians 3:28 proclaimed the unity and equality of all the members of the community called

Church. But that trajectory from Jesus moved along a path of cultural complexity. The reality of life in the Greco-Roman world did not always conform with the ideals of Christian living. Some Christians were freemen and freewomen; others were their slaves. Unable to change all the social structures of his time, Paul recommended living within them since he expected that all would soon pass: "Let each of you remain in the condition in which you were called" (1 Cor 7:20). One can debate whether Paul believed that slaves should seize the opportunity for freedom, or that they would be better off making the most of their slavery (1 Cor 7:21). He did challenge Christians to structure their community according to a different vision: "[W]hoever was called in the Lord as a slave is a freed person belonging to the Lord, just as whoever was free when called is a slave of Christ. You were bought with a price; do not become slaves of human masters" (1 Cor 7:22–23).

Slaves were not to be treated as lesser members of the Christian assemblies. Accordingly, from the very beginning, personal conversion to Christ or initiation into his living community had an impact upon social structures. The followers of Jesus, who came to serve and not to be served, were called to transform structures that smother freedom, peace, and love. The salvation offered by Jesus sought to heal not just individual humans but also their society with one another. Yet Jesus had not provided the early Church a detailed blueprint offering specific directions in advance for resolving every problem that would ever be confronted. With our hindsight, Paul's approach to the legal institution of slavery may seem too compromising; but he and the communities of his time simply had not worked out the Church's final position. Under the guidance of the Spirit, the first-generation Church did leave a sense of direction for those who came later. Our rejection of slavery goes beyond Paul (and Augustine and many others), but his powerful ideas about loving even one's runaway slave as a "beloved brother" (Phlm 16) was a trajectory from Jesus that called for further development.

In brief, the life and practice of the community called Church have never been static. There has always been discontinuity amid continuity, since the experiences of a faith community living in history have always required new responses to changing historical situations. As canon 6 of the First Synod of Orange in 441 indicates, even some of the ordained once owned slaves. In reaching its present position on the unacceptability of slavery, the Church was not unaffected by progress in human self-understanding. Such factors must also be kept in mind when considering the role of women.

Jesus never relegated women to the margins. The gospels portray him freely speaking to women and including them in his parables. They were among his friends and close followers.[121] If his impact erased the inequality between male and female, then it would make sense that we should find women assuming an active role in early Christianity. And we do find signs of that happening. In Matthew and John, the risen Jesus first appears to women. All four Gospels present women as the first to realize that Jesus was risen; they are portrayed as being given the mission of informing the male disciples. At Corinth, women were praying and prophesying (1 Cor 11:5) and apparently speaking out and asking questions in the assembly (1 Cor 14:34–35). In Romans (16:1) Paul commends Phoebe who is a deacon *(diakonon)* of the *ekklēsia* at Cenchreae. He also sends greetings to Junia (or Julia), whom he calls a prominent apostle (16:7).

Assuming that the directives in 1 Corinthians 11:2–16 are from Paul, it is significant that women are not told to stop praying and prophesying in the assembly, but only to do so with their heads covered. Paul did not impose an inactive silence on women, but he did stipulate prevailing patterns of dress and grooming and existing relational models ("the husband is the head of his wife": 1 Cor 11:3). A practical concern that the Christian gospel might find acceptance in the Greco-Roman society of Corinth may well have been operative.[122]

The post-Pauline churches more and more emphasized the patriarchal family structure of a father presiding over wife, children, and slaves (Col 3:18–22; Eph 5:22—6:9; Titus 2:4–9; 1 Pet 3:1–7). An active ecclesial role for women was gradually suppressed. In 1 Corinthians 14:34–35, we read: "As in all the churches of the saints, women should be silent in the churches. For they are not permitted to speak, but should be subordinate, as the law also says. If there is anything they desire to know, let them ask their husbands at home. For it is shameful for a woman to speak in church." This injunction to silence is difficult to reconcile with 1 Corinthians 11:5 and 13, which presume that women do pray and prophesy aloud, and supports the conclusion that 1 Corinthians 14:34–35 is very likely a later interpolation.[123]

The disciple who later wrote First Timothy, in Paul's name, demanded the complete submissiveness of woman (2:11–15), which is presented as a consequence of Eve's role in the Fall: "Let a woman learn in silence with full submission. I permit no woman to teach or to have authority over a man; she is to keep silent. For Adam was formed first, then Eve; and Adam was not deceived, but the woman was deceived and became a transgressor. Yet she will be saved through childbearing, provided they continue in faith and love and holiness, with modesty." Early Christianity was gradually adopting the patriarchal motifs prevalent in Jewish pseudepigraphal literature. Apocryphal works such as I Enoch, the Testament of the Twelve Patriarchs, and the Apocalypse of Moses buttressed a subservient role for women by holding them all responsible, in and through Eve, for the first human sin and even for the fall of the angels.[124] By contrast, Paul had emphasized Adam's transgression (Rom 5:12–21; 1 Cor 15:21–22).

In the third-century church, women did have an active role as deaconesses, who were to be honored by the people in the place of the Holy Spirit (*Didascalia* 2.26). But the ministry of such deaconesses was circumscribed in its functions. They could visit and minister to sick women in their homes and perform the baptismal anointings of women for the bishop (3.12), but they could not baptize. The *Didascalia* maintained that no woman could baptize, because otherwise Jesus would have been baptized by his mother Mary and not by John the Baptist (3.9). Women who were not deaconesses or officially appointed members of the order of widows (3.1–2) were to be subject to their husbands (1.8) and were to sit "apart" in the assembly for the Eucharist (2.57). On the street women were to cover their face with a veil and to walk looking downward (1.8 and 10).

The appreciation and implementation of human dignity and freedom have required a long process of development, maturation, and realization. For example, the Constitution of the United States was written in 1787, but the right to vote was not extended to African Americans until 1870. What had been recognized in theory began to be realized in practice only through the struggles of the 1960s. Women in the United States achieved the right to vote only in 1920; their efforts for a fuller role in society have likewise not been concluded. As a community living in history, the Church is not immune to such developments. Given the emerging role of women in society, and the living experience of the contemporary Christian community, the perspectives that developed within the post-Pauline communities and the exclusion of women from leadership roles in the Church appear less and less consonant with our responsibility to reimplement what Jesus did and said in our time.

As noted in section 5 of *Mysterium Ecclesiae*, the Declaration of the Congregation for the Doctrine of the Faith issued in 1973, formulas of faith may sometimes have to be rearticulated in order to convey what was intended in another worldview.[125] One might add that ecclesial structures and practices might likewise have to be adjusted when later cultures reconfront those "undigested blocks of information about Jesus which are historically reliable precisely because they did not fit the perspectives and theological views of those Christian writers who, unwittingly, happened to preserve such traditions."[126]

Confidence Amid the Passing of an Era

The ideal of the earliest *ekklēsia* was disciples of Jesus joined in "communion, peace, and love."[127] Union with Christ and with one another was effected and manifested in the celebration of the Eucharist within local churches or assemblies. In Christ, and later also through their bishops, those assemblies in many distant places were all bonded to one another within a catholic or universal communion of churches. As John Chrysostom said, "[Christ] made them one body; the one who sits in Rome considers the Indians members of himself" (*Homily on John* 65.1).

The first centuries were a time of persecution and tension, but also of growth, opportunity, and enthusiasm. The present Rite for the Christian Initiation of Adults seeks to retrieve the enthusiasm of a community wherein all the baptized experience themselves as Church. But ours is a culturally different Church. Unlike the directives found in the *Apostolic Tradition* (15 and 16), we no longer have to inquire at the outset whether persons are slaves or free, or whether they have their master's permission. Since we live after the Roman Empire's adoption of Christianity, teachers of young children, soldiers, or military commanders are no longer automatically excluded (although our technological, nuclear age has raised new questions about the morality of war). Nor do we require that women be veiled with an opaque cloth and stand in a separate part of the assembly for their prayers (*Ap. Tr.* 18). The regulations of the third and fourth centuries, assigning different places in the assembly to men, women, and children, and forbidding men and women to exchange the kiss of peace at the liturgy, seem foreign to our experience.[128] Relegating women to a balcony or behind a screen, as was the practice in a number of Eastern churches during the early centuries,[129] has become unthinkable in our culture.

Over the centuries, oneness in Christ *(koinōnia)* has been expressed through spiritualities and practices influenced by varying cultural perspectives. During the fourth century, Basil of

Caesarea taught that, by custom, a wife who was regularly beaten ought to endure it rather than be separated from her husband (*Ep.* 188.9). Augustine praised his mother because she counseled women with battered faces not to criticize the husbands who beat them. Monica's "joking" advice that women should view marriage as a contract for making them slaves (*Confessions* 9.9) seems appalling in the present sociocultural context. As we reshape the Church, we cannot accept everything that the early Christians held or admired, but we can still learn much from their imperfect efforts to live the way of Jesus in their time.

Augustine foresaw the end of an era during his lifetime. The Roman world to which he belonged, and in which the Church had emerged and become inculturated, was passing away. But he was not fearful, for he was confident that the destiny of the Church was not tied to the preservation of any one cultural or historical system. In his vision of the heavenly City on earth, the universal Church was a pilgrim community uniting citizens from all nations, calling them to live not in a selfish love of self and power, but in a love that seeks to serve (*City of God* 8:24, 13:16, bks. 14 and 28, and 19:17). A Church that was Catholic did not annul the cultural diversity of customs, laws, and traditions that worked for human peace, as long as they were not detrimental to Christian faith and worship (19:17). Augustine believed that at the end of history the Church will be among all the nations (20:11). The Church could thus be hopeful even in times of transition because it sought the only true peace, "the harmonious communion of those who find their joy in God and in one another in God" (19:17). That legacy and task now passed to the medieval Church.

4
A Changing Church: Struggling with Power, AD 600–1400

A tiny eighth-century church, barely holding thirty persons, stands at the edge of the village of Naturns, or Naturno, in the South Tirol region of Italy. Entering that stone church, dedicated to Saint Procolus, standing before its simple table-altar, and admiring its ancient frescoes, one wonders about the stories that could have been told by the persons who assembled there for Eucharist twelve centuries ago, in a region inhabited for thousands of years before Christianity. For just northwest of the village, a valley leads to a pyramid shaped mountain in whose glacier the frozen, five-thousand-year-old body of the "Iceman" was found in the latter part of the twentieth century.

The echo of those seeking to live the way of Jesus during the medieval period likewise resonates within the magnificent churches and cathedrals of Conques, Speyer, Vézelay, Lincoln, Canterbury, Chartres, Rouen, and Amiens. One can imagine those who long ago watched splendid processions preceding a bishop's Mass, knelt on the stone floor for the elevation of the host, or strolled about marveling at all the altars, artwork, or stained glass windows. Their faith lived in continuity both with the earliest centuries and with our own time. Yet, because their world was different from ours, there is also a certain discontinuity between their expression of faith and both earlier and contemporary efforts to live the way of Jesus. It is a conviction of this book that the community called Church ever mediates the presence of Jesus the Christ and calls his followers to holiness, but in ways that respond to the particular time and situation in which disciples are living.

During the fourth century, Christianity had spread into the countryside of Gaul through the efforts of missionary-minded bishops in the cities, such as Martin of Tours. The process of conversion was also a Romanization, in which the newly baptized peasants abandoned both their Celtic gods and their language. Adopting a popular or vulgarized form of Latin, they became a part of Roman culture. Jacques Le Goff has noted that between the fifth to the eighth centuries there was "a thinning of the middle classes in the cultural sphere, as the gap widened between the uncultured masses and a cultivated elite."[1] The cultural fault lines did not coincide with social stratification. Rather, the important division was between clerics and laymen, since with the collapse of the Roman Empire intellectual culture had become the monopoly of the Church.

Although there were great differences in degree in the culture of clerics, ecclesiastical culture of the early medieval period was "of a single kind," employing a previously schematized and simplified legacy of Greco-Roman culture, within the framework of the liberal arts. Church leaders were especially receptive to such intellectual influences because, particularly in the fifth and sixth centuries, bishops and abbots were largely drawn from the indigenous Roman aristocracies. Nonaristocratic prelates and abbots likewise adopted that sort of culture because it was the best way to be assimilated and to climb socially within the upper clergy. Thus, Christianity at the beginning of the Middle Ages was, sociologically speaking, caught between a higher clergy increasingly permeated by an aristocracy formed on Greco-Roman learning or *paideia* and a mainly rural lay population that culturally regressed after the crisis of the Barbarian invasions, which brought an infusion of new arrivals with their non-Christian folklore and practice. Clerical culture, nurtured in cathedral schools and monasteries, would have to make some effort to adapt culturally in order to evangelize. But there was no denying the gap, especially between the rural masses and the higher ecclesiastics in the cities, shaped by their aristocratic culture. Only over the longer run would clerical culture and its literature nurture a renaissance of western civilization.

One must keep in mind that the systems of education to which we are accustomed did not exist. A famous school of medicine would be established at Salerno during the ninth century. The University of Bologna was founded during the eleventh century. Universities also emerged at Paris in the early twelfth century and at Oxford by the end of that century. Compulsory elementary education, however, had to await the nineteenth century. Most of those assembled in medieval churches could not read or write.

The prevailing political structure of the medieval world was monarchical. Secular or temporal power and authority flowed downward from emperors and kings, princes and lords, nobles and knights; it was exercised over peasants and serfs who worked the land and wielded no power, and over the merchant class that later emerged in cities and towns. The pattern prevalent in secular society would be mirrored in the conception of the medieval Church as a papal monarchy, in which spiritual power and authority descended from the pope—down through archbishops, bishops, abbots, archdeacons, canons, and ordinary priests—and was exercised over the faithful. Although primarily supposed to be spiritual leaders within the Church, bishops would also be drawn into the temporal political power structure. As bishops within the Church, they were to lead their people to union with God; but, as lords within a feudal society, they also ruled their domains and worked with the king in ruling the kingdom.

Beginning from such a historical context, this chapter and the next will examine some of the factors that shaped the theological understanding of Church in the centuries between Pope Gregory the Great (590–604) and the First Vatican Council (1869–70). We shall consider how the leadership of the Church, responding to needs within the vacuum caused by the fall of the Roman Empire in the West, more and more came to possess power, originally unsought but later claimed and defended. Looking at the Church "from below," in a time in which the majority of the populace was minimally educated, we shall also see how the spirituality and practices that developed among rank-and-file medieval Christians constituted a distinctive experience of Church. From another perspective, we shall consider how bishops gradually relinquished their earlier spiritual, sacramental role and assumed a primarily administrative function, and, likewise, how the bishops of Rome, in their attempts to nurture reform and to overcome the problem of lay investiture, began to exercise a new dimension of administrative power. In consequence of such developments, theologians more and more related the Church to powers which the ordained "received from above," to "rule" and to "administer" sacraments.

Ecclesial Power as an Unintended Consequence of Service

After the imperial capital had been removed from Rome to Constantinople in the East, the borders of the West fell open to the "barbarians" whom the Roman armies had previously held off. Northern Gaul and the lower Rhine valley were soon controlled by the Franks, who found themselves ruling a Christianized and somewhat Romanized population headed and even militarily defended by bishops. Appropriating what they found appealing, the Franks gradually inculturated themselves into those whom they ruled. Clovis and his Burgundian wife had their first-born son baptized. Clovis's own baptism in 496 by Remigius, bishop of Rheims, further enhanced his relationship with the Romanized Catholic country folk whom he now ruled. Others followed his example, and the Franks gradually became Christians. Unlike the Visigoths, Vandals, Ostrogoths, and Lombards, who had arrived as Arian Christians from the East, the conversion of the Franks within the Western Church placed them in a special relationship with the bishop of Rome. This relationship ultimately contributed toward making their kingdom a powerful force that supplanted the vanishing remnants of the old Roman Empire in the West.

Although Emperor Justinian reconquered Italy for a brief period in the sixth century, the city of Rome soon found itself besieged by the Lombards, who had the undesirable practice of selling "old Romans" into slavery unless ransomed for a price. Since the imperial exarch at Ravenna and the praetorian prefect at Rome had no treasury, only the bishop of Rome, Pope Gregory I, had the resources to meet the people's needs of food and ransom. He also had at his disposal the communication network and managerial bureaucracy that had developed to administer the Church's now-vast holdings of donated lands. Thus, only the bishop of Rome with his staff could now do what the imperial government had previously done. The pope not only ransomed captives and fed the poor and hungry, but also appointed military governors for other cities and assumed the role of defender of Rome, now a decrepit capital where even the aqueducts were failing for lack of maintenance. Church leaders filled the vacuum created by the collapse of the Roman Empire in the West. Although Gregory acted to meet an emergency and not to gain power, the latter became the long-term effect.

The Church's growing relationship with power became one of Pope Gregory's constant concerns. Imbued with Augustine's doctrine of the two cities (the heavenly city motivated by love and the earthly motivated by power), Gregory was caught in a dilemma: "He on the one hand encourages bishops to undertake civil responsibilities out of necessity but on the other hand laments two dire effects of this necessity: bishops too easily assume airs of inflated authority inappropriate to their spiritual office, and they do not devote themselves to their proper office of preaching."[2]

Inspired by Augustine and by the monastic ideals of Benedict, Gregory longed for a Church ideally living in detached love for God. Instead, his Church was suffering like the faithful and innocent Job because so many, even within its own community, lusted for worldly power over others. Interpreting such abuses of power as portents of a coming anti-Christ, Gregory believed the end-time had begun.[3] Like Augustine, he also believed that the elect, whom God would finally save, were a minority in the Church.[4]

As a monk become pope, Gregory's heart was always rooted in monastic spirituality. Considering his administrative responsibilities a burdensome distraction from the ideal of contemplative holiness, he insisted that a good pastor should be a neighbor to all by compassion, but also be *above* all by contemplation (*Pastoral Rule* 2.5). Yet his own dedication to the contemplative life did not exclude decisive action to alleviate the needs of the poor or to correct injustices. Faced with the ecclesiastical meddling of an emperor who did nothing to save Italy from invasion by the Arian Christian Lombards, Gregory put his trust in monks like himself to accomplish the practical tasks of the Church. Despite his own longing to be rid of distractions from contemplation, he employed monks as missionaries, administrators, and legates.

Roman society had been composed of three "orders": the senators, the equestrians, and the people or plebs. Gregory now spoke of three "orders" in the Church: the rectors or preachers, the continent, and the married.[5] In his Platonic perspective, he believed that the grades and diverse orders of the earthly church mirrored a hierarchical diversity in a heavenly army of angels (*Epistle* 5.54). Given the fact that bishops of his time often acted as magistrates and assumed the tasks of defending their cities and of distributing food, Gregory could say that they "ruled" over "subjects" who were expected to give them the kind of respect given to secular rulers.[6]

The growing wealth of the Church allowed it to meet the needs of the oppressed but also created a new problem: it was transforming the Church into a unique kind of "meta-empire" that blurred the earlier distinction between a spiritual and a secular authority. The Roman Church's own solicitude for all the Churches now required a diversity of persons to help in "administration." Clerics employed by the pope to administer the patrimony or endowment of the Church were themselves given titles drawn from the vocabulary of imperial administration: *rector, defensor, chartularius*, and *notarius*.[7] Their duties as overseers of the far-flung holdings of the Church also enabled them to serve as informants on local bishops.[8] The remote beginnings of papal administrative centralization were being set in place. Unfortunately, some of the papal appointees would themselves not always be impervious to greed and the misuse of power.

Augustine had called all Christians "servants or disciples." As bishop of Hippo, he considered himself a coservant or codisciple with his people: "For them he was bishop, with them he was a Christian."[9] For them, he was a shepherd and teacher, with them he, too, was a sheep following Christ and a codisciple.[10] He was "a servant of Christ and of the servants of Christ."[11] Influenced by Augustine and also by the Rule of St. Benedict, Gregory referred to himself as "the servant of the servants of God."[12] As Walter Ullmann points out, that title could have been "an inverted exaltation of his office."[13] Emperor Justinian had similarly called himself "the ultimate least servant" (*ultimus servus minimus:* Code I.17.1), thereby portraying imperial authority as a burden, though he zealously claimed and exercised its fullness of power. Yet Gregory's self-designation as servant does not seem to have been merely empty words. In his *Pastoral Rule* (2.6), he clearly acknowledges the fortuitous character of power, observing that the ruler and the ruled are really equal in nature. And Gregory's practice was consistent with his words: he genuinely used all the resources at his disposition to serve human needs during the Lombard invasions.

Gregory also called himself "servant of all priests,"[14] but his dealings with the Churches of the West reveal that, like Leo before him, he simply presumed all were subject to the care and "*principatus*" of the Roman See.[15] He and his immediate predecessors encountered opposition in Gaul and northern Italy from those who felt that Pope Vigilius (543–53) had compromised the Church's faith by capitulating to imperial pressure (after being imprisoned in chains!) in accepting the controversial christological decisions of the Second Council of Constantinople. Gregory defended the papacy by emphasizing that the same faith was held by all the sees "founded by Peter" (Rome, Antioch, and Alexandria, to which Peter was believed to have sent his disciple Mark).[16]

The ongoing argument over the bishop of Constantinople's use of the title "ecumenical patriarch" led Gregory to make some careful distinctions about his own "universal" role. When the patriarch of Alexandria addressed him as "universal father," Gregory responded: "My honor is the honor of the universal Church. My honor is the solid strength of my brothers [bishops]. Then am I truly honored, when honor is not denied to the individuals to whom it is due. If Your Holiness calls me universal father, you deny for yourself what you profess me to be, universal. Let that not be. Words which inflate vanity and wound charity should cease" (*Ep.* 8.30). Even as he inaugurated the transition into the medieval papacy, Gregory was still rooted in the collegial, communion model of the early Church.

As bishop of Rome, Gregory had assumed responsibility for the human needs of the central Italian peninsula, but he had no legal claim over that territory. Technically, those lands remained part of the jurisdiction of the Roman emperor ruling from distant Constantinople. Gregory protested those imperial laws and decisions that he considered unjust, but he still thought it necessary to promulgate them. His successors, however, gradually turned away from the disengaged emperors of the East and began to look north, across the Alps, to the Frankish kings who were rapidly becoming the real secular power of the West. Pope Gregory II (715–31) refused to collect imperial taxes, disregarding the threats that came from Constantinople. Then Gregory III (731–41) wrote to Charles Martel asking his help against Lombard oppression. Next, Pope Stephen II (or III) (752–57) traveled across the Alps to meet with Pepin, asking him to be "defender" of the Church and to "restore" the territories seized by the Lombards.

The papacy's lack of a legal claim to the territory of central Italy was remedied by the *Donation* (or *Constitutum*) *of Constantine*, written in the first half of the 700s but purported to have existed from antiquity.[17] It "documented" how Constantine himself had given that territory to St. Peter through Pope Sylvester. In wresting those lands from Lombard control, the Franks could thus be assured that they were simply "returning" what already belonged to the popes. Such developments constituted the origins of the "papal states." The *Donation* further described how Constantine had given Pope Sylvester the imperial regalia, which he deserved as bishop of Rome. But because he thought it unseemly to wear the crown, Sylvester gave it to Constantine, who then left Rome, where the divinely appointed pope ruled, and moved to the newly established capital of Constantinople. Constantine there wore the crown given him by the pope.

Such fictitious history provided a desired precedent. If a bishop of Rome had given the first Christian emperor in Constantinople his crown, a later pope could do the same. On Christmas day in 800, Pope Leo III crowned Charlemagne while the people acclaimed him "emperor of the Romans." Western Christendom had emerged, nurtured by an idealized dream of a universal union of all Western Christians in one Church and state, under one pope and one Christian emperor, crowned by the pope who was "head" of the Church. Unfortunately, as we shall see in the following, that dream would soon be disturbed by the new secular power's growing intrusions into the affairs of the Church.

A Changing Experience of Church "From Below"

In the early centuries of Christianity, the Eucharist, presided over by the bishop, or by the presbyter who represented him, was a celebration in which the entire assembly of faithful was actively involved. The very term "*ekklēsia*" concretely signified the assembly of faithful who became what they received, the *Body of Christ*. During the medieval period, however, there would be a change in the relationship of the people to the Eucharist. The Eucharist came to be understood as an action of the priest, who celebrated silently and often privately. Such developments, in turn, altered the understanding of Church.

Most Catholic Christians have never been to Rome, and their day-to-day concerns are not focused on an analysis of papal or even episcopal authority. Their experience of Church begins "from below" and involves a local community that gathers in a town or neighborhood. So it was for the Christians who lived in the small fortified town of Dura-Europos, on the west bank of the Euphrates river in the region of Mesopotamia, during the early third century. The house where the Church of Dura-Europos once assembled has recently been excavated from the defensive embankment heaped over it by a Roman army in 265. On the outside, that corner house, in which Christians initiated new members and celebrated the Eucharist, was no different from others on the block. One entered through a baffled vestibule, which provided privacy, into a small square courtyard. One of the rooms opening off the courtyard had been enlarged to accommodate the community's meetings, and a small platform had been installed. Another room seems to have been used for dining. A third room had been transformed into a baptistery, with a bath covered by a canopy. Its walls were covered with paintings of Adam and Eve, the Good Shepherd with his sheep, Christ walking on the water, David and Goliath, and a procession of women with candles walking toward a lighted sarcophagus.[18] The community never bothered to remove the frieze of panpipes and theatrical masks with which the previous owner had decorated the main meeting room. The one who presided over the assembly may have lived on the second floor.

There were about eighteen such Christian assembly houses, called *tituli*, in third-century Rome. During the fourth and fifth centuries, they began to be replaced by larger structures. Not far from the Colosseum, where Christians had met in a house for which Clement had held the "title," the Church of St. Clement was built. On the Esquiline hill, where they had met in a house for which Equitius held the title, the Church of St. Martin was erected. On the Celian hill, the house church of Pammachius was replaced by the Church of Sts. John and Paul. The new structures were usually constructed according to the Roman "basilica" design (a rectangular interior with side aisles formed by rows of columns supporting the roof).

In approaching a fourth-century church for the *synaxis* or liturgy, especially in the east, one often encountered a group standing outside, perhaps covered with sackcloth and ashes, crying out for prayers that God might have mercy on them. Because of some serious sin after baptism, these "criers" had been excommunicated or excluded from the ranks of the faithful who could celebrate the Eucharist. As penitents in the first stage of a lengthy process of reconciliation (which could take fifteen to thirty years for someone guilty of murder or adultery, or seven years for fornication), they were not even allowed to enter the place of assembly.[19]

Those who were the "faithful" entered through separate doors for men and women and then went to their designated places, segregated according to whether they were men, women, or children.[20] (In some Eastern churches, women were relegated to a separate upstairs gallery; in Western churches, they would be assigned the north side.) Other sections at the rear of the assembly were assigned to catechumens preparing for baptism, and to penitents in the more advanced stages of reconciliation. Along the back wall were the "listeners" or "admitted," then came the "kneelers," and finally the "standers," positioned closest to the "faithful." Catechumens and the "listening" penitents were dismissed immediately after the Liturgy of the Word. After their departure, the "faithful" prayed for them and for others who could not be present because of travel, illness, etc., and then exchanged the kiss of peace among themselves. Penitents in the final stages of reconciliation were allowed to remain during the Eucharist, but only as observers. In some Western churches that had not developed elaborate rituals, the deacon simply warned penitents to distance themselves before communion. Outside the assembly, penitents were to live and dress like ascetics or monks, fasting, praying on their knees, abstaining from the use of marriage, and remaining disengaged from business affairs.

At the end of the fifth century, the tendency to distinguish the ordained from the baptized began to be reflected in the interior design of Eastern churches. A kind of semicircular dais called a *bema*, where the ordained sat around a lectern for the Liturgy of the Word, had been built into the middle of the main meeting room of the house church at Qirkbizé in northern Syria.[21] Even more significantly, a partition known as the iconostasis now separated the congregation from the altar table in Eastern churches. Only the ordained were admitted into immediate contact with the heavenly "mysteries" as they were celebrated on earth.

Originally, each church had only one altar, at which the one who presided faced the congregation. In third-century Rome and Carthage, a table, probably made of wood, was moved into place by deacons at the beginning of the eucharistic liturgy.[22] Metal and fixed stone altars emerged during the fourth century.[23] Eventually, stone altars began to be preferred, as in canon 26 of the Synod of Epaon, in Burgundy, in 517. The western practice of having more than one altar in a church began during the sixth century. In Rome, the oratories or private chapels with altars dedicated to apostles or martyrs, previously scattered about the city, began to be incorporated into the churches. The multiplication of altars was especially evident in Gaul, where one church was recorded to have thirteen in the year 590. After the year 600, as more and more monks were ordained priests, the number of Masses celebrated for personal devotion escalated. There was likewise a surge in the number of votive Masses celebrated for special intentions, often for the souls of the deceased, as stipulated by the stipend that was offered. As a result, private chapels or oratories, each with its own altar for an individual priest, especially proliferated in the monasteries. All those altars would later be gathered together as side altars in the main church.

During the ninth century, many priests began to celebrate two, three, or even seven to nine Masses a day. Because custom then allowed only one daily Mass per altar, more altars were constructed. Particularly in larger churches to which a number of priests were attached, side altars became the norm. Although the abusive multiplication of Masses was finally brought under control at the beginning of the thirteenth century, private Masses continued to increase because the number of priests grew. By 1500, some churches reflected an inflationary spiral in the number of altars: St. Mary at Danzig and the cathedral at Magdeburg each had forty-eight.[24] The symbolism of a local Church being united through its assembly for one Eucharist began to fade, since a local community was now often fragmented into groups attending different Eucharists at the same time, in the same building.[25]

In the Roman basilica of Pope Liberius, which Sixtus III (432–40) rededicated as St. Mary Major, side chapels and altars were not added until the sixteenth and seventeenth centuries. The main altar of that basilica, of St. John Lateran's, of St. Peter's, and of St. Paul's, always remained a table at which the one who presided could face the people. But, after 1000, partially in order to make room for the growing number of clerics, the main altar in most other western churches had been moved back and made into a shelf at which the priest prayed with his back to the people. Barriers, such as rood screens, separated the people from the area around the altar, which now began to be called the sanctuary.

To accommodate the proliferation of Masses all being celebrated at the same time, priests no longer sang the liturgy lest they disturb one another; instead, they now read in whispered tones. Such private, "low" Masses soon became standard. The priest "said" Mass in Latin for the particular intention of the person who had given a stipend. If any congregation attended, it passively "heard" the Mass. Often, no one except the "server" was in attendance, despite the fact that earlier episcopal directives, such as the *Capitulary* of Bishop Theodulph, had opposed solitary celebration of the Eucharist without a community of people who could respond standing around the priest.[26]

During the first four centuries, all the "faithful" who assembled for Sunday or weekday liturgies received the Eucharist, taking it in their hands and even carrying a portion home to be eaten before the first meal each day.[27] But at the end of the fourth century, John Chrysostom complained that the faithful of Antioch flocked to receive the Eucharist at Easter time by force of custom, often not properly disposed, while on other days of the year priests waited in vain for someone to partake.[28] Ambrose of Milan worried that his congregation was imitating the Eastern practice of yearly communion (*On Sacraments* 5.4.25).

Caesarius, bishop of Arles (470–542), later complained that "most, or even worse, almost all" simply left after the Liturgy of the Word (*Sermon* 73.2). Canon 18 of the Synod of Agde in Gaul (which Caesarius presided at in 506) insisted that communion should be received at least three times a year: at Christmas, Easter, and Pentecost. Chapter 21 of the Fourth Lateran Council in 1215 reduced the requirement to "at least once a year at Easter time." Thomas Aquinas and later the Council of Trent favored more frequent communion.[29]

One reason for the precipitous drop in reception of the Eucharist was a feeling of unworthiness among the faithful. Preachers like John Chrysostom did not alleviate that feeling by describing the Eucharist as a "table of fear" where "frightful" mysteries were celebrated, approached with "reverence and trembling."[30] In the West, the reaction to Arianism and Adoptionism emphasized Jesus' divinity in a way that overshadowed his humanity, making him seem less approachable. There was also a growing unwillingness to endure the protracted rigors of public penance; many instead simply chose to abstain from communion. Frequent reception was likewise not fostered by requiring three days of fasting prior to communion, along with abstinence from sexual relations for married persons.

In the early Church, there was a profound veneration for martyrs because it was believed that they had most closely imitated the way of Jesus. By contrast to the martyrs' heroism, ordinary

Christians bore witness to their faith in "nonverbal" everyday modes.[31] Following the gospel counsels, they cared for the poor, widows, the orphaned, and the sick, and they visited prisoners. Beginning with the second century, however, asceticism—or renunciation of possessions, marriage, food, and so on, previously also practiced by non-Christians—would more and more be chosen as a form of discipleship of Jesus. Thus, alongside martyrs and saintly bishops, ascetic monks with their practice of mortification became models for an ideal spirituality to be imitated by all Christians.

Moses was said to have commanded abstention from marital intercourse to prepare for the revelation of God on the third day (Exod 19:15). Paul advocated abstinence in order that couples might dedicate themselves to a time of prayer (1 Cor 7:5). At the beginning of the fifth century, Jerome insisted that married couples should abstain from intercourse before reception of the Eucharist, whether it was received in the church or at home, where a portion of the eucharistic bread was first reserved.[32] Later, Caesarius of Arles repeatedly advocated that married couples should practice sexual abstinence "for many days" before major feasts.[33]

Canon 46 of the sixth-century Penitential of Vinnian recommended sexual abstinence during "the three forty-day periods" (before Christmas and Easter, and after Pentecost), and also on Saturday nights and Sundays.[34] In the seventh century, the Penitential of Cummean (2.30) added the traditional penitential days of Wednesday and Friday. After claiming that the Greeks and Romans abstained from their wives three days "before the holy bread as it is written in the law" (1.12.3; cf. 1 Sam 21:4–5), the eighth-century Penitential (or Canons) of Theodore proposed likewise that married couples should abstain from sexual relations for three days before communion (2.12.1). Any married man who had sexual relations on a Sunday was to do penance "for one or two or three days" (1.14.20). Women were forbidden to enter a Church or to receive communion during menstruation and for forty days after childbirth (1.14.19; cf. Lev 12:1–5).

The regulations in the Penitential of Theodore seem to be negative parallels of the instructions found in Pope Gregory I's letter to Augustine of Canterbury. Viewing menstruation and birthing as natural, Gregory had concluded that they did not negate a woman's right to enter a church or to receive communion. He did stipulate that any man who had intercourse for pleasure should wash and allow some interval of time to pass before entering a church or receiving communion, "since such pleasure could not be exempt from fault."[35] That directive was optional if the intercourse was for procreation without the rapture of pleasure.

Despite Pope Gregory's attitude, which was remarkable for the time, the prevailing tendency was to devise ever-stricter regulations for married persons. The eighth-century Penitential of Egbert (7.4) imposed a one-year penance, which could be commuted to a monetary donation to the Church or the poor, on any man who refused to abstain from marital activity during Lent. The ninth-century St. Hubert Penitential added the feasts of martyrs to the days of marital abstinence (c. 49) and imposed three forty-day fasts on anyone who entered a church after intercourse, except on Sundays (c. 57).[36] Even some popes, such as Nicholas I and Innocent III, joined in advocating marital abstinence before communion. Edward Schillebeeckx observes that "holiness was thought to be impossible in the married state unless the married persons maintained the ideal of the monks."[37] Unlike contemporary theology that speaks of marriage as the sacrament in which human love is an effective sign of the love within the Trinity and of Christ's love for the Church (Eph 5:25), earlier medieval theologians, such as Peter Lombard, understood sacramental marriage not as a way to become holy but as a remedy for concupiscence.[38] Thomas Aquinas, with his more positive view of marriage, granted that abstention before communion might be appropriate, but maintained it was not necessary.[39] But whatever the reason, the practice of infrequent communion persisted.

In the early Church, the "faithful" had received the Eucharist in their hands and carried it to the sick at home.

Between the seventh and the thirteenth centuries various synods stipulated that the Eucharist had to be distributed by bishops or priests, or if necessary by deacons, and that it was to be placed directly into the mouth of communicants, which would prevent anyone from taking a portion home.[40] The fact that such regulations were repeatedly promulgated over a period of centuries indicates that the earlier practice of receiving communion in the hand, and of bringing a portion into one's home, refused to die out. With the introduction of an anointing for the hands of new priests, first found in the ordination ritual of the Missal of the Franks at the beginning of the eighth century,[41] the idea that only "consecrated priestly hands" were worthy enough to touch the host eventually emerged.[42]

The community called Church had always believed that Christ was present in and through the Eucharist. During the ninth century, however, a debate began about how to explain the presence of Christ in the Eucharist. Paschase Radbert, the Benedictine abbot of Corbie, emphasized, with almost literal realism, the physical presence of the real body of Christ in the Eucharist ("not other than that which was born of Mary, suffered on the cross, and rose from the tomb"), although he did distinguish between image *(figura)* and truth in the sacrament.[43] Ratramn, a monk of Corbie, by contrast, distinguished the historic, true body of Christ, glorified in heaven, from the spiritual and invisible or sacramental body internally present under the external "form" of what had "before" been bread.[44] Raban Maur, archbishop of Cologne, took a middle position, stressing that the body of the risen Christ and the sacramental body present in the Eucharist are not two bodies but one, although they differ in appearance.[45]

During the eleventh century, Berengar of Tours reopened and intensified the debate by denying that bread and wine could become the body and blood of Christ without changing in "appearance." Distinguishing sign and reality, Berengar argued that, if the bread and wine were a sacrament or visible sign, they could not be the invisible reality *(res)* signified, namely, Christ's body and blood. He therefore argued that the bread and wine, as sacramental signs signaling the presence of Christ's true body and blood, remain bread and wine, just as the water of baptism remains water.[46] Especially rejecting notions of a physical change in the elements of bread and wine, Berengar's sacramentalism envisioned a spiritual eating or communion of Christ's body. It also sparked a sharp reaction.

In a profession of faith imposed by Cardinal Humberto da Silva in 1059, Berengar had to affirm that the bread and wine become the true body and blood of Christ, handled and broken by the priests, and crushed by the teeth of the faithful (DH 690). Such exaggerated realism would have to be retracted. In 1079, Berengar had to subscribe to a revised formula, which declared that the bread and wine are "substantially changed" into the body and blood of Christ (DH 700). (The idea of transubstantiation—in which "substance" is understood as "that which makes a thing be and be what it is," thus denoting a change from "breadness" to "the body of Christ"—was beginning to emerge, although the term itself would not be used before the latter part of the twelfth century.) Because the wording of the earlier formula from 1059 had already affected the tradition, theologians such as Peter Lombard undertook the task of "interpreting away" the impact of its exaggerated realism.[47] Nevertheless, even some twentieth-century Catholics would be taught, during their childhood, not to chew the host.

The intensified emphasis on the Real Presence produced by all the controversies made believers in the medieval period more eager to "see" the Eucharist.[48] Thus the seldom-received Eucharist began to be "exposed" for the adoration of the faithful, who would rush into churches when they heard the bell signaling the now-heightened "moment of consecration." The elevation of the host, introduced during the twelfth and thirteenth centuries, would sometimes be prolonged for minutes. (The elevation of the cup began only at the end of the thirteenth century.) The practice of genuflecting before the Eucharist (in imitation of what one did before an earthly king or prince in that era) emerged after the controversies of the eleventh century and began to make its way into the rituals of the Mass during the fourteenth century. That same century also brought the practices of ceremonially exhibiting the host outside of Mass and of concluding with a blessing or benediction with the host. Likewise, the Feast of Corpus Christi (first introduced at Liège in 1246–47) now became a special focal point for eucharistic processions.[49] The custom of Forty Hours exposition, based upon a tradition that had calculated forty hours as the time from Jesus' death and entombment until his resurrection,[50] spread from Italy into Germany during the sixteenth century.

To be sure, the medieval Church did come to deeper insight about Real Presence, but it is worth remembering that no longer was one loaf of bread broken and shared by the many who thereby became one body (1 Cor 10:16–17). By the eleventh century, the priest was usually the only one who ate and drank the Eucharist. He came out to see if anyone else wished to receive only after removing his vestments at the end of Mass. It is no wonder that some theologians later characterized the communion of the faithful, who had become passive and marginalized observers at a liturgy celebrated by the ordained, as not essential for "the sacrifice of the Mass."[51]

The symbolism of "one bread broken and shared" also faded. Beginning in the ninth century, Western churches began to use unleavened bread (on the assumption that the Last Supper was a Passover meal) and then, during the eleventh and twelfth centuries, introduced the preformed small wafers still prevalent today. By the thirteenth century, some Western churches likewise gave communion only under the form of bread. Aquinas reasoned that the cup was received only by priests as a precaution lest "the blood of Christ" be spilled.[52] During the fifteenth century, the Council of Constance made that custom into a universal law, reacting to the arguments for communion under both kinds made by John Wycliff and John Hus.[53]

Jesus ate and drank with tax collectors and sinners during his ministry and celebrated a Last Supper with his friends before his death. The earliest postresurrection community gathered in homes such as Mary's (the mother of John Mark) in Jerusalem (Acts 12:12), Gaius's in Corinth (Rom 16:23), Prisca and Aquila's in Ephesus and Rome (1 Cor 16:19 and Rom 16:5), and Nympha's in Laodicea (Col 4:15) for the "breaking of bread" (Acts 2:42–46) or the Lord's supper; that is, they gathered to eat the bread that was a communion in his body and to drink the cup that was a communion in his blood, thereby proclaiming Jesus' death and resurrection until he comes again (1 Cor 10:16–17, 11:20–27). The faithful who gathered in the house-church at Dura-Europos or in the little church at Naturns, described at the beginning of this chapter, still ate and drank the Eucharist. Because of the developments after 1000, however, the presence of Jesus in the Eucharist would be emphasized and experienced in a different mode. Although there was continuity in Eucharistic faith, those who later knelt on the stone pavements of medieval churches and cathedrals to look at and adore the elevated host, but who came forward to receive perhaps only once or twice a year, experienced the presence of Christ in a different manner from those in earlier centuries. Henceforth, for many of the faithful, sacramental union with Christ was mediated visually, and by spiritual communion, rather than by a sacramental eating and drinking.

Instead of transforming the faithful into the body of Christ through their communion, the seldom-received Eucharist was transformed into the greatest of the relics so revered by medieval Christians. The earliest monstrances used to exhibit the eucharistic host were tower shaped and pinnacled, just like the reliquaries used for public veneration of the relics of saints. Only later would monstrances be designed to resemble the sun, with a circle of golden rays emanating from the eucharistic host, as prefigured in Raphael's 1509 fresco in the Vatican Palace (later entitled "The Dispute concerning the Holy Sacrament" during the seventeenth century).[54] Reservation of the Eucharist in a prominent container, either near to or suspended above the principal altar, emerged during the thirteenth century. Attaching a tabernacle to the main altar became common practice only after the sixteenth and seventeenth centuries.[55]

One must recognize that the medieval experience of Real Presence still challenges us today. As Karl Rahner has noted, "[E]ven in the future with all the changes that are possible in eucharistic piety, we will never be able simply to forget the knowledge that, in the twelfth century, was given to the Church about the presence of Jesus in the Lord's Supper and under the eucharistic signs, and which she professed officially in the dogma of Trent." Eucharistic worship will not simply return to the simplicity that it had in the time of the early Church. "The Church, having reached greater maturity, will not simply return to her childhood, even though we cannot say just what this worship will look like in Africa two hundred years from now."[56]

At the same time, one must acknowledge that all the changes in eucharistic practice during the medieval period profoundly impacted the theological understanding of Church. Latin writers of the seventh to the ninth centuries had still linked Eucharist and Church as cause to effect, in the manner of Augustine and John Chrysostom before them. But as fewer and fewer faithful received communion, the Eucharist began to be considered an end in itself, separated from its ecclesial effect. The previous emphasis on "all being united into the body of Christ" through the Eucharist was gradually replaced by a focus on individual, personal union with Christ through reception of the sacrament. A devotional aspect of that perspective endured in the pre–Vatican II practice whereby communicants, after returning to their pews, immediately covered their face with their hands to commune privately with Jesus in personal prayer.

The younger Thomas Aquinas, in his commentary on the Sentences of Peter Lombard, did acknowledge the ecclesial dimension of the Eucharist: "[O]nly the priest who consecrates the Eucharist, which is the sacrament of the universal Church, is able to consummate an act of the entire Church."[57] He taught that the Eucharist was the greatest sacrament because it perfected the union with Christ already established through baptism.[58] Because Eucharist perfected the union with "the head" that the members already had, incorporation into the mystical body of Christ was an effect.[59] Those who received Christ as spiritual food were changed or incorporated into him, but as Thomas added, reflecting the situation of his time, such incorporation could be achieved without sacramental reception of the Eucharist, through a spiritual communion.[60] In his later commentaries on First Corinthians and the Fourth Gospel, Aquinas more directly retrieved the causal relationship between Eucharist and Church.[61] Thus, in the *Summa theologiae*, he declared that the Eucharist is the greatest sacrament precisely because it effects the unity of the Church through the communion of all members to one head, Christ. He further noted that the reception of every other sacrament contains a desire of the Eucharist; and that neither grace and charity, nor incorporation into the body of Christ, could be obtained apart from it.[62] Yet, because of the persistence of infrequent communion, such perspectives receded during the fourteenth and fifteenth centuries.

Patterns of Popular Piety

The piety of many Christians had long been focused on relics of the saints and on the miracles that came from their power.[63] The role of the saint, which originated with the martyrs of the early Church, was originally to be a representative or patron acting for the community, rather than an individual with privileged access to a reality not accessible to the ordinary run of Christians.[64] A pilgrimage to a shrine such as Santiago de Compostela or the church of St. Faith at Conques, where one could touch the tomb or relics of a saint, was thought to connect one to the miraculous healing power of the holy one.[65] (By some estimates, as many as 500,000 pilgrims per year traveled the various roads to Compostela from 1100 to 1300.) As the Eucharist progressively became a cultic act performed by priests, passively observed by those attending, the devotion of the people ever more focused on the saints and especially on Mary, considered the Queen of all the saints. The first part of the "Hail Mary," taken from Luke's Gospel and ending with "blessed is the fruit of your womb," became a widespread popular prayer just before 1200. It also served to counter the Albigensian or Cathar heresy that viewed "matter," and thus the body, as evil and denied the bodily incarnation of Jesus. The popular devotion of the rosary developed out of practice in which those who could not read repeated the same prayers in three groups of fifty, using a knotted string to keep count, paralleling the way the literate prayed the one hundred and fifty Psalms in three groups of fifty.

At the end of the ninth century, reliquary busts had begun to be used as containers for the relics of saints.[66] This use marked the beginning of a new phase in Western Christian art, the emergence of "sculpture in the round" or statues (never accepted by the churches of the East). Reliquary statues, such as the doll-like figure of St. Faith at Conques, appeared during the tenth century. The earliest statues of Mary, made of wood and covered with gold and enamel, were also sculpted during the tenth century.[67] Eventually, it became a common custom to place statues above the numerous altars of western churches, in addition to the murals, mosaics, and icons found in earlier churches. The devotion of the people, often expressed in festivals where statues of "patron" saints were carried through the streets, was thereby brought onto the altars and connected with the liturgy celebrated by priests. Each day's Mass would also become a celebration of a saint's feast day.

The spirituality of the faithful reflected their level of education and understanding of the faith. In the early Middle Ages, many had been baptized under pressure from a king or prince. Knowing little about their new faith, some remained comfortably immersed in more familiar pagan practices. Writing to Charlemagne in 796, Alcuin referred to the infantile knowledge of the newly baptized. He observed that baptism is of no value when it is applied only to the body, without a previous rational understanding of the faith: "We are not required to receive the sacrament of baptism if the mind has not embraced the truth of the faith." Citing Matthew 28:19, Alcuin advocated: "First teach, then immerse."[68] But education was a difficult task. The portrayal of "clerical" persons reading and writing in the stained glass windows and sculptures of later medieval churches reflected the awe extended to a few. Even Charlemagne might not have learned to write, although he could read. And, although most of the literate were clerics, or "clerks," many priests in smaller towns and villages were not educated enough to preach more than the rudiments of the faith. Often they simply proclaimed a negative ethic, telling the faithful what they should not do. This practice was unfortunate for the unlearned who depended on the sermons they heard and the pictures they saw for their instruction in the faith. Such a situation also gave rise to a tendency to oversimplify or to leave some things unsaid in order "not to disturb the faithful."

Art provided an important source of information for those who could not read. As Pope Gregory the Great had observed, "pictures were for the unlearned what scriptures were for the literate" (*Register* 9.208; 11.10). And, since religion is itself "a way of seeing," art was also necessary "to orient individuals and communities, not only conceptually but also affectively to the reality that creates and nourishes, in solitude and in community, human life." In a time not inundated by the excess of images in modern media, an illiterate worshipper found the "knowledge conducive to living a fruitful life both in the present and after death" on the walls and ceiling of a local church.[69] For example, during the twelfth century, the paintings on the ceiling of the church of Saint Savin sur Gartempe, east of Poitiers, told the stories of the Pentateuch, while the panels of the church at Zillis in Switzerland told the story of Jesus beginning from his birth and childhood, through his miracles and teaching, to his Last Supper, agony, arrest, and crowning with thorns.[70] Despite medieval theology's emphasis on

Jesus' divinity, such art remarkably kept the humanity of the earthly Jesus before the eyes of the faithful.

The frescoes, paintings, and statues above the altars of the later Middle Ages also retold stories from the apocryphal gospels, those influential sources for popular piety and curiosity written since the second century.[71] In Giotto's frescoes for the Madonna della Arena or Scrovegni Chapel in Padua, painted between 1305 and 1306, the faithful could gaze on scenes from the life of "St. Ann" and "Joachim," the "mother and father" of Mary. Pope Leo III had earlier allowed their story to be portrayed in the church of St. Paul in Rome during the ninth century, despite the fact that Popes Damasus, Innocent I, and Gelasius had previously condemned the use of apocryphal infancy gospels, such as the one attributed to James, as sources.[72] Medieval Christians could also look at images of St. Joseph holding his miraculous rod or staff, the sign by which, according to the Apocrypha, he was divinely designated to be Mary's spouse.

The art of the twelfth and thirteenth centuries portrayed the Virgin Mary as the majestic Queen of Heaven, endowed with a unique power of intercession through her influence with her Son. Mary's power was also the theme of hymns in that time, such as the "Salve Regina" ("Hail Queen, Mother of Mercy"). The art of the fourteenth century would present a humble and very human Madonna nursing her child; she was nonetheless still perceived as powerful both because of her relationship to Jesus and because of her virginity. The frequent depictions of Mary Magdalene stood in contrast to those of the Virgin, who was said to be the Magdalene's lifelong friend. The Magdalene, usually portrayed with flowing red hair, was presented as a forgiven and reformed but once carnally sinful woman, a fictitious and false image earlier created through an unwarranted fusion of gospel passages.[73] Such a Mary of Magdala, in her loving relationship with Jesus, symbolized every ashamed and sorrowful sinner's hope for "forgiveness and acceptance."[74] Her role thereby complemented that of the sinless virgin Mary.

Instead of the very approachable young man or shepherd found in the murals of the Roman catacombs, medieval art frequently portrayed Jesus as majestic or enthroned (as in the cupola mosaic of Charlemagne's chapel at Aachen or Aix-la-Chapelle, in the ancient monastery of St. Gall, and in the Carolingian frescoes of the church at Müstair or Tuberis in Switzerland), or as the judge coming at the end of the world (on the tympanum over the west door of the pilgrimage Church of St. Faith at Conques, over the south door of the Abbey church of St. Peter in Moissac, and in the vivid sculpture signed by Gislebertus above the main entrance of Autun cathedral). There were also the bloody figures of a suffering Jesus hanging on the life-size, polychromed crucifixes which emerged during the tenth century.[75] The faithful were thus graphically reminded to prepare themselves for an ultimate encounter with a judge who had once died for their sins. Anselm of Canterbury and the later author (Thomas of Celano?) of the thirteenth-century hymn "Dies Irae" both described that encounter as a day of wrath and dread on which one pleaded for God's loving mercy.[76] Yet, the very positioning of Jesus above the church doorways of the twelfth century, either as judge or as the ascended, glorious Christ (in the Magdalene church at Vézelay), also offered a message of hope: it proclaimed that he was "the door to salvation."

Devotion to the passion of Jesus increased during the twelfth and thirteenth centuries. Fostered by the experiences of the veterans returning from the Crusades, it especially focused on Jesus' sufferings along the way to Calvary. Having been given responsibility for the holy places in Jerusalem during the fourteenth century, the Franciscans made the propagation of such devotion a special part of their mission. As a result, the stations of the cross (set at fourteen since the sixteenth century) eventually became a universal feature of Western Catholic churches during the eighteenth century.[77] The practice of placing a crucifix on every altar had begun in the thirteenth century.

In the theological perspective of Anselm's *Cur Deus Homo* or *Why God Became Human*, written between 1094 and 1098, Jesus' death on the cross was a vicarious satisfaction for the sin of Adam, which was considered an infinite offense inasmuch as it offended God who is infinite. Since finite, sinful humans were incapable of offering satisfaction for such an infinite offense, God out of love and mercy sent Jesus—God become human, so that a human might satisfy God's justice. The fully divine and fully human but sinless Jesus infinitely satisfied divine justice by freely accepting his undeserved death on the cross. By his death, the sinless Jesus restored humanity's relationship with God and the very order of creation, set askew by the sin of the first "Adam."[78] What was still of concern to medieval Christians, however, was whether they themselves had adequately "satisfied" for their own personal sins.

Between the sixth and ninth centuries, the practice of public or ecclesial penance began to be replaced by a system of private penance that Celtic monks introduced throughout western Europe.[79] Reconciliation back into the ranks of "the faithful" had previously been granted only after completion of a public penance lasting many years. By contrast, in the system of private penance, after a penitent's confession (whereby the priest made a judgment and assigned an appropriate penance for the sins committed), reconciliation or absolution was given on the subsequent Holy Thursday or, by the year 1000, immediately. Harsh but shorter private penances, as listed in the penitential books (for example, a considerable repetition of prayers, interspersed with genuflections and long periods of kneeling with hands outstretched in imitation of Jesus on the cross), were now offered as substitutes for the earlier public penances that had taken years to complete.[80] The commutation of penances lasting decades into penances of shorter duration ultimately generated a concern about dying without having fully "satisfied for" the "temporal punishment due to sin" in this life, and thereby the fear of being consigned to "purgatory."[81] As a result, the offering of Masses for the dead, for a stipend, increased and the granting of indulgences expanded.[82]

Indulgences came from the practice of commuting penances, wherein certain prayers or pious practices were substituted for a longer period of penance in one's lifetime. For example, Pope John the Twenty-Second (1316–34) granted ten thousand days of indulgence to those who recited the prayer Hail Holy Face *(Salve sancta facies)* while looking at the image of Christ's face on the "relic" cloth in St. Peter's Basilica. Technically, that pious practice, which also presupposed a pilgrimage to Rome, substituted for twenty-eight years of penance. In reducing the interval between the Roman Jubilee or Holy Years, inaugurated by Boniface VIII, to fifty years, Pope Clement VI's decree of 1343 observed that, although one drop of Christ's blood was sufficient to redeem the whole human race, the superabundance of Christ's sacrifice provided the Church with a treasury of infinite merit, to which were added the merits of Mary and all the saints. The decree concluded that God had committed that infinite treasury to the popes to use "for the full or partial remission of the temporal punishments of the sins of the faithful who have repented and confessed" (*Unigenitus Dei Filius:* DH 1025–27).

The fifteenth century especially gave rise to the practice of applying such indulgences, or remissions of temporal penances, to souls in purgatory, even though there is no measurement of time beyond death.[83] Pope Sixtus IV (1471–84), who expanded the practice of indulgences, explained that a "plenary remission" simply offered the suffrage or intercession of the official prayers of the Church for the relaxation of the "punishments" of the soul in purgatory: "We, to whom the fullness of power has been given from on high, from the treasury of the universal Church, which consists of the merits of Christ and his saints committed to us, offer help and intercession *[suffragium]* to the souls in purgatory."[84] Unfortunately, in the popular mind, and in the exaggerations of some who preached the indulgences offered for a donation to a cause, such plenary remissions were too often misinterpreted as guarantees that souls would be immediately liberated into heaven.

Western Christians now felt a need for mediators to intercede with the One who was supposed to be *the* Mediator between God and humans. In their feelings of unworthiness and in their fear of being condemned to hell, or sent to purgatory, medieval Christians turned to the saints and especially to Mary to be their intercessors with Jesus coming as the "judge."[85] The poignant hymn "*Stabat Mater,*" probably composed by Jacopone da Todi who died in 1306, invoked the Virgin Mary as a sorrowful mother tearfully beholding the sufferings of her son.[86] Those who sang the hymn asked to stand with her beside the cross and to share her grief, so that Mary might stand with them and be their advocate or defender on the day of judgment. The second part of the Hail Mary, added during the fifteenth century, epitomized their concern: "Holy Mary, Mother of God, pray for us sinners, now and at the hour of our death."

In this survey of medieval developments, we have actually been constructing the Church experienced "from below" by twentieth-century Catholics of the Latin rite in the years before the liturgical reforms initiated by the Second Vatican Council. On weekday mornings, in pre–Vatican II parishes, the priest was usually dressed in black vestments and silently "said" a Mass for the dead, in Latin, with his back to the people. Those who came forward to receive the Eucharist knelt at a communion rail, which, since the seventeenth century, replaced the earlier screen or wall separating the sanctuary from the people's part of the church.[87] Larger crowds came for the evening novenas, special devotions venerating Mary or one of the saints, whose statues often stood above the side altars. During Lent, many attended the stations of the cross. Both the novenas and the stations generally ended with Benediction. Two other details were also part of that experience: confessionals (originally open in the front), with a screen or grating separating the priest and the penitent, were introduced in 1565 by St. Charles Borromeo, the archbishop of Milan, and then required by the Roman Ritual of 1614; the holy water fonts at entrances to the church had been introduced during the ninth century.[88]

Recognizing what should be kept from that past and what should be let go calls for a subtle wisdom. Karl Rahner, in his later years, recalled that forty years earlier in Vienna he still saw people in a trolley car make the sign of the cross or tip their hat when the car passed a church. He acknowledged that "such a custom may have become strange for us, and not without reason, so that we should not try to revive such expressions of piety." But he went on to say that "in the Church of the future as well of the past...we should see Christians kneeling...alone and in silence, before the tabernacle....These Christians know that God is everywhere...and incredibly near to everything; the whole world is the cathedral....But these Christians also know that their own adoring love is not always near the God who is always near them."[89] In Rahner's view, God has created a few places and realities that make it easier to reach God's presence. Some of them emerged in the Church's medieval period, but along with other developments that might well be reconsidered.

A Diminishing Pastoral Role for Bishops

The "private" Eucharists at cemeteries and in small private chapels or oratories, celebrated in addition to the public liturgies of the basilicas, especially in Rome and North Africa at the end of the fourth century, marked the remote beginnings of a narrowing role for bishops. Ironically, at that very time, bishops were also extending their control over the countryside around their cities by building numerous rural churches and by replacing rural bishops with presbyters, or priests, who were responsible to the bishop in the city. (Rural bishops, called *chorepiskopoi* in the East, had earlier presided over the many small country churches in the East, in southern Italy, and in North Africa; presbyters had presided over those in northern Italy, Gaul, and Spain.) In some places, the presbyters who served the new churches may have initially traveled a circuit out of and back into the city where they still lived a collegial life around the bishop; but eventually the needs of the people required that they reside at the outlying chapels.

The metropolitan or city bishop's oversight of the countryside began to unravel during the sixth and seventh centuries, when the rural churches tended to become autonomous, with the local inhabitants administering the property, as directed by the Edict of Chlothacher in 614. Bishops retained only a right of supervision of such subordinate churches. The rise of the Germanic system of *Eigenkirchen* or private churches during the eighth century caused a further decentralization of the bishop's "church," since the priests who served those privately sponsored "Mass chapels" completely depended on the lay owner for their support. Within the feudal system of the tenth and eleventh centuries, the coveted financial benefits that flowed from the benefices or annuities attached to rural churches attracted even more lay lords. They nominated and paid a priest to be the "Mass sayer" for their church, thereby expending only a small part of the funds they reaped from such income-producing "property"; the bishop simply examined, approved, and ordained the "Mass-saying" priest.

The economic resurgence of the twelfth century brought both the growth of new cities and a multiplication of churches in those cities that were already the seat of a bishop. The institutional structure we call "parish" now formally emerged, inasmuch as all the inhabitants of a defined area were gradually required to attend one particular church for worship and the reception of the sacraments, for baptism, marriage, and burial, and particularly for yearly confession and communion (Fourth Lateran Council of 1215, chapter 21). Subsequently, the bishop and his cathedral were no longer the only pastor and parish of the city. The college of presbyters that had earlier gathered around the bishop would now be replaced by the priests who formed the cathedral chapter, which had its own patrimony or endowment separate from that of the bishop. Given their economic independence, some cathedral chapters even came into opposition with their bishops. The bishop's city was becoming thoroughly decentralized.

In the early centuries, the Greek term "*paroikia*" (sojourning or transient) designated a church led by a bishop as a community of God's "pilgrim" people. From the sixth to the thirteenth century, the West used the Latin term "*paroecia*" both for episcopal churches (the *episcopatum*) and the new rural communities headed by priests. Among the Eastern churches, the term "diocese" (originally applied to the civil divisions of the Empire under Diocletian in 294) was employed for the aggregate of many episcopal Churches within each of the civil dioceses. In the West, "diocese" initially referred to a country church; then it began to be used for a bishop's church, but still interchangeably with "*paroecia.*" During the thirteenth century, "diocese" exclusively came to indicate the larger community and territory presided over by a bishop; "*paroecia*" or "parish" was reserved for the smaller community and territory presided over by a priest.

From the tenth to the thirteenth centuries, many monasteries had also become parishes. Although theoretically under the supervision of the bishop, such monastic parishes were effectively controlled by religious communities that progressively emancipated themselves from the bishop until they were exempt from his control. The bishop may have always been technically considered the spiritual head of his diocese, and monks were always said to be responsible to the bishop for the souls under their care (First Lateran Council, canons 16 and 18); but, in fact, episcopal influence was considerably diminished over the parishes connected with monasteries.

During the thirteenth century, the bishop's role continued to be weakened by the large number of private or confraternity churches and by collegial churches under the patronage of secular communities, each with its unsupervised liturgies celebrated by priests paid simply to be "Mass sayers." The number of priests attached to each church also increased significantly. Although the First Lateran Council (1123) had placed the care of souls and the administration of property in the parishes under the control of the bishop, and the Second Lateran Council (1139) had reiterated the independence of churches from the laity, the power of the wealthy laity who controlled private churches had not diminished. They were perceived as a force to be feared and kept under control. To remedy the situation, canon law would devise a system of patronage and incorporation, but that system proved an unsuccessful solution. The bishop's role for unity within the community called Church was steadily eroded.

Likewise, during the thirteenth century, the Dominicans and Franciscans made their way into ministerial competition with the parochial priests. Bishops at first welcomed the preachers and friars since their learning and holiness usually exceeded that of the local priests. As John Peckham, archbishop of Canterbury from 1278, initially put it, they "are almost the only persons in these parts who understand the true doctrine."[90] But the archbishop, who had himself been a Franciscan friar, later had serious misgivings. In a letter written in 1285 he complains about the friars' errors and their defiance of his injunctions, since their papal recognition led them to presume themselves exempt from episcopal jurisdiction. In 1298, Archbishop Winchelsey of Canterbury was still trying to restrain friars and preachers who were absolving persons reserved to his jurisdiction.[91]

Pope Boniface VIII limited the rights of religious by his Bull "Super Cathedram," but Benedict XI abrogated it and again gave the Franciscans and Dominicans complete exemption. Boniface's Bull would later be reinstated after the Council of Vienne (1311–12). But during the fifteenth century, Sixtus IV once again restored many of the mendicants' privileges, and the atomization of the bishop's church continued. One must keep in mind that it was precisely their unitary, universal structure and their exemption from local control that made religious orders such as the Benedictines, Cistercians, Dominicans, Franciscans, and later the Jesuits invaluable allies of the papacy in various times of crisis.

In the canons of the Collectio Dionysio-Hadriana of 774, Pope Adrian I had unwittingly planted the seed of a future problem when he deputized Charlemagne to goad the bishops of northern Europe to reform. Beginning with Charlemagne, kings began to name new bishops, claiming that as a right stemming from the power that God gave them over the Church. Unfortunately, unlike Charlemagne, many later kings and emperors were not interested in genuine ecclesial reform and exercised their power in ways that were detrimental to the Church. An already-difficult situation was further aggravated by the rise of feudalism during the tenth and eleventh centuries. Feudalism brought the dawn of the benefice system, whereby offices in the Church became inseparably tied to the administration of a patrimony or endowment that supported the officeholder. Because of the extensive properties under their control, bishops found themselves incorporated into the hierarchical feudal nobility alongside the secular princes. Assuming an ever greater civil function, individual bishops were at once the vassals of the princes upon whom the bishops depended for their patrimony, and the lords of those who depended on them as bishops. Since bishops were now also territorial rulers, the problem of lay investiture intensified. Those with feudal power sought to expand it by having their relatives appointed to positions within the Church; nepotism and simony became rampant.

Unfortunately, a number of medieval bishops, elected under such circumstances, were more interested in serving on political missions for the king or on papal delegations than in pastorally serving their churches. If not off arbitrating some dispute, some were at the royal court or in the papal curia. Episcopal absenteeism became rampant, alongside the other problems of lay investiture and simony. Some bishops even held multiple dioceses, enjoying the revenues of their benefices or endowments without ever personally ministering in any of them. During such times, the bishop's *cathedra* or teacher's chair was transformed into an episcopal "throne," on which, after the twelfth and thirteenth centuries, a coat of arms could be emblazoned. Those whom the bishop "ruled" eventually knelt to kiss his hand or his ring, which had originally symbolized his marriage and fidelity to his church.[92]

During the twelfth century, bishops adopted the mitre, which the popes at Rome had previously borrowed from the court of Constantine. In the sixteenth century, bishops would begin to wear a regal shade of purple, copying the style of the prelates of the papal court, who had again earlier imitated the royal courts.[93]

To fill the gap caused by the prolonged absences of some bishops, the episcopal curia emerged. Modeled after the lay ruler's court, it became a permanent group of professionals whom the bishop could preside over from afar. Initially, the group was comprised of the episcopal chancellor, the preachers, and the officialis and notaries. The vicar general, temporarily at first, covered for the bishop during his *ad limina* visits to Rome to consult with the pope. By the thirteenth century, the vicar general had become a permanent administrative substitute. "Auxiliary" bishops, who could confirm and ordain in place of the absentee bishop, emerged at the end of the fourteenth century. The notion of a bishop presiding at his church assembled for the Eucharist was no longer the principal focus.[94] The bishop's primary function had become administration, which could also be delegated to another.

The Growth of Papal Administrative Power

Beginning with the ninth century, the need for general reform in local Churches, for which the papacy alone now seemed to have sufficient strength or concern, provided a legitimate justification for extending the administrative influence of papal power beyond the peninsula of Italy. Popes no longer restricted themselves to settling "major cases." *The Decretals of Pseudo-Isidore*, composed during the ninth century, probably in Rheims, enhanced the papacy's efforts for reform in the West by constructing an aura of legal antiquity for the contemporary expansion of papal administrative influence.[95] Responding to a deeply felt need, the document encouraged appeals to the bishop of Rome as an advocate who would be above the politics of the local scene. Stressing the primacy of Rome's spiritual authority, the

Pseudo-Isidoran decretals especially intended to curb secular rulers' interference into ecclesial matters. A related goal was the restoration of the authority of bishops, steadily weakened by the incursions of secular powers and of overbearing metropolitans. Only ecclesiastical synods approved by the pope, and not kings or princes, were to pass judgments on bishops.

Romanization had gradually become the mood of Christianized Europe. Southern Ireland dropped its different calendar for Easter during the 620s and 630s after some Irish abbots had visited Rome and come under its influence. At the Synod of Whitby convened by King Oswy of Northumbria in 664, Colman of Lindisfarne invoked the authority of St. Columba of Iona and of the apostle John for the calendar of the Scots. Bede reports that Wilfred of Ripon, who had visited Rome, responded that Christ had said "on this rock I will build my Church" only to Peter. Peter and not Columba had the keys to the kingdom (Ecclesiastical History 3.25). As a king who knew the importance of power, Oswy was impressed by Peter's authority and brought his people into conformity with Rome.

In 596, Gregory the Great had sent Augustine, the prior of St. Andrew's monastery in Rome, to convert the Angles of Britain. In 719, Pope Gregory II commissioned a Saxon called Winifred, later known as Boniface, to convert the Germanic tribes. Boniface pledged his loyalty "to you blessed Peter, prince of the apostles, and to your vicar the blessed Pope Gregory and to his successors." Deep bonds were being forged between Rome and the North. It is significant that the *Decretals of Pseudo-Isidore*, which created legal references inviting a stronger role for the bishop of Rome, were composed in northern Europe and not in Rome like the earlier Donation of Constantine.

During the eleventh century, the elections of new bishops were besieged by interference from the nobility. Even the elections of popes suffered from such interference, especially from the emperor. Pope Nicholas II took steps to remedy both of those problems. In 1059, it was decreed that the cardinal-bishops were to elect the new pope, with the consultation of the cardinal-priests and cardinal-deacons. Unfortunately, the political intrigues simply shifted into the ranks of the cardinals. In response, the Third Lateran Council in 1179 declared that cardinals of all ranks were eligible to vote and required a two-thirds majority for valid election.

Pope Gregory VII (1073–85), who had served as archdeacon and advisor under Nicholas II, implemented a centralized reform to deal with the continuing problem of lay investiture. Although he simply took over the personnel and the mechanisms used by his predecessor, the documents from his pontificate reflect the added element of his intense zeal.[96] His approach also seems to have been shaped by his years as a Benedictine monk at Cluny from 1047 to 1049. Enjoying a unique relationship with Rome that gave it independence or exemption from episcopal control, Cluny was supportive of the idea that Rome was the "head" to which all other churches, as "members," were to conform themselves. As Yves Congar has noted, the fact that Cluny was directly accountable only to the pope, and not to the local bishop or any secular authority, contributed to the notion "of a supranational Church, of one unified observance, dependent upon a papal monarchy and submissive to its teaching [or *magisterium*]," which Gregory would expound as pope.[97] That concept would be translated into a potent force for reforming an episcopacy caught up in feudal particularism. Significantly, just before Gregory became pope, the older profession of faith made by a new bishop was replaced by an administrative oath of office and fealty to St. Peter, the Church, the pope, and his successors, in which the bishop swore to defend the Roman papacy and the regalia or prerogatives of St. Peter.[98]

To overcome the problems of lay investiture, nepotism, and simony, Gregory VII vigilantly oversaw the elections of bishops and ensured their continued worthiness by ongoing surveillance through a system of papal legates who reported directly to him. Such initiatives for reform were further buttressed by the twenty-seven theoretical principles articulated in Gregory's *Dictatus*

Papae, issued in response to his confrontation with the emperor Henry IV about the matter of lay investiture: Gregory's *Dictates* explicitly placed the pope above all secular rulers. The Donation of Constantine, in the eighth century, had said that "the pope could use the imperial insignia." Three centuries later, Gregory instead declared that "the pope alone can use the imperial insignia" and added that the pope is "the only man whose feet all princes must kiss" (*Dictates* 8 and 9).[99] "Only the Roman pontiff has the right to be called universal," and his name is "unique in the whole world" (*Dictates* 2 and 11). Gregory further affirmed that the pope may depose emperors and absolve subjects from allegiance to unrighteous rulers (*Dictates* 12 and 27), and also depose or absolve bishops without a synodal assembly (*Dictates* 3 and 25). His legate, too, presides over all the bishops at a council even if he (the legate) is himself of lower rank; and he is able to depose bishops (*Dictate* 4). Moreover, Gregory asserted that the Roman Church may not be judged by anyone, that it "has never erred and, according to Scripture, never will err" (*Dicates* 19 and 22), and that, if canonically ordained, the Roman pontiff becomes holy by the merits of Saint Peter (*Dictate* 23).[100]

To say the least, such claims envisioned a role surpassing the kind of arbitration earlier exercised by Popes Celestine and Leo during the christological disputes sparked by Nestorius and Eutyches in the fourth and fifth centuries. Gregory's passion for obedience to God involved the realization of a universal order that, in his view, was willed by God—an order wherein the priest, more precisely the pope, was placed above royal rulers.[101] As "leader and priest" *(dux et pontifex)*, Gregory even considered leading or urging others "to take up arms against the enemies of God."[102]

This consideration soon passed into action. Calling for the First Crusade in 1095 and promising the full remission of sins to all who died repentant in that cause, Pope Urban II referred to himself as "spiritual ruler of the whole world."[103] Such claims gradually impacted the structure of the Church. By the time of Pope Alexander III (1159–81), Roman centralization and the legate system had diminished the role of intermediate structures in the Western Church. Primates and metropolitans no longer confirmed the election of suffragan bishops, nor judged their cases since most appeals were made directly to Rome. The first four Lateran Councils (in 1123, 1139, 1179, and 1215), which brought together bishops, abbots, the representatives of cathedral chapters, and even some laypersons in order to reform the Church, were all held in the papal residence at Rome.

By the end of Innocent III's reign (1198–1216), the central authority of the pope as an agent for reform was fully established and further enhanced by the title "Vicar of Christ." That title, first used by Christian emperors and then by all bishops as sacramental representatives of Christ, now came to designate the universal jurisdiction of the pope. According to Innocent, princes had the right to elect a new king or emperor "since that power came to them from the Apostolic See, which transferred the Roman Empire from the Greeks to the Germans in the person of Charles the Great." The right and authority to examine the person elected king or emperor belonged to the pope who would anoint, consecrate, and crown the king or emperor.[104] In the event of royal malfeasance, it was likewise the pope who could excommunicate a king, or even cause him to be deposed. Gregory VII had invoked Saint Peter at the beginning of his decrees to excommunicate (and thus to depose?)[105] Henry IV as king of Germany and Emperor.[106] Yet Innocent III did not consider it sufficient that one who could approve or depose kings and emperors should merely be "vicar of Peter." Innocent instead maintained that, although he was successor of the Prince of the Apostles who had assumed the fullness of power,[107] he was "not the vicar of Peter or of any other apostle or human, but only of Jesus Christ himself."[108]

Bernard of Clairvaux had earlier applied the title "Vicar of Christ" to his former student become Pope Eugenius III,[109] but Innocent III expanded its interpretation and application. Since Jesus Christ was "the King of kings and Lord of lords" (Rev 19:16) and "eternal high priest according to the order of Melchizedek"

(Ps 110:4; cf. Heb 5:6),[110] Innocent concluded that, "in the one person of the vicar of Christ, kingship and priesthood are united, as if they were body and soul."[111] The pope is "priest and king" precisely because he is vicar of Christ, and his "pontifical authority is prior, has greater dignity, and is more extensive than imperial authority."[112] The priestly power of the pope, who "presides over souls," is like the sun, while the power of kings, who "preside over bodies," is like the moon, which receives its light from the sun.[113] These two "great lights," spiritual and temporal power, "are the two swords" of Luke 22:38.[114] According to Innocent, the Lord intended that the priestly power should nurture the Church's sons and daughters, while the kingly power would subdue its adversaries.[115]

Innocent emphasized that "kings are anointed by priests, not priests by kings." He reasoned that "the one who is anointed is lesser than the one who anoints.... To princes is given power [only over bodies] on earth; to priests a power [even over souls] also in heaven" (Matt 16:19). Stretching the meaning of Exodus 22:28, he even suggested that the Lord called priests "gods," while kings were only called princes. Innocent further observed that "individual kings rule single kingdoms, but Peter, in fullness and in latitude, presides universally, because he is the vicar of him whose is the earth and its fullness, the entire earth and all its inhabitants." The priesthood *(sacerdotium)* of the papacy was thus "divinely ordained" while kingship *(regnum)* was instituted only "through human extortion."[116] Jesus "left not just the universal Church but the whole world to Peter's governance."[117]

The upshot of these claims is that, "seated higher than kings, and holding the throne of glory,"[118] "enjoying a fullness of spiritual powers and a breadth of temporal powers,"[119] "the Roman pontiff has no Lord except God."[120] As vicar of Jesus Christ and successor of Peter, the pope was "constituted as the medium between God and humans; beneath God but above humans; less than God but more than human."[121] While declaring himself "unworthy," Innocent claimed that he "held the place of God on earth" and acted as the "vicar *[vicem gerentes]*" of the "heavenly Father."[122]

Although he maintained that "the whole world and the general Church, not just some particular Church, were committed to Peter," since Peter was not just "called to a partial solicitude" but given "a fullness of power,"[123] Innocent nevertheless articulated some important distinctions:

> The Church called universal, which in Greek is the word Catholic, consists of all the Churches. According to this usage of the word, the Roman Church is not the universal Church, but part of the universal Church, clearly the first and preeminent part, as the head is to the body, since in her the fullness of power arises, while others derive a certain part of fullness. The Church called universal, in another sense, is that one Church which contains under itself all the Churches. According to this meaning of the term, only the Roman Church is called universal, since it alone by the privilege of singular dignity presides over all the others; just as God is called universal Lord...since everything *[universa]* is contained under the divine dominion.[124]

Yet, to reiterate lest the point is lost, there are *two* meanings to the "Church called universal," not just one.

Papal efforts for reform did ultimately succeed in making bishops less and less the choice of a king or prince. In that regard, "Innocent III's pontificate was the crucial one, for he secured the recognition of freedom of election in Sicily, Germany, and England, the very areas where royal influence had been greatest in the twelfth century...[T]hereafter the ruler's official part throughout most of Christendom was limited to the granting of a license to elect and subsequent approval of the candidate."[125]

A consequence of this reform, however, was that bishops would be more and more chosen by and therefore representative of the pope. Pope Celestine I (422–32) had declared that "a bishop should not be given to those who are unwilling [to accept him]. The consent and desire of the clergy, the people, and the civic leaders *[ordinis]* are required."[126] Pope Leo the Great had concurred, declaring that "the one who will preside over all should be chosen by all."[127] The Council of Rheims in 1049 still presumed (in chapter 1 of its decree) that bishops were to be elected by the clergy and the people, along with the neighboring bishops. But, around 1140, Gratian's collection of canons, known as the *Decretum*, stipulated that "the clergy is to elect, the people are to consent" (opening statement of Distinction 62). The laity were not to interfere in an election in any way (opening of Dist. 63). By the end of the twelfth century, bishops would be elected just by the clerics who formed the cathedral chapter. The people only voiced approval, by popular acclamation, of the one already elected. This practice supposedly eliminated meddling by the nobles, but it also reflected the growing subordination of the laity to the clergy.[128]

The reforms of Gregory VII had established Rome's role for oversight. By the end of the thirteenth century, multiple requests for Roman intervention to resolve the impasses arising from the internal politics of cathedral chapters had established a precedent whereby popes, invoking their "fullness of power," claimed the right to nominate candidates in disputed elections. In 1363, Urban V expanded that precedent and proclaimed his right to designate patriarchs, archbishops, abbots, and abbesses throughout Christendom. With rare exceptions, papal nomination had in fact taken the place of local election. And since the candidates appointed were, more and more, not from the diocese that they served as bishop or even from the region, and thus often felt no deep bond with the local Church, transfers became commonplace.[129] Given Rome's expanding role in the selection of new bishops, Robert Grosseteste (circa 1170–1253) put forth the idea that bishops received their power "through the mediation of the lord pope."[130] That notion would be debated at the Councils of Trent and Vatican I and then reconsidered at Vatican II.

The Pinnacle of Papal Power

The development of the medieval papacy climaxed with Pope Boniface VIII, whose reign marked an intensification of the ongoing papal struggle with emperors and kings. Boniface's decree *Unam Sanctam*, issued in 1302 to protest Philip IV's embargo on French contributions to Rome, categorized power into spiritual and temporal swords (cf. Luke 22:38). It declared that both those powers, or swords, were under the authority of the Church: the spiritual sword was to be used on behalf of the Church by priests; the temporal sword was to be used by the Church through the hand of kings and soldiers, but at the command and by the consent of the priest. According to Boniface, one sword should be under the other sword: temporal authority is subject to spiritual power.[131] Embracing the hierarchical worldview expounded by Pseudo-Dionysius, Boniface held that the spiritual power far exceeds the earthly power in dignity: "If, therefore, the earthly power err, it shall be judged by the spiritual power....But if the supreme spiritual power err, it can only be judged by God." Boniface claimed to exercise an authority that was "not human, but rather divine, given to Peter by the divine mouth and established on a rock [Matt 16:18] for him and his successors." Invoking a position once expressed by Thomas Aquinas,[132] Boniface declared that in order to be saved it is necessary "for every human creature to be subject to the Roman Pontiff."

The two ornamental rings of the tiara or papal crown, used since the eleventh century, were now magnified to symbolize the papal claims to spiritual and temporal power. Boniface's immediate successors added a third ring to the tiara, perhaps a forlorn act of defiance against the plotting of King Philip the Fair, at the dawn of the papacy's "captivity" in Avignon (1305–78). Despite the setback of Avignon, the papal vision of a fullness of power over the whole world did not die. It became an echo reverberating through the centuries that preceded Vatican I. The formula for the coronation of the pope in the Roman Pontifical of 1596 would declare the pope to be "father of princes and kings," "rector of the world," and "vicar of Christ."

The opening sentence of Pope Boniface VIII's decree *Clericos Laicos* issued in 1296 expressed the problematic legacy arising from the disputes between popes and temporal rulers: "Antiquity teaches us that the laity has been exceedingly hostile to the clergy."[133] Laity refers here to nobles scheming to despoil the Church and its leaders, and not to the community of baptized disciples genuinely trying to live the way of Jesus. Boniface was specifically protesting the royal plan to tax British clerics in order to cover the expenses of King Edward I's war with Philip IV of France. The notion of Christian kings taxing their "national" clergy in order to support the costs of waging war between their "states" severely conflicted with Boniface's ideal of all Christians united within a universal Church presided over by the pope. Unfortunately, the notion that the "laity" generally needed to be kept in their place would become endemic in the minds of Church leaders.

At the end of this discussion of papal power, we must keep in mind that achievement and ambiguity are ever conjoined within the humans who form the community called Church. It is tempting to lament the direction that the Church was taken by the ambitions, and it appears sometimes the arrogance, of its leaders. Yet succumbing to lamentation would be oversimplistic. William Henn has noted that twentieth century ecclesiologists, such as Yves Congar and Angel Antón,[134] lamented that the Gregorian reform gave rise to the predominance of a juridical vision of the Church in the West. In rejoinder, Henn observes that "in the situation of the eleventh century, recourse to law was the only possible way in which the pope could act effectively to defend the freedom of the local churches in selecting bishops." Yet Henn likewise acknowledges that "the fundamental 'sacramentality' of the Church was somewhat forgotten in the face of the overriding insistence that the Church is a juridically structured society"[135]—an acknowledgment of the fact that simple acclamation of the past is just as oversimplistic as simple lamentation. One might note further that

Congar and Antón lamented the predominance of a fundamentally juridical vision of Church because they were concerned that this vision no longer responded to the needs of the present situation.

The Persistence of Evangelical Ideals

A concern for service, evangelical simplicity, and even an active role for all the baptized was never forgotten or lost within the Church. During the tenth century, a reform that sought to correct the growing wealth and laxity of monastic life was initiated at the monastery of Cluny. In the eleventh century, religious reform became a vast movement shaped first by the monasteries and finally by the papacy itself, especially in the person of Gregory VII (who, as noted above, had been a monk at Cluny). For some, however, the customary regulations of the Benedictine Rule seemed to be hindering personal religious life. As a result, at the end of the eleventh century, the reform movement "swelled to a great tide," giving birth to new monastic orders such as the Cistercians who wished to retrieve the original spirit of Benedict, and the orders of Augustinians (including the more severe Premonstratensians) whose innovative approach sought to recapture the spirit of the Bible through the Rule of Augustine.[136] The twelfth century thus became the golden age of "religious" life, with Bernard of Clairvaux (1090–1153) as one of its principal spokespersons. The twelfth century, however, also gave rise to a wave of popular dissent. Papal and episcopal wealth and pomp were satirized and parodied by many anonymous authors, such as the one who declared, "Blessed are the rich, for theirs is the Curia of Rome."[137] Bernard of Clairvaux himself asked why bishops needed gold on their horses' bridles and so many changes of clothes, with ornamentation and furs.[138]

Criticism of hierarchical wealth and the trappings of power likewise permeated and reinforced the teachings of the Cathars or Albigensians. Proclaiming the material world to be the product of an evil creator, they claimed to have the power to enlighten and thereby to liberate human spirits from bodies and from all the enticements of the material world. Human spirits imprisoned in matter by an evil "creator" would thus be freed from the lust for wealth and power, and reunited with a previously "unknown," good God.[139] Given the mood of popular displeasure with ecclesiastical power and wealth, the Cathar movement unfortunately spread like wildfire after 1140. As noted earlier, its negativity about material creation, the human body, and thus the incarnation, would be prayerfully countered by the final words in the first part of the Hail Mary drawn from Luke's Gospel: "Blessed is the fruit of your womb."

Shortly after 1179, a lay poverty-movement intending to live according to the gospels gathered around Peter Valdès or Waldo, a once-wealthy merchant from Lyons. He and his followers began to speak out against the temporal wealth and pomp of the Church and the avarice and ostentatious pride of its clerics. Insisting that laypersons also had the gift of the Spirit, and therefore the right to preach on the scriptures, the Waldensians eventually refused obedience to the pope and bishops. They began to question the proliferation of relics and pilgrimages and to oppose certain sacramental practices, such as the multiplication of Masses offered for stipends for souls in purgatory (whose existence the Waldensians denied). Like the later Wycliff, they also rejected the concept of transubstantiation. Their growing anticlericalism and antisacramentalism, and their apparent advocacy of a priesthood of all believers, including an active role for women, soon sparked a reaction.

To quell "the heresies breaking out in modern times," Pope Lucius III placed the Cathars and certain poverty-movements including the Poor of Lyons, the *Humiliati* of Milan, and others, under a perpetual anathema for refusing to submit to ecclesiastical authority by their continued insistence on preaching without authorization. His decretal *Ad Abolendam* of 1184 also initiated the process of formal inquiry or "inquisition" in which suspects who were accused of heresy by three reputable persons or neighbors had to prove their innocence before their bishop. Those judged guilty were handed over to receive their punishment at the hands of secular authorities.[140] Canon 3 of the Fourth Lateran Council of 1215 directed civil authorities to exterminate all heretics in their territories, under pain of deposition. The Council of Toulouse in 1229 provided detailed instructions about searching for heretics and about destroying their homes (canons 1 and 6). It prescribed a special garb for reformed heretics and also prohibited lay persons from having the books of the Old or New Testaments, except for the Psalter (canons 10 and 14), lest they be tempted to preach. In 1231, Pope Gregory IX's decretal *Ille humani generis* established the Papal Inquisition, a tribunal with universal jurisdiction operating directly under the authority of the pope, rather than the local bishop. As the English law *De haeretico comburendo* of 1401 stipulated, heretics were burned in a prominent place so that such punishment might strike fear in others.

Some lay poverty-movements attempting to live according to the gospel (the *vita evangelica*) were not condemned, but instead blended into the mainstream of the Church. Such was the case with the followers of Francis of Assisi, also a layman with no formal training in theology, who chose to embrace poverty as "his Lady" at the beginning of the thirteenth century. With his deep loyalty to the Church, Francis convinced Pope Innocent III in 1210 to grant him authorization for an order that would live in poverty and preach repentance but not doctrine since its members were not ordained. Alongside his friars and Clare's community of women, Francis also established a "third order" for externs, which included married persons. Following a rule approved by Pope Honorius III in 1221, such "third order" members wore a scapular and cord under their outer clothing and were to live prayerfully, in accord with the commandments, with frequent reception of sacramental penance and the Eucharist, and practicing a form of poverty through moderation. Through its Militia of Jesus auxiliary established about 1225, Dominic's Order of Preachers likewise invited lay members to share in the "apostolic life" and in the Order's task of combating heresy. Despite the medieval tendency to identify "religious life," holiness, and spirituality with the orders of celibate monks and nuns and with the ordained, the idea that ordinary Christians could be holy, spiritual, and "seekers of perfection" without fully joining the "religious state" never completely disappeared.

Francis of Assisi's original vision of itinerants living in poverty and finding sustenance by begging soon began to be modified when friars teaching theology at the University of Paris, such as Bonaventure, and others ordained to the priesthood found that lifestyle problematic for their work. Within the intense debate that followed, the so-called "Spiritual" Franciscans, who argued for strict unconditional poverty, invoked the apocalyptic vision of Joachim of Fiore (1131–1202), who had founded a monastery in Calabria. He had prophesied that a new age of the Spirit, led by monks and characterized by contemplation of Truth, was supplanting a previous age of the Son, presided over by clerics and characterized by the wisdom of learning and discipline. (He likewise described an even earlier, "preparatory" age of the Father, shaped by the married and characterized by knowledge and work.) The Spiritual Franciscans declared Francis the "new leader" (Rev 7:2) of this dawning, "new age of the Spirit" in the Church, in which even the mediation of preaching and the sacraments would become obsolete for those with contemplative knowledge of God. It has been suggested that this wave of apocalyptic hope and rebellion reflected disillusionment with the complacency of the Franciscan movement, having itself become a powerful, established order. It was also a manifestation of a new mood, in which many felt hemmed in by the fixity of past structures that appeared closed to new possibilities.[141]

The Dominican friar-preacher Master Eckhart (c. 1260–1328) believed that religious life somehow had to be freed from the pressure of institutions. Rather than declaring the dawn of an age of contemplation presided over by religious, he proclaimed a call to perfection in which every individual emptied of self could be drawn into a personal, mystical union of love with

God, transcending even the need for sacraments and external practices. Eckhart never ceased advocating reception of the Eucharist, but always in a way that went beyond mere participation to union with God.[142] His emphasis was on the possibility of a direct, personal union with God in which there is "a changing into one."[143]

Eckhart reversed the traditional way of reading the story of Martha and Mary in Luke 10:38–42.[144] He considered Martha's active life preferable to Mary's contemplative life: "Martha is the type of soul who in the summit of the mind or depth of ground remains unchangeably united to God, but who continues to occupy herself with good works in the world that help her neighbor and also form her total being closer and closer to the divine image."[145] In Eckhart's view, learning to live with a deep sense of God's all-permeating presence does not require a flight from the world, running away from or shunning things, shutting oneself up in an external solitude. Rather, one "must practice a solitude of the spirit, wherever or with whomever [one] is. [One] must learn to break through things and grasp [one's] God in them, and to form [God] in [oneself] powerfully in an essential manner."[146] While granting that "praying is better than spinning [cloth], and that the church is a better place than the street," Eckhart also insisted that "whoever really and truly has God...has God everywhere, in the street and in company with everyone, just as much as in church, or in solitary places, or in [a monastic] cell."[147] He also argued that it would be far better to withdraw from the ecstasy of contemplation in order to serve a sick person some soup, out of the greater love of caring for another in need.[148]

In a time when the "laity" had become marginalized and "depositioned" in the Church, Eckhart's mystical vision empowered the baptized to find God within themselves, and within their world, in a way that was not totally dependent upon the clerically administered sacramental "system." In that regard, Herbert Vorgrimler has noted that, "[As] a consequence of the investiture struggle, Church and world were more sharply separated..., the

Church more strongly clericalized..., and the realm of sacraments became even more markedly a world unto itself." Sacraments, at this time, were usually not experienced as communal or ecclesial celebrations proclaiming and effecting God's presence and activity. Rather, they were predominantly understood as rituals administered by those "empowered" through ordination in order to "confer grace" on individuals. As Vorgrimler has observed, "interest in the liturgical context declined. Concentration on the 'essentials' of a sacrament led inevitably to a search for the minimum conditions under which it could come about." Ever more subject to a process of legalization and clericalization, "sacraments were transformed from symbolic liturgical actions and life-events to extremely brief, punctual gestures. In this shortened form it was no longer possible to accommodate any expressions of self-obligation to service and witnessing in the world." Vorgrimler has also acknowledged that the objections to the Church's sacraments that would be raised by the Protestant Reformers "can be explained to a great extent by the practical consequences of these developments."[149] The twentieth-century liturgical movement and the reforms initiated by Vatican II were delayed reconsiderations of such past developments.

Women likewise began to hope for new possibilities and opportunities in the medieval Church, and their initiatives took them beyond the roles assigned cloistered nuns. Visionary female ascetics like Mechtild of Magdeburg (1207–82 or 1298) criticized the corruption of the local diocesan clergy and friars.[150] Bridget of Sweden and Catherine of Siena even dared to criticize the papal curia and to challenge Pope Gregory XI (1370–78) to reform the Church by freeing it of greed, simony, and its concern for power. The mystic Julian of Norwich, reflecting on her experience of a vision in 1373, would write of the "motherhood" of God, expressed in the Second Person of the Trinity's taking on our human body and sensual soul in the incarnation, whereby we, joined to Christ as our savior and "true Mother," are *born* into the fullness of life.[151]

The beguinage movement, which peaked in the early fourteenth century, brought together women who took private vows of continence and simplicity of life, without following any "rule" from the past and without being confined in a cloister. "It was basically a women's movement, not simply a feminine appendix to a movement which owed its impetus, direction, and main support to men....It claimed the authority of no saintly founder; it sought no authorization from the Holy See." It allowed a liberating dedication to God in which "vows were a statement of intention, not an irreversible commitment to a discipline enforced by authority; and its adherents could continue their ordinary work in the world," sustaining themselves by their own labor, rather than depending upon donations from others.[152] In their independence, beguinage communities did find support in the Dominicans and Franciscans, around whose friaries their houses were clustered. But, in the end, their freedom from formal obedience to a rule or to male superiors led to their suppression by the sixteenth decree of the Council of Vienne in 1312. The beguines were systematically forced into Orders approved by the pope, leaving behind many hospitals and homes for the elderly as their memorial.[153]

R. W. Southern has argued that medieval religious Orders "were all based on one fundamental idea—that a life fully pleasing to God could not be lived in the secular world." They commonly assumed the need for a binding vow since it was their members' irrevocable, lifelong commitment to penitential discipline, self-abnegation, and prayer "that gave religious Orders a claim to the privileges they enjoyed." Anything less was considered a practical denial of total dedication to God.[154] Kenan Osborne has noted that "western church leadership, whether monastic or episcopal, did not provide the ordinary lay Catholic with very many facets of spirituality."[155] Except for an occasional pilgrimage to some place of holiness, the ordinary medieval Christian simply attended what had become a clericalized and monasticized liturgy, as an observer and a listener. Given that situation, it was inevitable that Gerard Groote's brief ministry of preaching, from 1377 to 1383, and the movement that he inspired, the "Brothers and Sisters of the Common Life," generated a great deal of opposition. For Groote proclaimed the possibility of a holiness that was not aloof from the world. He declared that persons had to "read and think for themselves," rather than just go to church and listen to the preacher, since all human beings, including the common people, were "endowed with a spark of divinity" and united with God by the bond of love.[156] Groote's approach to spirituality emphasized neither the existing forms of religious life nor the married state as a means of holiness, even though he acknowledged that marriage was a symbol of the union between Christ and the Church.[157]

Embracing Groote's perspectives, the Brothers and Sisters of the Common Life voluntarily lived together with freedom from any rule or vows, which was intended to allow them to experiment, to discover a way of life suited to experience, and to avoid the formalism seen in the great religious Orders.[158] They supported themselves by their own work, rather than by begging. Lay members were not subjected to second-class status, as in the major religious Orders, but were considered equal with the clerical, ordained members. In their search for interior union with God and in their avoidance of vows, the Brothers and Sisters of the Common Life shared Eckhart's "sense of alienation from the systems of the past," but they expressed it with great moderation. Not emphasizing ecstasy or withdrawal from the world, they lived and worked in the midst of towns. Their efforts to free the individual from the seeming tyranny of the medieval "group" involved no systematic reflection on the dynamics that shape society and history. They were not activists seeking to change the systems and structures of society or of the Church; they simply "retreated from the world's excesses and were indifferent to its large affairs."[159]

The moderation and lack of activism that characterized the Brothers and Sisters of the Common Life were not shared by the large popular movements known as the Lollards and Hussites, which emerged in England and Bohemia, before and after the turn of the fourteenth century. These movements respectively supported John Wycliff's condemnation of ecclesiatical abuses, especially the traffic in indulgences, and John Hus's criticism of simony and call for reform. They emphasized lay piety and reacted to the wealth and power of the hierarchical church with an intense spirit of anticlericalism. They opposed episcopal control over preaching and were particularly critical of the way papal power was exercised over the Church. Their divergent positions regarding the priesthood of the ordained, celibacy, vows of continence, the doctrine of transubstantiation, auricular confession, exorcisms, prayers for the dead, and the veneration of images would be condemned as heretical at the Council of Constance in 1415, where Hus was also burned at the stake. But such movements proved to be only a prelude for what was looming beyond the horizon, the Protestant Reformation of the sixteenth century.

5
The Birth of Ecclesiology: Theology Responding to Crises, AD 1400–1900

Medieval scholarship produced numerous collections and comparative studies of canon law, most notably Gratian's monumental *Concordia Discordantium Canonum*, which appeared about 1140 and was later known as the *Decretum*. However, no treatises solely focused on the theology of Church emerged until the fifteenth century. Neither the *Sentences* of Peter Lombard, nor the *Summa theologiae* of Thomas Aquinas, with its classical theological divisions, had a section dedicated specifically to a discussion of ecclesiology. Thomas's rich presentation of the Church was integrated into his Christology and his treatment of sacraments, particularly the Eucharist. His teaching on the "mystical body of the Church" emphasized the role of Christ as "head"[1] and acknowledged the role of the Spirit as the life-giving "heart" of the Church and the source of its unity.[2]

The absence of a theology of Church per se should not be taken to indicate that the questions with which the discipline of ecclesiology would occupy itself had not yet arisen. To the contrary, it is the purpose of this chapter to draw attention to the questions that gave birth to ecclesiology as a response to crises in the life of the Church. We begin our discussion with the medieval Church and end with the Church in modern times.

From Body of Christ to Mystical Body: Changing Ideas of Church

Until the eleventh century, the Eucharist had been called the mystical or sacramental body, and the Church the Body of Christ.[3] After the dispute about the Real Presence precipitated by Berengar of Tours, the terminology was transposed, so that the Eucharist was hereafter called the real Body of Christ and the Church his mystical body. That change signaled an even more profound shift in thinking about the constitutional foundations of ecclesial unity. The seldom-received Eucharist would henceforth be less and less perceived as grounding the unity of the Church. As a result, the idea that the Church was the community of persons incorporated into Christ through the Eucharist faded into the background. The biblical and patristic vision of Church as "the body of Christ," which had focused on Eucharistic communities, each presided over by a bishop serving as a personal symbol of sacramental unity, was replaced by a concept of Church as *corpus christianorum*, the corporate body of Christians as an organization unified by authority.

Given a situation in which the faithful seldom received the Eucharist while, at the same time, private masses proliferated, the "power to effect transubstantiation" effectively became separated from the role of building up the Church. Scholastic theologians thus distinguished the power of Orders—by which priests "confected" the *real* or Eucharistic Body of Christ—from the power of jurisdiction—by which the Mystical Body of the Church was unified.[4] A priestly "sacrificial" power was isolated from the role of gathering and presiding over an assembly that could "concelebrate" the Eucharist. Ordination was theologically understood to empower priests to change bread and wine into the Body and Blood of Christ, rather than to empower them to bring together a community by proclaiming the gospel and then to actualize the unity of that assembly, or "church," by presiding at a Eucharist through which those "assembled" become what they receive, the

Body of Christ (which had been the prevalent understanding until the first half of the twelfth century).[5]

The emerging Scholastic consensus, which adopted a Western tradition coming from Ambrosiaster and Jerome,[6] was reflected in Thomas Aquinas's teaching that bishops and priests were equal in their power of Orders over the "real Body of Christ," while bishops, as successors of the apostles, were superior in their jurisdiction over "the Mystical Body of the Church."[7] In Aquinas's view, bishops received a certain perpetual and indelible power ordered directly toward "the Mystical Body of Christ."[8] Having accepted that the power of bishops was superior to priests in jurisdiction but not in regard to the Eucharist, Thomas maintained that episcopacy was not a sacramental order beyond priesthood, but rather a "dignity," in which one was anointed or consecrated to rule.[9] He thereby adhered to the position previously developed by Alexander of Hales.[10] Embracing another theory earlier developed by canonists,[11] Thomas also held that "the keys [Matt 16:19] (namely, power [for ruling] and knowledge [for teaching]) came from Peter to the other apostles and from the pope to the bishops."[12] He thereby accepted that bishops received their jurisdiction from the pope, but in the sense that the pope designated or determined the subjects over whom the bishop exercised jurisdiction.[13] Invoking the Aristotelian principle that, "wherever many are ordered to one goal, there has to be a universal ruling power above particular ruling powers" (1 *Ethics* 1), Thomas goes on to argue not only that the pope must be above the bishops, but that power ought to descend from him to the bishops.[14]

In sum, episcopal authority, connected with the power of jurisdiction, now replaced the Eucharist as the source of ecclesial unity. Episcopacy was reduced to an office of external administration and government. Disconnected from its sacramental roots and its collegial dimension, the bishops' power of ruling, or jurisdiction, no longer reflected the structure of the Church as a communion of communions.[15] The churches over which bishops presided were instead more and more conceived as abstract administrative units, rather than as congregations of disciples whose unity was effected, actualized, and expressed in their assembly for Eucharist. In the mind of canonists, only the pope could create a diocese, and only a bishop could establish a parish. Even if all the members living in the particular territory disappeared, the abstract "legal personality"[16] of a diocese or parish did not die, but continued to exist in perpetuity until someone in authority abolished it. Such a notion of legal permanence dependent upon the will of pope or bishop prescinded from the existence of a real "community."

Legalistic tendencies gradually reshaped the conceptual understanding of Church into a juridical body of Christ, in which the institutional categories of corporation overpowered the liturgical and sacramental constitution of the Church as a community of disciples. In such a perspective, even the obligation of a bishop to reside in his diocese was considered more a matter of financial responsibility than a spiritual obligation to a community of believers. Amid the crisis of rampant absenteeism, legal concern for the proper administration of benefices or endowments sometimes overshadowed any concern about a bishop's duty to unify a Church by sacramentally presiding, especially at the Eucharist.

With regard to the universal Church, there was a shift of emphasis away from Christ as head of his body, the Church, to the pope as head of the Church's mystical body, which came to be seen as an "ecclesiastical, apostolic, or papal kingdom." Before the crisis at the beginning of the fourteenth century, claims for papal power were still moderated by concerns about its proper use and its relation to the rest of the Church. For example, although he referred to the pope as Vicar of Christ and invoked the notion of the two swords of spiritual and temporal power,[17] Bernard of Clairvaux counseled his former student become Pope Eugenius III (1145–53) not to exercise all the power at his disposal.[18] Observing that all the parts of a body are ordered to the unity of the whole, Aquinas, for his part, emphasized that the unity of the Church consisted both in the connection (or communication) of its members to one another and in the ordering of all members to one head, Christ, whose vicar in the Church was the pope.[19] Although he frequently emphasized the pope's fullness of power,[20] Aquinas likewise noted that each pope is head only of the pilgrim Church on earth, and only during the time of his pontificate, while Christ is head of the Church in every age, on earth, and in heaven.[21]

Debates about Papal Power and the Authority of Councils

At the end of the thirteenth century, a conflict erupted between Pope Boniface VIII and King Philip the Fair of France. This conflict led a whole series of papalist authors and theologians, such as Alexander of Saint Elpidio, Alvarez Pelagius, and the Augustinians Giles of Rome, Augustine Triumphus, and Giles of Viterbo, to defend the papacy by advocating centralization and absolutism.[22] They attempted "to condense the function of the whole Church into the function of the pope who had the plenitude of power."[23] In their perspective, the Church was the pope and the pope was the Church. Thus Alvarez Pelagius proclaimed, "[W]here the head is, namely the pope, there is the mystical Body of Christ."[24] What is more, "The pope alone has more power than the whole Catholic Church and councils together."[25] Augustine Triumphus declared that the pope's power was the same as God's, because the pope was God's delegate.[26] He also asserted that "hierarchical ordering in the community must follow from the principle that men are not equal: equality is opposed to the whole order of nature." To reject the hierarchical order within the Church was, in his view, to disregard the will of God.[27] Giles of Rome posited a papal supremacy of jurisdiction, which extended over every thing and every soul, and which was superior to royal or kingly power and prior to it both in time and in dignity.[28] His vision would be mirrored in Boniface VIII's *Unam Sanctam* issued one year later in 1302. Giles emphasized that "plenitude of power...truly resides in the pope with respect to all that is possible in the Church....

Accordingly…, whatever the pope can do with the mediation of any ecclesiastical persons, he can do without them." But Giles immediately added that "the pope should be God's imitator, and therefore should not employ this plenitude of power indiscriminately and without distinction, but only in certain specific cases."[29] Even for Giles, the fullness of the power of the pope "who holds [or occupies] the apex of the Church and can be said to be the Church"[30] had to uphold the active role of those with lesser authority.

The conflict about temporal and spiritual authority, or about kingship and priesthood (*regnum* and *sacerdotium*), continued during the first half of the fourteenth century. Marsilius of Padua and William Ockham aligned themselves with the emperor and opposed the claim that the pope held the two swords of spiritual and temporal power, and therefore bestowed temporal power on earthly rulers over whom he retained supremacy. But another conflict, concerning the internal structure of the Church or "the authority of its head and the proper interrelationship of its various members,"[31] would soon become even more pressing. After 1378, during the years of the Western Schism, multiple popes, each with their supporters, claimed full authority over the Church. The Spiritual Franciscans and imperial backers had proposed the idea of a general council as the way to resolve the divisions of the Western Church. That idea would also be embraced by those concerned for reform in a time of crisis.

Medieval thought had always interwoven the idea of the Church as a Spirit-filled community of believers with the idea of the Church "as a system of clerical offices deriving their authority from above, from outside the community."[32] Both conceptions could be expressed in terms of law and institutions; conflict arose if either was exaggerated at the expense of the other. During the twelfth and thirteenth centuries, the canonists or commentators on ecclesial discipline and structure pointedly argued that the unity of the whole Church could be ensured only by a thorough subordination of all the members to a single head, namely, the pope. But they likewise preserved another perspective, initially applied to individual churches and then at the beginning of the fourteenth century to the Roman Church and the Church as a whole. According to this perspective, the unity of the Church was rooted in the corporate association of the members of a Church, and thus allowed for an exercise of corporate authority by the members of a church even in the absence of an effective head.[33] The decretalists of the thirteenth century contributed the canonical notion of the prelate as proctor *(procurator)*, and not lord, of his corporation. Citing the scriptures, they insisted that all ecclesiastical authority was conferred for the good of the Church rather than for the personal glory of the prelates, "who were to be 'ministers' rather than masters."[34] During the fourteenth century, all these ideas were synthesized and further developed in such manner that "the most respected canonists held that in the corporate whole of the Universal Church all power was concentrated in the head by a direct act of the divine will; but they also held that, as a general principle of corporation structure, authority resided with all the members of a church, who conferred upon the head only a limited and conditional right to act on their behalf."[35]

The thirty-nine-year crisis of multiple popes (1378–1417) seemed to require an authority other than a pope to provide a resolution. Those who advocated a council supported their position by taking the idea of the Church as a corporation and injecting some rather undeveloped assertions coming from the twelfth-century decretists (not to be confused with the later decretalists) about an ultimate authority inherent in the totality of the faithful that could preserve the Church from error, about the authority of a pope surrounded by a council being greater than that of a pope alone, about a pope not acting against the well-being of the Church, and about the grounds for deposing a "heretical" pope.[36] A canonist writing around 1200 might have asked whether a pope and council were superior to a pope acting alone, for the sake of theoretical analysis. A publicist writing on Church structure about the year 1400 felt it necessary to inquire whether the authority of a general council was superior to a pope because the Church faced a problem of desperate practical urgency.[37]

Seeking a way to resolve the emergency of multiple popes, some joined the canonical idea of legal incorporation with the theological concept of the mystical unity of the Church as the Body of Christ. The canonical notion of the Church as a corporate entity enabled a more precise and concrete expression of the notion that an ultimate authority inhered in the community of the faithful as a whole. The further conviction that the corporate unity of the faithful was an integral part of "the whole Christ" inspired and motivated the intense effort to heal "the body of Christ" torn by the continuing schism.[38] From such a perspective, the conciliar position was not primarily juristic, but rather comprised a theology of Church, with a call for a return to scripture and patristic tradition.[39]

Brian Tierney has concluded that "the appeal to the underlying authority of the entire Church, understood as the congregation of the faithful, was the very essence of the conciliar position." However, some later advocates of a conciliar solution to the Church's crisis went a step further and argued that the pope possessed "only a derivative and limited right of government conferred on him by the Church; far from possessing absolute power, responsible to no human tribunal, he could exercise only such authority as was necessary for the 'edification' of the Church." Thus, if a pope's rule was destructive of the Church, these advocates argued that "he could be corrected or deposed by a General Council exercising the supreme authority inherent in the Church as a whole."[40] The underlying presupposition for asserting the superiority of a council acting against a pope was that "the whole Christian community was superior to any prelate, however exalted; the Pope was to be a servant of the Church rather than its master."[41] The question that remains is whether such assertions found any acceptance in the official position of the Council of Constance.

Meeting from 1414–18, the Council of Constance sought to resolve the crisis of the papacy. In reviewing various interpretations of the proceedings and intentions of the council, August

Franzen concludes that the council was not convened to attack the institution of the papacy, but to save it. Agreeing with Hubert Jedin,[42] Franzen contends that the majority at the council intended only to deal with an emergency situation, and not to establish any lasting control of a council over the pope, or to impose "any limitation of papal power in the normal government of the Church."[43] In that regard, he notes that in 1394 the University of Paris had proposed three ways to overcome the schism: "[T]wo appealed to the goodwill of the Popes themselves (yielding and compromise) and only the third way (through a council) attempted a solution without this appeal, more or less as a last way out." Important figures at the council, such as Jean Gerson (chancellor of the University of Paris, who led the theologians from there) and Cardinal Peter d'Ailly, were staunch defenders of the papacy who initially favored the first two approaches. In Franzen's view, the machinations and resistance of "Pope" John XXIII (1410–15), who had convened the council that then deposed him by applying the established canonical grounds for a judgment of "heresy," led a minority at the council to lapse into a radical conciliarism that the majority never accepted in its interpretation of the decrees.[44] Thus, the majority's support of a conciliar solution to an emergency situation should not be equated with "conciliarism."

In his speech at the Council of Constance on March 23, 1415, Jean Gerson addressed the situation in which a pope might have to obey a general council: "The council cannot abrogate papal supremacy, but it can restrict it if the welfare of the Church requires it. Christ's union with the Church is indissoluble—not so the Pope's."[45] In seeking to resolve the problem of multiple claimants to the papacy, Constance did seem to reinforce the idea that a council was above the pope in certain circumstances. Its decree *Haec sancta* of April 6, 1415 declared that the council "representing the catholic church militant...has power immediately from Christ; and that everyone of whatever state or dignity, even papal, is bound to obey it in those matters which pertain to the faith, the eradication of the said schism, and the general reform of the said church of God in head and members."[46] The decree went on to say that anyone, including the pope, who disobeyed a directive of that council or any other legitimately convened general council was to be subject to penance and punishment. In a later decree, *Frequens*, issued on October 9, 1417, Constance further ordered that general councils should be convened every decade.[47]

The dogmatic validity of the decrees of Constance, the ambiguities of their wording, and the further question of whether Popes Martin I and Eugene IV subsequently confirmed them are still debated among scholars. Franzen has proposed a moderate interpretation of the intention of Constance's decrees. Rather than asserting the autonomy of councils, in opposition to the papacy, Franzen believes that Constance considered councils to be subsidiary to the papacy: "The idea of the Church's co-responsibility at the councils should be stressed and in order to prevent an absolutist papacy, which convoked these councils once in a century, from letting them fall into oblivion, the Fathers laid down a minimum interval of ten years. It was even more important that the Church's right to convoke in future emergencies was legally formulated in the following decrees."[48] In Franzen's opinion, *Frequens* was a disciplinary decree that proposed the minimum interval of ten years only to keep councils from falling into oblivion and *not* to introduce a parliamentary system into the Church. By contrast, Hans Küng agrees that Constance did not aim "at introducing a new Church constitution along the lines of parliamentarianism," but he considers its decrees to be dogmatically binding and not just disciplinary. He believes they defined a conciliar control function, "a distinct kind of superiority of the council (along the lines of at least moderate 'conciliar theory')...on the premise that a possible future pope might again lapse into heresy, schism, or the like." In Küng's view, "all the participants at the Council, even the moderate Council Fathers and the pope, were in favor of the necessity of a definite control over the pope [who is heretical or schismatic] by an ecumenical council, viewed as the representation of the universal Church."[49]

To cite one further scholar on this question, Klaus Schatz notes that conciliarism had strong roots in the constitutionalism of its contemporary, late medieval world. However, he makes clear that conciliarism was also rooted in the ancient synodal tradition of the Church "and the awareness that the divine promise is given to the Church as a whole. The old *communio* ecclesiology was revived in it, after having been suppressed since the early Middle Ages not primarily by the papacy but because the Church was enmeshed in the political order of governance."[50] In that regard, Schatz describes how the earlier concept of divided sovereignty (in which a higher level of authority, such as the pope, was not seen as displacing a lower level authority, such as bishops, whose authority was not derived from the higher level) was displaced by the idea of an undivided, corporate sovereignty (as in the model of the medieval university). Then, in the latter part of the fifteenth century, the constitutional model of an undivided, corporate sovereignty gave way to the notion of a single, absolutist sovereignty, as reflected both in royal absolutism and "papalism" within the Church.

Defending the Papacy: Torquemada's *Summa de Ecclesia*

It was in the aftermath of Constance that conciliarism came to be seen as a threat that needed to be countered. At the Council of Basel (convened in 1431), the Dominican Juan de Torquemada mounted a vigorous defense of papal authority. Notwithstanding, the assembly at Basel, at which cardinals, bishops, and abbots were only a small minority of those voting, declared its supremacy over the pope and continued as an anticouncil after Pope Eugenius IV ordered it transferred to Ferrara in 1437. Nicholas Cardinal Cusa was among the minority who obeyed the pope's decree; however, his *On the Supremacy of General Councils in Church and Empire*, written in 1440, nevertheless maintained that all the other apostles were foundation stones for the Church along with Peter and that they were all equal in authority, sharing "one general episcopate, diffused throughout the world, without division into dioceses." He further concluded that "all bishops and perhaps even presbyters are of equal authority in respect to jurisdiction, although not in respect to the execution."[51]

It was in such a situation that Juan de Torquemada wrote his *Summa de ecclesia*, the first work dedicated solely to a treatment of the Church separate from Christology and sacramental theology. Reacting both to conciliarism and to the growing tensions between secular rulers and popes, Torquemada's *Summa* (in four books, treating the Church in its Nature or Mystery, Roman Primacy, Councils, and Schism and Heresy) was not a systematic theological reflection about the total nature of the Church. It was rather a defense of the rights and authority of the Roman primacy over the then-fragmenting Christendom of Europe. Torquemada argued that only Peter was made a bishop directly by Christ (*Summa* II, 32–34): "[He] received power for and before all others" (II, 22). Torquemada likewise maintained that all power in the Church hierarchically comes down from the pope who possesses it in its fullness (*Summa* II, 2, 52–55, 83); all other prelates derive their power of jurisdiction from the pope (II, 54). Pointedly attacking the position that authority and jurisdiction belonged to the Church collectively in all its members (*Summa* II, 24–26), he questioned whether "the mystical body" as a whole was even capable of exercising any authority, since an association of different members does not have a mind as a "whole" (universitas, *Summa* II, 71). In his view, the pope was empowered by Christ; consequently, as monarchical head of the mystical body of the Church, it was the pope who empowered the rest of the Church (*Summa* II, 55, 71). Torquemada did allow that a general council's unanimous agreement on a matter of faith should prevail over a contradicting pope,[52] and he conceded that a council could bring more reasoning power to an issue than an individual pope, and thereby exert more influence.[53] Yet Torquemada generally envisioned councils as in total dependence on the pope, whose jurisdiction was supreme. As Congar has observed, Torquemada's perspectives on the role of councils so determined later treatments that the West lost the chance to articulate a more refined and differentiated conciliar theology.[54] Instead polemics prevailed.

The papacy would henceforth reestablish its dominant role. At the Council of Florence in 1439, Pope Eugenius IV, with the agreement of the emperor, promulgated the decree concerning reunion with Greek Churches; not insignificantly, this decree also reaffirmed the prerogatives of the Apostolic See of Rome and the Roman pontiff.[55] (The Council of Florence is also distinguished for having made the now-reconsidered statement about no salvation outside the Catholic Church, declaring that "not only pagans, but also Jews, heretics and schismatics" were bound for the eternal fire of hell.)[56] During the Fifth Lateran Council in 1516, Pope Leo X moved to nullify the French or Gallican advocacy of conciliar superiority by personally promulgating *Pastor aeternus gregem*, in which he declared the authority of the pope to be above that of any council.[57] The decrees of the Council of Trent would be issued by the council itself, but papal confirmation was requested.[58]

Under different circumstances, the call for a conciliar response to ecclesial problems might have been recognized as an attempt to restore the structure of the Church as "communion," since ideally, at least, convening a council allows the mind of the entire communion of Churches to be expressed through dialogue. Such a conciliar or collegial structure within the Church should not be equated without further ado with "conciliarism." Such an equation would be far too simplistic. As Congar has emphasized, developing an idea also acknowledged by Torquemada, even though the "power" of a council is not above that of the pope, the council may contribute to the "credence" or "credibility" of what is taught.[59]

One can only wonder whether the tragic divisions of the sixteenth century might have been avoided, had an ongoing conciliar approach to reform been able to flourish in the period after

Constance. Unfortunately, history happened otherwise. And instead, the Protestant Reformation (with its critique of the Church of Rome and Luther's call for a "free Christian council in free German lands") provided another impetus for developing a theology of Church in the context of crisis. This context intensified the polemical and apologetic tone of Catholic ecclesiology, which focused on defending ecclesial authority and the sacramental and jurisdictional powers of the ordained rather than on providing an integrated explanation of the meaning and mission of the total community called Church.

The Protestant Reformation: A Church Divided

On October 31, 1517, the Augustinian monk Martin Luther published his Ninety-Five Theses, calling for a public disputation on the matter of indulgences, "out of love and concern for the truth." His theses were occasioned by events surrounding Albert of Brandenburg, who had become a bishop at the age of twenty-two, eight years short of the minimum age. Still in his twenties and not satisfied with already being Archbishop of Halberstadt and the administrator bishop of Magdeburg, Albert also sought to become Archbishop of Mainz, which would automatically make him a Prince-Elector of the German emperor. His appointment to Mainz on August 18, 1514, required a special dispensation from Rome, for which Albert paid a very considerable tax and honorarium amounting to 32,000 gold ducats, borrowed from the Fugger banking family. The loan was partially secured by Rome's promise to grant a special papal indulgence in Albert's three Sees. The Dominican friar John Tetzel was chosen to preach the indulgence, with half the receipts going into a building fund for the new St. Peter's Basilica, while the other half paid off the principal and interest on Albert's loan for the dispensation. In his Ninety-Five Theses, Luther's criticism of Tetzel's preaching was quite incisive: "There is no divine authority for preaching that the soul springs out of purgatory immediately when the money rings in the bottom of the chest" (Thesis 27).[60] Questioning how papal authority could be applied to souls beyond this life, Luther asked why the pope didn't free everyone from purgatory out of love and the need of souls, rather than for money to rebuild St. Peter's church (Thesis 82). As Thesis 91 indicates, Luther's original intention was not to attack Rome but to call for reform: "If, therefore, indulgences were preached in accordance with the spirit and mind of the pope, all these difficulties would be easily overcome, and indeed, cease to exist." But the matter rapidly escalated beyond a call for reform.

Luther's *Open Letter to the Christian Nobility of the German Nation*, written in August 1520, spoke of demolishing three walls by which the "Romanists" protected themselves.[61] The first wall involved calling the pope, bishops, priests, monks, and nuns the spiritual or religious class, but princes, lords, artisans, and farmers the secular or temporal class. Luther broke down that wall by declaring that all Christians belong to the religious class by one baptism, one gospel, and one faith: "[We] are all consecrated priests through baptism, as St. Peter says in 1 Peter 2[:9], 'You are a royal priesthood and a priestly realm.' The Apocalypse says, 'Thou hast made us to be priests and kings by thy blood' [Rev 5:9–10]."[62] In Luther's mind, when a bishop consecrates one who says Mass, or preaches, or gives absolution, "it is nothing else than that in the place and stead of the whole community, all of whom have like power, he takes a person and charges him to exercise this power on behalf of the others."[63]

The second wall that Luther intended to tear down was the claim that only Rome could interpret the scriptures. He believed that the third wall, namely, the papacy's pretensions to absolute power, would then fall by itself, once Christians used the scriptures to judge the pope when he acted contrary to the scriptures. Invoking as precedent the fact that Constantine and later emperors had convoked the first councils, Luther urged the princes of Germany to convene a "truly free council" in order to reform the Church that Luther saw as being harmed by the pope. He argued that "the Romanists have no basis in Scripture for their claim that the pope alone has the right to call or confirm a council."[64]

Cataloguing abuses he saw in the papal bureaucracy, especially regarding the process of appointing new bishops and the amount of money the process drained from the German people, Luther called for an end to Rome's expanding control of benefices, with the barbed observation that "it seems as though canon law were instituted solely for the purpose of making a great deal of money."[65] He thus called for bishops again to be chosen with the participation of neighboring bishops, according to the directives of canon 4 of the Council of Nicaea.[66] (Later, the Council of Trent would instead reaffirm the right of the pope to appoint bishops, but only after a prolonged debate in which some French and Spanish bishops also advocated a return to the practice of the early Church.)[67] Luther further argued that the papacy had usurped the authority and responsibility that rightfully belonged to bishops. In his view, the oaths of obedience imposed on new bishops made them servants unable to question the pope.[68]

Luther proposed in addition that an ordinary bishop's mitre take the place of the triple-crowned papal tiara, that the number of cardinals be reduced to twelve, and that ninety-nine percent of the papal court be abolished. In his view, the pope had no authority over the emperor; he was the vicar, not of the glorified Christ in heaven, but only of the crucified Christ who had walked on the earth. To resolve the continuing problem of the Hussite movement, Luther proposed using dialogue and persuasion, rather than power; heretics were to be overcome with books, not with fire.[69]

In his *Babylonian Captivity of the Church*, published two months later, Luther reiterated his emphasis on the priesthood of the baptized. Again invoking 1 Peter 2:9, Luther proclaimed "we are all priests, as many of us as are Christians. But the priests, as we call them, are ministers chosen from among us. All that they do is done in our name; the priesthood is nothing but a ministry." Complaining that the world is filled with priests, bishops, and cardinals who repetitiously mumble prayers as hour-readers and

Mass-sayers but do not preach, he concluded that "whoever does not preach the Word, though he was called by the church to do this very thing, is no priest at all, and that the sacrament of ordination can be nothing else than a certain rite by which the church chooses its preachers." According to Luther, "[it] is the ministry of the Word that makes the priest and the bishop," not blessing churches and bells, or confirming children.[70] Nevertheless, one must keep in mind that, although Luther proclaimed all Christians to be priests through their baptism, he did not consider all to be pastors. In brief, the role of "pastor" in the Church requires that "an office and a field of work" be committed to one's charge: "This call and command make pastors and preachers."[71]

Although he vehemently accused the Roman Church of falsifying the gospel of salvation by some of its additions, Luther likewise acknowledged Rome's crucial role in handing on Christian faith and practice, especially during his struggle with the Anabaptists:

> We confess that under the papacy there has been much, even all Christian treasure, and that it also came to us from there, because we confess that in the papacy there is the true holy scripture, the true baptism, the true sacrament of the altar, the true key to the forgiveness of sins, true preaching office, true catechism such as the Ten Commandments, the articles of faith, and the Our Father....I say that under the pope there is true Christianity, even the model of Christianity, and many devout great saints....We are not fanatics like the sectarians who reject everything to do with the papacy, for thus we would also reject Christianity, with all it has in Christ.[72]

But Luther's critique of the Roman Church gave rise to a persistent call for "a free Christian Council in German Lands." As Jedin has observed, that scenario was feared by many in the Roman Curia. A council bent on reform would threaten the curia's "traditional administration of benefices and their financial system, with a consequent loss of income and an end of the luxurious style in which they were wont to live."[73] Pope Clement VII had a much worthier motive for hoping to avoid a council, at which the divergent interests of the various nations and powers might further jeopardize the Church's unity. He asked the Dominican Cardinal Thomas de Vio, known as Cajetan, to draw up a memorandum outlining acceptable disciplinary concessions that might facilitate a "coming to terms" with the German Protestants. Cajetan's document, presented in 1530, recommended allowing the marriage of priests in Germany (on the model of the Greek Church) and communion in both kinds. He also proposed a general decree that Church laws regarding feast and fast days and reception of the sacraments were not binding under sin. Moreover, Cajetan suggested "that reunion with the Protestants could be brought about provided they gave an assurance that they believed all that the universal Church believed; [there is] no need to demand a formal recantation from their theologians." Warned by the canonist Accolti that he would risk deposition by granting such concessions, the pope took no action. Admittedly, it may have already been too late for reconciliation one way or another.[74]

Reformation movements had also emerged at Strasbourg, under the leadership of Martin Bucer; at Basel, under John Oecolampadius; and at Zurich, under Ulrich Zwingli. The latter's questioning of Real Presence in the Eucharist, it is worth remarking, made Luther uneasy. With the publication of the first edition of John Calvin's *Institutes of the Christian Religion* in 1536 (followed by his definitive edition of 1559), there was a further intensification of the reform movements in Geneva and Strasbourg. England and Scandinavia would also break with the Church of Rome. Ever more on the defensive, Clement VII's successor, Pope Paul III, finally convened a council in 1545 at Trent, a German-speaking town just outside the boundary of the German Empire at the edge of Italian-speaking lands. Besides responding to Luther's attacks on "the sacramental system," his emphasis on the priesthood of the baptized, and his position on faith, good works, and justification, the council also repeatedly reminded bishops of their responsibility to preach and teach, and therefore to reside, in their dioceses.[75]

One member of the papal curia who organized and participated in Trent's final sessions (1562–63) became an exemplar of that kind of bishop. Unlike Cardinal Ippolito d'Este who never left Rome to visit the archdiocese of Milan during the entire time he was its bishop from 1520 to 1550,[76] Cardinal Charles Borromeo, nephew of Pope Pius IV (1559–65), gave up the honors and power of the sixteenth-century papal court to take up residence in the diocese over which his uncle had much earlier appointed him administrator. That is, he lived and worked among the people for whom he was bishop. Given that no bishop had resided in Milan for the past eighty years, Borromeo's pastoral labors in his diocese between 1563 and 1584, so remarkable for the time, along with his contributions during Trent's final sessions, made him the ideal model of a Counter-Reformation bishop and ultimately contributed to his canonization as a saint in 1610.

The Ecclesiological Climate from the Council of Trent to Vatican I

The growth of nationalism during the later Middle Ages, including the notion of a French Church or English Church, which culminated in the establishment of state churches during the Reformation, would nurture a counter emphasis on the papacy, centralization, and uniformity. With half of Europe separated from the Catholic Church by the Reformation, there would be even stronger emphasis on the role of Rome for defending the faith. As the bulwark of a depleted Catholicism, the Church of Rome became more and more identified with the universal Church, and its bishop viewed almost as a universal bishop. Documents from the period in which the Council of Trent was held reveal a tendency to equate the terms "Apostolic Church" or "Holy See" with "Holy Church" or even "Universal Church."[77]

The name of one particular Church now began to define universal Church as "Roman Catholic Church."

In response to post-Reformation controversies during the sixteenth century, the Jesuit theologian and later cardinal Robert Bellarmine especially stressed the external visibility of the Church, under the "rule" of bishops and the pope, comparing it with that of secular states: "The one true Church is the community of humans brought together by profession of the true faith and communion in the same sacraments, under the rule of recognized pastors and especially of the sole vicar of Christ on earth, the Roman Pontiff....The Church is indeed a community *[coetus]* of humans, as visible and palpable as the community of the Roman people, or the kingdom of France, or the republic of Venice."[78]

Bellarmine's perspectives contributed to the later development of the notion of Church as a "perfect [or complete and self-sufficient] society," systematized by eighteenth-century canonists, and then widely influential among nineteenth-century theologians. In that view, like the Kingdom of France or the Republic of Venice, the Church as a juridical person, or institution, was thought to possess all the regulations and means necessary to procure its particular goal, salvation. Although some of its components had medieval roots (in the Gregorian reform and in the political categories used by Aquinas), the concept of Church as "perfect society" grew out of the Counter-Reformation's efforts to defend the Catholic system (of papacy, priesthood, sacraments, saints, etc.) and its tendency to conceive the Church along the lines of the absolutist states of the time: as a pyramidal society organized under the pope as monarch (with his curia and cardinals), and the bishops. As Congar has observed, the Church was viewed, not as the congregation of faithful disciples of Christ, or as an organism animated by the Holy Spirit, but as an organization established by Christ, in which the Spirit was the guarantor of authority.[79] In the perspective of the so-called naturalist ecclesiology of the Enlightenment, "God had created the hierarchy and thus provided more than was necessary for the Church until the end of time."[80]

The atmosphere of controversy did not diminish. In the aftermath of the French Revolution in 1789, many European governments moved toward a policy of "laicization." While emphasizing a separation of church and state, civil rulers such as Napoleon III in France, Bismarck in Germany, and Cavour in the emerging Italy sought to subordinate and control the Church by interfering in its ecclesiastical appointments and expropriating its land holdings. Challenged in its customary role in areas of public life by legislators who were supportive of "modern liberty" but hostile to the Church, the hierarchical Church increasingly resisted losing the entitlements that had accrued to it over the centuries. Many within the Church looked back to a time when governments favored the Catholic Church by proscribing non-Catholic proselytizing and prohibiting the sale of books holding "unacceptable" positions.[81] In this context, especially after the uprising against the Papal States in 1830—threatening the temporal power of the pope—a more authoritarian Catholicism emerged, seeking to recapture the position once enjoyed in the ancient regime. Catholicism began to assume a "closed" and defensive posture. There would be increasing emphasis on a theology of the kingship of Christ and on the ecclesiological notion of "perfect society."[82]

The nineteenth-century Roman theologian Giovanni Perrone, especially favored by Pope Gregory XVI (1831–46), conceded that the theological study of the Church had become equated with a treatment of authority.[83] Embracing an emphasis on the teaching Church introduced by Thomas Stapleton in the sixteenth century, and further elaborated into a distinction between a teaching and a believing Church during the eighteenth century,[84] Perrone said the word "Church" primarily referred not to the community of all the faithful who formed the "learning Church," but to the body of bishops with the Roman pontiff who formed the "teaching Church."[85] The faithful were to accept what they had been taught, based on the authority of the teaching Church. Perrone was convinced that the removal of authority would destroy the unity of the Church, leaving only individual liberty.[86]

Another motif significantly shaping nineteenth-century Catholic ecclesiology was an emphasis on the threefold office of Christ as prophet, king, and priest. (Ironically, this emphasis reflected the influence of Protestant theological themes.)[87] If Christ was prophet, king, and priest in relation to "the kingdom of God," Catholic writers asserted that the Church which manifested that "kingdom" succeeded to or carried on Christ's powers as prophet, king, and priest. Power and authority in the Church would henceforth be discussed in terms of the tripartite distinction of teaching, ruling, and sanctifying, supplementing the earlier distinction between orders and jurisdiction. The ground was thereby prepared for the assertion of a distinct *hierarchical* power of teaching or *magisterium.* Concurrently, with the growing emphasis on a juridical notion of Church as "perfect society," there was a narrowing of the scriptural sense of the kingdom or reign of God. Instead of including all humanity, God's kingdom or reign began to be identified with the Church, in a manner that emphasized the visibility of its hierarchy and authority, and its administration of sacraments as the means to salvation.[88] The very term "Church" more and more denoted its external organization, namely, its government by pope and bishops, and especially Roman teaching authority or *magisterium.*

As a further consequence of this development, the ancient idea of the "sense of the faithful," which acknowledged the role of the entire community of believers for keeping alive the beliefs of the Church, receded. Many Catholic theologians primarily stressed the prerogatives of the hierarchical magisterium, or official teaching authority of the pope and bishops.[89] A notable exception was John Henry Newman, especially in his essay "On Consulting the Faithful in Matters of Doctrine" published in 1859.[90] Newman "assumed a dynamic, non-static understanding of Christian truth" and "also...acknowledged a proper role for the faithful in the specific area of the formulation of the faith." He likewise spelled out a proper role for theologians at the heart of this process.[91] In his view, "the School of theologians" was "one of the principal parts of the body of the faithful." They had the important role of correcting both popular errors and overly narrow conceptions coming from the *magisterium*, thereby contributing to the preservation of the faith by the entire body of the faithful.[92] While sharing Newman's appreciation of the sacramental nature of the Church, Perrone and other Roman theologians would be disconcerted by his "seeming acceptance of historical change in the realm of dogma and his relative frankness about the historical reality of the church's past. They were not used to this...."[93] In the Roman climate established under Pope Pius IX, a commitment to historical research, especially as preserved in German theology, was not particularly welcomed.

Perrone and the professors who succeeded him at the Roman College, which was entrusted to the Jesuits, did begin to restore a theological dimension to the treatment of Church, thereby moderating the juridical emphasis found in earlier Counter-Reformation works. Carlo Passaglia, for example, introduced a methodology that consulted biblical and patristic sources; his successors, C. Schrader, J.-B. Franzelin, and (in Germany) M. J. Scheeben, applied this methodology. All of these figures were also influenced by the work of Johann Adam Möhler, who had been professor of theology at the University of Tübingen and afterward at Munich. Among continental theologians, Möhler was significant for having been consistently theological, rather than juridical, in his treatment of Church. Influenced both by German Romanticism and by the Christian writers of the first three centuries, his *Unity in the Church*, first published in 1825, recovered the idea of the Church as a community, ever seeking to incarnate or historically express an inner, spiritual life grounded in love. Accordingly, Möhler maintained that the unity of the Church was manifested or expressed when the community and its ministers embodied or gave form to the inner life of love. One could not have that inner life apart from the collective experience or living tradition of the Church, "the ever living and incarnate expression, through the centuries, of the Holy Spirit who animates the totality of the faithful."[94] Möhler's *Symbolik*, published in 1832, shifted the emphasis away from the Spirit's activity in tradition to that of "the living Word" remaining in the community of believers, and also gave more weight to the importance of teaching authority in the Church.[95] It spoke of the visible community of believers, which is the Church founded by Christ and directed by the Spirit, as the permanent incarnation of the Son of God in visible, human form. It presented the Church as the body of the Lord, through which Christ acts to reconcile humanity, while constantly renewing and rejuvenating himself.[96]

Yet the theological renaissance in ecclesiology initiated under Möhler's influence at the Roman College (later the Gregorian University) did not prevail. Especially with Joseph Kleutgen's arrival in Rome, such "positive" theology would be more and more displaced by a Neo-Scholastic "speculative" theology, which was thoroughly ahistorical in nature and opposed to contemporary philosophical developments. The Roman leadership, meanwhile, pursued what Congar has termed "a politico-clerical restoration."[97] In order to ward off attempts at control on the part of anticlerical lay governments, the leadership of the Church imitated those governments' very mode of conceiving authority in terms of "sovereignty" and coercive authority. For example, the tone of Gregory XVI's encyclical *Mirari vos* (1832), which invoked the reference to "using the rod" in 1 Corinthians 4:21, suggested that papal authority could coerce the proper expression of faith, instead of seeking to convince in the spirit of gentleness. As Giuseppe Alberigo observes, such a tactic tended to obscure "the evangelical call to service and even the exemplary dimension of authority."[98] Subsequently, the distinction between governing and teaching in the Church became more and more blurred, since the "hierarchical" governing activity was transferred to the doctrinal context, and more and more exercised as a centralized teaching authority. Proposition 24 of Pius IX's *Syllabus of the Principal Errors of Our Time*, issued in 1864, rebuked those who said the Church did not have the power of using force, nor any direct or indirect temporal power (DH 2924). It was unfortunate that the errors condemned in the *Syllabus* were simply listed, with no reference to their original context, since many involved very specific problems precipitated by the secularist Italian reunification movement, whose armies of revolution were then threatening the pope's temporal power over the Papal States.[99]

As evidenced by an increasing number of "instructions" (in the form of encyclicals, apostolic letters, and interventions by papal initiative, or *motu proprio*), the papacy now "also entered the domain of formulating the faith and concomitantly distinguishing errors." It thereby positioned an "official" *magisterium* between the Bible and tradition and the theologians.[100] Creative development within the theological faculties would subsequently be diminished. Reacting against the academic freedom advocated by a theological congress that Ignaz Döllinger had convened at Munich in 1863, Pius IX sent a letter of reprimand, *Tuas libenter*, to the Archbishop of Munich in which he insisted that scholarly research was to be guided, not only by the dogmas of faith defined by councils and popes, but by "the ordinary *magisterium*" of the entire Church, namely, the teaching of bishops dispersed throughout the world. Theologians were likewise to subject themselves to the doctrinal decisions of the Congregations in the Roman Curia.[101] An ultimate consequence was that theologians would be assigned the task of supporting the "definitive" teachings of the official *magisterium.*[102] It is significant that Denzinger's *Enchiridion* or handbook of sources for theology, first published in 1854, organized all its material under the reigns of popes, giving "equal status to creeds, definitions, and doctrinal declarations."[103]

In an era that produced Bismarck's Prussia, Bonaparte's dictatorship, and Emperor Franz Josef's "enlightened despotism," many believed that both church and state needed a strong centralized government dominating a unified and obedient people. In that context, some deemed it appropriate that Pope Pius IX, after consulting the bishops, should have defined the doctrine of Mary's Immaculate Conception on his own authority in 1854.[104] Sixteen years later, in 1870, the First Vatican Council would proclaim papal primacy and infallibility. Given the mood of the nineteenth century, Vatican I actually showed remarkable restraint in defining the role of the papacy. Perhaps it can be affirmed that the presence of the Spirit moderated any tendency toward excessive human zeal.

Vatican I: An Authoritative Petrine Ministry

The original plan was that Vatican I would develop its reflections on the papacy within the broader context of the theology of Church. A fifteen-chapter schema or draft on the Church was initially presented to the bishops for discussion.[105] Reflecting the influence of Möhler,[106] that preparatory draft began with a brief consideration of the Church as Mystical Body (ch. 1), but went on to declare that Christ founded the Church as a visible, perfect (or complete) society, necessary for salvation (chs. 2–7). The Church was also said to be permanent, indefectable, and untouched by error through the gift of infallibility, which was coextensive with the deposit of faith (chs. 8–9). In keeping with the then-prevalent paradigm, the Church was described as a hierarchical community, not of equals, but of unequals, in which clergy and laity, as well as varying degrees in the power of orders and of government, were to be distinguished (ch. 10). Chapters 11 and 12 respectively treated the primacy of the Roman pontiff (without reference to papal infallibility) and the temporal dominion of the Holy See. The last three chapters (13–15) dealt with issues concerning church and state relations.

The preliminary draft was not well received by the bishops. They considered its presentation of the Church as Mystical Body to be too vague and abstract and felt that the rights of the Church and the role of bishops were inadequately treated.[107] As a result, the moderators of the council withdrew the document for revision. The bishops kept only chapter 11 on papal primacy. With the subsequent addition of a section on papal infallibility (introduced through the efforts of Pius IX and the committee maneuvers of Cardinal Manning), chapter 11 eventually evolved into the document known as *Pastor Aeternus* or *Eternal Shepherd*, approved on July 18, 1870. The subsequent outbreak of the Franco-Prussian war, and the departure of many French and German bishops, led to the dissolution of the council. As a result, the chapters of a second, revised schema on the Church, prepared by Joseph Kleutgen, were never discussed. Cut short by external circumstances, Vatican I was limited to a definition of papal prerogatives in the very circumscribed context of responding to threats posed by secular states and of countering both Gallicanism (or French "ecclesial nationalism") and resurgent conciliarism.[108]

To take a step back in time, the four Gallican articles approved at an assembly of French clergy in 1682 asserted: (1) that the pope could not interfere in the civil affairs of France, since the papacy has no authority over temporal or secular power; (2) that the authority of councils is superior to that of the pope (for which the decrees of the Council of Constance were invoked); (3) that the exercise of papal authority is to be regulated according to the canons established by the Spirit of God and consecrated by the respect of the whole world, which means that the rules and customs of the French Church, and of other Churches, remain in force and are inviolable; and (4) that, although the pope has a primary role in matters of faith and his decrees pertain to each and every Church, his judgments or decrees are not irreformable unless the consent of the Church has been given.[109] (A similar outlook was reflected in the episcopalism and nationalism advocated in Germany by Febronianism, and in the Austro-Hungarian empire by Josephitism, which embraced the views, first, that religion is a personal and private matter and, second, that the Church is in the state, and the state is not in the Church.)[110] As Schatz observes, "Universal papal authority within the Church was, for the Gallicans, inseparably bound up with papal claims to superiority over secular authority,"[111] as found in a series of papal statements from Gregory VII's *Dictatus Papae* to Boniface VIII's *Unam Sanctam.* Ironically, Gallicanism emanated from the region of Europe that in the ninth century had forged the *Decretals of Pseudo-Isidore* to strengthen the role of the papacy. The earlier support for a strong papacy was now preserved by the group called Ultramontanes, who looked beyond the Alps (hence the name Ultramontanes) to the bishop of Rome for their theology and guidance. They considered the definition of papal infallibility to be indispensable for preserving papal sovereignty and the authority of the Church.

After much discussion and debate, the first two chapters of Vatican I's *Pastor Aeternus* or *Eternal Shepherd* solemnly defined that the bishops of Rome were successors *in perpetuum* to the "primacy of jurisdiction over the whole church of God" that was conferred on Peter by Christ the Lord.[112] Chapter 3 declared that the "successor in the chair of Peter," as "vicar of Christ" and "head of the whole Church," has a primacy "of full and supreme power of jurisdiction" that is "ordinary," "episcopal" (or pastoral), and "immediate," not only in matters concerning faith and morals, but also in discipline and government, over all pastors and faithful, "of whatever rite and dignity, both singly and collectively."[113] Chapter 4 of *Eternal Shepherd* further declared that the apostolic primacy of the pope also includes "the supreme power of teaching," described as follows:

> When the Roman pontiff speaks *ex cathedra,* that is, when in the exercise of his office as shepherd [pastor] and teacher of all Christians, in virtue of his supreme apostolic authority, he defines a doctrine concerning faith or morals *[de fide vel moribus]* to be held by the whole [universal] Church, he possesses, by the divine assistance promised to him in blessed Peter, that infallibility with which the divine Redeemer willed his Church to enjoy in defining doctrine concerning faith or morals. Therefore, such definitions of the Roman

> pontiff are of themselves *[ex sese]*, and not by the consent of the Church irreformable.[114]

The wording of the last phrase indicates that the council was directly rejecting the position espoused by the fourth Gallican article (to reiterate, that the pope's judgment or decrees are not irreformable unless the consent of the Church has been given).

In defining papal primacy and infallibility, Vatican I had no intention of diminishing the essential role of bishops, both within the universal church and within their particular churches. The council's earlier Constitution on Revelation and Faith, *Dei Filius*, promulgated in April 1870, was referring to the teaching authority of all the bishops when it declared that, "by divine and catholic faith all those things are to be believed which are contained in the word of God as found in scripture and tradition, and which are proposed by the Church as matters to be believed as divinely revealed, whether by her solemn judgment or in her ordinary and universal *magisterium*."[115] The council's silence about the role of the episcopal college in the universal Church, in its definition of papal primacy and infallibility, should not be interpreted as a negation of that role. Rather, given its defensive and traditional character, Vatican I was simply not preoccupied with matters thought to be "in tranquil possession."[116] In that regard, it should be noted that the episcopate's corporate or collegial power over the universal Church was affirmed both by Bishops Zinelli and Gasser in their explanation and defense of revisions prepared by the Deputation of Faith (the commission entrusted with the consideration of amendments proposed in the course of the conciliar debates), and by the Jesuit theologian Kleutgen, charged with rewriting the rejected chapters of the Constitution on the Church. In their view, the fullness of power exercised by the pope alone was the same as that exercised by all the bishops with the pope.[117] The Deputation of Faith likewise considered the infallibility attributed to the Roman pontiff to be the same as that which belongs to the pope united with all the bishops (as at an ecumenical council), not more or less.[118] (The Deputation further conceded that the position that maintained a bishop's power came from God, rather than from the pope, was not unacceptable.)[119]

In reporting on behalf of the Deputation of Faith, Bishop Zinelli noted that papal power is *ordinary*, because it comes to the pope by virtue of his office, and *immediate*, because it may be exercised without passing through an intermediary. Zinelli then brought up the question whether the pope could exercise episcopal powers in all dioceses by himself, without being obliged to use the medium of the bishop of the particular or local church. He further asked whether the pope had to ask permission from the local bishop in order to impart the sacrament of confirmation or to hear the confessions of the faithful.[120] In response, Zinelli explained that, if the pope used his ordinary and immediate jurisdiction to intervene in a diocese with no regard for the bishop, he would "not be using his power for building up but for destruction." Bishop Zinelli thus sought to assure the bishops that papal authority would uphold episcopal power, not weaken it.[121] To make that point clear, the final drafts of chapter 3, dealing with the power and nature of papal primacy, added a clarification: that the power of the pope "by no means detracts from that ordinary and immediate power of episcopal jurisdiction, by which bishops, who have succeeded to the place of the apostles by appointment of the holy Spirit, tend and govern individually the particular flocks which have been assigned to them." Instead, episcopal power "is asserted, supported and defended by the supreme and universal pastor."[122] Arguably, a more adequate resolution eluded the council because of its focus on the themes of jurisdiction and government *from above*, and not on the Church as a community of disciples. There were only brief allusions to the power of orders, and to the administration of sacraments and preaching as duties of a bishop who feeds his flock.[123]

Bismarck, the Chancellor of Prussia, precipitated a further clarification of the council's position when, in a ploy to weaken the German Church, he issued his circular letter of 1874 claiming that Vatican I's teaching on papal primacy established a totalitarianism that diminished or eliminated the role of bishops and also threatened the State. The German bishops issued a collective rebuttal in early 1875, declaring that Vatican I had not substituted papal jurisdiction (serving the unity of the universal Church) for territorial episcopal power and responsibility. Their response noted that "the pope is the Roman bishop, not the bishop of any other city or diocese; he is not the bishop of Cologne or Bratislava, etc."[124] Pius IX personally approved the German bishops' declaration in his Apostolic Letter, *Mirabilis illa constantia*, dated March 4, 1875 (DH 3117).

In defining the role of the papacy, Vatican I focused on the universal Church considered from above, and not on the local or "particular" churches. Although the term had appeared in the third and penultimate draft,[125] the final promulgated text made no reference to "particular churches"; it instead referred to bishops "as pastors assigned flocks." Within an ecclesiological paradigm emphasizing authority and jurisdiction, the particular church was understood, not as a Eucharistic community, but as a unit of spiritual administration determined by the flock and territory assigned to the jurisdiction of a bishop. Nonetheless, to reiterate, it is clear that the council did not propose to diminish the importance of particular churches or of bishops. Neither did some of the staunchest defenders of the papacy.

An article by Matteo Liberatore in *Civiltà Cattolica*, the publication of the Italian Jesuits that consistently championed papal authority, interpreted Vatican I's affirmation of all the prerogatives of the See of Peter to be reparation for the subversive negation of papal authority since the Council of Basel.[126] In another article, however, Liberatore pointed out that the definition of papal infallibility would not be a "definition through the Pope alone, but rather through the Council." He noted that it was false to claim "that the entire testimony of the Council boils down to the testimony of the Pope." Thus, "it is really not the Pope that bears witness to himself, but the Church with the Pope; it is the undoubtedly infallible Council which declares [that] the bearer of infallibility is the Pope with the Episcopate as well as the Pope alone." Remarkably, Liberatore, who was also an editor of *Civiltà Cattolica*, supported the idea of episcopal collegiality: "For the authority and infallibility of the Council is not simply the papal, but rather the conciliar, and rests on that universal authority which Christ bestowed first on the head for himself and then on the College of apostles in union with him, and thus also to the episcopate in catholic unity."[127] Since two other members of the editorial board, Secondo Franco and Francesco Berardinelli, also favored that position, perhaps under the influence of Giovan Vicenzo Bolgeni (1733–1811), Hermann Josef Sieben has concluded that it was the official position of *Civiltà Cattolica*, a journal famous for its militant papalism.[128]

The Conditions of Papal Infallibility

It should likewise be noted that Vatican I did not proclaim an unlimited papal infallibility subject to no conditions. The council's intention was clarified in the debates about the terms "absolute," "personal," and "separate." In the discussions, some bishops expressed concern lest the description of papal infallibility as "absolute" be taken to mean "without any condition." Others, reacting to the Gallican position that the consent of the bishops or the Church was necessary for a papal teaching to be infallible, were opposed to setting any conditions. But even they eventually acknowledged that certain conditions had to be fulfilled for a papal teaching to be considered "*ex cathedra*."[129] Speaking for the commission charged with revising the conciliar document, Bishop Gasser noted that the question before the commission was in what sense papal infallibility might be absolute. He answered, "in no sense." Insisting that absolute infallibility belongs to God alone, Gasser went on to explain that the infallibility of the Roman pontiff stands within certain limits and conditions. It must always be exercised in a public relation to the universal Church and is limited in regard to its subject, object, and act. To be infallible, the pope has to speak "as universal teacher and supreme judge, sitting in the Chair of Peter, that is to say, at the center." He has to be dealing with "questions of faith and morals" and he has to intend to "define something that all the faithful have to accept or reject."[130] In making an ex cathedra pronouncement, the pope *has to indicate* that he is acting not as a private teacher, or bishop of a diocese or province, but as pastor and teacher of all Christians, defining a matter to be held by the universal Church.[131] It was presupposed that the pope was under a moral obligation to exercise due diligence in preparing for an infallible teaching, but such diligence was never made a condition. Neither was consultation of all the bishops a condition for the exercise of papal infallibility. It was presumed that the pope would inform himself in regard to the tradition. That the pope might choose to consult the bishops or even call a council was not excluded.[132]

Gasser further clarified that, although papal infallibility is "distinct" from that "enjoyed by the entire teaching church joined with its head," the pope is not separated from the Church but is infallible only in union with it, a critical clarification.[133] In other words, the pope is endowed with the gift of personal infallibility not as a private person or teacher but only as a public person, exercising his charge of supreme *magisterium* as head of the church in relation to the universal church.[134] The pope enjoys the divine assistance on account of which he cannot err "only when exercising his function of supreme judge in controversies of faith and of teacher of the universal Church," and is "infallible only when by his solemn judgment he defines matters of faith and morals for the universal Church." In other words, the pope is infallible only when, in "representing the universal Church, he judges and defines what must be believed or rejected by all."[135] According to this understanding, officially presented on behalf of the Deputation of Faith, prior to the final vote of the bishops, Vatican I should be understood as intending to declare that the pope is infallible only in his *ex cathedra* or extraordinary *magisterium*, and not in his ordinary teaching.[136] The stated goal for such infallibility is "the conservation of truth in the Church."[137]

The record likewise indicates that Vatican I did not intend to declare that the pope could be infallible about *any* issue confronted by the Church, but only about revealed truths or those closely related to revelation. Bishop Gasser spelled out that the object of infallibility extended to truths that constitute "the deposit of faith" and also to truths not revealed but "requisite for maintaining the integrity of the deposit of revelation." He went on to clarify that it is not a dogma "of divine and catholic faith" but rather "theologically certain" that the pope is infallible about matters that were not revealed, but necessary for defending and explaining the faith.[138] This qualification is reflected in a change in the final draft of the canon defining papal infallibility; the final draft dropped an earlier reference exacting the assent of faith *(de fide tenendum)*, and simply said that what the pope teaches must be held *(tenendam)* by the universal Church.[139] One must also keep in mind that, although what is "defined" is "irreformable," the possibility of further clarification or the perfectibility of what was defined is not excluded.[140]

There has been some debate about the remote origins of the concept of papal infallibility. Thomas Aquinas had recognized the pope's authority to determine matters of faith with finality and to publish a revised edition of the creed,[141] but he never made any reference to infallibility. Brian Tierney has traced the idea to Peter Olivi, a Spiritual Franciscan and teacher of theology, who in 1280 published the *Question* "Whether the Roman pontiff is to be obeyed by all Catholics as an unerring standard *[tamquam regule inerrabili]* in faith and morals."[142] Olivi argued that "it is impossible for God to give to any one the full authority to decide about doubts concerning the faith and divine law with this condition, that He would permit him to err." That is, God would not oblige Catholics to obey the Roman pontiff "in faith and morals" and then permit the pontiff to err in faith.[143] While allowing for the possibility of personal error in a teaching involving the private opinions of a pope, Olivi excluded the possibility of magisterial error regarding the public teaching of a pope for the entire

Church. Olivi made a further distinction, however, between a pope "only in name and appearance" and a "true" pope who maintained the decrees of his predecessor. It was the true pope who could not err.[144]

It is worth remarking that the motive for Olivi's position was to guard against future popes revoking Pope Nicholas III's approval of Franciscan poverty and renunciation of property in his Bull, *Exiit*, of 1279. Yet the very situation that Olivi had sought to prevent actually occurred in 1323 when Pope John XXII reversed Nicholas III's decision and declared the position that Christ and the apostles did not own anything to be heretical. Maintaining that the issue of Franciscan poverty was a matter of canonical discipline open to change by the pope as sovereign, and not a biblical precept or article of faith or morals,[145] John XXII also went on to condemn the teaching of the anonymous Franciscan author of the Sachsenhausen appeal of 1324, which argued that the position of Nicholas III could not be reversed because "what the Roman pontiffs have once defined in faith and morals through the key [Matt 16:18] of knowledge is immutable....[It] cannot be called into doubt by any successor....[It] is true for all eternity and unchangeable by anyone."[146] Franciscan dissidents, such as William of Ockham, would continue defending such a stance about the immutability of papal teaching.

Francis Sullivan believes that Guido Terreni, a Carmelite become bishop, more directly anticipated Vatican I's teaching on papal infallibility.[147] As a counselor for John XXII, he had also served as one of the judges who condemned the position of Olivi. In a *Question* published around 1330, Terreni proposed that the pope cannot err in definitively *(sentencialiter)* determining matters of faith for the universal Church. He admitted that the pope can err as a single person; "nevertheless the Holy Spirit does not permit him to define anything contrary to the faith of the church for the sake of the community of the faithful and the universal church, for whose faith the Lord prayed [Luke 22:32]."[148] In the ensuing centuries, scholars such as Robert Bellarmine and

Francisco Suarez would consider papal infallibility to be a doctrine that was nearly a matter of faith.[149]

During the eighteenth century, theologians referred to an active infallibility of the teaching Church and a passive infallibility of the believing Church. Chapter 9 of the preparatory schema on the Church, rejected by the bishops at the beginning of Vatican I, had dealt with the infallibility of the Church. Unfortunately, since the council was curtailed due to the outbreak of the Franco-Prussian war, the bishops never returned to that issue, and so the relationship between papal infallibility and the infallibility of the Church was left undeveloped in conciliar debates. However, the Deputation of Faith did emphasize that, although the exercise of papal infallibility could be termed a separate or distinct privilege by which the successor of Peter maintains the unity of the church, that privilege does not involve any separation of the pope from bishops, or independence from the faith of the Church.[150] Speaking for the Deputation, Bishops d'Avanzo and Gasser both stressed that the infallibility of the Roman pontiff as head teaching the universal Church and the infallibility of the universal Church united with the head are one and the same.[151] Bishop d'Avanzo also noted that "the *magisterium* of the bishops implicitly remains in the *magisterium* of the pope to whom they adhere, and the *magisterium* of the bishops adhering to the pope contains the *magisterium* of the pontiff."[152]

The council's perspectives are well summarized in Sullivan's statement of Catholic belief regarding the dogma of papal infallibility. Acknowledging the importance of the indefectibility of the faith of the Church, and noting that definitive judgments on matters of faith are "normally the fruit of the deliberation of the whole episcopate with the pope," Sullivan explains that

> the "petrine ministry" on behalf of the faith and communion of the whole People of God includes the function, when circumstances warrant it, of pronouncing definitive judgments on matters of faith, which are equally as binding as the decisions of ecumenical councils....[T]he Church's charism of

> infallibility is present in a special way in the Roman pontiff when he makes a definitive statement about the faith. This is a kind of abiding assistance, which comes into play in a particular way to guarantee that the pope will not oblige the faithful to give their assent of faith to a teaching that is alien to the Gospel.[153]

In the wake of Vatican I, there would be an expanding emphasis on papal or Roman authority. The growing centralization of ecclesial authority in Rome was not, however, simply the result of Vatican I's definitions about the papacy. Rather, it may be attributed to a whole complex of developments such as the spread of a Roman approach to devotion, discipline, and theology throughout the Catholic Church, and a rapid improvement in travel and communications that enabled Roman authorities to exert a more immediate and, therefore, greater control over particular churches, and increased the number of pilgrims coming to Rome and the number of seminarians and priests attending Rome's colleges. In this context, "Roman authorities increasingly controlled or amended the decisions of provincial councils and encouraged the practice of consulting the Roman congregations on questions of worship, discipline or theology."[154] In addition, during the nearly thirty-two years of his papacy, Pius IX was able to replace almost all the bishops of the Church, usually with men devoted to him and the Holy See. He also revived the practice of *ad limina* visits to Rome, wherein bishops personally reported to the pope. "Few [bishops]," a scholar of the period notes, "ever complained if their decisions were overruled and some even took the initiative in submitting them for approval to the Pope."[155]

In a similar manner, some theologians exhibited a tendency toward extending the scope of papal infallibility to include the ordinary teaching of the popes (for example, in encyclicals) and not just extraordinary teaching.[156] (Others argued that such an expansion was not justified by Vatican I.)[157] The canonist Franciscus Wernz went so far as to describe the Roman pontiff as the individual to whom the whole world had been given as a diocese. While granting that the office of bishops in general is a divine institution, Wernz maintained that the office of an individual bishop placed over a particular diocese is a mere human institution subject to innovation or suppression by the pope.[158] In revising Wernz's work after the promulgation of the Code of Canon Law in 1917, Peter Vidal said that territorial divisions exist in the Church for the "convenient government" of the faithful who, besides the supreme pastor, ought to have other *immediate* pastors to rule them. He and most other canonists in the decades before Vatican II did not view particular churches (or dioceses) as communities of the faithful, but rather as practical units of spiritual jurisdiction and temporal administration. In that perspective, particular churches simply provided a convenient way of ruling the universal Church. Canonists generally stressed the jurisdictional power of a bishop, or his power to rule, which (in the then-prevalent opinion) was thought to come from the pope. There was little or no emphasis on the link between the power of orders and service to a community of believers. Unity was something achieved through law (and authoritatively imposed by one who governed), rather than through the celebration of the Eucharist. In regard to the positions of Wernz and Vidal, one might recall a remark by John Henry Newman: "The Catholic Church has its constitution and its theological laws in spite of the excesses of individuals."[159]

Openness to "A Desire of New Things"—*Rerum Novarum*

During the second to the fifth centuries, the key words applied to Church were "service" (*diakonia* or *ministerium*) and "communion" (*koinōnia*). The term "Church" denoted a participatory community of all the baptized. In that frame of reference, Cyprian, as bishop of Carthage, claimed that he made no major decisions without consulting his elders and deacons, or without the approval of his people (*Epistles* 14.4, 34.4, and 38:1; cf. 32). The entire community likewise participated in the election of a new bishop, who then exercised episcopal authority in a dialogue with the entire community. The "vicar of Peter" in Rome functioned within a "communion of bishops," for which his Church and his "persona" served as a center of unity. During the Middle Ages, the structural elements found in the Church of the second to the fifth centuries were preserved, but rearranged (as the studies of Copernicus and Galileo later rearranged the earth and the sun): pope, bishops, and baptized were placed into new relationships, organized vertically from above to below. Among the factors contributing to the shift were the monarchical worldview of that era and the emerging papal claim, articulated amid the struggle over lay investiture, that priesthood or *sacerdotium* was the source, not only of spiritual power over the Church, but of the temporal rule or *regnum* exercised by emperors and kings. As a result of the debate about who wielded ultimate authority over "Christian society" or Christendom, the new "shared model" or "paradigm" of Church was focused on a "mystique of authority." As Congar has noted, the new key words were "power, jurisdiction, rule, and Vicar of Christ."[160] In the period after the Council of Trent, even the term "Church" began to be equated with its leaders. Again to cite Congar, the key words became "the Hierarchy" and "the *Magisterium*." The very meaning of the terms "laity" and "apostolic" would be transformed by the way both were subordinated to the power and authority of "the Hierarchy."

Although foreshadowed by certain earlier developments, the paradigm or "shared model" that positioned the pope at the top of a pyramid of authority and jurisdiction, for ruling and teaching, had begun to take shape after 600. As we have seen, it was constructed not through some sudden burst of insight, but gradually, as certain Western ecclesial practices (including law, theory, and application) became more and more prevalent. Particular, time-conditioned traditions thus solidified into a new coherent "paradigm," whose presuppositions then became the "standard" or "normal" position.[161] Avery Dulles has described the net result in terms of a "military analogy of the Church": "It is almost a platitude to assert that the

Catholic Church from the Middle Ages until Vatican II was pyramidal in structure. Truth and holiness were conceived as emanating from the pope as commander-in-chief at the top, and the bishops were depicted as subordinate officers carrying out the orders of the pope."[162] The observation made by Cardinal Newman—"[W]ere the Pope as indistinct a power as he was in the first centuries, and the bishops as practically independent, the Church would still be the Church"—raises the question whether the developments of the second millennium are *absolutely* essential to the Church.[163]

Vatican I was convened by a pope beleaguered by the spirit of sweeping revolutionary challenges; its conciliar positions were undoubtedly conditioned by that historical context. Yet, in the wake of the council there would be hints of change or a new mood in the air. In 1864, Pius IX's encyclical *Quanta cura* and its appendix, *Syllabus of the Principal Errors of Our Time*, had censured "modern errors" and thus appeared to be predominantly restrictive. By contrast, the encyclicals of Pius IX's successor, Pope Leo XIII, provided a more positive teaching about the relations of church and state, and about the freedom of citizens.[164] Leo also revived the image of the Church as the Mystical Body of Christ of which the Spirit is the soul.[165]

Pope Gregory XVI's condemnation of liberalism in 1832 had responded to the reactionary wishes of the majority of the ruling classes; Leo XIII's encyclical letter *Rerum novarum*, issued in 1891, responded to the needs of workers in the newly industrialized society. Acknowledging that a thirst for innovation, "a desire of *new things [rerum novarum]*," was sweeping through the world, Leo's encyclical marked a move beyond the ancient regime that had simply presumed that power was wielded by an upper class. The encyclical recognized that ordinary workers had rights and could organize themselves into associations to protect their rights in the face of those with power and wealth. The ability to claim such rights would be strengthened by the emergence of compulsory, public elementary education and the subsequent spread of literacy during the nineteenth century.

The idea that the Church itself should respond to "the signs of the times" would be put forth by Pope John XXIII, soon after his election as Bishop of Rome in 1958. Besides advancing the discussion about the role of bishops in the Church, the Second Vatican Council, which he convened, would also give rise to a new set of expectations and understandings about the role of baptized persons in the Church. "A desire of new things" would emerge within the Church itself, among ordinary people who rediscovered that the Church is a "we" or a community of disciples, and not just a "they" or a hierarchy. Another paradigm shift would begin. The relationship among various roles within the Church would again begin to be rethought.

6
Vatican II: Toward "A New Order Of Things," 1900–

In deciding to convene the Second Vatican Council, Pope John XXIII opened the community called Church to the risk of living with hope. "Risk" is the appropriate term since this council would revisit many seeming certainties and put the Church on a new and sometimes unsettling path. Yet it is also appropriate to speak of hope. For the council would call the Church to change—without fear of the "uncontrollable" dimensions of the future, and in trust and confidence. In convening the council, John manifested both a profound historical consciousness of the Church's living tradition and an openness to contemporary experience, evidenced by his repeated calls for "*aggiornamento*," or updating and renewal of the Church. In his speech opening the council on October 11, 1962, at the end of his fourth year as bishop of Rome, Pope John chided "prophets of gloom" who "say that our era, in comparison with past eras, is getting worse and behave as though they had learned nothing from history, which is nonetheless the teacher of life."[1] By contrast, he envisioned Divine Providence "leading us to a new order of things," as Abram had been led from his country to a new land (Gen 12:1). For John, the future mattered; it was the context in which God offered new possibilities. This openness to the future must be kept in mind in the sometimes revisionist discussions about whether Pope John really envisioned where Vatican II would take the church. He may have been somewhat surprised, but it seems that he would not have been surprised to be surprised.

For he embraced precisely this risk while trusting in the Providence of God.

John XXIII signaled his openness to the arrival of a "new order" by symbolic gestures. On October 4, 1962, one week before the opening of Vatican II, he made a pilgrimage to the Marian shrine at Loreto, near Ancona in the Marches Province, and to Assisi in Umbria. The choice of Loreto and the mode of transportation there were both significant. The last pope to visit Loreto had been Pius IX, who arrived there in May of 1857 "as head of the Papal States" in a horse-drawn carriage. Pius IX was also the last pope to journey by railroad, but his official train, still on display at the Museum of Rome in the Braschi Palace, was never able to travel on the tracks from Bologna to Ancona. Pius, as head of state, had ordered and paid for the construction of this rail line, but, before it was completed in 1861, the armies of the Italian Reunification Movement, or *Risorgimento*, seized that territory from the troops defending the Papal States. After the papacy's complete loss of temporal power over the Papal States, marked by the invasion of Rome on September 20, 1870, no subsequent pope traveled on a train while in office. By journeying through the Marches and Umbria on Italian National Railways, "as the bishop of Rome," without any nostalgia for the Papal States, John XXIII proclaimed the Church's new freedom from the burdens of the past.

On May 11, 1963, about five months after the first session of Vatican II, and less than a month before his death, John XXIII also paid an official visit to the President of Italy in the Quirinale Palace and gave his blessing from the balcony over the main entrance. No pope had set foot in the Quirinale since Pius IX fled that residence to make himself a "prisoner of the Vatican," when the armies of the *Risorgimento* occupied Rome in 1870. This occupation took place only two months after the abrupt dissolution of Vatican I, which had just defined papal primacy in terms of full and supreme jurisdiction. Giancarlo Zizola has rightly observed that John's line of conduct was more ecclesiological than political. In recognizing Italy's freedom to be Italy, as expressed in his "A

Wider Tiber" speech of April 11, 1961, Pope John gave the Church the freedom to be truly universal.[2] By a deliberate move toward "noninvolvement" in the politics of Italy, he freed the papacy and the Church of Rome for the kind of multicultural universality espoused by Vatican II.[3]

The popes who succeeded John XXIII continued his initiatives in the way that they confronted elements from the papacy of the past. Pope Paul VI sold the papal tiara given him for his coronation and donated the money to the poor. Pope John Paul I, who led the Church for only a month, did away with his coronation. He was inaugurated simply by being invested with the pallium, and then presided at a Eucharist celebrated in the piazza before St. Peter's Basilica. Pope John Paul II has symbolized the papacy's universal ministry by flying to visit Churches around the world. Such developments were consistent with Pope John's call for *aggiornamento* and "for reading the signs of the times."

One other anecdote deserves mention by way of introduction. In the month before his death, as he formally accepted the Balzan Peace Prize, standing in the papal throne room decorated with frescoes depicting a Church of power, with sword-wielding popes on horseback and kings kneeling before the papal throne, John recalled the day that workers came to the Vatican during the pontificate of Leo XIII, after his encyclical *Rerum novarum* (Of new things) appeared in 1891. These men, John remarked, "were no longer just the representatives of temporal power, they were the sons of the people who had found their road back to the Vatican"—a pregnant phrase.[4] In calling for "updating" and for "reading the signs of the times," John sensed that the social patterns that had emerged during the nineteenth century, particularly the notion that ordinary workers could claim their rights by challenging the powerful, were not without impact on the Church. The development of universal public education during the past one hundred years, to choose just one change among many, would require a rethinking of the earlier system in which the masses, who had once been illiterate serfs or peasants, were simply expected to do what they were told by nobles or by clerics. Many more "new things" were on the horizon for the Church.

The purpose of this chapter is to summarize the reforms instituted by the council. As the time of Vatican II becomes more and more distant from the Church of today, it is important that we again read the conciliar documents. There is a need to be clear about what they did and did not say, and to realize what agendas were left unfinished and what questions were unanswered or not even asked.

Vatican II and *Aggiornamento*: Updating by Creative Retrieval

Charged with the task of *aggiornamento* or updating, the Second Vatican Council, over the course of four years, came to some crucial decisions about what we as Catholics should not forget and about what we might leave behind us. The council did not introduce something completely new, particularly in its liturgical reforms and its theology of Church, but rather it retrieved perspectives and practices prevalent in the earliest centuries, adapting these perspectives and practices to the present, sometimes juxtaposing them with the developments of more recent centuries.

Avery Dulles has listed ten basic principles unquestionably endorsed by Vatican II, which he believes have to be accepted in order to accept the results of that council.[5] Three principles—religious freedom, ecumenism, and dialogue with other religions—clearly represent new horizons (although Francis of Assisi had personally initiated a dialogue with Muslims, thereby suggesting an alternative to the Crusades). Two principles—*aggiornamento* and the reformability of the Church—might be seen as recapturing the early Church's readiness to adapt to new situations and cultures. The remaining five principles—renewed attention to the Word of God, collegiality, the active role of the laity, regional and local variety, and the social mission of the Church, with its emphasis on solidarity with the poor and powerless rather than with the powerful—retrieve dimensions that were more prominent before 600, when the Church, as a communion of Churches proclaiming the gospel, had itself suffered persecution by the Roman imperial establishment. Especially before 380, when Theodosius made Christianity the official religion of the empire, church leaders focused more on nurturing unity than on claiming power. As has already been discussed, bishops were chosen by and, on important issues, also advised by the baptized who formed the local communities called churches. Although all bishops together shared responsibility for the universal Church, one particular Church, Rome, and its bishop were recognized as having a primacy of special service for preserving the unity of all the Churches in the universal communion.

Back to the Future: Church as Worshiping Community

Beginning with the Constitution on the Liturgy *(Sacrosanctum Concilium)*, Vatican II sought to retrieve the early centuries' vision of Church as a particular or local community gathered for the Eucharist presided at by a bishop. Section 2 of the constitution emphasizes that "it is through the liturgy, especially, that the faithful are enabled to express in their lives and manifest to others the mystery of Christ and the real nature of the true Church."[6] That statement drew opposition from a minority group of bishops clinging to the ecclesiology of the eighteenth and nineteenth centuries, which primarily identified the essence of the Church with its juridical organization as a "perfect society."[7] Section 2 further declares that the liturgy "builds" those within the Church into the Lord's temple, a dwelling for the Spirit, and empowers the faithful to proclaim Christ. To those outside the assembly, the liturgy is said to reveal the Church as a sign raised above the nations, under which the scattered sons and daughters of God are being gathered into one.

Section 7 of the constitution speaks of the ongoing, manifold presence of Christ within the Church: in those who minister, in the Eucharist, in all the sacraments, in the proclamation of the scriptures, and wherever two or three are gathered together in his name (Matt 18:20). Section 10 describes the liturgy as the summit toward which the activity of the Church is directed and at the same time as the fount empowering the Church. Citing Cyprian of Carthage, section 26 observes that "liturgical services are not private functions, but are celebrations of the Church, which is 'the sacrament of unity,' namely, 'the holy people united and arranged under their bishops.'" Liturgical services therefore pertain to, manifest, and have effects upon the whole Body of the Church. Referring to the Epistles of Ignatius of Antioch, section 41 emphasizes that "the principal manifestation of the Church consists in the full active participation of all God's holy people in the same liturgical celebrations, especially in the same Eucharist, in one prayer, at one altar, at which the bishop presides, surrounded by his college of priests and by his ministers." Section 42 declares that communal liturgical celebrations in parishes, "under a pastor who takes the place of the bishop, are the most important, for in some way they represent the visible Church constituted throughout the world." The Constitution on the Liturgy thus initiated Vatican II's retrieval of the concept of the particular or local Church, which understands that the universal Church is actualized in and through the community of a particular locale, most especially when it assembles in prayer, thanking God for sharing and transforming our humanity in Jesus and for sending the Spirit into our midst. That foundational role of the Eucharist would be reiterated throughout the Constitution on the Church, particularly in sections 3, 7, 10, 11, and 26.

In the postconciliar implementation of liturgical "renewal," altars again became tables at which the ordained presider faced the assembly, and the rail that had separated the people from the sanctuary was removed. During a Sunday celebration of the Eucharist at the main altar of a church, there was to be no other celebration at a side altar, since this practice would divide the oneness of the assembly or church. It bears reiterating that such changes were not something "new" but a creative retrieval of the eucharistic experience of the assemblies of the earliest centuries.

Yet, while retrieving the earlier paradigm of Church as a community of disciples actualized at a eucharistic assembly, the Constitution on the Liturgy likewise held onto the paradigm of a hierarchical Church. The subtitle preceding section 26 refers to "Norms Drawn from the Hierarchic and Communal Nature of the Liturgy." Section 26 declares that liturgical services "touch individual members of the Church in different ways, depending on their orders, their role in the liturgical services, and their actual participation in them." This is an early indication of Vatican II's approach to reform: the conciliar documents often put communal perspectives retrieved from the first millennium alongside hierarchical perspectives from the second millennium.

The Birth Pains of Vatican II's Theology of Church

Vatican II's ecclesiological perspectives were specifically developed in its Constitution on the Church, *Lumen gentium* (or Light of all peoples), whose genesis has a complex history. During the two years before the council, a subcommittee of the Commission on the Doctrine of Faith and Morals composed a preliminary draft. Presented to the bishops gathering for Vatican II, the first eight chapters of that initial document treated these topics:

1. The nature of the Church militant
2. The members of the Church and its necessity for salvation
3. The episcopate as the highest grade of sacramental orders
4. Residential bishops
5. The states of evangelical perfection

6. The laity
7. The teaching office of the Church
8. Authority and obedience in the Church[8]

During Vatican II's first session in 1962, many bishops expressed their dissatisfaction with the preparatory draft's content and with the order of its material. They particularly criticized its shortcomings in regard to biblical and patristic sources and its tendencies toward "triumphalism" and "clericalism." Faulting the preliminary document's excessive emphasis on Church as society and institution, juridically conceived, a number of bishops called for a new perspective, more precisely the retrieval of the most ancient and original emphasis on the Church as community, animated and united by love, and not simply by laws.[9]

A revised draft was presented to the bishops at Vatican II's second session in 1963. It now treated these four topics:

1. The mystery of the Church
2. The hierarchical constitution of the Church and the episcopate in particular
3. The people of God and the laity in particular
4. The call to holiness in the Church

Following a suggestion made by Cardinal Suenens of Belgium, all the material dealing with "the people of God in general" was subsequently removed from chapters 1 and 3 in order to be combined into a separate, new chapter.[10]

Thus, by comparison with the first draft discussed in 1962, the content, order, and spirit of the final constitution, *Lumen gentium*, promulgated in 1964, were significantly different. It now had eight chapters:

1. The Mystery of the Church
2. The People of God
3. The Hierarchical Structure of the Church, with Special Reference to the Episcopate
4. The Laity

5. The Call of the Whole Church to Holiness
6. Religious
7. The Eschatological Nature of the Pilgrim Church and Her Union with the Heavenly Church
8. The Role of the Blessed Virgin Mary, Mother of God, in the Mystery of Christ and the Church

The order of the first three chapters clearly indicates that Vatican II intentionally shifted the starting point for a discussion of Church away from the hierarchy to a treatment of the Church as "mystery."

Church as Sacrament of Unity

In presenting the Church as Mystery, chapter 1 of *Lumen gentium* describes the Church "as a kind of sacrament, or sign and instrument of intimate union with God and of unity among all humans" (section 1).[11] The theological developments that preceded the council's conception of the Church as "a kind of sacrament" have been discussed in chapter 1 of the present work. We should recall here that the Pauline Epistle to the Ephesians 1:3–9 used the Greek term *mysterion* (translated as *sacramentum* in Jerome's Latin Vulgate edition) in reference to God's plan, existing before creation, to unite all humans in and through Jesus the Christ. The First Epistle to Timothy 3:16 spoke of the great mystery (or sacrament) "revealed in flesh, vindicated in spirit." Likewise in *Lumen gentium*, it is Christ who is the "Light" of all peoples; the Church is sign and instrument of that Light.

Lumen gentium relates the origins of the Church to the trinitarian activities of creation, incarnation, and sanctification. Sections 2 through 4 speak of the Church as prefigured in God's decisions to create humans, to offer them a share in the divine life, and to call Israel to be God's people. Before creation, the Father is said to have already decided to call humans into unity as adopted daughters and sons (Eph 1:4–5). Then, through the incarnation, all humans are called into unity with Jesus who in his life, death, and resurrection is "the image of the invisible God, the firstborn of all creation" (Col 1:15; RSV). The sanctifying Spirit, sent to dwell in the Church and in the hearts of the faithful, is said to be guiding the Church toward truth and unifying the communion and ministry of the Church by various hierarchical and charismatic gifts. By virtue of the good news of the gospel, that indwelling Spirit makes the Church "ever youthful." Section 4 thus concludes that the Church is "a people brought into unity [*adunata:* made one] from the unity of the Father, Son, and Holy Spirit." Section 5 emphasizes that the Church continues the mission of Jesus who proclaimed the kingdom or reign of God by his deeds and words. United with the crucified but risen Christ, its members are constituted into the Body of Christ through the sacraments, particularly by baptism and the Eucharist—which effects our communion with him and with one another (section 7).

In treating the Church as a "visible structure," *Lumen gentium* deliberately moves beyond the perspectives of Robert Bellarmine, who, as noted above, compared the visibility of the Church to the unity of the kingdom of France or the Republic of Venice.[12] Unlike Pope Pius XII's encyclicals *Mystici Corporis* and *Humani Generis*, issued in 1943 and 1950 respectively, the constitution does not simply identify "the society structured with hierarchical organs" with "the mystical body of Christ," or "the visible society" with "the spiritual community," or "the earthly Church" with "the Church endowed with heavenly riches." While emphasizing that the elements of each pair do not represent "two realities," section 8 describes them as "one complex reality which comes together from a human and a divine element," analogously invoking the incarnation uniting the human and divine. Section 8 likewise reflects the bishops' explicit decision not to say that the Church of Christ is the Catholic Church. It instead declares that the Church of Christ "constituted and organized as a society in the present world subsists in the Catholic Church, which is governed by the successor of Peter and by the bishops in communion with him." Further, section 8 affirms that "many elements of sanctification and of truth" are found outside the visible confines of the Catholic Church.

Theologians will undoubtedly continue to interpret the surplus of meaning, to put it positively, in the council's choice of the wording "subsists in." A narrow interpretation put forth by the Congregation for the Faith in 1985 has led to an examination of the conciliar records in order to make clear the actual intent of the council. (According to the Congregation, "the council had chosen the word *subsistit*—'subsists'—exactly in order to make clear that one sole 'subsistence' of the true church exists, whereas outside her visible structure only *elementa ecclesiae*—elements of church—exist.")[13] From his analysis of the successive revisions of section 8 and a comparative reading of the Decree on Ecumenism, Francis Sullivan concludes that, by saying the church of Christ "subsists in" the Catholic Church, Vatican II intended to say

> that it is there alone that the Church which Christ founded continues to exist with the fullness of the means of grace which Christ gave to his church and wants it always to have. With regard to other Christian churches,...the council recognized the presence of more than just "elements of church" in them; it explicitly recognized the separated eastern churches as particular churches, and acknowledged the ecclesial character of the separated "ecclesial communities" of the west, seeing "significance and importance in the mystery of salvation," not only in the sacraments and other "elements of sanctification and truth" present in them, but in these Christian communities as such.[14]

The report of the commission charged with revising the text of section 8 explicitly stated that the "elements of sanctification and truth" found outside the Catholic Church are "ecclesial in nature."[15]

Church as the Priestly People of God

Chapter 2 of *Lumen gentium* declares that God makes humans holy and saves them not just as individuals without any mutual connection, but by making them into a people, like the Jewish people. In that regard, the Church as the people of God (1 Pet 2:9–10) is a historical community of humans living in time and place, but always simultaneously permeated by an essential universality. As "the visible sacrament of saving unity...destined to extend to all regions of the earth, [the Church as the people of God] enters into human history, though it transcends at once all times and all racial boundaries" (section 9).

Section 10 describes the people of God as a priestly people, meaning that all the baptized and the ordained together share a "common priesthood of the faithful" in which all have equal dignity. That common priesthood of all who form the Church is said to be essentially different from "the ministerial or hierarchical priesthood," although there was much discussion within the council about the ways in which the "priesthood of the faithful" and the "ministerial priesthood" are dissimilar and similar.[16] The final text describes ministerial priests as endowed with a sacred power by which they "form and rule" the priestly people, but at the same time emphasizes that the common priesthood of the faithful and the ministerial priesthood are mutually ordered to one another. Both participate, in distinctive modes, in the one priesthood of Christ. The "priestly community" of all the faithful is said to be actualized both in the celebration of the sacraments and in virtuous living. The unity of God's priestly people, deputized to worship by the baptismal character, is most aptly signified and effected by their celebration and reception of the Eucharist (section 11).

Lumen gentium recognizes that all of the people of God share in Christ's prophetic office. Section 12 affirms that, in witnessing to Christ, the body of the faithful, anointed by the Holy One (cf. 1 John 2:20), "cannot err in matters of belief." The entire people together reflect "a supernatural sense of the faith," when all baptized members of the Church, from bishops to nonordained, exhibit a universal consent on matters of faith and morals. (Section 10 of the Constitution on Revelation will later declare that "in maintaining, practicing, and professing the faith that has been handed on, there should be a remarkable harmony between the bishops and the faithful.") The council acknowledges that the Spirit may work through every member of the Church; the faithful of every rank are endowed with various charismatic gifts of the Spirit. These gifts are to be authenticated but not extinguished by those who preside in the Church. To be sure, there is a challenge here in moving from theory to practice.

Church as a Communion of Churches: A Unity in Diversity

Section 13 is connected to section 12 by a common interest in the diversity of "gifts" among the faithful. According to the text, the "one" people of God, to which all humans are called, is spread throughout the entire world, but all its faithful are in communion with one another in the Spirit, "so that the one who sits at Rome knows those in India to be his members." From that perspective, section 13 goes on to emphasize that the Church "fosters and takes to herself, in so far as they are good, the abilities, the resources and customs of various peoples." By virtue of the catholicity or universality of the Church gathered from all peoples, each part contributes its own gifts to other parts and to the whole Church. Making a passing reference to an internal diversity of rank within the Church, stemming from different duties or states of life, the text proceeds to articulate Vatican II's vision of the Church's unity as a "communion of Churches," in which "particular Churches retain their own traditions, without prejudice to the Chair of Peter." That Chair, in the Church of Rome, "presides over the whole assembly of charity, and protects legitimate differences, while at the same time taking care that these differences do not hinder unity but rather contribute to it." Writing as the council was ending, Joseph Ratzinger noted "that for the early Christians the first and predominant meaning of the word 'Church' was the local Church....The local Churches were not administrative branches of a large organization; they were the living cells, in each of which the *whole* mystery of the *one* body of the Church was present, so that each was simply called *Ecclesia*, Church."[17]

Declaring that the pilgrim Church on earth is necessary for salvation, section 14 adds that those who are aware of its necessity but do not enter or remain within it will not be able to be saved. What it means to be "aware of its necessity," to be sure, calls for further elaboration. Sections 15 and 16 proceed to recognize the Church's multifaceted relationship with all baptized Christians not united in communion with the successor of Peter, and also with those who have not yet received the gospel. With regard to the latter, section 16 specifically acknowledges God's ongoing covenant with the Jewish people, and recognizes that the plan of salvation includes those, particularly Muslims, who acknowledge the Creator. It affirms that those who do not know the gospel but seek to do God's will, as they know it, can be saved. Chapter 2 then concludes with a reaffirmation of the Church's mission to proclaim the gospel, so that all may become the people of God. In carrying out that mission of evangelization, the Church is said to preserve and perfect the good already existing in the hearts and minds, rituals and cultures, of those to whom the gospel is proclaimed. Catholicism understood in that way involves an openness to accepting truth and goodness wherever they are found. (But how they are to be discerned is surely not always so simple.) Concluding the council's treatment of the Church as the people of God, section 17 declares that every disciple of Christ has the obligation of spreading the faith.

Toward Retrieving a Collegial Leadership of Pope and Bishops

Chapter 3 of *Lumen gentium* turns to the hierarchical structure of the Church, beginning with the declaration that Christ "instituted various ministries in his Church, which strive for the good of the whole Body."[18] Strengthened by a sacred power, ministers serve their brethren, so that the entire people of God might achieve salvation, "freely and orderly working together toward the same end." Having characterized hierarchy as a power to serve, the rest of the chapter concentrates on the role of bishops within the Church, described as a "hierarchically structured society" (section 19). The continuing strength of the hierarchical paradigm is apparent.

Section 18 declares that Jesus, having entrusted his mission to the apostles, "willed that their successors, namely the bishops, should be the shepherds in his Church until the end of the world." Section 20 simply says "that by divine institution bishops have succeeded to the place of the apostles as shepherds of the Church," without taking any position about what was traceable to the historical Jesus. The manner of the "divine institution" was left open to interpretation, which was wise given that *Lumen gentium* was promulgated before the conclusion of the debates about the Constitution on Revelation, with its distinction between the deeds and words of Jesus and postresurrection developments. As already noted, contemporary scholarship recognizes that there was a development in leadership structures—moving from the Twelve and the disciples called by Jesus, to a "pluriformity" of diverse types of leadership in the earliest postresurrection communities, to the eighties' universalizing of a collegial leadership pattern interchangeably called overseers/elders *(episkopoi/presbyteroi)* working with the group known as deacons, and finally, at the beginning of the second century, to the emergence of the *mono-episkopos* (or bishop) presiding over the elders and deacons. The letter from the Church of Rome to the Church of Corinth, written about the year 97 and later attributed to Clement, identified the collegial group of *episkopoi/presbyteroi* as successors of the apostles; the *mono-episkopos* or bishop became designated as successor to the apostles during the course of the second century.

In discussing the role of bishops within the Church, chapter 3 reflects an intense concern for specifying their relationship to the pope. The entire chapter is "full of additions designed to block at the start every attack on the primacy of the pope."[19] By way of introduction, section 18 emphasizes that Vatican II is following in the footsteps of the First Vatican Council and reiterates that earlier council's teaching regarding the institution, permanence, nature, and import of the sacred primacy of the Roman pontiff and his infallible teaching. To safeguard the unity of bishops as shepherds in the Church, this section affirms that Jesus put Peter at the head of the apostles as a perpetual, visible principle and foundation of unity of faith and communion. It declares that bishops, as successors of the apostles, direct the living house of God, together with Peter's successor who is the Vicar of Christ and the visible head of the whole Church. Gérard Philips, the coordinator of the conciliar commission charged with redrafting the constitution, has observed that an "overloading of the text" with "soothing precautions" and "reassuring clauses" about the primacy of the pope successfully lessened the misgivings of many Western bishops, but in the eyes of the Eastern Churches weakened the text in regard to the episcopacy.[20]

Sections 19 to 23 develop the theological concept of collegiality, wherein all the bishops, united with the bishop of Rome at their head, are understood as forming a corporate body or "college" succeeding to the college of apostles, namely the Twelve with Peter at their head. The crucial foundation for collegiality is the council's definitive declaration, in section 21, that the "consecration" of a new bishop is a sacramental ordination bestowing the apostolic gift of the Spirit. This statement means that bishops receive their offices (functions or duties: *munera*) of sanctifying, teaching, and governing through ordination, and not from the pope. The text adds, however, that these functions, by their very nature, are able to be exercised only in hierarchical communion with the "head" and members of the college of bishops. Reflecting the concern for specifying the bishops' relationship with the pope, section 22 makes clear that both sacramental consecration and hierarchical communion with the head and members of the college constitute one a member of the episcopal body. The college or body of bishops is said to have no authority, unless it is understood together with its head, the Roman pontiff, Peter's successor. The bishops' exercise of collegiality, in an ecumenical council or dispersed throughout the world, has to be confirmed or recognized by the pope, who is described in terms drawn from Vatican I as having "full, supreme, and universal power over the whole Church." As composed of many members, the college of bishops is said to express the variety and universality of the people of God; as gathered under one head, the college expresses the unity of God's people.

The concern for safeguarding papal primacy is particularly evident throughout the explanatory prefatory note, produced by the Doctrinal Commission and appended to the official Latin text of *Lumen gentium*. This note spells out four clarifications regarding episcopal collegiality, which especially apply to section 22 of *Lumen gentium*. First, the note insists that the term "college" is not to be understood in the juridical sense of a group of equal partners who hand over their powers to a presider. More expansively, the parallel drawn between the relationship of Peter with the rest of the Twelve and the relationship of the pope with all the other bishops, found in section 22 of *Lumen gentium*, is not to be understood as implying that the extraordinary powers of the apostles have been transmitted to their successors, or that there is an equality of head and members in the college; rather, only a proportionality or similarity is intended.

Second, the note intends to explain why one becomes a member of the college by virtue of episcopal consecration *and* hierarchical communion with the head and members of the college (*Lumen gentium* 22). Distinguishing the terms "*munera*" (functions, duties, or offices) and "*potestates*" (powers), the note maintains that episcopal consecration confers "an ontological participation" in sacred functions or duties *(munera)*. The exercise of these functions as active powers *(potestates)* requires canonical or juridical determination by hierarchical authority, for example, through the concession of a particular office or the assignment of subjects. The canonical or juridical determination makes possible the hierarchical cooperation needed among the many who exercise the functions imparted through episcopal ordination. Section 22 of *Lumen gentium* refers to the bishops' communion with the pope and one another as "a bond of unity, charity, and peace." Acknowledging that "communion" had historically shaped applications in the life of the Church before it became "codified" in Church law, the note insists that communion is not to be understood as "some sort of vague affection, but as an organic reality which requires a juridical form [or structure] and is simultaneously animated by charity."[21] This reality is termed "hierarchical communion."

Third, the note reiterates that, as "the subject of supreme and entire [full] power over the whole [universal] Church," the college of bishops cannot exist without and thus always presupposes its head. According to the note, this needs to be recognized lest the fullness of power of the Roman pontiff be jeopardized. The pope, as head of the college, fully preserves his function as Vicar of Christ and Pastor of the universal Church. Therefore, collegiality, properly understood, never distinguishes between the pope and all the bishops as a body, but only between the pope acting alone and the pope together with the bishops. As head of the college, the pope is said to have tasks or functions distinct from those of the other bishops as members. Entrusted with care for the whole flock of Christ, the pope determines the mode in which that care will be put into practice—whether in a personal or a collegial manner. Only the pope can convoke and direct the college and approve its norms of action. Thus, in organizing, fostering, and approving the exercise of collegiality, the pope can proceed according to his own discretion, always taking into account the good of the Church. Summarily stated, all official initiatives regarding the universal Church must involve the pope.

Fourth, the note emphasizes that the pope may always exercise his power, according to his own judgment, but the college is not permanently in act and can act collegially only with the pope's "consenting." The term "consenting" is said to indicate not dependence on someone external to the college, but communion; it implies the necessity of an act proper to the head of the college. In sum, the college of bishops always acts in conjunction with the pope and never independently from him. As section 22 of *Lumen gentium* stipulates, if the pope as head is not acting with them, the bishops cannot act collegially. (Some theologians have argued that actions initiated by the pope as head should likewise be understood as always presupposing and expressing his unity with all the other bishops, but this argument takes us beyond the text of the constitution. Yet it might well be asked how the metaphor of pope as head and the bishops as body finally ought to be understood.)[22]

In concluding, the note once again distinguishes a canonical-juridical aspect from the "sacramental-ontological functions" received in episcopal ordination and reiterates that the sacramental-ontological functions cannot be exercised without hierarchical communion. Whether exercise of those functions without hierarchical communion would be invalid or merely illicit was left open to theological discussion. It is difficult to shake the feeling, however, that the explanatory note's defensive emphasis on papal primacy over the universal Church was meant to offset the council's attempt to retrieve the understanding of Church as a communion of churches and the idea that the universal Church is actualized in and through local Churches.

Section 23 of *Lumen gentium* envisions both the pope and the bishops as symbols of unity within the Church conceived as a communion of churches that is both catholic, or universal, and particular. Examining various layers of collegial unity, section 23 envisions the pope, as successor of Peter, to be the visible source and foundation of the unity of all the bishops and of all the faithful. Individual bishops are the visible source and foundation of unity within their own particular Churches, which are essential to the very existence of the universal Church. The one Catholic Church is said to exist in and to be formed out of those particular Churches. Again retrieving the ancient communion model of Church, the council speaks of each bishop representing his own Church, while all the bishops together with the pope represent the whole Church in a bond of peace, love, and unity. Individual bishops preside over only their own particular Churches, each being a "portion" of the universal Church; but all the bishops, as a college succeeding the apostles, are called to have care and solicitude for the entire mystical Body, which is a "Body of Churches," and to collaborate with one another and with Peter's successor. Particular Churches are thus not parts that dissolve into the universal Church; rather, retaining their particular identities, disciplines, liturgical usages, and theological traditions, they make the universal Church present within a particular culture and local context. The catholicity or universality of the Church involves, accordingly, a unity embracing the diversities of all the particular Churches. Recalling past models of "organically united" groups of churches, such as the ancient patriarchates, the council declares episcopal conferences to be contemporary manifestations of collegial cooperation among bishops.

The Ministries of Teaching, Sanctifying, and Leading

Following section 23's discussion of the unifying roles of the pope and bishops within the Church seen as a communion of churches, section 24 turns to a specific consideration of the ministry of bishops. Section 24 speaks of bishops as entrusted with the mission of teaching all peoples and of proclaiming the gospel to every person. Terming the office of bishop a "service," in continuity with the scriptural emphasis on *diakonia* or ministry, the text goes on to declare that the canonical mission whereby bishops are assigned a particular office "can be made by legitimate customs that have not been revoked by the supreme and universal authority of the Church or acknowledged by the same authority, or directly by Peter's successor himself." In that regard, any bishop who objects to or refuses apostolic communion cannot be admitted to office.

Invoking the threefold distinction developed in the post-Reformation period, section 20 of *Lumen gentium* affirmed that bishops, assisted by presbyters and deacons, undertake a pastoral ministry to their communities as teachers of doctrine, priests of sacred worship, and ministers of government. Specific treatments of the bishops' exercise of the functions of teaching, sanctifying, and governing are presented in sections 25 to 27.

Section 25 begins by declaring that preaching the gospel is eminent among the duties of a bishop, thereby establishing it as foundational to the bishop's task of teaching. In other words, witnessing to the faith precedes claims to authoritative judgments about the content of faith. The text goes on to discuss the everyday teaching of individual bishops in communion with the pope, the noninfallible (or *non–ex cathedra*) teaching of the pope, and the kind of assent that should be given to such teachings. Next, the text considers the collective teaching of all the bishops dispersed throughout the world. In regard to this "ordinary magisterium" of the bishops, the constitution states that they can "infallibly" proclaim the doctrine of Christ under the conditions that they preserve communion among themselves and with the pope and that, "in their authoritative teaching concerning matters of faith and morals, they are in agreement that a particular teaching is to be held definitively and absolutely." The passage does not explain how such unanimity among all the bishops becomes clearly evident to the members of the Church. Declaring that the infallibility with which Christ wished to endow his Church is bounded by the deposit of revelation, the section turns to the extraordinary exercise of infallible teaching. Interrupting its analysis of episcopal teaching, the text first summarizes and thereby reaffirms Vatican I's definition of the extraordinary exercise of papal infallibility, including the assertion that such infallible definitions are irreformable of themselves and not from the consent of the

Church. It then declares that the charism of infallibility promised to the Church is likewise present in the body of bishops when that body, together with Peter's successor, exercises the supreme teaching office. It further insists that such teaching will never lack the consent of the Church. Section 25 closes with a brief discussion of the "suitable means" by which the pope or the body of bishops should proceed in preparing to define a doctrine, emphasizing that they "do not accept any new public revelation as pertaining to the divine deposit of faith."

The bishop's responsibility for sanctifying his community is treated in section 26. His fullness of Orders is said to be especially operative in the Eucharist, "which he himself offers, or ensures that it is offered." The next few sentences, inserted during the revision of the text between the second and third sessions of the council, again reflect the communion model of Church. They speak of the Church of Christ as truly present in all legitimate local congregations of faithful, which, joined to their pastors, are called Churches in the New Testament. Celebrating the mystery of the Lord's Supper, the faithful as a community around the altar symbolize that charity and "unity of the Mystical Body without which there is no salvation."[23] By receiving the flesh and blood of the Lord's Body, the entire community is united and transformed into what all its members have received. Each of these communities, no matter how small or poor, thus makes Christ present, by whose power the one, holy, catholic, and apostolic Church is gathered. As Karl Rahner has observed, "from this starting point one can come to understand the Church as a whole, because it is truly there *(vere adest)* in the local Church."[24] At the center of each particular Church, the council envisions the bishop, not acting primarily as an administrator having little contact with individual faithful, but praying and working for the people by overseeing the sacramental activity of the faith community. That ideal perspective on the office of bishop has its roots in the early centuries when episcopal communities were smaller than many contemporary parishes and bishops' duties were more pastoral than those of some modern pastors weighed down by financial management of a large complex. How the modern bishop, who carries administrative responsibility for a diocese with many parishes, and in some places even a school system, can regain a personal role in the spiritual life of individual believers requires imagination and creative initiatives—beyond issuing letters to be read at Sunday liturgies, public statements, and visits on the occasion of confirmation or the dedication of a building. Again there is a challenge in moving from theory to practice.

Section 27 speaks of bishops governing their particular Churches as vicars and legates of Christ. Besides counseling, exhorting, and giving example, they are said to exercise authority and power, but only to build up their flocks in truth and holiness. Yet a tension between two approaches is apparent in the text's descriptions of the bishop's exercise of leadership. Some sentences reflect a juridical terminology, focusing on rights, duties, legislation for subjects, authority, and the bishop's power, which is described as "proper, ordinary, and immediate." Others have a more pastoral tonality, speaking of habitual and daily care for people, service, compassion, listening, and collaborating. The text emphasizes that bishops are not to be regarded as vicars of the pope. They are said to exercise the power that they possess "in their own right," and truly to be prelates of the people they "rule." At the same time, the pope's role in relation to the bishops is once again carefully clarified. The text affirms that the authority of bishops is not impaired, but strengthened and defended by the supreme and universal power of the pope. In governing his family, a bishop should imitate Jesus who came not to be served but to serve (Mark 10:45; Matt 20:28). A bishop is to be compassionate; he should not refuse to listen to his "subjects," cherishing them as sons and daughters and urging them to cooperate or work with him. Chapter 3 ends with sections 28 and 29, which discuss the indispensable roles of priests and deacons—including a restored married permanent diaconate—carrying on a collaborative ministry with their bishop.

The Mission of the Nonordained and Nonvowed Faithful

Chapter 4 of *Lumen gentium* focuses on the role and mission of the laity, beginning with the reminder that everything previously said about the people of God applies equally to laity, religious, and clerics. (The constitution never pauses to discuss how the distinctions laity, clergy, and religious emerged.) Section 30 states that Christ never established that pastors should carry out the whole salvific mission of the Church to the world by themselves; it recognizes the need for a cooperative effort in that regard. Having loosely defined "laity" as all baptized faithful who are not ordained or vowed members of the religious state, section 31 speaks of their special vocation to seek the kingdom of God by engaging in temporal affairs and directing them according to God's will. Called by God and led by an evangelical spirit to be involved in worldly affairs, the laity can act as the leaven sanctifying the world from within. Referring to a "wonderful diversity within the Church," section 32 cites Galatians 3:28 ("There is no longer Jew or Greek,...slave or free,...male and female") to declare that there is no inequality in the Church based on race, nationality, social condition, or sex (a place where we might pause to wonder). Section 32 likewise affirms that all members of the Church are called to sanctity, although all do not follow the same path. Because they have a mutual need for one another, the laity and the ministers who teach, sanctify, and govern God's family should cooperate and collaborate. All are called to follow the example of Christ who became our brother in order to serve.

Section 33 speaks of the laity having a vocation to build up the Church and describes the "lay apostolate," commissioned by baptism and confirmation, as a participation in the saving mission of the Church. It adds that the laity can further be called to a more immediate cooperation in the apostolate of the hierarchy. In section 34, the laity are said to share in the priestly office of Christ. All their works, prayers, and apostolic initiatives, including family, married life, work, and relaxation may become spiritual sacrifices, offered in their celebration of the Eucharist, thereby consecrating the world to God. Section 35 says the laity also share in the prophetic ministry of Christ. They have been constituted as witnesses endowed with "a sense of the faith" *(sensu fidei)*. As a result, the power of the gospel can radiate through all the dimensions of their lives. In times of crisis, the laity may even assume some of the functions usually carried out by the ordained.

Section 36 treats the laity's role in advancing the "kingdom." Jesus, exalted as the Christ though his death and resurrection, is said to have desired that his kingdom be spread by the lay faithful. In a significant paragraph deserving attention, the faithful are called to recognize God's profound relationship with all of creation. Then, "by their competence in secular disciplines and by their activity, interiorly raised up [or elevated] by the grace of Christ," they are to strive to assure that the goods created by human labor, technology, and culture benefit all people and be more equitably distributed, in keeping with God's plan for creation. The laity are further urged to transform the sinful tendencies of the institutions and conditions of the world and to inculcate moral values into the culture.

Section 37 discusses the rights and duties of the laity within the Church. Beyond their right to the ministrations of their pastors, they are said to have the responsibility to offer their informed, competent opinion where needed for the good of the Church. With Christ's "obedience unto death" invoked as an example (!), lay persons are likewise urged to a "Christian" obedience toward pastors. Pastors, at the same time, are reminded to acknowledge and to promote the dignity and responsibility of the laity by using their prudent advice and assigning them duties in the service of the Church, leaving them freedom and room for acting. Pastors should encourage initiatives coming from the laity, and be open to their suggestions. Chapter 4 concludes with section 38, which declares that every layperson is to be a witness to the death and resurrection of Christ and a sign of the living God.

Christians in the world should be like the soul in the body, that is, *informing* the world. (The relation of soul to body is to be conceived as Aquinas does.) In the council's vision, the laity are no longer simply passive believers and "obeyers." Rather, they are empowered to contribute to decision making and to collaborate in the work of the Church. Unfortunately, the institutional structures that would enable a fuller implementation of that vision have not been adequately developed.

Chapter 5 of *Lumen gentium* considers the holiness to which all members of the Church—baptized, religious, and ordained—are called, in union with Christ our self-emptying, suffering savior. Chapter 6 then treats the religious state and the relation of religious to the hierarchy, particularly local bishops. The priority given to the holiness of all the members of the Church indicates a significant shift in perspective. The initial draft of the Constitution on the Church gave priority to the states of evangelical perfection.

The Eschatological Dimension of the Church

Chapter 7, entitled "The Eschatological Nature of the Pilgrim Church and Its Union with the Heavenly Church," was originally a separate document drafted in response to Pope John's proposal that Vatican II treat the veneration of saints in relationship to the Church. In the course of the conciliar discussions, it became clear that the council's teaching about the Communion of Saints appropriately belonged within the Constitution on the Church. Christians on their earthly pilgrimage come together in one Church and are united to one another in Christ, but they are likewise united with those who "sleep in the peace of Christ," which brings innumerable spiritual benefits to the earthly Church (section 49). Since the saints are members of the heavenly Church already united to Christ, the discussion of their relationship to the Church within history was situated within an exploration of the pilgrim Church's eschatological dimension. Hence the title of the chapter. Declaring the final age of the world already with us, and the renewal of the world "irrevocably under way," the chapter's eschatology has an "otherworldly" focus. Looking to the "end" of this world that is "passing" (section 48), it reflects a theology of hope for the afterlife and the heavenly Church of holiness. *Lumen gentium* thereby reminds us that the community called Church anticipates and already foreshadows the eschatological fullness of God's heavenly reign. In contrast to this "otherworldly" focus, one must turn to the Constitution on the Church in the Modern World, *Gaudium et spes,* for a complementary "this-worldly" eschatology—a theology of hope more fully focused on the future of worldly history. *Lumen gentium* concludes with chapter 8, which treats the Blessed Virgin Mary, relating her motherhood and role in salvation to the Church as "mother."

Themes Reprised in a Chorus of Documents

Some of the themes in the Constitution on the Church are reiterated and even amplified in the other documents promulgated by the council. The Decree on Eastern Catholic Churches (*Orientalium Ecclesiarum,* 1964) especially emphasizes the theology of Church as a communion of Churches retaining their diverse traditions, and it recognizes the role of the "patriarchs" and the patriarchal synods within the groups of Churches forming the structure known as patriarchates (sections 2 and 7–11). The Decree on Ecumenism (*Unitatis redintegratio,* 1964) encourages initiatives toward Christian unity and, in that regard, affirms the need for reform and renewal in the Church (section 6). It reminds Catholic theologians that, in comparing doctrines in ecumenical dialogue, they must recognize "an order or 'hierarchy' of truths, since they vary in their relation to the foundation of the Christian faith" (section 11). The decree stresses the apostolic role of bishops, with the successor of Peter at their head (section 2). It likewise highlights the essential importance of the Eucharist as a sign and cause of the unity of the Church and as a means of sharing in grace, and relates those teachings to arguments for and against intercommunion (sections 2 and 8). With regard to the celebration of the Lord's Supper by Protestant assemblies, the decree raises the issue of a lack of Orders in their ministers and calls for further dialogue on that question (section 22). Noting that the Churches of the East and the West went their own ways for many centuries, the decree says that they were nevertheless connected by a fraternal communion of faith and sacramental life. It further remarks that, when disagreements about faith or discipline arose, the Roman See acted as moderator, by common consent (section 14).

Emphasizing yet again that the episcopal function is to be exercised in communion with the Roman pontiff and subject to his authority, the Decree on the Pastoral Office of Bishops in the Church (*Christus Dominus*, 1965) analyzes the role of bishops in relation to the universal Church, in relation to their own particular churches, and with regard to their mutual cooperation for the good of many churches. In relation to the universal Church, section 5 specifically calls for the formation of a council to assist the pope, to be known as the Synod of Bishops. Composed of bishops from various parts of the world, chosen in a manner determined by the pope, it was to act in the name of the entire Catholic episcopate.[25] The synod would thus signify that all bishops in hierarchical communion share solicitude for the universal Church. Turning to the mutual cooperation of bishops, section 36 acknowledges the great benefit that regional synods and councils of bishops have historically provided the Church and calls for their renewed vigor. Then section 37 declares the more recent formation of national or regional episcopal conferences an opportune development of the Church's longstanding synodal tradition and provides some basic guidelines for their foundation and procedure.

The Decree on the Missionary Activity of the Church (*Ad gentes divinitus*, 1965) emphasizes that the assembly of the faithful within a particular Church should be rooted in the social life and adapted to the culture of the locale. The assembly should have its own indigenous priests, religious, and laity, and should develop the ministries and institutions necessary for its life (section 19). Since it is obligated to represent the universal Church as perfectly as possible, each particular Church, through the lives of its individual faithful and of the entire community, should be a sign of Christ not just to believers but also to all nonbelievers in its locale. The decree affirms that the Church is not truly established, nor fully living, nor a perfect sign of Christ among humans, unless there is a mature, active laity working with the hierarchy. Only then will the gospel impact the talents, life, and work of the people (section 21). In other words, the gospel cannot be inculturated into the lives of people by a hierarchy acting alone.

A Wider Horizon for the Church's Self-Understanding

Within the context of a pluralistic world in which the entire human community is forming ever more extensive bonds of communication, the Declaration on the Relation of the Church to Non-Christian Religions (*Nostra aetate*, 1965) has a special import. In a crucial development, this declaration recognizes that other religions genuinely mediate the restless search for the meaning of human existence and for deeper understanding of the ultimate, ineffable divine mystery (section 1). It acknowledges that there is a loving, trusting ascent toward God within Hinduism. It speaks positively of the liberation and illumination sought by Buddhists. In the words of the declaration, "The Catholic Church rejects nothing of what is true and holy in these religions" (section 2). The declaration likewise declares the Church's esteem for Muslims and many of their beliefs (section 3). With regard to the Jewish people with whom God established a covenant, the declaration affirms that "God does not take back the gifts he bestowed or the choice he made" (section 4). These declarations of Vatican II stand in contrast to the proclamation of the Council of Florence (1442) that "all those who are outside the catholic church, not only pagans but also Jews or heretics and schismatics, cannot share in eternal life and will go into the everlasting fire."[26] The Spirit has drawn the Church to acknowledge God's relationship with all humans, including those outside the Church.

The Reception of Vatican II's Theology of Church

The Spirit brings forth the unexpected. Ten years before Vatican II, few Western Catholics dreamed that there would ever be a change from Latin to the vernacular in the liturgy. The idea of once again receiving communion in the hand, or of again standing to receive, was even more remote. That women would be lectors and eucharistic ministers, or that some would raise the question of the possibility of ordaining women, was hardly conceivable.

Whether the perspectives of Vatican II have achieved full reception and implementation is an open question. The teachings of the Council of Nicaea in 325 did not have full reception until about fifty years later. Immediately after that council, a number of bishops became uneasy with its teaching that the Father and the Son, or Eternal Word, were *homoousios*, meaning that they were of the "same essence" or "one in being." Some began to fear that the term *homoousios* could be misunderstood as implying monarchian modalism, which contended that the persons of God are really only three different appearances or manifestations and that God is essentially one rather than triune. Only after decades of debate, and, as John Henry Newman has maintained, under pressure from rank-and-file believers, was what the Council of Nicaea taught fully accepted.[27] One may trust that the Spirit is likewise working in this time of ours.

In speaking of "the pope, who can be said to be the Church," Giles of Rome, a fourteenth-century curial theologian, expressed a viewpoint on Church order that "would never have crossed the mind of anybody in the tenth" century and that was still hotly contested in the fourteenth. The fact that Giles dared to use such language shows that a shift in consciousness was emerging.[28] Vatican II opened the door to another shift in consciousness by its reaffirmation of "the priesthood of all believers" and by its references to the Church as the people of God. In contrast with the decades before Vatican II, after the council, many of the nonordained would no longer think of the Church as a "they" identified with the hierarchy, but would instead understand it as a "we" intrinsically including all the baptized.

The Second Vatican Council was truly remarkable for how much it accomplished during its deliberations. As Ratzinger commented at the end of the council, "looking back objectively, we must bear in mind that it is difficult for an assembly of 2,500 men, each accustomed to having the last word, to get used to working together."[29] He noted that the participants at Vatican II not only learned to work together, but in so doing also retrieved a "horizontal Catholicity," nurturing "cross connections among those who call themselves Catholic." Such horizontal connections, which "had actually been lost in the Church's practical life," were a necessary complement "to the 'vertical' unity joining all to the center of the Church." In Ratzinger's words, the bishops at Vatican II "had taken a giant step beyond being a mere sounding board for propaganda" to become, as an "independent body of bishops," a force which the papal curia or central administrative bureaucracy had to reckon with and engage as a partner in dialogue.[30]

Given that opposition between the Roman curia and the world episcopate had marked the debates of councils since the late Middle Ages, Ratzinger commented that popes had previously considered any reform of the curia as a matter of personal competence on which a council had no right to intrude. The reason for such defensiveness was fear of conciliarism: the view that sought to put the council not merely above the curia, but also above the pope himself. This fear had loomed over the papacy since the events surrounding the Council of Constance. It is Ratzinger's argument that Vatican I's clarification of the papacy's role in the Church enabled the pope to leave behind such a defensive attitude. Thus, during the second session of Vatican II in 1963, Pope Paul VI invited the council to deal with curial reform. In Ratzinger's view, at the end of the council, "the traditional solidarity between pope and curia was now giving way to an unprecedented new solidarity between pope and Council."[31]

Discussing Vatican II's teaching about collegiality, Ratzinger argues that *Lumen gentium* contains two theologies of Church that were never completely integrated. One begins from the universal Church and the college of bishops who are said to have full and supreme power over it, always with and under the pope as head; the other begins from the particular or local church and its bishop.[32] Ratzinger claims that the key to overcoming the tension between the two starting points is the ancient concept of communion. Elsewhere, he observes that "the *one* Church comprises the plurality of Churches.... [T]he individual Church is a self-contained unity fully embodying the entire essence of the Church of God, but...it is open on all sides through the bond of communion."[33] Each local church, in communion with all the other churches, makes present the whole Church.

In some ways, *Lumen gentium* is an ambiguous text. Balancing two concerns, renewal of the Church and preservation of continuity, Vatican II employed the method of juxtaposition: "alongside a doctrine or thesis couched in preconciliar language is set a doctrine or thesis that formulates some complementary aspect."[34] That approach satisfied the council's further concern for preserving unity among the bishops, that is, for seeking a middle ground or consensus between those more committed to the past and those more open to reform. As a result, the debates about *Lumen gentium* produced a compromise document wherein differing positions or understandings were more often accommodated than made to come to terms with one another. The reintroduced paradigm of communion was presented alongside, and in tension with, the pyramidal hierarchical paradigm that had developed during the Church's second millennium. *Lumen gentium* recovered the concepts of communion and episcopal collegiality, thereby setting the office of the bishop of Rome in relationship to the college of bishops, in succession to the college of apostles with Peter at their head (sections 20–23). But it simultaneously retained and juxtaposed the perspectives and language of Vatican I, describing the bishop of Rome as having "full, supreme, and universal power over the Church" (section 22). Nonetheless, within a transitional council such as Vatican II, such juxtaposition must be counted as *progress*, "because by being complemented the older thesis is relativized as one-sided and bearings are given for further development in understanding of the faith"[35]

Vatican II's recovery of an ecclesiology of communion has been characterized as "hesitant and unsystematic,"[36] but the council's hesitancy and lack of "systematicness" are not the only reasons why its ecclesiology remains a delicate issue. In the decades after Vatican II, many of the bishops who during the time of the council had contributed to shaping the "horizontal connections," so essential for the communion of particular or local Churches within the universal Church, were replaced by bishops who had not shared the experience of Vatican II and who had other priorities. Consequently, the conciliar solidarity that had developed between pope and bishops has been practically eroded by a resurgent solidarity between pope and curia. Thus, the communion paradigm has not been put into practice. It remains primarily a theoretical model with multiple interpretations generating ongoing theological discussion. This chapter concludes with consideration of this discussion.

The Unfinished Task of Theological Synthesis

Much of Vatican II's "new vision" retrieved the spirit of the earliest centuries of the Church in an attempt to renovate an understanding of Church focused on the authority of a centralized, pyramidal hierarchy. The council could not, however, discard all the developments that had emerged during the centuries of the second millennium. Vatican II's very creation of the compromise formula "hierarchical communion," which juxtaposed a sacramental communion ecclesiology with a juristic unity ecclesiology, was not simply a tactic that made it possible for an uneasy minority of bishops to vote for *Lumen gentium.* Rather, as Walter Kasper has insisted, that formula also recognizes that "the Catholic principle about living tradition makes it impossible simply to eliminate the tradition of the second millennium. The continuity of tradition demands a creative synthesis of the first millennium and the second." Kasper concedes that the synthesis attempted by Vatican II was "highly superficial and in no way satisfactory," but he insists that theological synthesis is really not the task of the council, but a matter for theology that comes afterward. The council provides "the indispensable 'frame of reference.'"[37]

Kasper and Ratzinger agree that the ecclesiology of Church as a communion of Churches is an indispensable frame of reference coming from Vatican II. What the council left unfinished is the daunting and delicate task of theological synthesis of the new and the old. In this regard, two operative principles should be kept in mind: first, the structures and patterns of the earliest six centuries of the Church cannot simply be restored, since contexts differ and new categories have emerged in the interim; second, although a Catholic approach to reform, as reflected by Trent and by Vatican II, cannot discard developments in leadership patterns during the second millennium of the Church, it can seek to reshape them. The Congregation for the Doctrine of the Faith's recognition of the need to restate doctrines in differing historical contexts, found in *Mysterium Ecclesiae* (1973), can analogously be applied to structural development.[38] "The needed synthesis…is a task of reception, which is far from being a merely passive process."[39] Instead, it involves a creative retrieval of the ecclesiological tradition through a process of interpretation, translating the structures that met the needs of a past horizon into a form that responds to the contemporary situation. As Pope John Paul II recognized in his encyclical *Ut unum sint*, contemporary theology has to ask how the papacy and episcopacy might function in ways that creatively respond to new needs and situations.[40]

At the Extraordinary Synod about Vatican II in 1986, some bishops expressed concern that certain post–Vatican II interpretations of the "people of God" encouraged civil democratic thinking in the Church.[41] Bluntly put, this concern attests to a narrowness of mind, closed to new possibilities. Given that the Church of the past has always borrowed from the structures of the times, it is not inconceivable that the biblical notion of the Church as "the people of God" might be able to assimilate some "democratic" patterns of dialogue and consensus. Rather than writing off democratic patterns as a threat, the leadership of the Church might better consider both the compatibility of this model to the Church and its limits. At the least, a process of discernment should be applied. Within the spirit of *aggiornamento*, structures from the past should respond to the expectations of new times.

One need not presume that only a totally monarchical, centralist organization is compatible with the structure of the Catholic Church, despite the fact that such a pattern has permeated ecclesial self-understanding over the course of the second millennium. Hermann Pottmeyer's analysis of the complex discussions that shaped Vatican I's teaching on the papacy has led him to conclude that even Vatican I's position was not simply equivalent with a monarchical, centralist interpretation of the papacy. He argues that reform of the papacy is possible without relativizing Vatican I's teaching on papal primacy and infallibility, and that reducing Vatican centralization does not mean a weakening of papal authority.

Whether such voices will make any difference, however, is another question. At present, it often seems that Rome is primarily intent on defending rather than rethinking the role of the papacy and of the Roman curial offices. The rather centralist ecclesiology of the letter to bishops entitled "The Church as Communion," issued in 1992 by the Congregation for the

Doctrine of the Faith under Cardinal Ratzinger as its Prefect, offers an example.[42]

The introductory section of the congregation's letter is remarkably positive. Quoting Pope John Paul II's "Address to the Bishops of the United States," it affirms that the notion of communion lies "at the heart of the Church's self-understanding," insofar as communion is the mystery of the personal union of each human being with both the Trinity (an invisible, vertical dimension of communion) and with the rest of humankind (a visible, horizontal dimension). Citing multiple passages in *Lumen gentium*, the letter explains that communion should express both the nature of the Church as the sacrament of salvation, making present Christ in whom the love of the triune God is communicated to humans, and the nature of the Church as the body of Christ, uniting all members into one and the same body, an organically structured community, a visible and social union, open to missionary and ecumenical endeavor. The Eucharist is identified as the creative force and source of communion among the members of the Church. The letter speaks of a "common visible sharing in the goods of salvation (the holy things), especially in the Eucharist," which is the source of the invisible communion. Communion brings a spiritual solidarity and fosters a union in charity among all the members who together form one body.[43]

The congregation's letter offers valuable insights about the universality of the Church, particularly in observing that "in the Church no one is a stranger" and that "it is precisely the Eucharist that renders all self-sufficiency on the part of the particular Churches impossible."[44] Yet some of its positions give pause. Affirming that "the universal Church is the body of the Churches" and viewing "the universal Church as a communion of Churches," the letter says that the concept of communion can be applied only "in analogous fashion" to the union existing among particular churches. The Congregation thereby appears determined to restrict the concept of communion. Why? The answer is: "Sometimes,...the idea of a 'communion of particular

Churches' is presented in such a way as to weaken the concept of the Church at the visible and institutional level." The letter expresses concern about "ecclesiological unilateralism" wherein particular Churches seek to become self-sufficient and thus weaken their "real communion with the universal Church and with its living and visible center."[45] One suspects that this concern might be restated in less spiritual, more bureaucratic language. As Michael J. Buckley has observed, "The will-to-power constitutes one of the strongest, yet unrecognized passions within human engagements, and the history of the Church indicates how ravaging and destructive an effect it can produce even while advancing under the flag of the most religious of vocabularies."[46]

Because "the universal Church becomes present in [particular churches] with all her essential elements," the letter affirms that particular Churches "are therefore constituted after the model of the universal Church."[47] Each is said to be "a portion of the People of God entrusted to a bishop to be guided by him with the assistance of his clergy."[48] Insofar as they are "part of the one Church of Christ,"[49] particular Churches are said to have "a special relationship of 'mutual interiority' with the whole, that is, with the universal Church." Wrapping itself in somewhat abstract terms, the Congregation then insists that the universal Church is "a reality ontologically and temporally prior to every individual particular church." It declares that "the Church that is one and unique...precedes creation and gives birth to the particular Churches as her daughters. She expresses herself in them; she is the mother and not the offspring of the particular Churches." According to the letter, "the one unique Church" preexisted any local Churches: "the Church is manifested, temporally, on the day of Pentecost in the community of the one hundred and twenty gathered around Mary and the twelve apostles, the representatives of the one unique Church and the founders-to-be of the local Churches, who have a mission directed to the world."[50] Apparently, on that occasion, Jerusalem is not to be considered a local Church. One might want to ask why not.

The assertion of the priority of the universal Church leads to the claim that particular Churches receive their ecclesiality from the universal Church. To buttress that claim, the letter remarkably declares Vatican II's formula of "The Church in and formed out of the Churches" *(Ecclesia in et ex Ecclesiis)*[51] to be inseparable from a formula found in Pope John Paul II's talk to the Roman Curia,[52] "The Churches in and formed out of the Church" *(Ecclesiae in et ex Ecclesia)*.[53] The letter insists that one "does not belong to the universal Church in a mediate way, through belonging to a particular Church, but in an immediate way, even though entry into and life within the universal Church are necessarily brought about in a particular Church." The next sentence is a much more nuanced statement, resonating with Vatican II's approach to describing the complexity of the Church (e.g., in *Lumen gentium* 8): "From the point of view of the Church understood as communion, the universal communion of the faithful and the communion of the Churches are not consequences of one another but constitute the same reality seen from different viewpoints."[54] This more balanced perspective is developed in an unsigned letter published a year later in *l'Osservatore Romano* (June 23, 1993): "Every particular Church is truly Church, although it is not the whole Church; at the same time, the universal Church is not distinct from the communion of particular Churches, without, however, being conceived as the sum of them.…[I]ncorporation into the universal Church is as immediate as is incorporation into a particular Church. Belonging to the universal Church and belonging to a particular Church are a single Christian reality."[55]

The congregation's letter was also concerned that the rediscovery of a eucharistic ecclesiology has sometimes placed one-sided emphasis on the principle of the local Church: "It is claimed that, where the Eucharist is celebrated, the totality of the mystery of the Church would be made present in such a way as to render any other principle of unity or universality inessential."[56] This concern signals what appears to be the letter's primary aim, namely, safeguarding the role of the bishop of Rome. In an unusual mix of images, the letter speaks of the Roman Church as the head of "the body of Churches."[57] While acknowledging that the bishop is a visible source and foundation of the unity of the particular Church, the letter emphasizes that, "for each particular Church to be fully Church, that is, the particular presence of the universal Church with all its essential elements, and hence constituted after the model of the universal Church, there must be present in it, as a proper element, the supreme authority of the Church: the episcopal college 'together with their head the supreme pontiff, and never apart from him'" (*Lumen gentium* 22, par. 2; cf. also 19). Again quoting from Pope John Paul II's "Address to the Roman Curia," the letter stresses that "the primacy of the bishop of Rome and the episcopal college are proper elements of the universal Church that are 'not derived from the particularity of the Churches,' but are nevertheless interior to each particular Church." Citing John Paul II's "Address to the Bishops of the United States," the letter goes on to state that the ministry of the successor of Peter is to be seen "not only as a 'global' service, reaching each particular Church from 'outside,' as it were, but as belonging already to the essence of each particular Church from 'within.'" In that regard, the letter also invokes Vatican I's teaching that "the ministry of the primacy involves, in essence, a truly episcopal power, which is not only supreme, full and universal, but also immediate, over all, whether pastors or other faithful." It concludes that the ministry of Peter's successor "as something interior to each particular Church is a necessary expression of that fundamental interiority between universal Church and particular Church." That is, "the unity of the Eucharist and the unity of the episcopate with Peter are not independent roots of the unity of the Church" because Christ instituted the Eucharist and the episcopate as essentially interlinked realities. "[E]very celebration of the Eucharist is performed in union not only with the proper bishop, but also with the pope, with the episcopal order, with all the clergy, and with the entire people."[58] One might note that a genuine theology of communion has always recognized that the celebration of the Eucharist by any particular Church presupposes and expresses its unity with the entire Catholic communion of Churches, which includes its center. No person and no community can be Catholic alone. Yet, as J. M. R. Tillard has observed, "[i]t is necessary also, and before everything, not to err over the fundamental points of the faith. The Church is made by Eucharist and baptism, not by the papacy. The purpose of the papacy is to give the Eucharist its full dimensions."[59]

Addressing the issue of unity in diversity, the Congregation's letter acknowledges that plurality and diversification do not obstruct the unity of the universal Church, "but rather confer upon it the character of 'communion.'" The plurality within the Church is said to involve a diversity of ministries, charisms, and forms of life and apostolate within each particular Church, and a diversity of liturgical and cultural traditions among the various particular Churches. The fundamental task of the Roman pontiff is to foster a unity that does not obstruct diversity, and a diversification that does not obstruct unity but rather enriches it. Yet everyone in the Church shares the task of building up and preserving a unity "on which diversification confers the character of communion."[60]

In brief, it seems fair to say that the overall tone of the congregation's letter does not sustain Ratzinger's much earlier observation, as a theologian, that Vatican I's clarification of the papacy's role in the Church had the positive effect of enabling Rome to leave behind the defensive attitude precipitated by conciliarism. Nor does the tone of the letter reflect Ratzinger's earlier praise for Vatican II's retrieval of "horizontal connections" within the Church, or his earlier enthusiasm for "an independent body of bishops" in communion with Rome, who "had taken a giant step beyond being a mere sounding board for propaganda" toward acting as a force which the papal curia or central administrative bureaucracy would have to reckon with.[61] Perhaps it should not come as too much of a surprise, however, that pre–Vatican II tendencies still exert a powerful influence upon those who come to

Rome to assume the mantle of ecclesial leadership. In describing how the higher clergy of seventh-century Rome proceeded to their churches, in the very manner in which Roman consuls had processed in the early sixth century, "greeted by candles, scattering largesse to the populace, wearing the silken slippers of a senator," Peter Brown observed that the mantle of eternal Rome would be draped over medieval papal Rome and added, "a city, its habits and associations change slowly."[62]

A more adequate harmonization of the "Church universal" and the "local church," and of papal primacy and the episcopacy, is still "widely considered to be one of the most pressing theological tasks of the Church today."[63] One possible way toward advancing that task is suggested by Miroslav Volf's analysis of the underpinnings and presuppositions of trinitarian elements within the theology of Church as communion.[64] Volf argues that Ratzinger's recent writings understand the Church "from the perspective of the whole" because of a focus on the oneness of substance in the Trinity, leaving aside the differentiation of three persons who always act collegially within the Trinity as communion/community.[65] Focusing on the oneness of the substance of the Trinity grounds a hierarchical focus in which "one" (either pope or bishop) has power over the many. Though keeping in mind that a nonhierarchical "Free Church" commitment colors Volf's theology, it is surely right to say that his insights that the trinitarian communion involves "three," and that catholicity thus calls for more attention to "otherness,"[66] merit attention within Catholic theology. The theme of "otherness" or differentiation in communion, which bears a relationship to Vatican II's motif of "unity in diversity," calls for deeper reflection and analysis. Focusing on the three-in-oneness of the Trinity grounds a collegial focus that sees the pope and the church of Rome always communally engaged with "others," namely, the bishops and their local churches, in the exercise of coresponsibility for the Church; this focus likewise sees each bishop always communally engaged with the ministers and faithful of the local church in the exercise of coresponsibility. It sees leadership as recognizing the coresponsibility of others.

The Congregation for the Faith's letter about the Church as communion does acknowledge that the Spirit unites the entire communion and that its members and particular communities are endowed with different gifts and reflect a liturgical and cultural diversity. As noted above, the letter likewise refers to a unity "on which diversification confers the character of communion."[67] There remains a need, however, to develop what the universal Church receives from each individual member, and what the universal Church receives from particular or local Churches, to counterbalance the past tendency of simply accentuating what individual persons receive from the whole (by way of liturgy, sacraments, spirituality, and the teaching of pope and bishops). Given that the Church as the Body of Christ is a communion in the image of the Trinity, it cannot be claimed that individual members and local communities are simply absorbed into a whole; rather, it must be affirmed that the communion is expressed in and through their specific identities and contributions. Volf puts the point as follows: "According to the New Testament witness, the Spirit of the new creation is not only the Spirit of salvation common to all, but simultaneously the Spirit of gifts unique to each."[68] Catholic theology and practice might ponder Volf's further claim that the "twofold activity of the Spirit in unifying and differentiating prevents false catholicity of either church or persons from emerging in which the particular is swallowed up by the universal. The Spirit of communion opens up every person to others, so that every person can reflect something of the eschatological communion of the entire people of God with the triune God in a unique way through the relations in which that person lives."[69]

In our time, we have come to understand that humans deal with the world and with one another by means of conditioned models of interpretation.[70] Given that some of these models presume centuries of historical development, it takes considerable time to change ingrained patterns of thought. "Analysts of culture have shown that, even after a successful political and social revolution, eighty percent of the old, rejected structures 'recur' in one way or another." Moreover, when a major change occurs, it does not affect every sector of the culture at the same time. The notion of "a sudden switch in the mental or material cultural pattern…turns out therefore to be wrong—a 'myth.'"[71] "Even where life changes violently, as in ages of revolution, far more of the old is preserved in the supposed transformation of everything than anyone knows, and it combines with the new to create a new value."[72] Such observations must be kept in mind when considering the documents promulgated by Vatican II and the subsequent reception of what they proclaimed. Further progress is required in the efforts to harmonize the ecclesiologies of the first and second millennia, to rearticulate the relationship of pope and bishops and of baptized and ordained, and to put into practice a renewed theology of communion. In the postconciliar period, those who receive and implement the council's teachings sometimes interpret them in ways that reveal the unconscious presuppositions of deeply ingrained, contrasting models of thinking. For example, the concept of communion can be invoked to buttress the pyramidal, monarchical paradigm: one may insist that all the bishops in communion with the pope must implement the decisions and teachings received from the pope, but without equal concern for clarifying what the pope should receive from the bishops spread throughout the world. Yet, it is true, in the postconciliar period, much of "new value" has to be recognized as well. The next and final chapter goes on to consider another indispensable "frame of reference" coming from Vatican II, the eschatological vision of the Constitution on the Church in the Modern World, *Gaudium et spes.* The richness of this text, it will become evident, has yet to be fully exploited.

7
Restoring a Future to a World Church

As Karl Rahner has noted, the future is not simply the prolongation of our past, nor merely the actualization or implementation of our present plans. Such an understanding of the future would primarily be a projection of a static present. The real future is "uncertain" and is not just the unfolding of our present ideas or strategies. It is not simply a calculated human creation involving "plans plus time." Rather, the open future that comes to meet us brings surprises. That unforeseen future requires provisionality, since it cannot be controlled or calculated; "it rips up the nets of all our plans."[1] Planning for the future is certainly a justifiable necessity, but genuine possibility involves boldly committing ourselves to the unplanned: "we dare to enter upon that which has not been planned."[2]

As Christians, we trust that the triune God who created our universe and then became fully human in Jesus of Nazareth will ever be coming toward us through the very darkness that conceals the unknown future of our freedom. In and through Jesus, God has shared our human experience of the uncontrollable future and, as Spirit, still dwells within us. Thus, we do not hope simply because we act; rather, we act because we hope, trusting in God's presence and love. Living into the unforeseen future, we encounter the self-giving God who makes possible the kind of love that can transform the world. That is the mystery that the Church as sacrament points to in the here and now, in the midst of ongoing history. "The Church does not exist for its own sake."[3] It exists for the world and for history. It exists because there has to be a community coming from Jesus, proclaiming that only in love and community do humans find their deepest meaning and fulfillment.

Unlike Augustine, who reckoned creation to be six thousand years old,[4] we today speak of a universe that is about fourteen billion years old and estimate that our human species, *homo sapiens*, has been in existence at least fifty thousand years. Like Abraham responding to God's call to go to a new land, or the Jewish people journeying through the wilderness on their way to freedom, we are still a pilgrim people, ever moving into the new future of God's vast creation. As Christians, we live into the future, not as isolated individuals, but as members of a believing community, ever responding to a call and partaking in the liberating power of our faith tradition. The faith tradition of our mothers and fathers lives in us as we move into the future of the creation we are called to reshape in love. It pulsates in our efforts to live out an identity forged by the biblical narrative and empowered by the incarnational, sacramental expressions of our life in faith.

A "This-Worldly" Eschatology

Jesus proclaimed the coming of the kingdom or reign of God, which he saw as already present and growing, but he did not provide any absolute timetable for its fulfillment.[5] In the decades after the resurrection, Christians hoped and prayed for the immediate return of Jesus. At the end of the first century, some complained that, when they were young, they had been told Jesus was coming; now they were old and it had still not happened.[6] Augustine, by contrast, refused to speculate about when the end would take place.[7] Then again, Gregory the Great, pope from 590–604, believed the end was imminent, but the year 1000 came and went. As Christianity begins its third millennium, those who have gone before us can teach us to be cautious about how long the final time will be.

Our perspectives on time and space vastly surpass what Augustine or Gregory might ever have imagined. As stated in the

Introduction, we understand that we are living about fourteen billion years after the moment called the Big Bang. Our planet, Earth, is about four-and-a-half-billion-years old. It orbits around a moderate-sized star at the outer edge of a galaxy called the "Milky Way," composed of a hundred million stars. It takes light, moving at 186,000 miles a second, a hundred thousand years to cross our galaxy. And our galaxy is but one of millions. We have come to realize the immensity of the universe that God brought into existence through creation.

The theology of Church must be developed in a dialogue not only with Christology and sacramental theology but also with a renewed eschatology. Avery Dulles has observed that "the panoramic vision" implied in an eschatological view of the Church has been narrowed in modern ecclesiology because the prevalent definitions do not include the heavenly Church.[8] That is, the way we often conceive of the Church is limited to the here and now. Vatican II did give some attention to this important Catholic theme. Under the title "The Eschatological Nature of the Pilgrim Church and its Union with the Heavenly Church," chapter 7 of *Lumen gentium* declares that the final age of the world is already coming upon us, citing 1 Corinthians 10:11. The renewal of the world is said to have been not only irrevocably initiated, but even anticipated in this world through the authentic but still imperfect sanctity of the Church. In the meanwhile, the Church travels as a pilgrim, carrying in her sacraments and institutions the mark of this passing age. The Church is described as living amid the groans and travails of creatures awaiting the revelation of the sons and daughters of God, looking forward to the end of the world when the Lord will come in glory (section 48).

Without speculating about any timetable, *Lumen gentium's* eschatological perspective looks primarily to the end of the world and the heavenly Church. For his part, Dulles has proposed that we "consider more carefully the condition of the Church in the centuries between Pentecost and the Parousia." He maintains that, "in the Catholic view, the Church at this stage already participates in a real, definitive, though imperfect manner, in the fullness of God's gift in Christ" and that such participation in fullness "brings about a real continuity or communion between different generations of Christians." He further recognizes, however, that "different periods of the Church, notwithstanding this continuity, have their own distinctive character, so that the later is able to complement and complete what has been initiated by the earlier."[9] Yet such a dynamic, historical understanding of the Church's relationship to the ongoing history or future of this world is not fully developed in *Lumen gentium.* One must instead turn to Vatican II's Constitution on the Church in the Modern World.

Gaudium et spes

At the Fifth Lateran Council (1512–17), which convened just before the Protestant Reformation, the inaugural address of Giles of Viterbo, prior general of the Augustinian order, reflected what was then a prevalent understanding of Catholic reform: that humans were to be changed by the Church, and not the Church by humans. A classicist mentality predominated, which simply presumed that the Church moved through history without being affected by it. Nearly four hundred and fifty years later, Vatican II's perspective was rather different. The council explicitly intended "to end the stance of cultural isolation…[and] to initiate a new freedom of expression and action within the Church."[10] In particular, the Constitution on the Church in the Modern World, *Gaudium et spes* ("Joy and hope"), discusses the Church's relationship to the world. It speaks of a new age of history in which the human mind, with a keen sense of freedom, is broadening its mastery over time. And it acknowledges the accelerated pace of history. What is more, "a dynamic and more evolutionary concept of nature" has displaced "a static one," giving rise to "an immense series of new problems" (sections 4 and 5).

Some have suggested, with hindsight, that *Gaudium et spes* is too optimistic and idealistic, overly embracing a modern trust in human potential. Such an appraisal seems to forget that the constitution is predicated upon hope. As Dermot A. Lane has so well explained, hope arises out of a certain darkness or crisis in life. It presupposes a certain unease or dissatisfaction with the way the world is.[11] In that regard, *Gaudium et spes* pointedly declares that humanity's growing mastery over nature, as well as our shaping of the world's political, social, and economic order, is overshadowed by injustice, unfair distribution, and widespread hunger. The paradox of our world is that human freedom faces ever-new forms of slavery, and human unity is threatened by racial and ideological antagonism and by the specter of a war of total destruction. In a world that is simultaneously powerful and weak, noble deeds are matched by villainous, progress contends with decline, and brotherhood and sisterhood coexist with hatred (sections 4 and 9). Furthermore, the Church in the Modern World does not expect total emancipation through human effort alone, or a purely earthly paradise, since every individual human (thus all humans together) brings a divided self to the struggle with good and evil, having a freedom weakened by sin. Nevertheless, humans have the freedom to turn themselves toward what is good (sections 10, 13, and 17).

The constitution repeatedly acknowledges that God has created humans with freedom. It emphasizes the dignity and the inviolable rights and duties of persons, declaring that discrimination in basic personal rights on the basis of sex, race, color, social conditions, language, or religion must be eradicated (sections 21, 26, 29, and 59). That theme is likewise central to Vatican II's Declaration on Religious Liberty (*Dignitatis humanae* 2), which proclaims the dignity of all persons, and their right to be immune from coercion even if they are considered to be in error. *Gaudium et spes* (33) further recognizes that a human "now produces by his [or her] own enterprise many things which in former times he [or she] looked for from heavenly powers." It admits that God has given the world a certain autonomy: "By the very nature of creation, material being is endowed with its own stability, truth and excellence, its own order and laws" (section 36). Human achievements, too, can be the fulfillment of God's mysterious design (section 33). "Trusting in the design of the creator and admitting that progress can contribute to [humanity's] happiness," the Church, in the words of the constitution, reminds humans that they "can, indeed...must love the things of God's creation," while ever acknowledging that all comes from God and putting love of self aside (sections 37 and 38).

Gaudium et spes also reminds us that Sacred Scripture teaches what has been confirmed by humanity's own experience, namely, that the progress of the world is always threatened by humanity's pride and inordinate self-love. Jesus assures those who put their faith in God's love "that the way of love is open to all [humans] and that the effort to establish a universal brotherhood [and sisterhood] will not be in vain." True progress is said to require the kind of self-giving love that Jesus showed in dying for us. It is not a love reserved for important matters, "but must be exercised above all in the ordinary circumstances of daily life" (section 38).

Gaudium et spes further emphasizes that we do not know when the consummation of the earth and of humanity will take place, nor the way the universe will be transformed. At the same time, it insists that the expectation of a transformed, new earth should stimulate rather than diminish our concern to develop this earth. For, although earthly progress must be distinguished from the increase of the kingdom or reign of God, it is of vital concern to that ultimate reign of truth and life, holiness, justice, love, and peace (section 39). The Church itself is envisioned as "a leaven and, as it were, the soul of human society in its renewal by Christ and transformation into the family of God." The Church seeks to contribute to humanizing the human family and its history, both through its individual members and its whole community, and recognizes the considerable help that the Church can receive from the world in preparing for the proclamation of the gospel (section 40). In this regard, the constitution affirms that only God can satisfy the restless searching of the human heart, and that being a follower of Christ, who is the perfect human, enables one to become more human. It stresses that the gospel safeguards the personal dignity and freedom of humans, and specifically refers to the dignity of conscience and its freedom of choice. God as creator and savior does not suppress the "autonomy of the creature," but restores and consolidates a true human autonomy (section 41).

To say that the Church was not given a mission in the political, economic, or social order does not mean that the Church has no function to fulfill in those areas. Accordingly, *Gaudium et spes* emphasizes that, by reason of its universality, which can unite diverse peoples and nations, the Church as a Sacrament of unity cannot be tied to any one culture, or to any political, economic, or social system (sections 42, 58, and 76). At the same time, the Church as a historical reality "is not unaware how much it has profited from the history and development of humanity,...from the experience of past ages,...from the progress of the sciences, and from the riches hidden in various cultures." The constitution recalls that, from the very beginnings of its history, the Church learned to express the message of Christ with the help of the concepts and language of diverse peoples, and attempted to clarify that message with the wisdom of philosophers. Such adaptation remains the norm, and makes it crucial for the Church to foster vital contact and exchange with different cultures. The words of the council still ring true: "Nowadays when things change so rapidly and thought patterns differ so widely, the Church needs to step up this exchange by calling upon the help of people who are living in the world, who are expert in its organizations and its forms of training, and who understand its mentality, in the case of believers and nonbelievers alike" (section 44).

In different terms, Christians are to follow the example of Christ who worked as a craftsman. Although this world is not the lasting city that is to come, Christians should carry out their earthly activity in a manner that brings "human, domestic, professional, scientific or technical efforts into a vital synthesis with religious values." The fulfillment of earthly responsibilities toward one's neighbor is viewed as inseparable from one's salvation. In the debates which will inevitably emerge about difficult issues, the council advocates looking to pastors for guidance, while admitting that pastors "will not always be so expert as to have a ready answer to every problem (even every grave problem)" (section 43). In aiding and benefiting from the world, the Church is intent on one goal—that God's reign or kingdom come and all of humanity attain salvation. It thus continues the ministry of Jesus in whom the Word of God, through whom all things were made, became human (section 45).

In discussing the development of culture, *Gaudium et spes* recognizes that "historical studies tend to make us view things under the aspects of changeability and evolution." It likewise points out that the customs and mores of life are becoming more and more uniform, and industrialization and urbanization are creating a new mass culture, which generates new ways of thinking and acting (section 54). Increasingly, groups of men and women in each nation and social group are aware of being shapers of their community's culture. The constitution considers the worldwide, growing sense of human autonomy and responsibility crucially significant for the spiritual and moral maturity of humanity, and deeply related to the need to unify the world and to construct a world of truth and justice. In that regard, *Gaudium et spes* speaks of the birth of a new humanism, in which humans are defined above all by their responsibility toward their brothers and sisters and toward the shaping of history (section 55). (At the same time, the constitution notes, ascertaining the legitimate claims of autonomy requires careful discernment, in order that one not embrace a purely earthbound humanism, which construes religion as an adversary [sections 56 and 59].)

By way of summary, Christians "must be convinced that they have much to contribute to the prosperity of humanity and to world peace" (section 72). That message has been received. As the bishops of Latin America gathered at Medellin in 1968 and at Puebla in 1979 affirmed, the Church must proclaim an "integral salvation" in which hope for heaven is inseparable from concerted action for economic and social justice on earth. Based on the belief that the life, death, and resurrection of Jesus mark the beginning of a new creation, Christian joy and hope underwrite a confidence that no particular time, including our own, is irredeemable. That is the good news effectively proclaimed by Jesus' life (especially by his parables and his meals with "outcasts"), his death, and his resurrection. Never forgetting suffering and the "scandal" of the cross, Christian joy and hope have their ultimate foundation in God's pledge that the destructive forces of sin and evil will not have the last word.

Foundations for a "This-Worldly" Eschatology

Nevertheless, *Gaudium et spes* marks a beginning, rather than the culmination, of theological reflection about God's relationship to a world in which humans have a certain autonomy.[12] Whereas *Lumen gentium* relates the beginnings of the Church to God's initiative in creation, and roots its theology of Church in the trinitarian relationship within God, *Gaudium et spes* provides a complementary frame of reference with its eschatological perspective and its affirmation of a certain human autonomy within history. Yet contemporary Christian understanding of human freedom's role in shaping history prompts a question never fully confronted by Vatican II, namely, to what extent the autonomy with which God has endowed humanity for shaping the world has also been given for shaping the Church. It would seem that the Church should be open to the possibility that God, acting through the Spirit in our midst, is also inviting and enabling something "new" to emerge through human freedom and creativity *within* the Church.

The constitution's repeated references to the cross and resurrection of Jesus provide a place to begin.[13] Jesus, as God become truly human, fully experienced the inner struggle that human freedom sometimes involves. The Synoptic Gospels portray him as distressed and sorrowful in the face of death (Mark 14:33–34; Matt 26:37–38; Luke 22:44). Hanging upon the cross, he is depicted praying psalms of trust. In Mark 15:34 and Matthew 27:46, the first verse of Psalm 22, "My God, my God, why have you forsaken me?" is on his lips. In Luke 23:46, we find a verse from Psalm 31, "Father, into your hands I commend my spirit." Jesus truly "died our death": "[If] he really became like us in everything but sin, as the Epistle to the Hebrews says, then he became like us in death, too, and his death cannot be similar to ours merely in externals."[14] The crucified Jesus, like every human, was confronted by the radical powerlessness and darkness of human death. As Walter Kasper puts it, "Jesus' faith did not give way, but he experienced the darkness and distress of death more deeply than any other man or woman." For "he experienced God as the one who withdraws in his very closeness."[15] On this understanding, God is like a lover who lets the beloved go free—an act that, truly speaking, it is unlikely any human lover ever achieves. The dying Jesus, in his "dark night of faith," "trusts in God [and] knows that he is still held in God's hand, even though there is no help that he can touch or feel, and in utmost emptiness will not let go of this hand." Yet, as the Fourth Gospel makes clear, "the deepest reality does not lie on the surface": despite his helplessness and seeming failure as one rejected and condemned, "Jesus was successful by virtue of his living communion with God, which is stronger than death."[16] As he hung upon the cross, Jesus' success was his "once and for all" affirmation of love for God and humans, even his enemies.

As Jesus was hanging on the cross, the Father in whom he trusted and the Spirit, who is the relationship of love eternally expressed within God, were present and active. That is, the cross was a trinitarian event, revealing God's freely chosen vulnerability and defenselessness in relation to human freedom. During Jesus' crucifixion, God sustained not only Jesus' freedom but the freedom of those who put Jesus to death. The fully human but sinless Jesus, "the image of the invisible God" (Col 1:15), distressed and sorrowful in his dark night of faith, on the cross expressed what the triune God "is": a self-giving, self-emptying Love, who in the Word become human truly shares the struggle of human freedom.[17]

Human freedom is "sustained"—upheld, or even affirmed—even in this most awful, awesome moment. In other words, in that moment, Jesus is God's liberating embrace of the human condition. "God's overcoming of human failure is historically incorporated in Jesus' never ceasing love for God and [humans], during and in the historical moment of his failure on the cross."[18]

From Unmoved Mover to the Death of God

To say the least, Christians have not always thought about God or Jesus as just described. So before pursuing the implications of what might be called a theology of the cross for ecclesiology, it is worth reviewing—admittedly only in broad outlines—earlier models of God and God's relation to the world to which earlier Christians had recourse in thinking about the Church.

Plato's *Timaeus*, probably written in the latter part of his life (428/7–348/7 BCE), envisioned the universe as a perfect sphere with the earth fixed in its center. All the planets and stars were thought to rotate around the earth in perfectly circular orbits, always moving at absolutely unvarying speed. As the realm of becoming or change, where one found birth and death, generation and decay, the world was considered but a shadow of a more substantial and unchanging reality called Being. As an immaterial order, Being was the realm of all intelligence, including the rational part of human souls. Earth, by contrast, was the visible, material shadow of the unchanging perfection of a purely intelligible order, the realm of Ideas or Forms, beyond the orbit of the farthest star. The most transcendent Idea, "the Good," was defined as pure being, having no limitation or becoming, and approachable only through contemplation.

Aristotle's vision of the universe likewise had an immobile earth encircled by concentric, transparent spheres to which the moon, planets, and stars were attached. (Aristotle [384–22 BCE] was a student at Plato's academy.) Only on Earth, inside the innermost sphere of the moon, did one find change or incomplete motion (up and down, forward and back, right and left, generation and deterioration). The outermost layers of the universe were the spheres of the fixed stars, which were said to move in perfect, fixed circles at unvarying speed. In Aristotle's view, that was the only perfect motion. Unpredictable movement was imperfect. Outside the sphere of the farthest star lay the realm of the Prime Mover who was pure act *(energeia)*, having a completeness and perfection that excluded any potentiality. That Prime or First Mover was thus absolutely unmoved, causing change without being changed, by means of final causality—by attracting or drawing forth as the object of desire—and not by efficient causality. (Aristotle's First Mover was not a creator; the material universe eternally existed.) Being unmoved, the First Mover rules totally from outside, having no interaction with the world. Aristotle thus emphasized that there could be no friendship with the Unmoved Mover. Perfection is identified with Being and sameness. Becoming and change reflect imperfection.

During the second century, two Christian apologists, Aristedes of Athens and Justin Martyr, introduced Aristotle's concept of the Unmoved Mover into Christian thought. Justin Martyr imported this concept from Middle Platonism (a synthesis of Platonic and Aristotelian perspectives) to make clear that the God of Christians is both transcendent and immanent. He used the term "Unmoved Mover" to emphasize the Father's total transcendence, while affirming that the Word and the Spirit had become immanent within creation. Justin thereby carefully countered the pantheism of the Stoics who maintained that the divine, which they called Logos, was entirely immanent in this world. Justin did not, however, seem to have been troubled by the inconsistency of designating the *Abba*, whom Jesus experienced as unconditionally loving, as an Unmoved Mover. Nor did Justin seem to have asked how one could pray to the Father whom he called unmoved.

The introduction of the philosophical concept of the Unmoved Mover into Christian thought shaped a classical concept of God, which specified God's perfection primarily in terms of omnipotence and omniscience. God was defined as the Being who knows everything in one eternal act of self-consciousness and who exercises mastery over everything, while enjoying a completeness that needs nothing and depends on no one, being essentially unaffected or unmoved. Some Christian writers, particularly Origen and Anselm, acknowledged the problem of calling God both compassionate and unmoved, but without resolving the dilemma.[19] The presumption of a perfection rooted in omnipotence became so primary that, for centuries, no one considered abandoning the philosophical view of God as an Unmoved Mover essentially unaffected by creation, even though that conceptualization seems to be in some tension with the God of love revealed through the deeds and words of Jesus.

Also for centuries, Christians likewise shared the earth-centered worldview held by Plato, Aristotle, and later Ptolemy (second century CE). Thus, in publishing his concept of a sun-centered universe in 1543, Nicholas Copernicus initiated a revolution in the way the Western world viewed its relationship to the universe and to God. Taking on the project of verifying the Copernican world view, Galileo Galilei (1564–1642) expressed a profound confidence in scientific method. He argued that a discussion of physical problems should begin not from the authority of scriptural passages, but from sense experiences and necessary demonstrations: "nothing physical which sense-experience sets before our eyes, or which necessary demonstration proves to us, ought to be called in question (much less condemned) upon the testimony of biblical passages which have some different meaning beneath their words."[20] Galileo's scientific confidence was not shared, however, by Robert Bellarmine, the cardinal-inquisitor of the Congregation of the Holy Office in Rome. Despite Galileo's telescopic discoveries, the cardinal wrote the following in 1615:

> If there were a true demonstration that the sun was in the center of the universe...and that the sun did not travel around the earth, but the earth circled around the sun, then it would be necessary to proceed with great caution in

> explaining the passages of Scripture which seemed contrary, and we would rather have to say that we did not understand them than to say something was false which has been demonstrated. But I do not believe that there is any such demonstration; none has been shown to me....[I]n a case of doubt, one may not depart from the Scriptures as explained by the holy Fathers.[21]

In 1616, the views of Copernicus were condemned as "false and erroneous," and Galileo was silenced. But his insistence that experience was to be considered a resource along with the scriptures was not to disappear.

Cardinal Bellarmine was not in disagreement with Copernicus and Galileo about the components of the universe. All spoke about the earth, sun, moon, planets, and stars. The problem involved the ways those components were placed in relationship.[22] If Bellarmine were to relinquish the worldview articulated by Plato, Aristotle, and Ptolemy, in which the earth was at the center of a spherically shaped universe, he would have had to dismantle a whole network of theory and fact, the presuppositions through which his historical community previously perceived and explained the universe. Copernicus and Galileo had introduced an epochal "shift of paradigms," one of those significant moments when human understanding of the world undergoes a change affecting "the entire constellation of beliefs, values, techniques, and so on shared by the members of a given community."[23] The Copernican insights dismantled "a world-view that had previously made the universe meaningful for the members of a whole civilization, specialist and non-specialist alike." That dismantling necessitated changes even in the formulation of theological questions and answers.[24] In his *Dialogue Concerning the Two Chief Systems of the World*, Galileo himself moved toward a somewhat mechanistic conception of the universe: in his view, God simply created "the atoms of a fundamentally independent and self-sustaining natural order."[25] That position was certainly not unproblematic for Cardinal Bellarmine. Nor should it have been.

At the heart of the Copernican paradigm shift was a new "puzzle-solution" that placed all the components of the previous paradigm in a different relationship: Earth was no longer at the center. This reshuffling precipitated a communication breakdown between the adherents of the old and new paradigms, since there was no neutral language that both could use in the same way.[26] Bellarmine recognized that, if Copernicus and Galileo were correct, a new set of theological presuppositions would have to emerge, to be "reconstructed" into the new vision. But he chose not to be "converted" to the new paradigm.[27] Galileo would be silenced yet another time, in 1633.[28]

Bellarmine's response was itself conditioned by the shared values or symbols of a particular, historically conditioned paradigm, which molded the operational style of Church leaders in his time. The "ecclesial paradigm" in which he had been trained, and to which he contributed by his own writing, was closed to new ideas and evidence. Since the Middle Ages, "antiquity" connoted something tested by time and tradition; what was old was authoritative and valued. Something "modern" or "new" was suspect; novel ideas and innovation were not welcomed.[29]

Only some two hundred years later, in 1822, were works that taught the motion of the earth finally removed from the index of forbidden books. In the meantime, Johannes Kepler (1571–1630) had concluded that the orbits of the heavenly bodies were not circular. Isaac Newton (1642–1727) formulated the laws of gravity, which explained why orbits are elliptical and enabled Edmund Halley (1656–1742) to predict the return of the comet ultimately named after him. Humans were discovering what *Gaudium et spes* so well describes: "By the very nature of creation, material being is endowed with its own stability, truth and excellence, its own order and laws" (section 36).

As science began to realize that God has given the world a certain autonomy, humans also started to think about themselves and their relationship to the world in new ways. The foundations for this shift were gradually set in place by a philosophical revolution that turned from God to humans as the starting point of reflection. About the time of the Galileo affair, René Descartes (1596–1650) developed a philosophical method that proposed to deal with the great metaphysical questions by starting from the *ego*, as indicated by his famous saying, in the *Discourse on Method*, "I think, therefore I am." For Descartes, the solidity of self-awareness served as an antidote to the worldview of nominalist thinkers, according to whom God exercised omnipotence via random acts of the divine will, so that creation represented no overall order but only God's arbitrary decisions, which could have been totally otherwise. Well read in scientific thought, including Newtonian physics, and an accomplished scientist himself, Immanuel Kant (1724–1804) maintained that human intellectual understanding does not passively reflect objects, as if the intellect were shaped by the world around it, but that intellectual understanding is an activity in which a priori concepts provided by the intellect form and shape the way the world "appears." Kant's position drew critical reactions, but it pushed open the door to the realization that human understanding is not simply shaped by an objective world; more and more, human understanding would be seen as shaping the world.

Thomas Aquinas had acknowledged that God worked through the secondary causality of human freedom, but God's ultimate control over creation remained unquestionable for Christians.[30] In that regard, the great earthquake of Lisbon on November 1, 1755, posed a serious problem. If God controls everything, why were so many killed in churches? Voltaire's *Candide*, published in 1759, embraced a solution known as deism: God exists and created the world, but is completely uninvolved in the world after its creation. For Voltaire, an uninvolved God is not concerned about the well-being of humans. They are like the mice on board a ship, for whom a ship owner has no real concern. No instructions about their care are given at the beginning of a voyage. Humans are completely on their own, and God is unconcerned about their destiny. Yet that kind of unmoved God is certainly not the God to whom Christians entrust themselves.

Some thinkers soon moved beyond deism to atheism. Marquis de Condorcet (1743–94) and Auguste Comte (1798–1857) were fascinated by human potential. Judging faith in God to be deleterious to the actualization of human potential, Pierre-Joseph Proudhon (1809–65) argued that the very notion of God was anticivilization and antiprogress. Belief in God was labeled antihuman. By contrast, Georg Wilhelm Friedrich Hegel (1770–1831) sought to develop a philosophical explanation of human history wherein God's Spirit, "the cunning of reason," was shaping history through the very dialectic of human freedom. But Hegel's philosophical vision of God's Spirit shaping history was turned upside down in Ludwig Feuerbach's *Essence of Christianity* (1841). Rather than viewing history as the actualization of God's idea, Feuerbach insisted that God and heaven were nothing but human ideas, projecting an absolutized image of humanity's own potential and dreams onto the clouds. Humans created God in the image of what they wished to be. In seeking to expose God and heaven as mere human projections, Feuerbach intended to liberate humans from depending on God to bring about ultimate justice and happiness in heaven. Rid of the notion of God and heaven, humans would realize that only they themselves shape the future of history. This premise was subsequently embraced by Karl Marx (1813–83). In Marx's socioeconomic view of history, belief in God and in a heaven, where the suffering of the oppressed masses would finally be overturned, was a false "opiate" that encouraged passivity in the face of oppression. Belief in God and heaven reflected a self-alienation from the world, which prevented the historical overcoming of injustice, and thereby empowered oppressors. Similarly, for Sigmund Freud (1856–1939), religion was an infantile illusion in which humans sought security through an obsessive-compulsive enactment of rituals. In opposition to the classical concept of an omnipotent God who controlled everything, "moderns" set in place the notion that humans, rather than God, could control everything. The culmination of this shift in thought was perhaps best expressed by Friedrich Wilhelm Nietzsche

(1844–1900) in his book *The Joyful Science;* there his character, the madman, declares that "God is dead."

An Eschatological Catholicity

Obviously, a new vision of the future of the Church cannot begin with the death of God, at least as proclaimed by Nietzsche's madman. From this perspective, there is no future in the Church; there is only a long goodbye. But, to return to the theology of the cross articulated in the previous section (and all the more in the work of Schillebeeckx and Kasper), it is possible to envision or reenvision a future for the Church beginning with the revelation of God's love—or, of the God who is love—in Jesus' death and resurrection.

Arguably, during the nineteenth century, the flame of eschatology (in the sense of a concern for shaping the future of history) was kept alive by atheists.[31] Christians were primarily focused on individual salvation in afterlife and did not adequately recognize the need to rethink their, and God's, relationship to the future of history. Against this background, Vatican II's acknowledgment that a human "now produces by his [or her] own enterprise many things which in former times he [or she] looked for from heavenly powers" and that God has given the world a certain autonomy can be seen as a momentous event (sections 33, 36, 41, and 56). To reiterate, *Gaudium et spes* also affirms that humans are shapers of history, which requires a heightened sense of Christian responsibility and action for the world. Christians share the human hope that things can be "otherwise" in this world.

Our universe is not completely predetermined and closed to human intervention. God has chosen to leave room for human creativity, empowering us to shape the world through our developing understanding. To be sure, the limitations and ambiguity of our human potential are ever more apparent in our technological era. As already noted, we humans build hospitals and concentration camps.[32] Two world wars, with poison gases in the trenches and whole cities destroyed by conventional and nuclear bombs, have vividly reminded us of the foolishness of putting all our trust in ourselves. Our freedom is always in need of redemption because of our sinfulness. From that perspective, a relationship with God enhances rather than diminishes human freedom. The community of faith called Church walks in the midst of human history proclaiming that an Infinite Love initiated the process of development in which humans participate. Further, according to the Church, humans are called to transform that process through the freedom with which they have been endowed and by the grace given them by that Fullness of Love called God. Our faith, as an openness to God's constant but nonintrusive closeness, draws us to ask what humanity should and should not be doing, giving direction to our freedom. In that light, a relationship with God does not diminish human freedom but enhances it, enabling it to actualize its deepest potential.

Now the question to ask is, would God create through a process in which humans can choose among a surplus of possibilities for shaping a new future, but then completely predetermine the shape of the Church for all time? It seems unlikely. *Lumen gentium* linked the origins of the Church to the trinitarian activities of creation, incarnation, and ongoing sanctification. *Gaudium et spes* added a complementary frame of reference with its eschatological perspective affirming a certain human autonomy within history. Taking our bearings from the council, and likewise from what was revealed about God in the event of the cross, we are empowered to move beyond the question whether Jesus intended to found the Church, and beyond the presupposition that the Church was completely predetermined as it came from Jesus. If we accept that God chose to create us with a certain autonomy, and freely embraced the vulnerability and defenselessness revealed in the event of the cross, the presumption of predeterminism that has characterized the theology of Church falls away. Given, moreover, the historical evidence for the fact that the Church has continually been developing over the centuries, it appears that God has left room for genuine possibility and surprise in the future of the Church. Surely, if it is to serve and to be credible to the generations of the future, the Church cannot be less open to the risk of creative human freedom than is God.[33]

But what does Jesus teach us? During his ministry, Jesus valued persons whom others considered irrevocably lost. He offered a new future to those who had no worldly reason to hope. His parables daringly proposed that a publican and a Samaritan might have a more genuine relationship with God than some professional religious leaders. He proclaimed a reign of God in which the poor, the empty, and the sorrowful would be filled and laughing. Sharing a meal with him was likened to the celebration at a wedding. He proposed a way of living in which one risked turning the cheek or going the extra mile in order to create new possibilities in our human relationships. On the cross, he lived out what he had proclaimed, loving even his enemies. In the dark night of his vulnerability and defenselessness, he reaffirmed his trust in the saving Love who can overcome the hopelessness stemming from human history.[34] He thereby manifested God's love and compassion, and revealed that God is omnipotent in love rather than simply omnipotent. Such a memory of Jesus must reshape the Church as the Body of Christ for our time. To be true to Jesus, the Church must be a "pro-future" community, open to the risk of new possibilities.

Like the story of creation, the story of the Church includes room for freedom. Yet more can be said. Through Jesus' resurrection, the disciples he had left behind in death came to understand fully who he had always really been. Experiencing his continuing presence, they now lived as a community filled with his kind of hope. Led by the Spirit, they had to decide the ways to proclaim Jesus and the ways to structure the community which enabled that proclamation. Initially thinking they were already living within the chronological end-time, the disciples hoped that Jesus would return in the not-too-distant future. They gradually came to understand that the future to which God opened them through the Easter event was much more complex. Since then, followers of Jesus have come to a deeper understanding of the original intuition that Jesus' death and resurrection had initiated a new creation. For example, we have come to understand that the end-time is really a vast "final time" of immense possibility, within a universe existing billions of years. More importantly, we see that Jesus is truly the paradigmatic new Adam or "new human" whose way of living and dying revealed the way to be fully human in God's image and likeness. The new creation that exploded into reality through the resurrection of Jesus is the fulfillment of God's original intention for creating. It is actualized within history by humans who, in the way of Jesus, have opened themselves to being empowered by self-giving Love, which is to say, by God. To believe in the risen Jesus is to trust that the risk of self-giving love will prevail, in history and beyond. Like Jesus, his disciples, in both the past and the present, trust that the God who is love comes to meet us in the uncontrollable future.

Looking Ahead

"What humanity is," the philosopher Wilhelm Dilthey writes, "only history tells us."[35] Like human life, the life of the catholic or universal Church is lived forward but understood backward. Catholic tradition does not, however, simply involve remembering and preserving the past. The final chapters of Catholic identity are a work in progress, like a book without a final chapter and a back cover. The Church's catholicity includes sweeping spatial and temporal dimensions. It involves an ever-expanding memory, embracing the immense richness of past and present times, places, and cultures, and at the same time an openness to assimilating, and possibly being transformed by, a future history in which God offers a surplus of possibilities. What the Church is, only the entirety of its history will fully reveal.

The Church seeks to pass on the heart of a vision of reality so that it can be lived by new generations, which involves making decisions about what should not be forgotten, and about what is best left behind. In that regard, certain developments are not essential to the catholicity of the Church. We have considered how, in the eleventh century, Gregory VII's *Dictatus Papae* declared that only the pope, and not the emperor or king, had the right to have his foot kissed by all. That feudal practice was rather novel for the community in which Jesus was remembered as washing his disciples' feet. Even in the early decades of the twentieth century, those admitted to a private audience with the pope still knelt to kiss his slipper.[36] Today, that practice has been forgotten. What else may be dropped and forgotten, or be open to change? And what, by contrast, is so essential that it can never be changed? Determining the boundaries confronted by such questions is ever more crucial for the Church of our time. In that regard, genuine Catholicism cannot absolutize any particular moment, even though it is incarnated in and cannot live outside of any and every historical and cultural moment.

The beginning of the third millennium is a time in which some think of themselves as being "after" so many things, rather than "before." In our so-called postmodern era, many experience the absence of God more than God's presence. Yet, as herald of a new creation, the community called Church must resist the temptation to turn its gaze inward, within its own walls, or over its shoulder to the past. Succumbing would represent a loss of nerve in its mission of service to all times and places. A prophetic memory is aware that the past has never been perfect. To proclaim the good news of hope, the Church must ever nurture a critical openness to the future. In the words of Pope John XXIII at the opening of Vatican II: "Divine Providence is leading us to a new order of human relations."[37] So we can hope.

The God who shared our struggle of freedom in and through Jesus of Nazareth is best proclaimed by a Church that truly shares the human struggle in history with a compassion that risks vulnerability and defenselessness just as God did. As precursor of God's present and "not yet" reign, the Church certainly has to remember the past, but it likewise has to invite humans to look ahead to a new future, both within history and beyond history. It has to focus both on what has been done and on what might yet emerge. As the pilgrim people of God, the Church is called to nurture hope by its own openness to new possibilities. Such an eschatological perspective is not without implications for the issues being debated in the Church of today. For a Church made ever young by the Spirit, this can be a time of new beginnings and not simply of ending. The Church of the future may already be becoming in our midst, even if the institutional Church cannot yet recognize it.

For Catholics, the Petrine function of the bishop of Rome is essential and vital. It would be a mistake, however, to make Vatican I's perspectives into a timeless model for the future, since they were defensively developed in response to a particular historical situation.[38] In Carl J. Peter's words, the teachings of Vatican I and Vatican II have to be accepted "with the proviso that both need to be interpreted to see how they help express the gospel in the situation of the present day."[39] That includes asking *how* the bishop of Rome might best fulfill the Petrine function for unity. The medieval papacy's struggle with the burden of unsought power has left behind a legacy focused on fullness of power *(plenitudo potestatis)* and on full and supreme jurisdiction *(plena et suprema jurisdictio)*, giving rise to an ever-increasing centralization of decision making. There is, however, reason to ask whether such an emphasis is required by the essential nature of the Church called Catholic.[40] In our pluralist and changing world, arguably, there is a profound need for the successor of Peter to serve as a center of unity—as both a watchman and sentinel for genuine unity in faith, and yet a protector of legitimate diversity.[41] Our moment in history calls for a Petrine service that is effective because it is authoritative and convincing in a dialogical manner.

Further, it is worth asking how Roman primacy should be exercised in this day and age of telecommunications and electronic mail, where the "near" has lost much of its distance from the "far," or to put it another way the "local" (as in "local church") has had its bounds massively expanded. On the first Pentecost, Peter is described standing with the Eleven as he proclaimed the risen Jesus to persons of many cultures and languages. Arguably, Rome's tendency to appoint like-minded bishops supportive of all its positions might not best serve the future of the Church. The unity of the catholic or universal Church, spread throughout the world and across time, is sustained both by papal leadership *and* by the leadership initiatives arising from the oversight *(episkopē)* of bishops serving diverse communities in different cultures. It is instructive that Irenaeus, the first to stress Rome's position of leadership and authority, who insisted that "every Church, that is the faithful everywhere, has to agree with the Church at Rome, since in her the faithful from all parts of the world have preserved the faith tradition coming from the apostles" (*Against Heresies* 3.3.2), later sent a letter chiding Victor of Rome for threatening to break communion with the churches of Asia Minor over a dispute about the day on which Easter was to be celebrated. Surely, there is a need for committed and courageous bishops like Irenaeus in every time. "What the Church needs today, as always, are not adulators to extol the status quo, but [persons] whose humility and obedience are no less than their passion for truth." The Church benefits from "that obedience which is forthright truthfulness and which is animated by the persistent power of love."[42]

Psalm 104:30 prayerfully acknowledges that God's Spirit is sent forth to renew the face of the land. If we listen closely, we can hear perhaps that Spirit, sent by the risen Jesus to dwell in our midst, likewise calling the "Unfinished Church" to newness, to be made young again on its ongoing pilgrimage.

Epilogue: A Future for Women in the Church?

Vatican II's Constitution on the Church in the Modern World notes that women are presently involved in just about all spheres of life and says that it is fitting that they assume their proper role (section 60). One might ask what the proper role of women should be within the Church. In asking that question, one must keep in mind how much the role of women has already changed over the course of the Church's history. In the Gospels of Matthew and John, the risen Jesus first appears to women. In the Epistle to the Romans (16:1–2, 6–7), Paul commends Phoebe "the deacon or minister *(diakonos)* of the church of Cenchreae" for being "a benefactor of many." He sends greetings to Mary "who has worked very hard among you [at Rome]," and refers to Junia (or Julia) as "prominent among the apostles." Unfortunately, under the influence of the prevalent culture, women were eventually excluded from any active ministerial role in the Church and relegated to the home or the cloister. There were always, however, women who broke through such barriers.

A renewed effort to enable women to dedicate their lives to God through active service within society emerged during the sixteenth century. In 1535, Angela Merici brought together a "company" of women, under the patronage of St. Ursula, to work for the revitalization of family life in their native Brescia. They intended to live under a rule that "was the first in the Western Church drawn up for women by a woman," with no habit, no cloister, and a private vow of chastity.[1] But the bishops under whom they worked had different ideas. A simple habit was required by the bishop of Brescia in 1546. After their spread to Milan, further conditions were imposed by Cardinal Charles

Borromeo. Thereafter, the women went out only with permission, and no longer taught in homes but only within the community. The most extreme modifications came during the "company's" spread into France, where Angela's group of apostolic women living and working in the family circle was finally transformed into the cloistered nuns known as the Ursulines. The expectations of the time—that women should be either married or cloistered, but certainly not "freelance charitable workers"—eventually prevailed.

In 1610, Francis de Sales, as bishop of Geneva, founded a community of women with simple vows living in a flexible cloister, which would allow the "daughters of the Visitation" the freedom to do external works of charity for the needy. But since visiting the sick and teaching children, particularly boys, were not considered suitable tasks for consecrated virgins, they, too, were eventually forced into a totally cloistered life. To avoid a similar fate for his Daughters of Charity, begun in 1633, Vincent de Paul insisted that they were not "religious" or a "congregation." They would have no "grille" or enclosure, but only regulations about contact on the streets. Making private vows, they wore no religious garb or veil, but adopted the ordinary gray serge dress worn by young women in the area around Paris. Instead of having a chaplain, they prayed and confessed in their local parish. When their private rule was officially approved by the Archbishop of Paris in 1646, the matter of clerical supervision was specifically spelled out for the future. But the Daughters of Charity managed to escape the cloister and soon added the ministry of teaching to their care of the sick.[2]

Mary Ward had earlier founded the Institute of the English Ladies at St. Omer, in France, with the bold idea of establishing schools for girls, the way the Jesuits had for boys.[3] Rather than using a rule approved for nuns, her community adapted the rule of the Jesuits in 1611 and wore the ordinary dress of the time. Although the bishop of St. Omer defended them, many others expressed outrage and shock. A group of English clerics complained to Pope Gregory XV, arguing that women had never undertaken an apostolic office in the Church and that the present was no time to begin. Stereotyping the female sex as "soft, flexible, slippery, inconstant, erroneous, always grasping for novelties, and subject to a thousand dangers," the clerics concluded that women should not be living outside a cloister.[4]

Having already requested Rome's approval, Ward personally presented her case there in 1621 and 1624, asking for the papal recognition that would prevent the interference of bishops, an innovation never previously considered for women. Rome's approval never came because the Ladies would not give up their apostolate and stay in their convents to pray, and because they refused to wear a habit. After founding new institutes in Italy, Ward did the same in Munich until three clerics from the Holy Office arrived there and imprisoned her in a convent. She was freed through the intervention of Pope Urban VIII, but the opposition prevailed and her Institute was officially suppressed in 1631. It survived only in Munich and, remarkably, in Rome, where it continued under the personal invitation of the pope.

Although Ward's initiatives were ahead of her time and were thus considered too revolutionary, they ultimately contributed to the gradual recognition (in papal documents dated 1706, 1749, 1889, 1900, and 1901)[5] of religious communities known as "sisters." Unlike "nuns," "sisters" would not be cloistered and were thereby free to exercise a public apostolate. The earlier insistence on a permanent enclosure or cloister was reshaped into a plethora of directives imposing a kind of portable cloister. Until Vatican II, in order to obtain recognition as religious, congregations of women usually had to accept the imposition of the religious habit and veil, rules regarding contact with others, and detailed regulations regarding the use of parlors for visitors, the need for sister companions, and the avoidance of contact with strangers via "custody of the eyes" on the street. As that epoch passed with Vatican II, women assumed more significant roles in the Church. In our time, religious and "lay" women, with degrees in theology, liturgical studies, pastoral ministry, and religious education, are making enormous contributions in service to the Church.

Some women have begun to press for an even more significant ministerial role in the Church. As documented in the commentary issued with the promulgation of the Congregation for the Doctrine of Faith's Declaration concerning the Question of the Admission of Women to the Ministerial Priesthood, the initiatives to ordain women are fairly recent.[6] The first appointment of women as pastors took place in 1958, in the Swedish Lutheran Church. The first ordinations of women to the priesthood took place in 1970 and 1974 in the Episcopal Church. In response, in 1976 the Congregation for the Doctrine of Faith declared that women cannot be ordained to the priesthood.[7] Pope John Paul II reaffirmed that position in 1994 in his apostolic letter *Priestly Ordination*, which stated that the Catholic Church does not have the authority or faculty (power) to ordain women.[8]

How did the Congregation for the Doctrine of Faith and the pope arrive at their conclusion? Vatican II taught that the bishops dispersed throughout the world can teach infallibly when, in communion with one another, they unanimously concur that a particular teaching on a matter of faith or morals must be held conclusively (*Lumen gentium* 25). Invoking that text, the Congregation for the Doctrine of the Faith, in 1995, declared infallible the teaching that women cannot be ordained; this teaching is a matter of faith, and the Congregation asserted that it has always been the ordinary, constant, and definitive teaching of all bishops through the world. The Congregation further concluded that Pope John Paul II's letter *Priestly Ordination* had confirmed, or handed on, this same teaching by a formal declaration, thereby making explicit what is always and everywhere to be held by all as belonging to the deposit of faith.[9]

It should, however, be noted that the Congregation's declaration is itself noninfallible,[10] and was proclaimed without prior consultation to verify whether that is the de facto position of all bishops serving today. These are the crucial issues that are still being debated and questioned by theologians studying the Vatican's statements, and more discussion is likely to develop in the years ahead. The perspectives developed in this book suggest that a crucial element of that ongoing discussion should be an eschatological view of the Church open to the possibilities of a new future. Vatican II's Decree on Ecumenism declares that the Church is perennially in need of reform (section 6). The question that remains is whether reform also makes room for the possibility of something "new." One might recall the words of Isaiah 43:18–19:

> Do not remember the former things,
> or consider the things of old.
> I am about to do a new thing;
> now it springs forth, do you not perceive it?

Notes

Introduction

1. "Virtute Evangelii iuvenescere facit Ecclesiam eamque perpetuo renovat...." *Lumen gentium*, section 4. Latin text in *Decrees of the Ecumenical Councils*, vol. 2, *Trent to Vatican II*, ed. Norman P. Tanner (London: Sheed & Ward, and Washington, D.C.: Georgetown University Press, 1990), p. 851. Translation here is mine.

2. English text in *Documents of Vatican II*, eds. Walter M. Abbott and J. Gallagher (New York: Herder and Herder/Association Press, 1966), pp. 710–19, cited text from 712–13.

3. Unless otherwise noted, biblical passages are cited from *The Holy Bible*, New Revised Standard Version, with the Apocryphal/ Deuterocanonical Books (New York/Oxford: Oxford University Press, 1989).

4. Hans-Georg Gadamer, *Truth and Method*, second revised edition, tr. Joel Weinsheimer and Donald G. Marshall (New York: Crossroad, 1992), p. 304.

5. *Gaudium et spes*, sections 36, 41, and 56.

6. Walter Kasper, *Theology and Church*, tr. Margaret Kohl (New York: Crossroad, 1989), pp. 55 and 33.

7. Dermot Lane, *Keeping Hope Alive: Stirrings in Christian Theology* (New York/Mahwah, NJ: Paulist Press, 1996), p. 13.

8. I am here applying Hans-Georg Gadamer's notion of the positive function of "prejudice," in the sense of prejudgment within a living tradition, which is always in a process of reconstitution: *Truth and Method*, pp. 270–77. See also Richard J. Bernstein, *Beyond Objectivism and Relativism: Science, Hermeneutics, and Praxis* (Philadelphia: University of Pennsylvania Press, 1983), pp. 127–31.

9. *Ut unum sint*, Encyclical Letter on Commitment to Ecumenism, John Paul II (Vatican City: Libreria Editrice Vaticana, 1995).

Chapter 1

1. See Karl Rahner, *Foundations of Christian Faith*, tr. William V. Dych (New York: Seabury–Crossroad Book, 1978), pp. 126–37, 178–227; "On the Theology of the Incarnation," *Theological Investigations*, vol. 4, *More Recent Writings*, tr. Kevin Smyth (London:

Darton, Longman and Todd; Baltimore: Helicon, 1966), pp. 87–117; "Jesus Christ," *Sacramentum Mundi* 3 (New York: Herder & Herder, 1969), p. 207–8; *The Trinity* (New York: Herder & Herder, 1970), pp. 34–40, 82–103.

2. See Walter Kasper, *The God of Jesus Christ*, tr. Matthew J. O'Connell (New York: Crossroad, 1986), pp. 194–97; Edward Schillebeeckx, *Church: The Human Story of God*, tr. John Bowden (New York: Crossroad, 1990), pp. 121–31.

3. See Vatican II's Constitution on Divine Revelation *(Dei verbum)*, section 2; Kasper, *God of Jesus Christ*, pp. 315–16.

4. See Edward Schillebeeckx, *The Understanding of Faith* (New York: Seabury, 1974), pp. 3–5, 95–100; *Christ: The Experience of Jesus as Lord*, tr. John Bowden (New York: Crossroad, 1981), pp. 669–70; Kasper, *God of Jesus Christ*, pp. 98–109.

5. Gabriel Daly, *Creation and Redemption* (Wilmington, DE: Michael Glazier, 1989), pp. 208–13.

6. Abraham J. Heschel, *God in Search of Man: A Philosophy of Judaism* (New York: Farrar, Straus & Cudahy, 1955), p. 377.

7. *Against the Heresies* 4.37.4; 4.38.1–2; 4.39.1–2; *Proof of the Apostolic Preaching* 12.

8. Augustine, *Confessions* 1.1; Abraham J. Heschel, *Who Is Man?* (Stanford, CA: Stanford University, 1965), pp. 72–74; Rahner, *Foundations of Christian Faith*, p. 32; Schillebeeckx, *Understanding of Faith*, pp. 95–100; Kasper, *God of Jesus Christ*, pp. 79–87.

9. Mircea Eliade, *The Sacred and the Profane: The Nature of Religion* (New York: Harcourt, Brace & World, 1959), pp. 201–13; Michael H. Barnes, *In the Presence of Mystery: An Introduction to the Story of Human Religiousness*, rev. ed. (Mystic, CT: Twenty-Third Publications, 1990), pp. 29–44, 70–88.

10. Edward Schillebeeckx, *Interim Report on the Books Jesus and Christ*, tr. John Bowden (New York: Crossroad, 1981), pp. 3–9; *Jesus: An Experiment in Christology*, tr. Hubert Hoskins (New York: Seabury Press–Crossroad Book, 1979), pp. 44 and 71–85; *Christ*, pp. 813–14.

11. Schillebeeckx, *Jesus*, pp. 57 and 112–14; *Interim Report*, pp. 11–19.

12. Schillebeeckx, *Jesus*, pp. 577–79; *Christ*, p. 38; *Interim Report*, pp. 3–4, 18–19.

13. Sandra M. Schneiders, "From Exegesis to Hermeneutics: The Problem of the Contemporary Meaning of Scripture," *Horizons* 8 (1981), p. 72; "The Paschal Imagination: Objectivity and Subjectivity in New Testament Interpretation," *Theological Studies* 43 (1982), pp. 57 and 62;

Gadamer, *Truth and Method*, pp. 362–438; Schillebeeckx, *Christ*, pp. 36 and 76.

14. Rahner, *Foundations*, pp. 101–2.

15. See Paul Ricoeur, *The Conflict of Interpretations: Essays in Hermeneutics* (Evanston: Northwestern University Press, 1974), pp. 12–13; "The Hermeneutics of Symbols and Philosophical Reflection," in *The Philosophy of Paul Ricoeur: An Anthology of His Work*, eds. Charles E. Reagan and David Stewart (Boston: Beacon Press, 1978), pp. 36–58.

16. John Bowker, *The Sense of God* (London: Oxford University Press, 1973), pp. 66–85, 114–15; Eliade, *The Sacred and the Profane*, pp. 179–201.

17. R. S. Solecki, "Shanidar Cave: A Paleolithic Site in Northern Iraq," *Annual Report of the Smithsonian* (1954), pp. 389–425; "Three Adult Skeletons from Shanidar Cave," *Annual Report of the Smithsonian* (1959), pp. 603–35; T. D. Stewart, "Restoration and Study of the Shanidar I Neanderthal Skeleton in Bagdad, Iraq," *Year Book of the American Philosophical Society* (1958), pp. 274–78.

18. Schillebeeckx, *Christ*, pp. 30–64; Thomas F. O'Meara, "A History of Grace," in *A World of Grace*, ed. Leo J. O'Donovan (New York: Crossroad, 1981), pp. 76–90.

19. Raymond E. Brown, "'And the Lord Said'? Biblical Reflections on Scripture as the Word of God," *Theological Studies* 42 (1981), pp. 3–19.

20. See Richard Kearney, "Religion and Ideology: Paul Ricoeur's Hermeneutic Conflict," *Irish Theological Quarterly* 52 (1986), pp. 109–26; Mary Barbara Agnew, "Liturgy and Christian Social Action," *Liturgy* 7 (1984), pp. 18–19.

21. 1 QS 2:19–25; 9:7; CD 14:3–12; Flavius Josephus, *Jewish Wars* 2, 8, 129–32; *Antiquities* 18, 1, 19–22; Philo, *Quod omnis probus vir sit* 86; *Apologia pro Judaeis* 11, 5, and 11; J. T. Milik, *Ten Years of Discovery in the Wilderness of Judaea* (Naperville, IL: Alec Allenson, 1959), p. 105; James D. G. Dunn, "Jesus, Table-Fellowship, and Qumran," in *Jesus and the Dead Sea Scrolls*, ed. James H. Charlesworth (New York: Doubleday, 1992), pp. 254–72.

22. Schillebeeckx, *Jesus*, pp. 200–18; N. T. Wright, *Christian Origins and the Question of God*, vol. 2, *Jesus and the Victory of God*, Anchor Bible Reference Library (Minneapolis: Fortress Press, 1992), pp. 149–50.

23. Wright, *Jesus and the Victory of God*, p. 104; see also Gerhard Lohfink, *Jesus and Community: The Social Dimension of Christian Faith*, tr.

John P. Galvin (Philadelphia: Fortress; New York/Ramsey, NJ: Paulist Press, 1984), pp. 26–29.

24. Wright, *Jesus and the Victory of God*, p. 172.

25. Schillebeeckx, *Jesus*, p. 160; Etienne Trocme, *Jesus as Seen by His Contemporaries* (Philadelphia: Westminster, 1973), pp. 90–91.

26. Wright, *Jesus and the Victory of God*, p. 182.

27. Eugene A. LaVerdiere and William G. Thompson, "New Testament Communities in Transition: A Study of Matthew and Luke," *Theological Studies* 37 (1976), pp. 571–77.

28. Mark 3:31–35; Matt 12:46–50; Luke 8:19–21.

29. Wright, *Jesus and the Victory of God*, p. 276.

30. 1 QS 5:5–7, 8:4–10, 9:3–6; CD 3:18—4:10; Bertil Gärtner, *The Temple and the Community in Qumran and the New Testament* (Cambridge: Cambridge University Press, 1965), pp. 16–46; L. Gaston, *No Stone on Another* (Leiden: E. J. Brill, 1970), pp. 151–54, 163–79; Joseph A. Fitzmyer, "Qumran and the Interpolated Paragraph in 2 Cor 6, 14—7,1," *Catholic Biblical Quarterly* 23 (1961), pp. 271–80; Donald Juel, *Messiah and Temple*, SBL Dissertation Series 31 (Missoula, MT: Scholars Press, 1977), pp. 160–63; G. Klinzing, *Die Umdeutung des Kultus in der Qumrangemeinde und im Neuen Testament* (Göttingen: Vandenhoeck and Ruprecht, 1971), pp. 51–68.

31. Cf. Matt 9:17; Luke 5:37–39. See C. H. Dodd, *The Interpretation of the Fourth Gospel* (Cambridge: Cambridge University Press, 1953, reprinted 1968), p. 298; George Brooke, "The Feast of New Wine and the Question of Fasting," *The Expository Times* 95 (1984), pp. 175–76; Wright, *Jesus and the Victory of God*, p. 433; John P. Meier, *A Marginal Jew: Rethinking the Historical Jesus*, vol. 2, *Mentor, Message and Miracles* (New York: Doubleday, 1994), p. 494 n. 182.

32. Raymond E. Brown, *The Gospel According to John*, *The Anchor Bible* 29 (Garden City, NY: Doubleday, 1966), pp. 124–25; Dodd, *Interpretation of the Fourth Gospel*, pp. 301–3; Juel, *Messiah and Temple*, pp. 156 and 139; Eduard Lohse, "xeirōpoíētos," *Theological Dictionary of the New Testament* IX (Grand Rapids, MI: Eerdmans, 1974), p. 436; Vincent Taylor, *The Gospel According to St. Mark* (London: Macmillan, 1963), p. 566.

33. Wright, *Jesus and the Victory of God*, p. 434.

34. Schillebeeckx, *Jesus*, p. 245.

35. Dodd, *Interpretation of the Fourth Gospel*, pp. 297–303; Meier, *A Marginal Jew*, vol. 2, pp. 942–46.

36. Gerhard Lohfink, "Das Weinwunder zu Kana. Eine Auslegung von Joh 2, 1–12," *Geist und Leben* 57 (1984), pp. 169–82; "The Miracle at Cana," *Theology Digest* 32 (1985), pp. 243–246.

37. Lohfink, *Jesus and Community*, p. 29.

38. See sections 6–10. English translation by Joseph A. Fitzmyer in "The Biblical Commission's Instruction on the Historical Truth of the Gospels," *Theological Studies* 25 (September 1964), pp. 404–6; also in *A Christological Catechism: New Testament Answers, New Revised and Expanded Edition* (New York/Mahwah, NJ: Paulist Press, 1991), pp. 153–59.

39. *Decrees of the Ecumenical Councils*, vol. 2, p. 978.

40. Schillebeeckx, *Jesus*, pp. 180–92; Wright, *Jesus and the Victory of God*, pp. 191–96.

41. See Kasper, *Jesus the Christ*, tr. V. Green (New York: Paulist Press, 1977), pp. 118 and 121; Schillebeeckx, *Jesus*, p. 317; David M. Stanley, *Jesus in Gethsemane: The Early Church Reflects on the Suffering of Jesus* (New York/Ramsey, NJ: Paulist Press, 1980), p. 274.

42. Wolfhart Pannenberg, *Jesus—God and Man*, tr. Lewis L. Wilkins and Duane A. Priebe, second edition (Philadelphia: Westminster, 1977), pp. 136 and 362–3; Schillebeeckx, *Jesus*, pp. 72–74.

43. See Bernard P. Prusak, "Bodily Resurrection in Catholic Perspectives," *Theological Studies* 61 (2000), pp. 99–105.

44. Raymond E. Brown, *An Introduction to New Testament Christology* (New York/Mahwah, NJ: Paulist Press, 1994), pp. 57–58; Meier, *A Marginal Jew*, vol. 2, pp. 336–39 and 350–51.

45. Kasper, *Jesus the Christ*, pp. 107–8; Gerald O'Collins, *Interpreting Jesus* (Ramsey, NJ: Paulist Press, 1983), pp. 61–65; Schillebeeckx, *Jesus*, pp. 467–72; Stanley, *Jesus in Gethsemane*, p. 36.

46. *Jesus*, pp. 506–7.

47. Mark 10:47–48; Matt 9:27, 20:30–31; Luke 18:38–39.

48. See Raymond E. Brown, Karl P. Donfried, and John Reumann, eds., *Peter in the New Testament* (Minneapolis, MN: Augsburg, and New York: Paulist Press, 1973), pp. 65–69, 159–60; Fitzmyer, *A Christological Catechism*, pp. 62–66 and 103–4; Kasper, *Jesus the Christ*, pp. 106, 114–15; Schillebeeckx, *Jesus*, pp. 193, 297–98, 322–23, 505; Stanley, *Jesus in Gethsemane*, p. 37.

49. Brown et al., *Peter in the New Testament*, pp. 83–107; Fitzmyer, *A Christological Catechism*, pp. 64–66.

50. Ioachim Salaverri, *De Ecclesia Christi*, in *Sacrae Theologiae Summa*, vol. 1, ed. Patres Societatis Jesu (Madrid: Biblioteca de Autores Cristianos, 1958, 4th edition), pp. 515–615.

51. See Timotheus Zapelena, *De Ecclesia Christi: Pars Apologetica* (Rome: Gregorian University, 1955, 6th edition), pp. 196–313.

52. *The Churches the Apostles Left Behind* (New York: Paulist Press, 1984), pp. 105–6.

53. *Summa Theologiae* 3, q. 9, a. 1–4.

54. *Summa* 3, q. 10, a. 2, resp.; cited from the translation by Fathers of the English Dominican Province, *Summa Theologica*, vol. 2 (New York: Benziger Brothers, 1947), p. 2087.

55. *Summa* 3, q. 15, a. 8, resp.

56. English Dominican Province, *Summa Theologica*, vol. 2, p. 2278.

57. International Theological Commission, "Select Questions on Christology," section III, D, 6–6.1; cf. II, C, 7 (Washington, DC: United States Catholic Conference, 1980); Latin text in *Gregorianum* 61 (1980), pp. 609–32. The statement is also found in *International Theological Commission: Texts and Documents* 1969–1985, ed. Michael Sharkey (San Francisco: Ignatius Press, 1989), pp. 185–205.

58. See Kasper, *Jesus the Christ*, pp. 114–21; Hans Küng, *On Being a Christian* (Garden City, NY: Doubleday, 1976), pp. 320–24; O'Collins, *Interpreting Jesus*, pp. 79–92 and *Christology: A Biblical, Historical and Systematic Study of Jesus* (Oxford/New York: Oxford University Press, 1995), pp. 71–72; Schillebeeckx, *Jesus*, pp. 297–98; John P. Galvin, "Jesus' Approach to Death: An Examination of Some Recent Studies," *Theological Studies* 41 (1980), pp. 713–44.

59. O'Collins, *Interpreting Jesus*, p. 186.

60. Schillebeeckx, *Jesus*, p. 306.

61. Kasper, *Jesus the Christ*, pp. 120–21; O'Collins, *Interpreting Jesus*, pp. 193–95; Pannenberg, *Jesus—God and Man*, pp. 224 and 354–64; Schillebeeckx, *Christ*, p. 823; cf. *Jesus*, p. 600.

62. See Karl Rahner, "Dogmatic Reflections on the Knowledge and Self-Consciousness of Christ," *Theological Investigations*, vol. 5, tr. Karl-H. Kruger (London: Darton, Longman and Todd; Baltimore: Helicon, 1966), pp. 193–215; Bernard Lonergan, *De Verbo Incarnato*, second edition (Rome: Pontifical Gregorian University, 1961), pp. 269–312; 333–62; Elizabeth Johnson, *Consider Jesus* (New York: Crossroad, 1991), pp. 35–47.

63. Schillebeeckx, *Church: The Human Story of God*, p. 118.

64. Schillebeeckx, *Jesus*, p. 666.

65. *Summa theologiae* 3, q. 9, a. 2 and q. 10, a. 4.

66. *The Knowledge of Christ* (London/New York: Continuum, 1999), p. 124; for the text of the statement, see *International Theological Commission: Texts and Documents* 1969–1985, pp. 305–16.

67. See Schillebeeckx, *Jesus*, pp. 256–71; Rahner, "Dogmatic Reflections on the Knowledge and Self-Consciousness of Christ," p. 215; Raymond E. Brown "Moving All Christians to Think," in *The Critical Meaning of the Bible* (New York: Paulist Press, 1981), p. 87 n. 8.; also in *Origins*, p. 10 n. 47 (May 7, 1981), p. 743. As Brown observes, "Many of the most respected Catholic theologians today, including Rahner, Ratzinger, Lonergan, and von Balthasaar, have reinterpreted the theory of Jesus' beatific vision without producing any indication of ecclesiastical disapproval." O'Collins embraces Rahner's position and approvingly quotes Brown: *Interpreting Jesus*, pp. 184–85 and 199 n. 5; also see his *Christology*, pp. 235–37, 240–41, 247–49, and 254–62; Moloney, *The Knowledge of Christ*, pp. 82–138.

68. See Raymond E. Brown, "*Episkopē* and *Episkopos:* The New Testament Evidence," *Theological Studies* 41 (1980), pp. 323–24 and n. 4.

69. See Kasper, *Jesus the Christ*, pp. 117–18; O'Collins, *Interpreting Jesus*, pp. 88–91; Schillebeeckx, *Jesus*, pp. 306–12.

70. "Select Questions on Christology," section IV, B, 2.1—C, 3.4.

71. O'Collins, *Christology*, p. 81.

72. Kasper, *Jesus the Christ*, p. 158.

73. *Jesus*, p. 355.

74. Wright, *Jesus and the Victory of God*, pp. 172 and 660.

75. Schillebeeckx, *Church: The Human Story of God*, p. 110.

76. Kasper, *Jesus the Christ*, pp. 159 and 120.

77. O'Collins, *Christology*, p. 76.

78. See Kasper, *Jesus the Christ*, pp. 117–18; O'Collins, *Interpreting Jesus*, pp. 88–90 and *Christology*, pp. 72–77; Schillebeeckx, *Jesus*, pp. 307–11 and *Interim Report*, p. 146 n. 28; Ted Schoof, ed., *The Schillebeeckx Case* (New York/Ramsey, NJ: Paulist Press, 1984), pp. 86–89, 128–29; Stanley, *Jesus in Gethsemane*, p. 274, cf. 127.

79. Kasper, *Jesus the Christ*, p. 158.

80. Schillebeeckx, *Jesus*, p. 325.

81. Section 8; text in Fitzmyer, "The Biblical Commission's Instruction," p. 404; *A Christological Catechism*, pp. 156–57.

82. Joseph Ratzinger, *Eschatology: Death and Eternal Life*, tr. Michael Waldstein, tr. ed. Aidan Nichols, *Dogmatic Theology* 9, eds. Johann Auer and J. Ratzinger (Washington, DC: Catholic University of America Press, 1988), p. 102; also see pp. 93 and 217–18.

83. Schillebeeckx, *Christ*, pp. 824–25; also *Jesus*, p. 317: "The Father, however, did not intervene. Nowhere did Jesus see any visible aid come from him whose cause he had so much at heart. As a fact of history it can hardly be denied that Jesus was subject to an inner conflict between his consciousness of his mission and the utter silence of the One whom he was accustomed to call his Father. At least in its hard core the struggle in Gethsemene is not to be cogitated out of existence." Also see Kasper, *Jesus the Christ*, p. 118.

84. International Theological Commission, "Select Questions on Christology," IV, B, 2.2–2.5; O'Collins, *Christology*, pp. 76–77; Pannenberg, *Jesus—God and Man*, pp. 362–63; Schillebeeckx, *Jesus*, p. 638 and *Christ*, pp. 825–29.

85. International Theological Commission, "Select Questions on Christology," IV, C, 3.3—D, 6; Ratzinger, *Eschatology*, p. 100.

86. Kasper, *The God of Jesus Christ*, pp. 194–97.

87. Schillebeeckx, *Christ*, pp. 830 and 728–30; *Church: The Human Story of God*, pp. 120–29.

88. Schillebeeckx, *Christ*, p. 830.

89. Ratzinger, *Eschatology*, p. 97.

90. Schillebeeckx, *Jesus*, pp. 344–45, 354–55, 382–90.

91. Mark 14:66–72; Matt 26:69–75; Luke 22:56–62; John 18:25–27. In Luke, as Schillebeeckx notes, "at a glance from Jesus Peter is 'turned again'" (22:32 and 22:61). Nevertheless even "the man at the top" has his failings: *Jesus*, p. 327.

92. Gerald O'Collins and Daniel Kendall, "Mary Magdalen as Major Witness to Jesus' Resurrection," *Theological Studies* 48 (1987), pp. 631–46.

93. Kasper, *Jesus the Christ*, pp. 137–39, 158–59.

94. "La experiencia del resucitado se sitúa en otro régimen que la visión corporal. Se sitúa en el terreno de la fe." Juan Martín Velasco, *La experiencia cristiana de Dios* (Madrid: Editorial Trotta, 1995), p. 76.

95. Lohfink, *Jesus and Community*, p. 76.

96. Brown, "*Episkopē* and *Episkopos*," pp. 324–25; cf. Schillebeeckx, *Jesus*, p. 350.

97. "How the Priest Should View His Official Ministry," *Theological Investigations*, vol. 14 (New York: Seabury, 1976), p. 207.

98. "Teaching and canons on the most holy sacrifice of the mass" (Session 22, September 17, 1562), chapter 1 and canon 2, *Decrees of the Ecumenical Councils*, vol. 2, pp. 733 and 735. See also "The true and catholic doctrine of the sacrament of order, to combat the errors of our

time" (Session 23, July 15, 1563), chapter 1 and canon 1, *Decrees of the Ecumenical Councils*, vol. 2, pp. 742 and 743.

99. Maurice Vidal, "Ministère et ordination," in Jean Delorme, ed., *Le ministère et les ministères selon le Nouveau Testament* (Paris: Éditions du Seuill, 1974), p. 484; see also Raymond E. Brown, *Priest and Bishop: Biblical Reflections* (New York: Paulist Press, 1970), pp. 40–43; Fitzmyer, *A Christological Catechism*, pp. 75–76; Edward Schillebeeckx, *The Church with a Human Face* (New York: Crossroad, 1985), pp. 40–73.

100. The principal focus for such perspectives was Robert Bellarmine's definition of Church as a visible community, comparable to the kingdom of France or the republic of Venice: *De controversiis Christianae fidei adversus nostri temporis haereticos*, vol. 2: *Prima Controversia generalis*, book 3: *De Ecclesia militante*, chapter 2: "*de definitione Ecclesiae*" (Ingolstadt, 1601 edition), cols. 137–38.

101. Alfred Loisy, *The Gospel and the Church*, tr. Christopher Hume (Philadelphia: Fortress, 1976 reprint), p. 166.

102. Ibid.; also see pp. 165–69 and 147–51. Loisy was responding to Adolf von Harnack's *Das Wesen des Christentums* (1900, translated as *What Is Christianity?*) (New York: Harper & Row, 1957).

103. *The Gospel and the Church*, p. 171.

104. *Enchiridion symbolorum definitionum et declarationum de rebus fidei et morum*, ed. H. Denzinger, rev. P. Hünermann, 38th edition (Freiburg: Herder, 1999), no. 3452 (hereafter cited as DH); cf. Loisy's *The Gospel and the Church*, pp. 146–48 and 165–67.

105. "The Provenance of the Church in the History of Salvation from the Death and Resurrection of Jesus," in Karl Rahner and Wilhelm Thüsing, *A New Christology*, tr. David Smith and Verdant Green (New York: Seabury, 1980), p. 21.

106. "Aspects of the Episcopal Office," *Theological Investigations*, vol. 14 (New York: Seabury, 1976), p. 187.

107. Kasper, *Jesus the Christ*, p. 158.

108. Lohfink, *Jesus and Community*, p. 76.

109. Donald Senior, *Jesus: A Gospel Portrait*, revised and expanded edition (New York/Mahwah, NJ: Paulist Press, 1992), pp. 143–46.

110. See the commentary on section 20 by Karl Rahner in *Commentary on the Documents of Vatican II*, vol. 1, ed. Herbert Vorgrimler (New York: Herder & Herder, 1967), pp. 190–92.

111. Walter Kasper, *Theology and Church*, p. 158.

112. *The Gospel and the Church*, p. 166.

113. Wright, *Jesus and the Victory of God*, p. 660.

114. Francis Schüssler Fiorenza, *Foundational Theology—Jesus and the Church* (New York: Crossroad, 1984), pp. 156–73.

115. Ibid., p. 171, also 163.

116. Rahner, "Provenance of the Church," pp. 26–27.

117. Gerhard Lohfink, "Hat Jesus eine Kirche gestiftet?" *Theologische Quartalschrift* 161 (1981), pp. 92–93; "Did Jesus Found a Church?" *Theology Digest* 30 (1982), p. 234.

118. *The Community of the Beloved Disciple* (New York: Paulist Press, 1979), pp. 84–88; *The Churches the Apostles Left Behind*, pp. 84–94, 104–9.

119. Brown, *The Churches the Apostles Left Behind*, p. 108.

120. See Leonardo Boff, *Die Kirche als Sakrament im Horizont der Welterfahrung* (Paderborn: Verlag Bonifacius-Drukerei, 1972); Kasper, *Theology and Church*, pp. 113–14 and 217, notes 7–9.

121. *Catholicism: A Study of Dogma in Relation to the Corporate Destiny of Mankind*, from 4th French ed. (New York: Longmans, Green & Co., 1950), p. 29; *The Splendour of the Church (Méditation sur l'Église)*, from 2nd French ed. (New York: Sheed & Ward, 1956), p. 147.

122. See Karl Rahner, *The Church and the Sacraments* (New York: Herder and Herder, 1963), pp. 11–24; Edward Schillebeeckx, *Christ the Sacrament of the Encounter with God* (New York: Sheed & Ward, 1963), pp. 13–63; Otto Semmelroth, *Die Kirche als Ursakrament* (Frankfurt: J. Knecht, 1953, 3rd ed. 1963).

123. Walter Kasper and Gerhard Sauter, *Kirche-Ort des Geistes* (Freiburg: Herder, 1976), pp. 38–43; Leonardo Boff, *Church: Charism and Power—Liberation Theology and the Institutional Church* (New York: Crossroad, 1985), pp. 144–53; Joseph Ratzinger, "Kirche, III. Systematisch," *Lexikon fur Theologie und Kirche* (Freiburg: Herder, 1961), vol. 6:174–77, and *Das neue Volk Gottes; Entwürfe zur Ekklesiologie* (Düsseldorf: Patmos, 1969), pp. 75–89.

124. *Ecclesiogenesis: The Base Communities Reinvent the Church* (Maryknoll, NY: Orbis, 1986), p. 58; *Church: Charism and Power*, p. 146.

125. *Church: Charism and Power*, pp. 146–50.

126. Ibid., p. 152.

127. Ibid., p. 147.

128. Karl Rahner, "The Theology of the Symbol," in *Theological Investigations*, vol. 4, p. 239, and "On the Theology of the Incarnation," *Theological Investigations*, vol. 4, pp. 112–19.

129. See Kenan B. Osborne, *Sacramental Theology: A General Introduction* (New York/Mahwah, NJ: Paulist Press, 1988), pp. 35–36 and 40.

130. Henri de Lubac, *Catholicism*, p. 154.

131. See *Gaudium et spes* 45.

132. Rhabanus Maurus (died 856), *De Universo* 22.3: "omnis gens secundum suam patriam in Ecclesia psallit auctori" (*Patrologia Latina* 111, 598).

133. de Lubac, *Catholicism*, pp. 153–54.

Chapter 2

1. See Jacques Dupont, "The First Christian Pentecost," in *The Salvation of the Gentiles: Studies in the Acts of the Apostles* (New York/Ramsey, NJ: Paulist Press, 1979), pp. 56–59.

2. Church in English and *Kirche* in German come from the later Greek *kyriakos* or Lord's (house). The Romance and Celtic languages draw upon the Latin word *ecclesia*, which was simply a transliteration of *ekkl¯esia*, meaning the "assembly" or community of believers. Regarding *ekkl¯esia* in the scriptures, see John P. Meier, "Antioch," in Raymond E. Brown and John P. Meier, *Antioch and Rome: New Testament Cradles of Catholic Christianity* (New York/Ramsey, NJ: Paulist Press, 1983), p. 66; K. L. Schmidt, "*ekklēsia*," *Theological Dictionary of the New Testament*, ed. Gerhard Kittel (Grand Rapids, MI: Wm. B. Eerdmans, 1965), vol. 3, pp. 501–36.

3. See Joseph Cardinal Ratzinger, *Called to Communion: Understanding the Church Today*, tr. Adrian Walker (San Francisco: Ignatius, 1996), pp. 56–60; Ben F. Meyer, *The Aims of Jesus* (London: SCM Press, 1979), pp. 185–97.

4. See John P. Meier, *A Marginal Jew: Rethinking the Historical Jesus*, vol. 3, *Companions and Competitors* (New York: Doubleday, 2001), pp. 228–38; Rudolph Pesch, "The Position and Significance of Peter in the Church of the New Testament," in *Papal Ministry in the Church*, ed. Hans Küng, *Concilium*, vol. 64 (New York: Herder & Herder, 1971), pp. 26–29; J. Blank, "The Person and Office of Peter in the New Testament," in *Truth and Certainty*, eds. Edward Schillebeeckx and Bas van Iersel, *Concilium*, vol. 83 (New York: Herder & Herder, 1973), pp. 42–55; Brown et al., *Peter in the New Testament*, pp. 84–93; Daniel J. Harrington, *God's People in Christ: New Testament Perspectives on the Church and Judaism* (Philadelphia: Fortress, 1980), pp. 29–30; J. M. R. Tillard, *The Bishop of Rome* (Wilmington, DE: Michael Glazier, 1983), p. 108; Meier, "Antioch," pp. 63–72; Fiorenza, *Foundational Theology*, pp. 87–90; Leonardo Boff, *Ecclesiogenesis*, pp. 52–53; Frederick J. Cwiekowski, *The Beginnings of the Church* (New York/Mahwah, NJ: Paulist Press, 1988), pp. 154–59; and Simon Légasse, "L'Évangile selon Matthieu," in J. Delorme, ed., *Le ministère et les ministères…*, p. 198, regarding Qumran and Matt 18.

5. See Fiorenza, *Foundational Theology*, pp. 141–42.

6. See Wayne A. Meeks, *The First Urban Christians: The Social World of the Apostle Paul* (New Haven: Yale University Press, 1983), p. 80; Fiorenza, *Foundational Theology*, pp. 126 and 185 n. 219; K. L. Schmidt, "*ekklēsia*," pp. 513–18; Raymond E. Brown, "The New Testament Background for the Emerging Doctrine of 'Local Church,'" in *Biblical Exegesis and Church Doctrine* (New York/Mahwah, NJ: Paulist Press, 1985), pp. 115–19.

7. See Lohfink, "Did Jesus Found a Church?" p. 231.

8. Richard J. Dillon, "Acts of the Apostles," in *The New Jerome Biblical Commentary*, eds. R. E. Brown, J. A. Fitzmyer, and R. E. Murphy (Englewood Cliffs, NJ: Prentice-Hall, 1990), pp. 724–25; Gerhard A. Krodel, *Augsburg Commentary on the New Testament: Acts* (Minneapolis, MN: Augsburg, 1986), pp. 14–18; Ernst Haenchen, *The Acts of the Apostles: A Commentary* (Philadelphia: Westminster, 1971), pp. 60–71 and 90–110; Richard J. Dillon and Joseph A. Fitzmyer, "Acts of the Apostles," in *The Jerome Biblical Commentary*, eds. R. E. Brown, J. A. Fitzmyer, and R. E. Murphy (Englewood Cliffs, NJ: Prentice-Hall, 1968) vol. 2, pp. 166–67.

9. Krodel, *Acts*, pp. 17 and 375–79.

10. See Daniel Harrington, *Light of All Nations: Essays on the Church in New Testament Research* (Wilmington, DE: Michael Glazier, 1982), p. 65; Hans Conzelmann, *Acts of the Apostles* (Philadelphia: Fortress, 1987), p. xliii, and n. 106 for pertinent literature; Haenchen, *Acts*, pp. 190–96, 230–35, and 242–46; Krodel, *Acts*, pp. 92–95.

11. The Greek terms are *proskarterountes* and *homothumadon*.

12. Walter Kasper and Gerhard Sauter, *Kirche-Ort des Geistes*, p. 38; Hans Küng, *On Being a Christian* (New York: Doubleday, 1976), pp. 283–86, 478; Boff, *Ecclesiogenesis*, pp. 49–51; Brown, *Biblical Exegesis and Church Doctrine*, pp. 60 and 143; Harrington, *God's People in Christ*, pp. 28–30; Ben F. Meyer, *The Early Christians: Their World Mission and Self-Discovery* (Wilmington, DE: Michael Glazier, 1986), pp. 38–52.

13. Paul J. Achtemeier, "An Elusive Unity: Paul, Acts, and the Early Church," *The Catholic Biblical Quarterly* 48 (1986), pp. 18–22; *The Quest for Unity in the New Testament Church* (Philadelphia: Fortress, 1987), pp. 47–55.

14. Achtemeier, "An Elusive Unity," p. 25.

15. Meier, "Antioch," pp. 40–44; James D. G. Dunn, *Unity and Diversity in the New Testament: An Inquiry into the Character of Earliest Christianity* (London: SCM, 1977), pp. 245–52; Brown, *Churches the Apostles Left Behind*, pp. 128–29.

16. See Schillebeeckx, *Jesus*, pp. 385–90; Meyer, *The Early Christians*, p. 102.

17. Kasper, *Jesus the Christ*, p. 145.

18. See Michael McDermott, "The Biblical Doctrine of *KOINŌNIA*," *Biblische Zeitschrift* 19 (1975), pp. 64–77 and 219–33; Schuyler Brown, "*Koinōnia* as the Basis of New Testament Ecclesiology," *One in Christ* 12 (1976), pp. 157–67; Brown, *Biblical Exegesis and Church Doctrine*, pp. 118–26; J.-M. R. Tillard, *Church of Churches: An Ecclesiology of Communion*, tr. R. C. De Peaux (Collegeville, MN: Liturgical Press–Michael Glazier Book, 1992), pp. 1–105; Jacques Dupont, "L'union entre les premiers Chretiens dans les Actes des Apôtres," *Nouvelle Revue Théologiques* 91 (1969), pp. 903–8, and "Community of Goods in the Early Church," in *The Salvation of the Gentiles*, pp. 85–102; Bernard P. Prusak, "Hospitality Extended or Denied: *Koinōnia* Incarnate from Jesus to Augustine," *The Jurist* 36 (1976), pp. 89–126.

19. 1 Thess 4:3, 5:23; 2 Thess 2:13; 1 Cor 1:2, 6:1, 16:1, 15; 2 Cor 1:1, 8:4, 13:12; Phil 1:1, 4:21–22; Rom 1:7, 12:13, 15:25–31, 16:2, 15; Phlm 5, 7; Acts 9:13, 32; 1 Pet 1:15, 2:5, 9; see Exod 19:6.

20. Gerd Theissen, *The Social Setting of Pauline Christianity*, ed. and tr. John H. Schütz (Philadelphia: Fortress Press, 1982), pp. 96 and 147–67; Meeks, *The First Urban Christians*, pp. 67–68.

21. See John E. Lynch, "The Limits of *Communio* in the Pre-Constantinian Church," *The Jurist* 36 (1976), pp. 159–90; Kenneth Hein, *Eucharist and Excommunication: A Study in Early Christian Doctrine and Discipline* (Bern: Herbert Lang, 1973), pp. 411–49.

22. Douglas R. Hare, *The Theme of Jewish Persecution of Christians in the Gospel According to Matthew* (Cambridge: Cambridge University Press, 1967); Brown, *The Community of the Beloved Disciple*, pp. 22–23, 63, 71–73, and 172–74.

23. See 1 Thess 5:26; 1 Cor 16:20; 2 Cor 13:12; Rom 16:16; 1 Pet 5:14; *Didache* 14:2; Justin Martyr, *1 Apology* 65.2; Tertullian, *On Prayer* 18; Hippolytus, *Apostolic Tradition* 18 and 21 (22); *Didascalia* II, 54.1; Cyril of Jerusalem, *Mystagogic Catechesis* 5.3; Pseudo-Dionysius, *On the Eccesiastical Hierarchy* 3.3.8.

24. See Brown, *The Churches the Apostles Left Behind*, pp. 47–60; Harrington, *God's People in Christ*, pp. 67–74 and *Light of All Nations*, pp. 71–72; Tillard, *Church of Churches*, pp. 45–53.

25. *The Churches the Apostles Left Behind*, p. 51.

26. See Meeks, *The First Urban Christians*, pp. 75–84; Brown, "*Episkopē* and *Episkopos*," p. 333; Edward Schillebeeckx, *The Church with*

a Human Face: A New and Expanded Theology of Ministry, tr. John Bowden (New York: Crossroad, 1985), pp. 46–50.

27. See Brown, "*Episkopē* and *Episkopos*," pp. 323–25; Schillebeeckx, *Jesus*, p. 389; Dunn, *Unity and Diversity*, pp. 104–6; Wright, *Jesus and the Victory of God*, pp. 147, 299–300, 338, 444; E. P. Sanders, *Jesus and Judaism* (Philadelphia: Fortress, 1985), pp. 98–106, and *The Historical Figure of Jesus* (London/New York: Penguin, 1995), pp. 107, 120, 124, 184–90.

28. See note 4 above and also Raymond E. Brown, "The Meaning of Modern New Testament Studies for an Ecumenical Understanding of Peter and a Theology of the Papacy," in *Biblical Reflections on Crises Facing the Church* (New York/Paramus, NJ: Paulist Press, 1975), pp. 63–77; *Priest and Bishop*, pp. 49–51.

29. Brown et al., *Peter in the New Testament*, pp. 114–19 and 140–41.

30. Ibid., pp. 100 n. 231, 106–7, 143 n. 306; Brown, *The Churches the Apostles Left Behind*, pp. 142–45; Meier, "Antioch," pp. 68–72; cf. C. H. Dodd, *The Interpretation of the Fourth Gospel*, p. 441.

31. Dunn, *Unity and Diversity*, pp. 107–9 and 270; Augustin George, "L'Oeuvre de Luc: Actes et Évangile," in J. Delorme, *Le ministère et les ministères...*, pp. 215–17.

32. See Theissen, *The Social Setting of Pauline Christianity*, pp. 31–32, 38–40.

33. Schillebeeckx, *The Church with a Human Face*, pp. 57–58; cf. André Lemaire, "Les épîtres de Paul: la diversité des ministères," in J. Delorme, *Le ministère et les ministères...*, pp. 57–73.

34. *Church with a Human Face*, p. 85.

35. "*Episkopē* and *Episkopos*," p. 331.

36. Brown, *Community of the Beloved Disciple*, p. 88.

37. Ibid., pp. 82–88, 158–62; "*Episkopē* and *Episkopos*," pp. 337–38; *Churches the Apostles Left Behind*, pp. 92–101; Xavier Léon-Dufour, "L'Évangile et les épîtres Johanniques," in Delorme, *Le ministère et les ministères...*, pp. 257–61.

38. See Brown, *Priest and Bishop*, pp. 41 and 55; *The Critical Meaning of the Bible*, pp. 77–78; *Biblical Exegesis and Church Doctrine*, pp. 47–48; Jean Delorme, "Diversité et unité des ministères d'après le Nouveau Testament," in *Le ministère et les ministères...*, pp. 308–9.

39. Alexandre Faivre, *The Emergence of the Laity in the Early Church*, tr. David Smith (New York/Mahwah, NJ: Paulist Press, 1990), pp. 5–40.

40. "*Episkopē* and *Episkopos*," p. 331.

41. See James D. G. Dunn, *The Living Word* (Philadelphia: Fortress, 1988), p. 75; and David G. Meade, *Pseudonimity and Canon* (Grand Rapids, MI: W. B. Eerdmans, 1987), pp. 128–33 and 160–61.

42. See John P. Meier, "*Presbyteros* in the Pastoral Epistles," *Catholic Biblical Quarterly* 35 (1973), pp. 323–45; Brown, "*Episkopē* and *Episkopos,*" p. 334; Bernard Cooke, *Ministry to Word and Sacraments: History and Theology* (Philadelphia: Fortress, 1976), pp. 61 and 70 n. 35.

43. See Col 3:18—4:1; Eph 5:21—6:9; Titus 2:1–10; Cf. 1 Pet 3:1–7; Elisabeth Schüssler Fiorenza, *In Memory of Her: A Feminist Theological Reconstruction of Christian Origins* (New York: Crossroad, 1983), pp. 251–84.

44. See J. H. Elliott, "Ministry and Church Order in the New Testament," *Catholic Biblical Quarterly* 32 (1970), pp. 367–91; Brown, "*Episkopē* and *Episkopos,*" pp. 333–35.

45. See E. S. Fiorenza, *In Memory of Her*, pp. 292–93.

46. The Letter of the Romans to the Corinthians, in *The Apostolic Fathers*, second edition, tr. J. B. Lightfoot and J. B. Harmer, ed. and rev. Michael W. Holmes (Grand Rapids, MI: Baker Book House, 1989), pp. 52–53.

47. Faivre, *The Emergence of the Laity*, pp. 16–21.

48. "Rome," in *Antioch and Rome*, pp. 208–10.

49. Meier, "Antioch," pp. 40–44.

50. William R. Schoedel, *Ignatius of Antioch: A Commentary on the Letters of Ignatius of Antioch* (Philadelphia: Fortress, 1985), p. 244; cf. James F. McCue, "Bishops, Presbyters, and Priests in Ignatius of Antioch," *Theological Studies* 28 (1967), pp. 828–34.

51. In regard to the Judaizers, see Mag 8–10; Philad 6; for docetism, see Tral 9 and 10; Smyr 2–3 and 5–6.

52. Schoedel, *Ignatius of Antioch*, p. 109.

53. Patrick Burke, "The Monarchical Episcopate at the End of the First Century," *Journal of Ecumenical Studies* 7 (1970), pp. 499–518.

54. Schoedel, *Ignatius of Antioch*, pp. 22 and 116.

55. See *Didascalia* II, 57.4; Albano Vilela, *La condition collégiale des Prêtres au IIIe siècle* (Paris: Éditions Beauchesne, 1971), p. 393; Giuseppe D'Ercole, "The Presbyteral Colleges in the Early Church," *Historical Investigations, Concilium* 17 (New York: Paulist Press, 1966), pp. 20–33.

56. W. R. Schoedel, "Theological Norms and Social Perspectives in Ignatius of Antioch," in *Jewish and Christian Self-Definition*, vol. 1, ed. E. P. Sanders (London: SCM Press, 1980), p. 55.

Chapter 3

1. It was originally a baptismal creed used in Jerusalem. Cyril of Jerusalem explained it in his *Catechesis* and Epiphanius included it in his *Ancoratus* written about 374.

2. For an overview of such literature, see E. S. Fiorenza, *In Memory of Her*, pp. 304–6. Texts may be found in Edgar Hennecke and Wilhelm Schneemelcher, *New Testament Apocrypha*, 2 vols. (Philadelphia: Westminster, 1963 and 1966).

3. *Against the Heresies* 1.10.1–2, 3.2.2, 3.3.1–3; see James F. McCue, "The Roman Primacy in the Patristic Era: The Beginnings Through Nicaea," in *Papal Primacy and the Universal Church*, eds. Paul C. Empie and T. Austin Murphy (Minneapolis: Augsburg, 1974), pp. 55–57.

4. Eusebius, *Ecclesiastical History* 4.22.1; see Hans von Campenhausen, *Ecclesiastical Authority and Spiritual Power in the Church of the First Three Centuries* (Stanford, CA: Stanford University Press, 1969), pp. 163–68.

5. See James L. Ash, "The Decline of Ecstatic Prophecy in the Early Church," *Theological Studies* 37 (1976), pp. 227–52; Bernard Sesboüé, "Ministères et structure de l'Église: Reflexion théologique à partir du Nouveau Testament," in J. Delorme, *Le ministère et les ministères…*, pp. 413–17; von Campenhausen, *Ecclesiastical Authority and Spiritual Power*, pp. 187–92.

6. Maurice Vidal, "Ministère et ordination," in Delorme, *Le ministère et les ministères…*, p. 484; also Brown, "*Episkopē* and *Episkopos*," pp. 331–32 and notes 21 and 23.

7. Chapters in the *Apostolic Tradition* are cited according to Bernard Botte's critical edition, *Hippolyte de Rome: La Tradition Apostolique, D'après les anciennes versions*, second edition, *Sources Chrétiennes* 11 (Paris: Éditions du Cerf, 1968), pp. 40–69. Botte omits the material that comprises chapter seven in Gregory Dix's edition: Gregory Dix and Henry Chadwick, *The Treatise on the Apostolic Tradition of St. Hippolytus of Rome* (London: S.P.C.K., 1968).

8. See *Epistle* 33:1; Robert F. Evans, *One and Holy: The Church in Latin Patristic Thought* (London: S.P.C.K., 1972), p. 58.

9. *Homily on Leviticus* 6.3 and 6; *Commentary on Matthew* 14.22; *Against Celsus* 3.48; see Aaron Milavec, "The Office of the Bishop in Origen," in *Raising the Torch of Good News: Catholic Authority and Dialogue with the World*, ed. Bernard P. Prusak (Lanham, MD: University Press of America, 1988), pp. 14–18.

10. For Origen that meant a "spiritual ascetic"; see Hans von Campenhausen, *Ecclesiastical Authority and Spiritual Power*, p. 251.

11. *Communio: Church and Papacy in Early Christianity* (Chicago: Loyola University Press, 1972), pp. 16 and 48–56.

12. *Eucharist and Church Fellowship in the First Four Centuries* (St. Louis: Concordia, 1966), p. 52.

13. Franciscus X. Funk, *Didascalia et Constitutiones Apostolorum* (Paderborn, Germany: F. Schoeningh, 1905), vol. 1, pp. 168–69; English translation in R. Hugh Connolly, *Didascalia Apostolorum: The Syriac Version Translated and Accompanied by the Verona Latin Fragments* (Oxford: Clarendon Press, 1929, reprinted 1969), p. 122.

14. See Cyprian, *Epistles* 1.2; Justin Martyr, 1 *Apology* 65; Theodoret, *Ecclesiatical History* 5.34.10; Ludwig Hertling, *Communio*, pp. 28–36, 47–51; Werner Elert, *Eucharist and Church Fellowship*, pp. 138–39, 149–59; Giuseppe D'Ercole, *Communio-Collegialitá-Primato e Sollicitudo Omnium Ecclesiarum dai Vangeli a Costantino* (Rome: Herder, 1964), pp. 160–204.

15. Eusebius, *Ecclesiastical History* 5.23–25; cf. Cyprian, *Ep.* 75.7.

16. See Bernard P. Prusak, "The Roman Patriarch and the Eastern Churches: The Question of Autonomy in Communion—Part One," *The American Ecclesiastical Review* 166 (1972), pp. 628–33.

17. *The Churches the Apostles Left Behind*, p. 137; also see p. 125.

18. See Ludwig Hertling and Engelbert Kirschbaum, *The Roman Catacombs and Their Martyrs* (London: Darton, Longman & Todd, 1960); Margherita Guarducci, *The Tomb of St. Peter: The New Discoveries in the Sacred Grottoes of the Vatican* (New York: Hawthorne Books, 1960) and *Le Reliquie di Pietro sotto la Confessione della Basilica Vaticana* (Vatican City: Libreria Editrice Vaticana, 1965).

19. See Maurice Bevenot, *St. Cyprian: The Lapsed; The Unity of the Catholic Church, in Ancient Christian Writers* 25, eds. J. Quasten and J.C. Plumpe (Westminster, MD: Newman, 1957), pp. 103–4 and n. 28; "'*Primatus Petro Datur*': St. Cyprian on the Papacy," in *Journal of Thological Studies*, n.s. 5 (1954), pp. 19–35; G. S. M. Walker, *The Churchmanship of St. Cyprian, Ecumenical Studies in History*, No. 9 (Richmond, VA: John Knox Press, 1969), p. 26.

20. See Cyprian, *Ep.* 71.3 and 75.17.

21. See Maurice Bevenot, *Cyprian: De Lapsis and De Ecclesiae Catholicae Unitate* (Oxford: Clarendon Press, 1971), pp. xi–xvii, 61–65; *St Cyprian: The Lapsed; The Unity of the Catholic Church*, pp. 6–8 and 102–7; *The Tradition of Manuscripts: A Study in the Transmission of St. Cyprian's Treatises* (Oxford: Clarendon Press, 1961); James F. McCue, "The

Roman Primacy in the Patristic Era: The Beginnings Through Nicaea," pp. 62, 68–71.

22. See Maurice Bevenot, *Cyprian*, p. xiv; *St. Cyprian*, p. 7.

23. Optatus, *Donatist Schism* 2, 6; 3, 2; 6, 3; Augustine, *Against Cresconius* 2.37.46 and *Ep.* 43.7.

24. *Explanation of Psalms* 108.1; *Ep.* 53.2.

25. *On John* 124.5; *Retractions* 1.21.1; *Sermon* 76.3; see J. M. R. Tillard, *The Bishop of Rome* (Wilmington, DE: Michael Glazier, 1983), pp. 108–9.

26. *Against the Epistle of Manichee Entitled Fundamental* 4.5.

27. *Post has omnes* in *PL* 13, 374 and *PL* 19, 793; the decree is also attributed to Pope Gelasius: *PL* 59, 159.

28. *Epistle* 1 to Himerius of Tarragona, found in *PL* 13.

29. *Epistle* 25 to Decentius of Gubbio; *Ep.* 1 to Anysius; *Ep.* 17 to Rufus and others; *Ep.* 2 to Victricius of Rouen; *Ep.* 13 to Rufus of Thessalonica; *Ep.* 29 to Aurelius and the Council of Carthage; *Ep.* 30 to Silvanus and the synod of Milevis. Innocent's epistles are found in *PL* 20.

30. *Epistle* 12 to Aurelius of Carthage and the African bishops. The epistles of Zosimus are found in *PL* 20.

31. *Epistle* 14 to the bishops of Thessalia; *Ep.* 15 to Rufus and the bishops of Macedonia, and others. Pope Boniface's epistles are found in *PL* 20.

32. Text is found in *PL* 50, 422–27 and in *Corpus Christianorum, Series Latina*, vol. 149: *Concilia Africae A. 345–A. 525*, ed. C. Munier (Tournai, Belgium: Brepols, 1974), pp. 169–72 (hereafter CCSL).

33. *Epistle* 6 to John, bishop of Antioch. The epistles of Sixtus III are found in *PL* 50.

34. The sermons and epistles of Pope Leo are found in *PL* 54.

35. See Tillard, *Bishop of Rome*, pp. 124–25.

36. Joseph Lécuyer has shown that such a perspective was common among popes of the fifth century: "Collégialité épiscopale selon les papes du Ve siècle," in *La collégialité épiscopale, Unam sanctam* 52 (Paris: Éditions du Cerf, 1965), pp. 41–57.

37. See Walter Ullmann, *The Growth of Papal Government in the Middle Ages: A Study in the Ideological Relation of Clerical to Lay Power*, third edition (London: Methuen, 1970), pp. 7–14; "Leo I and the Theme of Papal Primacy," *The Journal of Theological Studies* n.s. 11 (1960), pp. 25–51; Cornelius Ernst, "The Primacy of Peter: Theology and Ideology—I," *New Blackfriars* 50 (1969), pp. 352–55.

38. See Arthur Carl Piepkorn, "From Nicaea to Leo the Great," in *Papal Primacy and the Universal Church*, eds. Paul C. Empie and T. Austin Murphy, pp. 94–95.

39. *Ep.* 8 to Emperor Anastasius in *PL* 59 = *Ep.* 12.2 in Andreas Thiel, ed., *Epistolae Romanorum pontificum genuinae et quae ad eos scriptae sunt a S. Hilario usque ad Pelagium II*, vol. 1 (Brunsberg: E. Peter, 1868; Hildesheim, Germany: G. Olms, 1974 reprint). As indicated, the numeration differs in Migne and Thiel.

40. *Ep.* 4 to Faustus in *PL* = 10.9 in Thiel.

41. Gelasian Decree: "*Post (has omnes) propheticas,*" in *PL* 59, 159 (cf. 167–68).

42. Tractate within *Ep.* 11 in *PL* 58, 950 = *Ep.* 1.10 in Thiel.

43. *Tome on the Bond of Anathema—"Ne forte"* in *PL* 59, 110 = *Tractate* 4.10–13 in Thiel.

44. *Ep.* 4 in *PL* 59 = 10.5 in Thiel; and *Ep.* 13 to the bishops of Dardania = 26.5 in Thiel.

45. See Arthur Carl Piepkorn, "From Nicaea to Leo the Great," p. 97.

46. *Explanations of Psalms* 30.4, 127.3; *Sermon* 341.1 and 10.

47. *Sermons* 267.4, 268.2, 272; *Homilies on 1 John* 6.10, 10.3.

48. *Against the Epistle of Parmenian* 2.13.28; *On Baptism* 1.1.2; *Sermon to the Church of Caesarea* 1.

49. *Sermon to the Church of Caesarea 2; Against the Epistle of Parmenian* 2.13.29; *On Baptism* 1.4.5, 3.19.25, 6.1.1; *Ep.* 185.6.

50. *On Baptism* 1.1.2, 5.23.33; *Ep.* 98.2; *Sermon* 269.2–3.

51. *On Baptism* 1.12.18, 4.1.1, 4.17.24, 5.8.9, 6.1.1, 6.5.7, and 7.44.87.

52. G. W. H. Lampe, "Christian Theology in the Patristic Period," in *A History of Christian Doctrine*, ed. Hubert Cunliffe-Jones with Benjamin Drewery (Philadelphia: Fortress Press, 1980), pp. 175–76.

53. *On Baptism* 1.15.24, 3.14.19, 4.15.22.

54. Yves Congar, *L'Église: De saint Augustin à l'époque moderne* (Paris: Éditions du Cerf, 1970), p. 15.

55. *On the Gospel of John* 5.18, 6.7–8, 15.3; *Against the Ep. of Parmenian* 2.15.34; *On Baptism* 5.14.19; *Against Cresconius* 4.20.23.

56. *Epistle to Catholics "On Unity"* 13.33, 20.56; *Ep.* 49.3, 93.23.

57. *Against Cresconius the Donatist* 3, 35, 39; *On Baptism* 3, 21; *Sermon* 71.18.

58. *Explanation of Psalms* 21.28f., 95.11; *Ep. to Catholics* 9.23.

59. *Sermon* 269.2, 271; *On the Gospel of John* 6.10; *Explan. of Psalms* 54.9, 95.15; Peter Brown, *Augustine: A Biography* (Berkeley & Los Angeles: University of California Press, 1967), p. 224.

60. *Sermon* 268.3–4; *City of God* 12.22 and 28, 13.14, 14.11, 16.27.

61. *Against the Ep. of Parmenian* 2.21.40–41; *On Baptism* 4.9.13; *City of God* 20.11.

62. *On Baptism* 5.27.38, 6.2.3; *On Condemnation and Grace* 39–42.

63. *On Baptism* 5.21.29; *Against the Letter of Petilian* 3.49.59.

64. *Ep.* 93.23; *On Baptism* 3, 4, 6; *Ep.* 54.1, 1.

65. *L'Église: De saint Augustin à l'époque moderne*, p. 16; Augustine, *Sermon to the Church of Caesarea* 6; cf. *Sermon* 268.2; *On Baptism* 1.1, 2; 4.17, 24; 5.8, 9; 6.5, 7; 7.44, 86–87; 7.52, 100; 7.54, 103; *Against Cresconius* 1.29.34; *Epistle* 61.1.

66. Origen, *Homily on the Book of Joshua* 3.5; Cyprian, *Ep.* 73.21; *On the Unity of the Catholic Church* 6.

67. Augustine, *On the Spirit and the Letter* 52 and 60; *On Grace and Free Will* 31–33.

68. *On Condemnation and Grace* 12–14, 31–34, 44; *On the Gift of Perseverance* 21 and 35.

69. *On Baptism* 7.51.99–52.100; *On Catechizing the Uninstructed* 25.48; *City of God* 1.35.

70. *Explan. of Psalms* 98.4; *City of God* 8.24, 13.16, 14.28.

71. *City of God* 1.35, 10.7, 18.49, 19.27, 21.25; *City of God* 11.9, 15.15; *Confessions* 12.11.13.

72. *City of God* 22.1; *Enchiridion* 29, 62.

73. Cf. Aquinas, *Summa theologiae* 1, q. 23, a. 3–7; 1.2, q. 112, a. 4.

74. Faivre, *The Emergence of the Laity*, pp. 74–82; *Naissance d'une hiérarchie*, pp. 49–50.

75. See Cyril of Jerusalem, *Mystagogic Catecheses* 1.2–9; Ambrose, *On the Mysteries* 2.5–7.

76. See Jean Gaudemet, *L'Église dans l'empire Romain (IV*[e]*-V*[e] *siecles)*, in *Histoire du droit et des institutions de l'Église en occident*, dir., G. Le Bras (Paris: Sirey, 1958), p. 101.

77. See P. M. Gy, "Notes on the Early Terminology of Christian Priesthood," in *The Sacrament of Holy Orders* (Collegeville, MN: Liturgical Press, 1962), pp. 109–12.

78. *Code of Theodosius* 16.2.3.

79. See Innocent I, *Ep.* 25.3; Zosimus, *Ep.* 9.3.

80. See Council of Nicaea (325), canon 2; Council of Sardica (343/44?), canon 10; Pope Siricius, Ep. 1.9, 13–13, 17; Canons of the Roman Synod, "*Dominus inter,*" to the bishops of Gaul, canon 12

(Siricius, *Ep.* 10.5, 15 in *PL* 13, 1181–1194); Pope Zosimus, *Ep.* 9.3, 5; Second Synod of Arles (443?), canon 1; Pope Gelasius, *Ep.* 9. An English translation of the canons of the early synods and councils may be found in Charles J. Hefele, *A History of the Christian Councils*, 5 vols. (Edinburgh: T. & T. Clark, 1883–96).

81. Council of Nicaea (325), canons 4 and 6; Council of Antioch (341), canon 19; Synod of Laodicea in Phrygia (343/81), canon 12; Basil, *Ep.* 28.3; John Chrysostom, *On Priesthood* 2.4 and 4.2 (3.5 acknowledges the problem of factions); Augustine, *Ep.* 213.1 and 4; Synod of Hippo (393), canon 20; disputed "Fourth Synod of Carthage" (398?), canon 27; Pope Celestine I, *Ep.* 4.5; Second Synod of Arles (443?), canon 5; Leo I, *Ep.* 10.4 to the bishops of the province of Vienne; *Ep.* 14.5 to Anastasius; *Ep.* 167 to Rusticus, response to Question 1. Canon 23 of the Council of Antioch (341) stipulated that bishops were not to appoint their own successors, even at the time of their death.

82. Council of Arles (314), canons 2 and 21; Council of Nicaea, canons 15–16; Council of Antioch (341), canons 3 and 21; Council of Sardica (343/44?), canon 1; disputed "Fourth Synod of Carthage" (398?), canon 27; Canons of the Roman Synod, "*Dominus inter*," to the bishops of Gaul, canon 13 (Pope Siricius, *Ep.* 10.5, 16: the church left behind is "like an abandoned wife"); Council of Chalcedon (451), canon 5.

83. *Book of Questions on the Old and New Testament* 101.2: *On the Boasting of the Roman Deacons.* Latin text is found in *Corpus Scriptorum Ecclesiasticorum Latinorum*, vol. 50, ed. Alexander Souter (Vienna: F. Tempsky, 1908) (hereafter CSEL).

84. *Book of Questions* 101.5.

85. *Commentary on 1 Timothy* 3.10; cf. *Book of Questions* 101.5 and *Commentary on Ephesians* 4.12. Latin text found in *CSEL*, vol. 81, 1–3, ed. Henry J. Vogels (Vienna: Hoelder-Pichler-Tempsky, 1966–69).

86. *Commentary on Ephesians* 4.11–12; *Commentary on 1 Corinthians* 12.28; *Commentary on Philippians* 1.1.

87. *Comm. on Eph.* 4.12.

88. *Ep.* 146 to Evangelus; *Commentary on Titus* 1.5; *Dialogue against the Luciferians* 9.

89. *Comm. on Titus* 1.5.

90. John Chrysostom, *Homily* 11 on 1 Tim 3.8; *Homily* 13 on 1 Tim 4.14; *Homily* 1 on Phil 1.1.

91. See Athanasius, *Life of Antony;* Palladius, *Lausiac History (Paradise of the Holy Fathers); Life of Pachomius;* Jean Décarreaux, *Monks and Civilization* (Garden City, NY: Doubleday, 1964), pp. 72–116; Peter Brown, *The Body and Society: Men, Women, and Sexual Renunciation in*

Early Christianity (New York: Columbia University Press, 1988), pp. 213–84; and J. C. O'Neill, "The Origins of Monasticism," in *The Making of Orthodoxy: Essays in Honor of Henry Chadwick*, ed. Rowan Williams (Cambridge: Cambridge University Press, 1989), pp. 270–87. O'Neill argues that monasticism did not begin with Antony and Pachomius but "was always simply there in the life of the Church."

92. See Christian Cochini, *Origines Apostoliques du Célibat Sacerdotal* (Paris: Éditions Lethielleux, 1981), pp. 23–37, 183–203, 209–27.

93. See John Chrysostom, *On Priesthood* 3.4–5.

94. See Daniel Callam, "Clerical Continence in the Fourth Century: Three Papal Decretals," in *Theological Studies* 41 (1980), pp. 3–50. Callam analyzes Siricius, *Ep.* 1 to Himmerius of Tarragona and *Ep.* 5 to the bishops of Africa, and the Canons of the Roman Synod, "*Dominus inter,*" to the bishops of Gaul, canon 3 (Siricius, *Ep.* 10.2.5–6).

95. *Ep.* 2 to Bp. Victricius of Rouen, 9.12 (*PL* 20, 475C–477A).

96. *Ep.* 6 to Bp. Exsuperius of Toulouse, 1.2 (*PL* 20, 496B–498A). Priests who had fathered children during the time of their ministry were termed *unworthy* and were to be removed from office: *Ep.* 38 to Maximus and Severus (*PL* 20, 605B–C).

97. *Ep.* 167 to Bp. Rusticus of Narbonne, response to question 3 (*PL* 54, 1204A).

98. See Cochini, *Origines Apostoliques du Célibat Sacerdotal*, pp. 128 and 136.

99. See Peter Brown, *The Body and Society*, pp. 138–39.

100. Ibid., pp. 138, 358–59.

101. See Faivre, *The Emergence of the Laity*, p. 37.

102. Ibid., p. 133.

103. Peter Brown, *The Body and Society*, pp. 359–61. See Ambrose, *De Virginibus* 1.3–7, and Pope Siricius, *Ep.* 1.10, 14, which refers to the unmarried clerical state as "better."

104. Peter Brown, *The Body and Society*, pp. 426–27.

105. *Against the Epistle of Parmenian* 2.8.15–16.

106. Peter Brown, *The Body and Society*, pp. 410, 435, and 248–49.

107. Ibid., pp. 431–32; Suzanne F. Wemple, *Women in Frankish Society* (Philadelphia: University of Pennsylvania Press, 1981), pp. 134–35.

108. *On the Grace of Christ* 2.34; *On condemnation and grace* 12–14; *On the Gift of Perseverance* 35; *To Simplicianus* 1.16; Ep. 166.10; *Unfinished Work against Julian* 6.22; *On the Merits of Sins* 1.29f.

109. *Against Julian* 5.41; *Enchiridion* 93.

110. See Pope Siricius, *Ep.* 1.10, 14; First Council of Orange (441), canon 22; Second Synod of Arles (443), canons 2 and 55; Synod at Agde or Languedoc (506), canon 16.

111. *On Divine Names* 3.1; 4.2 and 6–10; 5.3; 6.1; 8.2.

112. *The Heavenly Hierarchy* 3.1; *Ecclesiastical Hierarchy* 1.3.

113. *Heav. Hier.* 6; *Eccl. Hier.* 5.1, 1–2.

114. The triad of three orders is described in *Eccl. Hier.* 5.1, 4–7. The bishop is called the "head of the hierarchical order." See 1.3; 5.1, 5; and 7.3, 7.

115. *Eccl. Hier.* 5.3, 7, which explains the bishop's role as teacher or illuminator; cf. 5.1, 7 and 5.2; *Heav. Hier.* 1.1–2 and also the *Apostolic Constitutions* 8.4.6.

116. *Eccl. Hier.* chs. 2–4.

117. *Eccl. Hier.* 6.1, 1–3.

118. *Eccl. Hier.* 5.1, 3; 6.3, 5.

119. See James M. Robinson and Helmut Koester, *Trajectories through Early Christianity* (Philadelphia: Fortress, 1971), pp. 14–17 and 274–79.

120. See Karl Rahner, *Concern for the Church, Theological Investigations XX* (New York: Crossroad, 1981), pp. 82–83.

121. Even Rudolf Bultmann, despite his doubts about the possibility of retrieving the historical Jesus, acknowledged that to be a characteristic of Jesus: "The Primitive Christian Kerygma and the Historical Jesus," in *The Historical Jesus and the Kerygmatic Christ*, eds. Carl Braaten and Roy A. Harrisville (Nashville: Abingdon, 1964), pp. 22–23.

122. See E. S. Fiorenza, *In Memory of Her*, pp. 226–33; Edward Schillebeeckx, *The Church with a Human Face*, pp. 54–55.

123. See Jerome Murphy-O'Connor, "Interpolations in 1 Corinthians," in *The Catholic Biblical Quarterly* 48 (1986), pp. 90–92; cf. Elisabeth Schüssler Fiorenza, *In Memory of Her*, pp. 230–33.

124. Bernard P. Prusak, "Woman: Seductive Siren and Source of Sin? Pseudepigraphal Myth and Christian Origins," in *Religion and Sexism: Images of Woman in the Jewish and Christian Traditions*, ed. Rosemary Radford Ruether (New York: Simon and Schuster, 1974), pp. 89–116.

125. *Acta Apostolicae Sedis*, 65 (1973), pp. 396–408, here pp. 402–4. An English translation is found in *Catholic Mind* 71 (1973), pp. 54–64; section 5 is on pp. 58–60.

126. James M. Robinson and Helmut Koester, *Trajectories through Early Christianity*, p. 278.

127. Hertling, *Communio*, pp. 18–22.

128. *Apostolic Tradition* 18; *Didascalia* 2.57.5–9; *Apostolic Constitutions* 8.11.9–11.

129. See Alphonsus Raes, *Introductio in Liturgiam Orientalem* (Rome: Pontifical Oriental Institute, 1947), p. 31.

Chapter 4

1. *Time, Work, & Culture in the Middle Ages*, tr. Arthur Goldhammer (Chicago: University of Chicago Press, 1980), pp. 155–57. The cultural shifts and the high class and culture of bishops are also treated by Peter Brown in *The World of Late Antiquity, AD 150–750* (New York: Harcourt Brace Jovanovich, 1971), pp. 126–35 and *The Cult of the Saints: Its Rise and Function in Latin Christianity* (Chicago: University of Chicago Press, 1981), pp. 39–40, 53–56.

2. Robert F. Evans, *One and Holy*, p. 143; Pope Gregory I, *Epistles* (in *PL* 77) 1.36; 2.11, 31, and 47; 9.4; 10.62; 5.20 ; *Moralia in Job* 19.23 (*PL* 76, 111–12); 20.79 (*PL* 76, 186–88); 22.53 (*PL* 76, 246–47); *Pastoral Rule* 3 (PL 77, 49–126).

3. *Moralia in Job* 14.27 (*PL* 75, 1053–54); 15.32–33 and 69 (*PL* 75, 1097, and 1117); 16.15 (*PL* 75, 1128); 32.25–28 (*PL* 76, 650–54); 34.8 (*PL* 76, 722).

4. *Moralia in Job* 7.30 (*PL* 75, 781–82); 8.66 (*PL* 75, 841–42); 20.77 (*PL* 76, 185); 25.20–21 (*PL* 76, 332–33).

5. *Moralia in Job* 32.35 (*PL* 76, 657); *Homily on Ezechiel* 2.4.5–6; 2.7.3 (*PL* 76, 976–77, and 1014).

6. *Pastoral Rule* 2.6; cf. 1.3; *Epistle* 14.17 (*PL* 77, 1323–25).

7. See *Epistles* 4.6, 14.4, 13.18, 10.67; Evans, *One and Holy*, p. 143.

8. See *Epistles* 1.72, 13.18, 14.4.

9. *Sermon* 340.1.

10. *Explanations of Psalms* 126.3.

11. *Ep.* 130 and 217.

12. *Ep.* 13.1 (*PL* 77, 1253); *Register* 9.214 and 219 (CCSL 140, 772, and 782).

13. Walter Ullmann, *The Growth of Papal Government in the Middle Ages*, pp. 37 and 465.

14. *Ep.* 5.20 (PL 77, 747= *Register* 5.37).

15. *Register* 5.37 (= 5.20 in *PL);* cf. 1.24 (=1.25 in *PL*); 7.37 (=7.40 in *PL*).

16. *Ep.* 1.25. 3.10, 4.3 and 39, 6.2, 7.4 and 40.

17. English translation in *Church and State Through the Centuries*, eds. and trs. Sidney Z. Ehler and John B. Morrall (Westminster, MD: Newman Press, 1954), pp. 16–22.

18. See Jean Lassus, *The Early Christian and Byzantine World* (London: Paul Hamlyn, 1967), p. 11.

19. See Basil of Caesarea, *Ep.* 188, canon 7; *Ep.* 217, can. 56–58.

20. See *Apostolic Constitutions* 8.11, 11; *Didascalia* 2.57, 3–5 (Funk, vol. 1, pp. 158–61 and 494–95); and also Hippolytus, *Apostolic Tradition* 18, 2–5.

21. Lassus, *Early Christian and Byzantine World*, pp. 11–12.

22. See Ambrosiaster, *Questiones exemplares Veteris et Novi Testamenti* 101 (*PL* 35, 2301); and Cyprian, *Ep.* 45.2. For the following centuries, see Athanasius, *Historia Arianorum ad Monachos* 56; and Augustine, *Ep.* 185.7 (*PL* 33, 805).

23. See John Chrysostom, *Homily 20 on 2 Cor* 3.

24. See Joseph A. Jungmann, *The Mass of the Roman Rite: Its Origins and Development* (New York: Benziger, 1959), pp. 159–63.

25. Regarding the impact of private masses on the understanding of Eucharist, and their proliferation, see Theodore Klauser, *A Short History of the Western Liturgy*, 2nd ed., tr. John Halliburton (New York: Oxford University Press, 1979), pp. 96–97, 101–8.

26. *Capitula*, VII in *PL* 105, 194.

27. Basil, *Ep.* 93; Augustine, *Ep.* 54, 2–4.

28. *Homily on Eph* 3.4; *Hom. on Heb* 17.4.

29. *Summa Theologiae* 3, q. 80, a. 10, to 5; and Trent, session 22, ch. 6, *Decrees of the Ecumenical Councils*, vol. 2, pp. 734 (also in DH 1747).

30. *Homily on John* 46.3–4; *Hom. on 1 Cor* 24.4–5.

31. See Norbert Brox, *A Concise History of the Early Church*, tr. John Bowden (New York: Continuum: 1995), pp. 116–17.

32. *Ep.* 48: Apologetic to Pammachius; in *PL* 22, 505–6.

33. Sermons 19.3 (in CCSL, [Tournai: Brepols, 1953], 103, 89); 44.3 (CCSL, 103, 196); 68.2: in Lent (103, 290); 187.4 (104.765); 188.3 (104, 768); 199.7 (104, 806); 201.3 in Lent (104, 813); 229.4 (104, 908).

34. See Pierre J. Payer, *Sex and the Penitentials: The Development of a Sexual Code, 550–1150* (Toronto: University of Toronto Press, 1984), pp. 24–25.

35. Ibid., pp. 35–36; Gregory I, Register 11, 56a, 2. 331–43; and *Bede's Ecclesiastical History of the English People*, ed. Bertram Colgrave and R. A. B. Mynors (Oxford: Clarendon Press, 1969), pp. 1.27, 78–103.

36. See Payer, *Sex and the Penitentials*, pp. 26 and 61.

37. Edward Schillebeeckx, *Church with a Human Face*, pp. 165.

38. *Commentary on the Sentences* 4, d. 2, c. 1.

39. *Summa* 3, 80, 7, to 2nd.

40. See Nathan Mitchell, *Cult and Controversy: The Worship of the Eucharist Outside Mass* (New York: Pueblo, 1982), pp. 276–80.

41. *Rerum ecclesiasticarum documenta, series major, Fontes*, 2, eds. L. C. Mohlberg, L. Eizenhöfer, P. Siffrin (Rome: Herder, 1957), n. 33–34.

42. See Thomas Aquinas, *Comm. on Sent.* 4, d. 24, q. 2, a. 3; *Summa*, 3 supplement, 37, 5, resp.

43. *On the Body and Blood of the Lord* 1.2 (*PL* 120, 1269). English text is available in *Early Medieval Theology*, eds. and trs. George E. McCracken and Allen Cabaniss, vol. IX in *The Library of Christian Classics*, eds. John Baillie, John T. McNeill, and Henry P. Van Dusen (Philadelphia: Westminster Press, 1957), p. 94. For further analysis of Paschasius's position, see Mitchell, *Cult and Controversy*, pp. 74–80.

44. *On the Body and Blood of the Lord*, see sections 2, 9–10, and 69–71 (*PL* 121, cols. 128–29, 130–31, and 154–58). English text in *Early Medieval Theology*, pp. 118, 120–21, and 137–38. Also see Mitchell, *Cult and Controversy*, pp. 80–86.

45. *Ep*. 3. 3 and 7: to Egiles, abbot of Prum (*PL* 112, 1513–14 and 1517–18).

46. *De Sacra Coena adversus Lanfrancum, liber posterior*, eds. A. F. and F. Th. Vischer (Berlin: Haude et Spener, 1834), pp. 67, 78, 112, 150–53, 194, 209, 220, 222, and 251. Also see Mitchell, *Cult and Controversy*, pp. 142–45.

47. See Gary Macy, "The Theological Fate of Berengar's Oath of 1059: Interpreting a Blunder Become Tradition," in *Interpreting Tradition: The Art of Theological Reflection*, ed. Jane Kopas, *The Annual Publication of the College Theology Society*, vol. 29 (Chico, CA: Scholars Press, 1984), pp. 27–38; reprinted in Gary Macy, *Treasures from the Storeroom: Medieval Religion and the Eucharist* (Collegeville, MN: Liturgical Press, 1999), pp. 20–35.

48. See E. Dumoutet, *Le désir de voir l'hostie et les origines de la dévotion au Saint-Sacrement* (Paris: G. Beauchesne, 1926); and V. L. Kennedy, "The Moment of Consecration and the Elevation of the Host," *Medieval Studies* 6 (1944), pp. 121–50.

49. See Mitchell, *Cult and Controversy*, pp. 175–76; Miri Rubin, *Corpus Christi: The Eucharist in Late Medieval Culture* (Cambridge: Cambridge University Press, 1991), pp. 164–212 and 243–71.

50. See Augustine, *On the Trinity* 4, 6. During the tenth century the Eucharist began to be "buried" in a tomb constructed within the church as part of the reenactment of Jesus' burial and resurrection in the Holy Week "mystery plays" so popular at that time. See Mitchell, *Cult and Controversy*, pp. 133–36.

51. See, for example, Iosephus A. De Aldama, "De Actione Sacrificali Sacrificii Eucharistici," in *Sacrae Theologiae Summa* IV (Madrid: Biblioteca de Autores Cristianos, 1956), p. 337.

52. *Summa* 3, 80, 12.

53. See *Decrees of the Ecumenical Councils*, vol. 1: *Nicaea to Lateran* V, ed. Norman P. Tanner (London: Sheed & Ward, and Washington, DC: Georgetown University Press, 1990) pp. 418–19, also in DH 1198–1200; the Bull of Martin V, *Inter cunctas*, article 18: DH 1258.

54. See Pietro Redondi, *Galileo Heretic* (Princeton: Princeton University Press, 1987), pp. 205–6; Rubin, *Corpus Christi*, pp. 290–91.

55. See Mitchell, *Cult and Controversy*, pp. 164 and 168; W. H. Freestone, *The Sacrament Reserved*, Alcuin Club Collections, XXI (London: A. R. Mowbray, 1917) and Archdale A. King, *Eucharistic Reservation in the Western Church* (London: A. R. Mowbray/New York: Sheed & Ward, 1965).

56. "Devotion to the Sacred Heart Today," in *Theological Investigations*, vol. XXII, *Final Writings*, tr. Joseph Donceel and Hugh M. Riley (New York: Crossroad, 1992), pp. 121–22.

57. *Comm. on Sent.* 4, d. 24, q. 2, a. 2, to 2nd.

58. Ibid., 4, d. 8, q. 1, a. 1, qc. 1, resp. and ad 1.

59. Ibid., 4, d. 4, q. 2, a. 2, qc. 5, ad 2; and d. 9, q. 1, a.3, qc. 1, resp. According to the latter text, the *res et sacramentum* or intermediate effect of the sacrament was union with Christ; the *res tantum* or ultimate effect was the mystical Body of Christ; reception of the Eucharist was said to signify that the recipient "tended toward" the unity of the mystical body.

60. Ibid., 4, d. 9, q. 1, a. 2, qc. 4, resp.; and d. 9, q. 1, a. 1, qc. 2, ad 3.

61. See *Commentary on John* 6.7.2, 4 and 6; *Comm. on 1 Cor* 11.7.

62. *Summa* 3, q. 73, a. 2 and 3; q. 79, a. 3; q. 80, a. 1 and 9; q. 83, a. 4, ad 3.

63. See Peter Brown, *The Cult of the Saints*, pp. 1–68.

64. Robert Markus, *The End of Ancient Christianity* (Cambridge: Cambridge University Press, 1990), pp. 23 and 25–26.

65. See Gregory of Tours, *Libri Miraculorum* (*PL* 71, 705–828) and *De Miraculis Sancti Martini Episcopi, Libri Quatuor* (*PL* 71, 913–1010); Albert Mirgeler, *Mutations of Western Christianity*, tr. Edward Quinn (New York: Herder and Herder, 1964), pp. 44–62; Margaret Ruth Miles, *Practicing Christianity: Critical Perspectives for an Embodied Spirituality* (New York: Crossroad, 1988), pp. 46–47.

66. See Pierre Riché, *Daily Life in the World of Charlemagne*, tr. Jo Ann McNamara (Philadelphia: University of Pennsylvania, 1978), p. 234.

67. See Victor-Henry Debidour, *Christian Sculpture*, vol. 122 in *Twentieth Century Encyclopedia of Catholicism*, ed. Henri Daniel-Rops (New York: Hawthorn Books, 1968), pp. 60–64; George Zarnecki, *Art of the Medieval World* (Englewood Cliffs, NJ: Prentice-Hall/New York: Harry N. Abrams, 1975), pp. 169–71 and 183 (colorplate 30).

68. *Ep.* 33 (*PL* 100, 188).

69. Margaret R. Miles, *Image as Insight: Visual Understanding in Western Christianity and Secular Culture* (Boston: Beacon Press, 1985), pp. 2, 4, and 6.

70. See Ernst Murbach, and Peter Heman, illus., *Zillis: die romanische Bilderdecke der Kirche St. Martin* (Zurich: Atlantis Verlag, 1967); *The Painted Romanesque Ceiling of St. Martin in Zillis* (New York: Praeger, 1967).

71. Such as the second century *Protevangelium of James*, or the eighth or ninth century compilation called *The Gospel of Pseudo-Matthew*. See Edgar Hennecke and Wilhelm Schneemelcher, *New Testament Apocrypha*, vol. 1, *Gospels and Related Writings*, tr. R. McL. Wilson (Philadelphia: Westminster Press, 1963), pp. 368–79 and 405–7.

72. Hennecke and Schneemelcher, p. 368, also point out that during the sixteenth century there would be an attempt, under Pope Pius V, to remove Joachim and the apocryphal story of Mary's presentation in the temple from the Roman breviary.

73. Compare the following passages: (1) Luke 7:36–50, (2) Luke 10:38–42, (3) John 11:1–45, (4) John 12:1–8, (5) Mark 16:9 and Luke 8:2, (6) Mark 15:40–41, Matt 27:55–56, Luke 23:49, John 19:25, (7) Mark 16:1–8, Matt 28:1–10, Luke 24:1–10, John 20:1–10, (8) John 20:11–18, Mark 16:9–11. See Victor Saxer, *Le culte de Marie Madeleine en Occident, des origines à la fin du Moyen Age* (Paris: Auxerre, 1959), p. 2; Margaret R. Miles, *Image as Insight*, p. 177 n. 62. Gregory the Great, Homily 33.1 (*PL* 76, 1238) and Raban Maur, *Life of St. Mary Magdalene (De Vita Beatae Mariae Magdalenae: PL* 112, 1431–1508) provide examples of such conflation.

74. See Miles, *Image as Insight*, pp. 75–81 and 89.

75. See Kenneth Clark, *Civilisation: A Personal View* (New York: Harper & Row, 1969), p. 29.

76. See Meditations I and II, in *The Prayers and Meditations of St. Anselm*, tr. Benedicta Ward (Harmondsworth: Penguin, 1973), pp. 221–29.

77. The sixth Station, where Veronica wipes the face of Jesus, preserves a fourteenth-century embellishment of a story from the apocryphal Death of Pilate. That tale of "Veronica," or "true *[vero]* image *[nika]*," had been spun around an image cloth venerated in St. Peter's Basilica since the end of the tenth century.

78. English translation in Eugene R. Fairweather, *A Scholastic Miscellany: Anselm to Ockham* (New York: Macmillan, 1970), pp. 100–83.

79. See Bernhard Poschmann, *Penance and the Anointing of the Sick* (New York: Herder & Herder, 1964), pp. 122–54.

80. See John T. McNeill and Helena M. Gamer, *New Medieval Handbooks of Penance: A Translation of the Principal Libri Poenitentiales and Selections from Related Documents* (New York: Columbia University Press, 1938).

81. See Jacques Le Goff, *The Birth of Purgatory*, tr. Arthur Goldhammer (Chicago: University of Chicago Press, 1984).

82. See R. W. Southern, *Western Society and the Church in the Middle Ages* (London: Penguin Books, 1970, 1990 reprint), pp. 136–43.

83. On the concept of time and purgatory, see Le Goff, *The Birth of Purgatory*, pp. 290–95; on pp. 330–31 he notes that on Christmas Day in the Jubilee Year of 1300, Pope Boniface VIII granted a plenary indulgence to all pilgrims who died while on pilgrimage en route to or in Rome.

84. *Salvator noster:* DH 1398; *Romani Pontificis provida:* DH 1405–7.

85. See Elizabeth A. Johnson, "Marian Devotion in the Western Church," in *World Christian Spirituality: High Middle Ages and Reformation Spirituality*, eds. Jill Raitt et al., vol. 17 of *An Encyclopedic History of the Religious Quest*, ed. Ewert Cousins (New York: Crossroad, 1989), pp. 392–414.

86. Latin text and translation in Joseph Connelly, *Hymns of the Roman Liturgy* (London: Longmans, Green, 1957), pp. 186–91.

87. The communion rail, built low for kneeling, had evolved out of the sixteenth-century practice of receiving communion at a table or bench covered with a cloth (which previously, since the thirteenth century, had been held by two acolytes). In earlier centuries, there were varying procedures. The Roman *ordines* describe the Eucharist being

carried to the people who remained in their place in the church. In other locales, such as Gaul during the fourth to the seventh centuries, the people approached the Lord's table, coming forward to stand in front of the main altar to receive the Eucharist. The gates separating the sanctuary (now the place of the clergy) would have been opened at that time in the liturgy. After 800, communion was often distributed at a side altar since many churches in northern Europe now had a high wall or screen separating the main altar from the nave. In other regions, including North Africa during the early centuries, the faithful came forward and stood at a chest-high rail or chancel that surrounded the altar. Even when the Eucharist was received standing, various expressions of reverence emerged in different places, such as genuflecting before receiving, receiving with bare feet or with lowered eyes and joined hands, kissing the floor before receiving, or even kissing the hand of the one distributing communion. Come the twelfth century, the practice of giving communion under the form of the cup generally disappeared in churches of the West. See Jungmann, *The Mass of the Roman Rite*, pp. 506–13.

88. The Sunday aspersion or sprinkling of the community by the priest, first practiced in the monasteries, thereby developed into a self-sprinkling on weekdays.

89. "Eucharistic Worship," in *Theological Investigations*, vol. 23, *Final Writings*, pp. 115–16.

90. See Richard Hart, *Ecclesiastical Records of England, Ireland, and Scotland from the Fifth Century till the Reformation* (Cambridge: Macmillan, 1846), pp. 104–5.

91. Ibid., pp. 160–61.

92. See the episcopal consecration ritual in *Ordo* 35B.35, in M. Andrieu, ed., *Les Ordines romani du haut moyen-âge*, 5 volumes (Louvain, 1931–61); *Pontificale Romanum saec. XII* 10.28, in M. Andrieu ed., *Le Pontifical romain au moyen-âge* (Vatican City, 1938–41); Hugh of St. Victor, *De sacramentis christianae fidei* 2, 4,15 (*PL* 176, 438).

93. Medieval bishops seem to have favored green (which is still considered the episcopal color), although other bright colors were also used, since clerical dress was not uniformly determined before the sixteenth and seventeenth centuries. See John Abel Nainfa, *Costume of Prelates of the Catholic Church, According to Roman Etiquette* (New York: Blase Benziger & Co., 1925), pp. 204–6.

94. Rupert von Simmern, bishop of Strasbourg from 1440 to 1478, never celebrated the liturgy, and only received communion once a year on Holy Thursday: see E. de Moreau, P. Jourda, and P. Janelle, *La*

Crise religieuse du XVIe *siècle*, vol. 15 in *Histoire de l'Église*, founded by A. Fliche and V. Martin (Paris: Bloud & Gay, 1956), pp. 7–9.

95. See, for example, the spurious epistles of Clement, "bishop of Rome," to James, "bishop of Jerusalem," in Paulus Hinschius, ed., *Decretales Pseudo-Isidorianae et Capitulae Angilramni* (Aalen: Scientia Verlag, 1963, reprint of 1863 Leipzig edition), pp. 30–52; text also in *PL* 130.

96. See R. W. Southern, *The Making of the Middle Ages* (New Haven & London: Yale University Press, 1953, reprinted 1976), p. 142.

97. See Congar, *L'Église: De saint Augustin à l'époque moderne*, p. 91.

98. See Ernst H. Kantorowicz, *The Kings's Two Bodies: A Study in Medieval Political Theology* (Princeton: Princeton University Press, 1957), pp. 348–49.

99. Kissing the pope's foot was a practice that survived beyond 1925: "It is well known that the Pope wears for everyday shoes, red, thin-soled, flat-heeled slippers, made of cloth or silk, according to the season. On the vamp of these shoes a gold cross is embroidered, which faithful Catholics, admitted to a private audience, kiss after having made three genuflections, according to etiquette." Nainfa, *Costume of Prelates of the Catholic Church*, p. 124.

100. Text in *Register* 2.55a, in *Bibliotheca Rerum Germanicarum*, vol. 2, *Monumenta Gregoriana*, ed. Philipp Jaffé (Aalen: Scientia Verlag, 1964, reprint of 1865 Berlin ed.) pp. 174–76; also in *PL* 148, 407–8.

101. Congar, *L'Église: De saint Augustin à l'époque moderne*, p. 103.

102. Letter to Henry IV, *Register* 2.31 (Jaffé, *Monumenta Gregoriana*, p. 145); cf. *Register* 1.7, 2.51, 4.28 (Jaffé, pp. 16–17, 168, and 285).

103. Text in *Readings in Church History*, vol. 1, *From Pentecost to the Protestant Revolt*, ed. Colman J. Barry (Westminster, MD: Newman Press, 1960), p. 326.

104. *Decretal Venerabilem Fratrem* to the Duke of Zähringen (March 1202): *Registrum de Negotio Romani Imperii*, 62 in *PL* 216, 1065 or *Corpus Iuris Canonici*, vol. 2, *Decretalium Collectiones*, ed. Aemilius Friedberg (Leipzig: Bernhard Tauchnitz, 1881), col. 80; English text in Ehler and Morrall, *Church and State Through the Centuries*, pp. 69–73.

105. The decrees refer only to excommunication; two of Gregory's letters include the threat of deposition: see *Register* 4.3, 8.21 (Jaffé, *Monumenta Gregoriana*, pp. 245 and 456): see Karl F. Morrison, "Canossa: A Revision," in *Traditio: Studies in Ancient and Medieval History, Thought and Religion*, vol. XVIII, eds. Stephan Kuttner et al. (New York: Fordham University Press, 1962), pp. 121–48.

106. *Register* 3.10a, 7.14a (Jaffé, *Monumenta Gregoriana*, pp. 223–24 and 401); cf. *Register* 1.63, 3.6, 8.20 (Jaffé, pp. 82, 212, and 452).

107. *Sermons* 2 and 3, *"In Consecratione Pontificis Maximi"* (*PL* 217, 658, and 665).

108. *Register* 1.326; *PL* 214, 292); for a review of the literature about this title, see Yves Congar, "Titres donnés au pape," reprinted from *Concilium: Revue internationale de théologie* 108 (Tours, 1975) in *Droit ancien et structures ecclésiales* (London: Variorum Reprints, 1982), VI, p. 61.

109. *Epistle* 251; *De Consideratione* 2.8, 16; 4.7, 23; *De Moribus et Officio Episcoporum* 8, 31; 9, 36 (*PL* 182, cols. 451, 752, 788, 829, and 832).

110. See *Sermon* 3: *In Consecratione Pontificis* (*PL* 217, 665); *Sermon* 7: *in festo D. Silvestri Pont. Max.* (*PL* 217, 481); *Register* 16.131 (*PL* 216, 923); *Registrum de Negotio Romani Imperii* 2 (*PL* 216, 997).

111. *Register* 16.131 (*PL* 216, 924).

112. *Sermon* 7 (*PL* 217, 481–82).

113. *Sicut universitatis conditor*, *Register* 1.401 (*PL* 214, 377; also 216, 1186); *Appendix ad Regesta Tit.* 2, 2: *Solitae benignitatis* to Emperor Alexis of Constantinople (*PL* 216, 1184). The analogy of sun and moon had been previously suggested by Gregory VII in an Epistle to William I (the Conqueror), *Register* 7.25 (Jaffé, *Monumenta Gregoriana*, p. 419).

114. *Registrum de Negotio Romani Imperii* 2 (*PL* 216, 997).

115. *Register* 7.79 (*PL* 215, 361).

116. *Registrum de Negotio Romani Imperii* 18: *In Genesi legimus;* (*PL* 216, 1012–13).

117. *Register* 2.209 (*PL* 214, 759).

118. *Sermon* 2 (*PL* 217, 657).

119. *Sermon* 3 (*PL* 217, 665).

120. *Sermon* 4: In Consecratione Pontificis (*PL* 217, 670).

121. *Sermon* 2 (*PL 217*, 658).

122. *Register* 1.485: *Cum inter alios;* 3.44 (*PL* 214, 453, and 931–32).

123. *Register* 7.1 (*PL* 215, 279).

124. *Register 2.209* (*PL* 214, 763).

125. Colin Morris, *The Papal Monarchy: The Western Church from 1050 to 1250* (Oxford: Clarendon Press, 1989), pp. 527–28.

126. *Ep.* 4.5; in *PL* 50, 434.

127. *Ep.* 10.6; in *PL* 54, 634. He likewise believed the process of selecting a new bishop was to include the votes of the citizens, the testi-

monies of the people, the judgment of esteemed persons, and election by the clerics (*Ep.* 10.4; *PL* 54, 632).

128. See Jean Gaudemet, "Bishops: From Election to Nomination," in *Electing Our Own Bishops,* eds. Peter Huizing and Knut Walf, *Concilium* 137 (New York: Seabury, 1980), pp. 11–12.

129. Ibid., pp. 14–15.

130. *Epistle* 127. W. Ullmann observed that Augustinus Triumphus and Juan de Torquemada later held that all power, both spiritual and temporal, was derived from Christ through the mediation of his successor Peter, whose person is represented by the Roman pontiff: *Growth of Papal Government*, p. 443 n. 4, and p. 477.

131. Latin text in *Corpus Iuris Canonici,* vol. 2 (*Extravag. Commun.*, Bk. I, Title VIII: "*De Majoritate et Obedientia,*" ch. 1), cols. 1245–46; also in DS 870–74; English text in *Documents of the Christian Church*, second edition, ed. Henry Bettenson (Oxford: Oxford University Press, 1963, 1982 reprint), pp. 115–16.

132. See his *Opusculum, Contra Errores Graecorum (ad Urbanum IV)* Pt. 2, ch. 38; *Opera Omnia*, vol. 40, eds. Friars Preachers (Rome: Sancta Sabina, 1969), p. A 103.

133. Latin text in *Corpus Iuris Canonici,* vol. 2 (Sexti Decretal., Bk. III, Title XXIII: "De immunitate ecclesiarum...," ch. 3), cols. 1062–63; English text in Barry, *Readings in Church History*, vol. 1, pp. 464–65.

134. See Congar, *L'Église: De saint Augustin à l'époque moderne*, p. 103–6; A. Anton, *El misterio de la Iglesia*, vol. 1 (Madrid/Toledo: BAC, 1986), pp. 171–74.

135. William Henn, *The Honor of My Brothers: A Brief History of the Relationship Between the Pope and the Bishops, in Ut Unum Sint: Studies on Papal Primacy* (New York: Crossroad–Herder & Herder, 2000), p. 107.

136. See Southern, *Western Society and the Church*, pp. 231–42.

137. In the Gospel according to the Mark of Silver: see Paul Joachim Georg Lehmann, *Die Parodie im Mittelalter* (Munich: Drei Masken Verlag, 1922), pp. 43–69; and *Parodistische Texte, Beispiele zur lateinischen Parodie im Mittelalter* (Munich: Drei Masken Verlag, 1923), pp. 7–10.

138. *De Moribus et Officio Episcoporum* 2, 4–7 (*PL* 182, 812–16).

139. A number of scholars believe that the Cathars initially maintained a mitigated dualism, in which the "spirit of evil" had been produced by the good God and ultimately subordinated to that God, and that an absolute dualism, in which good and evil were eternal and independent principles, was a later position that emerged among some only

toward the end of the twelfth century. See Edward Peters, ed., *Heresy and Authority in Medieval Europe: Documents in Translation* (Philadelphia: University of Pennsylvania Press, 1980), p. 106.

140. Eighty Waldensians were reportedly burned at the stake in Strasbourg in 1211.

141. Southern, *Western Society and the Church*, p. 302.

142. See Ray C. Petry, *Late Medieval Mysticism*, vol. XIII of *The Library of Christian Classics* (Philadelphia: Westminster Press, 1957), pp. 174–75.

143. See *Counsels on Discernment*, 20; *Meister Eckhart: The Essential Sermons, Commentaries, Treatises, and Defense*, eds. and trs. Edmund Colledge and Bernard McGinn (New York/Ramsey, NJ: Paulist Press, 1981), p. 272. Eckhart there describes the mystical union of the soul with God achieved through the Eucharist as so intimate that even the angels could not distinguish between the soul and God. Such blurring of the distinction between God and created reality ultimately gave rise to questions about Eckhart's doctrinal soundness.

144. *German Sermon* 86; text in *Meister Eckhart: Teacher and Preacher*, ed. Bernard McGinn, tr. Frank Tobin (New York/Mahwah, NJ: Paulist Press, 1986), pp. 338–45, here 341–44.

145. Bernard McGinn, "Theological Summary," in *Meister Eckhart: The Essential Sermons*, p. 60.

146. *Counsels on Discernment* 6, p. 253.

147. Ibid., pp. 252 and 251.

148. *Counsels on Discernment* 10, p. 258.

149. Herbert Vorgrimler, *Sacramental Theology*, tr. Linda M. Maloney (Collegeville, MN: Liturgical Press, 1992), pp. 51 and 53–55.

150. See Caroline Walker Bynum, *Jesus as Mother: Studies in the Spirituality of the High Middle Ages* (Berkeley/Los Angeles: University of California Press, 1982), pp. 240–42 and 245.

151. *Showings* (Long text), chapters 57–58, in *Julian of Norwich: Showings*, tr. Edmund Colledge and James Walsh (New York/Ramsey, NJ: Paulist Press, 1978), pp. 290–95.

152. Southern, *Western Society and the Church*, p. 321.

153. Ibid., pp. 327–31.

154. Ibid., pp. 340–41.

155. Kenan B. Osborne, *Ministry, Lay Ministry in the Roman Catholic Church: Its History and Theology* (New York/Mahwah, NJ: Paulist Press, 1993), p. 326.

156. Albert Hyma, *The Christian Renaissance: A History of the "Devotio Moderna,"* second edition (Hamden, CT: Archon Books, 1965), pp. 14, 17, and 20–22.

157. See Jean Leclercq, François Vandenbroucke, and Louis Bouyer, *The Spirituality of the Middle Ages,* tr. Benedictines of Holme Eden Abbey, Carlisle (New York: Seabury Press–Crossroad Book, 1968), p. 429; Hyma, *Christian Renaissance*, pp. 32–33.

158. Southern, *Western Society and the Church*, pp. 344–46.

159. Ibid., p. 357; also see John Van Engen's "Introduction" in *Devotio Moderna: Basic Writings* (New York/Mahwah, NJ: Paulist Press, 1988), pp. 22–25; and Hyma, *Christian Renaissance*, pp. 44–46.

Chapter 5

1. *Summa theologiae* 3, q. 8, a. 1–6.

2. Spirit as "heart": *Summa* 3, q. 8, a. 1 ad 3; as source of unity: *Commentary on the Sentences* 3, d. 13, q. 2, a. 2, sol. 2; *Summa* 2, 2, q. 183, a. 2, ad 3; *Commentary in Ioannem*, c. 6, lect. 7, 4; cf. *Summa* 3, q. 68, a. 9 ad 2.

3. See Henri de Lubac, *Corpus Mysticum* (Paris: Aubier–Ed. Montaigne, 1949), pp. 39–46.

4. For example, see Thomas Aquinas, *Comm. on Sent.* 4, d. 18, q. 1, a. 1, sol. 2; d. 24, q. 2, a. 1–3; and q. 3, a. 2.

5. See de Lubac, *Corpus Mysticum*, pp. 23 and 97.

6. See Seamus Ryan, "Episcopal Consecration: The Legacy of the Schoolmen," *Irish Theological Quarterly* 33 (1966), pp. 6–26; the positions of Ambrosiaster and Jerome were discussed above in chapter 3.

7. See *Comm. on Sent.* 4, d. 7, q. 3, a. 1; d. 24, q. 1, a. 3, sol. 2; also q. 2, a. 1; q. 3, a. 2; d. 25, q. 1, a. 1 ad 3 and a. 2, ad 2; *Summa contra gentiles* 4, 74–76; *Opusculum de Perfectione Spiritualis Vitae* 21–22, 24, and 27–28; *Summa theologiae* 2, 2, q. 184, a. 6; 3, q. 82, a. 1, ad 4; cf. 3, q. 67, a. 2, ad 1 and q. 72, a. 11.

8. *Comm. on Sent.* 4, d. 25, q. 1, a. 2, ad 2.

9. *Comm. on Sent.* 4, d. 24, q. 3, a. 2; *Opusculum* 25 and 28; *De Articulis Fidei et Ecclesiae Sacramentis* 2.

10. *Glossa in Libros Sententiarum* IV, d. 24, n. 2.

11. For example, Huguccio of Pisa, *Summa* ad Dist. 21, c. 1; and Rufinus, *Summa* ad Dist. 21, c. 2.

12. See Congar, *L'Église: De saint Augustin à l'époque moderne*, p. 237, and Aquinas, *Comm. on Sent.* 2, d. 44, exp. textus; 4, d. 18, q. 2, a. 2, sol. 1 ad 1; d. 20, q. 1, a. 4, sol. 3; d. 24, q. 3, a. 2, sol. 3, ad 1; *Summa contra gentiles* 72 and 76; *Commentary on Mattthew* 16.

13. *Comm. on Sent.* 4, d. 18, q. 1, a. 1, sol. 2, ad 2; d. 19, q. 1, a. 2, sol. 3; and a. 3, sol. 1 and 2; see J. Lécuyer, "Orientations présentes de la théologie de l'épiscopat," in *L'Épiscopat et l'Église Universelle*, eds. Y. Congar and B.-D. Dupuy (Paris: Les Éditions du Cerf, 1964), p. 804.

14. *Comm. on Sent.* 4, d. 24, q. 3, a. 2, q. 3, sol. 3 and ad 1.

15. Ryan, "Episcopal Consecration," p. 33.

16. Especially meaning its right to acquire and hold property.

17. *De Consideratione* 2.8, 16; 4.3, 7; 4.7, 23 (*PL* 182, cols. 752, 776, and 788).

18. *De Consideratione* 3.4, 14 (*PL* 182, 766–67).

19. *Summa* 2, 2, q. 39, a. 1.

20. *Comm. in Sent.* 4, d. 7, q. 3, a. 1, sol. 3; d. 20, q. 1, a. 4, sol. 3; d. 25, q. 1, a. 1, ad 3; *Contra impugnantes Dei cultum et religionem* 4; *Summa* 2, 2, q. 88, a. 12, ad 3; q. 89, a. 9 ad 3; 3, q. 72, a.11, ad 1.

21. *Summa* 3, q. 8, a. 6 resp.

22. See Michael Wilks, *The Problem of Sovereignty in the Later Middle Ages: The Papal Monarchy with Augustinus Triumphus and the Publicists* (Cambridge: Cambridge University Press, 1963), pp. 15–64.

23. Anton Weiler, "Church Authority and Government in the Middle Ages: A Bibliographical Survey," in *Concilium*, vol. 7, No. 1, eds. Roger Aubert and Anton Weiler (London: Burns & Oates, 1965), p. 65.

24. *Collirium*, in *Unbekannte Kirchenpolitische Streitschriften aus der Zeit Ludwigs des Bayern (1327–1354)*, vol. 2 (Bibliothek d. Preussischen Historischen Instituts in Rom, IX–X), ed. Richard Scholz (Rome: Loescher & Co. [W. Regenberg], 1911–14), p. 506.

25. *De planctu Ecclesiae* 1.6.

26. *Summa de potestate ecclesiastica* 45.2.

27. Wilks, *Problem of Sovereignty*, pp. 59–60: citing Augustinus Triumphus, *Summa* 6.2–3, 22.5.

28. See *On Ecclesiastical Power by Giles of Rome*, tr. Arthur P. Monahan (Lewiston, NY: Edwin Mellen Press, 1990), 1.2–6, pp. 8–33.

29. *On Ecclesiastical Power* 3.9: Monahan, pp. 264 and 267.

30. *On Ecclesiastical Power* 3.12: Monahan, p. 288.

31. Brian Tierney, *Foundations of the Conciliar Theory: The Contribution of the Medieval Canonists from Gratian to the Great Schism* (Cambridge: Cambridge University Press, 1955), p. 1.

32. Ibid., pp. 23–24.

33. Ibid., p. 240.

34. Ibid., p. 242.

35. Ibid., p. 244.

36. Ibid., pp. 41–43, 53–55, 84, and 245.

37. Ibid., p. 24.

38. Ibid., p. 246.

39. J. Black, "What Was Conciliarism? Conciliar Theory in Historical Perspective," in *Authority and Power: Studies on Medieval Law and Government Presented to Walter Ullmann on his Seventieth Birthday*, eds. Brian Tierney and Peter Linehan (Cambridge: Cambridge University Press, 1980), pp. 216–17.

40. Tierney, *Foundations of the Conciliar Theory*, pp. 4–5.

41. Ibid., p. 6; cf. p. 55.

42. Hubert Jedin, *Bischöfliches Konzil oder Kirchenparlament. Ein Beitrag zur Ekklesiologie der Konzilien von Konstanz und Basel* (Basel: Helbing & Lichtenhahn, 1963), p. 12.

43. August Franzen, "The Council of Constance: Present State of the Problem," in *Concilium*, vol. 7, No. 1, pp. 29–30 and 32–34. (Cf. n.23 above.)

44. Ibid., pp. 21, 27, and 30.

45. See Hubert Jedin, *Ecumenical Councils of the Catholic Church* (New York: Paulist Press, 1960), pp. 91–92.

46. *Decrees of the Ecumenical Councils*, vol. 1, p. *409.

47. Ibid., pp. 438–42.

48. Franzen, "The Council of Constance: Present State of the Problem," p. 31.

49. *Structures of the Church* (Edinburgh/New York: Thomas Nelson, 1964), p. 285; also see pp. 278–84.

50. Klaus Schatz, *Papal Primacy: From Its Origins to the Present* (Collegeville, MN: Liturgical Press, 1996), p. 105.

51. Text in *Readings in Church History*, vol. 1, ed. Colman J. Barry (Westminster, MD: Newman Press, 1960), pp. 506–10.

52. *Summa de ecclesia* III, 64; *Oratio synodalis de primatu* 70.

53. *In Gratiani Decretorum primam Commentarii*, on Dist. 19, c. 8; *Oratio synodalis de primatu* 36.

54. *L'Église: De saint Augustin à l'époque moderne*, p. 343.

55. *Laetentur caeli*, July 6, 1439, *Decrees of the Ecumenical Councils*, vol. 1, pp. 523 and 528 (DH 1307).

56. *Cantate domino*, Bull of Union with the Copts (or Decree for the Jacobites), Feb. 4, 1442, *Decrees of the Ecumenical Councils*, vol. 1, p. 578 (DH 1351).

57. Ibid., p. 642 (DH 1445).

58. Decree on the end of the council and seeking confirmation from the pope, Session 25 (Dec. 3–4, 1563): *Decrees of the Ecumenical Councils*, vol. 2, p. 799.

59. Yves Congar, "Reception as an Ecclesiological Reality," *Election and Consensus in the Church*, vol. 77 of *Concilium*, eds. Giuseppe Alberigo and Anton Weiler (New York: Herder and Herder, 1972), p. 68.

60. "The Ninety-Five Theses," in *Martin Luther: Selections from His Writings*, ed. John Dillenberger (Garden City, NY: Doubleday–Anchor Books, 1961), pp. 490–500.

61. See Martin Luther, *Three Treatises* (Philadelphia: Fortress, 1970), pp. 12–23.

62. *Three Treatises*, p. 12.

63. Ibid.

64. Ibid, p. 22.

65. Ibid., pp. 42 and 32–46. From the middle of the thirteenth century, a newly appointed bishop had to reimburse the papal chancellery for the expenses incurred in processing his appointment. He was also expected to make a financial contribution to the pope and other "staff," which all amounted to a third of the annual revenues from the benefices attached to the bishopric.

66. Ibid., p. 46.

67. Session 23, Decree on the Sacrament of Order, canon 8; Session 24, Reform Decree, chapter 1: *Decrees of the Ecumenical Councils*, vol. 2, pp. 744 (DH 1778) and 760; for an analysis of the debates, see Jean Bernhard, "The Election of Bishops at the Council of Trent," in *Electing Our Own Bishops*, pp. 24–30.

68. Ibid., pp. 46–52.

69. *Three Treatises*, pp. 26–30, 53–54, and 88.

70. Ibid., pp. 244–45 and 247.

71. Martin Luther, *Commentary on Psalm 82*, section 4, in *Luther's Works*, vol. 13, *Selected Psalms II*, ed. Jaroslav Pelikan (St. Louis: Concordia Publishing House, 1956), p. 65.

72. *Sendschreiben an zwei Pfarrherren von der Wiedertaufe*, 1528, in the Weimar edition of Luther's work, vol. 26, p. 257f.: cited by Lorenz Cardinal Jaeger, *A Stand on Ecumenism: The Council's Decree*, tr. Hilda Graef (London: Geoffrey Chapman, 1965), p. 117.

73. Hubert Jedin, *A History of the Council of Trent*, vol. 1, *The Struggle for the Council* (Edinburgh: Thomas Nelson, 1957), pp. 211 and 195.

74. Ibid., pp. 195 and 274–75.

75. Regarding preaching, see Session 5, Decree on Preaching, c. 2 and 9; Decrees of Reformation, Session 23, c. 1; Session 24, c. 4; in *Decrees of the Ecumenical Councils*, vol. 2, pp. 668, 669, 744, and 763.

Regarding the obligation of residence, see Decrees of Reformation, in Sessions 6, 7, 13, 14, 21, 22, 23, 24, and 25 in *Decrees of the Ecumenical Councils*, vol. 2, pp. 681–83, 686–89, 698–701, 714–18, 728–32, 737–41, 744–53, 759–73, 784–96.

76. Hubert Jedin, *A History of the Council of Trent*, vol. II, *The First Sessions at Trent* 1545–47, tr. Ernest Graf, OSB (Edinburgh: Thomas Nelson, 1961), p. 321.

77. Alphonse Dupront, "Le Concile de Trente," in *Le concile et les Conciles* (Chevetogne: Editions de Chevetogne, 1960), pp. 229–30.

78. *De controversiis Christianae fidei adversus nostri temporis haereticos*, vol. 2, *Prima Controversia generalis*, book 3: De Ecclesia militante, chapter 2, "*de definitione Ecclesiae*" (Ingolstadt, 1601), cols. 137–38.

79. See Congar, *L'Église: De saint Augustin à l'époque moderne*, pp. 381–84.

80. As summarized by Johann Adam Möhler, *Theologische Quartalschrift* 5 (1823), p. 493.

81. Roger Aubert, "Religious Liberty from 'Mirari vos' to the 'Syllabus'," in *Concilium*, vol. 7, no. 1, p. 52. (Cf. n.23 above.)

82. Giuseppe Alberigo, "The Authority of the Church in the Documents of Vatican I and Vatican II," *Journal of Ecumenical Studies* 19 (1982), p. 120.

83. Yves M. J. Congar, "L'ecclésiologie, de la Révolution française au Concile du Vatican, sous le signe de l'affirmation de l'autorité," in *L'ecclésiologie au XIX*[e] *siècle*, ed. Maurice Nédoncelle (Paris: Les Éditions du Cerf, 1960), pp. 99–100.

84. *Principiarum fidei doctrinalium Demonstratio methodica*, *Controv.* IV, bk. VIII, c. 12 (1572 and Paris, 1579); cited by Congar, *L'Église: De saint Augustin à l'époque moderne*, p. 371. Stapleton maintained the early fathers were teachers only because they had the episcopal or priestly grace or charism: *Principiarum fidei...Demonstratio methodica*, *Controv.* III, bk. VII, c. 12.

85. Congar has traced the distinction between a "learning" and "teaching" Church to the theological discussion of passive vs. active infallibility in the eighteenth century. He noted that the distinction became frequent in the early nineteenth century: *L'Église: De saint Augustin à l'époque moderne*, p. 389.

86. *Praelectiones theologicae quas in Collegio Romano habebat* (Rome: Collegio Urbano de Propaganda Fide, 1835–42) I, n. 333; cited by Congar, *L'Église, De saint Augustin à l'époque moderne*, p. 431 n. 9.

87. The theme of participation in the threefold office of Christ was especially developed by the nineteenth-century canonist Georg

Phillips, who converted to Catholicism in 1828. See Giuseppe Alberigo, *Lo Sviluppo della Dottrina sui Poteri nella Chiesa Universale: Momenti essenziali tra il XVI e il XIX secolo* (Roma: Herder, 1964), pp. 391–94; Richard R. Gaillardetz, *Witnesses to the Faith: Community, Infallibility and the Ordinary Magisterium of Bishops* (New York/Mahwah, NJ: Paulist Press, 1992), pp. 15–16 and 194, note 23; Joseph Fuchs, "Origines d'une trilogie ecclésiologique a l'époque rationaliste de la théologie," *Revue des sciences philosophiques et théologiques* 53 (1969), pp. 186–211; Herman Josef Pottmeyer, *Unfehlbarkeit und Souveränität: Die päpstliche Unfehlbarkeit im System der ultramontanen Ekklesiologie des 19.* Jahrhunderts (Mainz: Matthias Grünewald Verlag, 1975), pp. 145–72. For earlier perspectives, consider Herbert Grundmann, "Sacerdotium-Regnum-Studium: Zur Wertung der Wissenschaft im 13. Jahrhundert," *Archiv für Kulturgeschichte* 34 (1952), pp. 5–21.

88. See, for example, Timotheus Zapelena, *De Ecclesia Christi, Pars Apologetica*, sixth revised edition (Rome: Gregorian University, 1955), pp. 120–38; and Ioachim Salaverri, "De Ecclesia Christi," in *Sacrae Theologiae Summa I: Theologia Fundamentalis* (Madrid: Biblioteca de Autores Cristianos, 1958), pp. 524–26 and 555–56.

89. See Gustave Thils, *L'Infaillibilité du peuple chrétien "in credendo": notes de théologie posttridentine* (Paris: Desclée de Brouwer/Louvain: E. Warny, 1963).

90. Originally in *The Rambler* 1 (1859), pp. 198–230; a revised summary appeared as "Note 5" in the Appendix to the third edition of *The Arians of the Fourth Century* (London: Longmans, Green & Co., 1891); for recent editions, see John Coulson, ed., *On Consulting the Faithful in Matters of Doctrine by John Henry Newman* (London: Geoffrey Chapman, 1961); or Jean Guitton, *The Church and the Laity* (Staten Island, NY: Alba House, 1965), pp. 64–121.

91. Alberigo, "The Authority of the Church," p. 129.

92. Ibid., pp. 128–29; see Newman's letter of July 28, 1875, to Isy Froude, in *The Letters and Diaries of John Henry Newman*, vol. 27, eds. Charles S. Dessain and Thomas Gornall (Oxford: Clarendon Press, 1975), p. 338.

93. Paul Misner, *Papacy and Development: Newman and the Primacy of the Pope* (Leiden: E. J. Brill, 1976), p. 180; see John Henry Newman's *The Development of Christian Doctrine* (London & New York: Sheed & Ward, 1960).

94. *Die Einheit in der Kirche; oder, das Prinzip des Katholizismus dargestellt im Geiste der Kirchenväter der drei ersten Jahrhunderte*, rev. by

E. J. Vierneisel (Mainz: M. Grunewald, 1925 [orig. ed., Tübingen: Heinrich Laupp, 1825]), p. 34.

95. *Symbolik, oder Darstellung der dogmatischen Gegensätze der Katholiken und Protestanten nach ihren öffentlichen Bekenntnisschriften*, fourth edition (Mainz: F. Kupferberg, 1835), pp. 334–37, 360–62, and 374–76; *Symbolism, or Exposition of the Doctrinal Differences between Catholics and Protestants as Evidenced by Their Symbolical Writings*, fifth edition, tr. James Burton Robertson (London: Gibbings & Co., 1906) pp. 258–59, 278–79, and 289–90.

96. *Symbolik*, pp. 301, 334–37, 360; *Symbolism*, pp. 236, 258–59, and 278.

97. *L'Église: De saint Augustin à l'époque moderne*, p. 429.

98. "The Authority of the Church," pp. 120–21, and 125.

99. See J. Derek Holmes, *The Triumph of the Holy See: A Short History of the Papacy in the Nineteenth Century* (London: Burns & Oates/Shepherdstown, WV: Patmos Press, 1978), pp. 146–47.

100. Alberigo, "The Authority of the Church," pp. 121–22 and 127; Yves Congar, "Pour une histoire sémantique du terme 'magisterium'," *Revue des sciences philosophiques et théologiques*, vol. 60 (1976), p. 95; "Bref historique des formes du 'magistère' et de ses relations avec les docteurs," *Revue des sciences...*, vol. 60 (1976), p. 107–9; Herman J. Pottmeyer, "Das Lehramt der Hirten und seine Ausübung," *Theologisch-praktische Quartalschrift*, vol. 128 (1980), pp. 336–48.

101. DH 2879–80. This is the first reference to a magisterium ordinarium, whose teachings are said to demand the assent of faith, in an official ecclesiastical document. The use of the term by Pius IX later facilitated its inclusion in chapter 3 of Vatican I's Dogmatic Constitution on Revelation and Faith, *Dei Filius*, in 1869: *Decrees of the Ecumenical Councils*, vol. 2, p. 807 (DH 3011). See Francis A. Sullivan, *Magisterium: Teaching Authority in the Catholic Church* (Mahwah, NJ: Paulist Press, 1983), p. 122; Gaillardetz, *Witnesses to the Faith*, pp. 25 and 30–31.

102. See Pope Pius IX, "*Inter gravissimas*," in *Pii IX Acta*, Part 1, vol. 5, col. 260; Pope Pius XII, *Humani generis* in DH 3886.

103. Alberigo, "The Authority of the Church," p. 122.

104. See Holmes, *The Triumph of the Holy See*, pp. 139–42. Holmes observes that some even found a way to link devotions with secular and ecclesiastical politics. For example, French monarchists "adopted the cult of the Sacred Heart, which signified the submission of political authority to that of Christ."

105. Text in J. D. Mansi, *Sacrorum Conciliorum nova et amplissima collectio*, revised and augmented by J. B. Martin and L. Petit, 53 volumes

in 60, anastatic edition (Paris, 1901–27), vol. 51, 539–53; English text of chapters 1–10 in *The Teaching of the Catholic Church*, ed. Karl Rahner, orig. eds. Josef Neuner and Heinrich Roos (Staten Island, NY: Alba House, 1967), pp. 211–20.

106. He was cited three times in the notes to the schema.

107. For a summary of comments about the inadequate treatment of bishops, see Gustave Thils, *Primauté pontificale et prérogatives épiscopales: "potestas ordinaria" au Concile du Vatican, Bibliotheca Ephemeridum Theologicarum Lovaniensium*, vol. XVII (Louvain: É. Warny, 1961), pp. 35–39.

108. See Gustave Thils, *La primauté pontificale. La doctrine de Vatican I* (Gembloux: Éditions J. Duculot, 1972).

109. DH 2281–84; English text in Schatz, *Papal Primacy*, pp. 188–89.

110. Congar, *L'Église: De saint Augustin à l'époque moderne*, p. 409.

111. *Papal Primacy*, p. 137.

112. *Decrees of the Ecumenical Councils*, vol. 2, pp. 812–13 (DH 3053–58).

113. Ibid., pp. 813–15 (DH 3059–64).

114. Ibid., pp. 815–16 (DH 3065–75).

115. Ibid., p. 807 (DH 3011); see Gaillardetz, *Witnesses to the Faith*, pp. 30–31.

116. Alberigo, *Lo Sviluppo della Dottrina sui Poteri*, pp. 436–38.

117. Ibid., pp. 438–45; Mansi, 52, 1109B–1110B and 1204D–1205C; 53, 310BC and 321BC.

118. Mansi 53, 271C, cf. 268D–269A.

119. Bishop Zinelli said that Trent let the question stand because "in practice it makes no difference whether one follows one or the other opinion" (Mansi 52, 1110D); Vatican I likewise left it an open question (Mansi 52, 1109C, 1110C–D, 1314A–C).

120. Mansi 52, 1105B–C.

121. Ibid., 1105B–D.

122. See Jean-Pierre Torrell, *La théologie de l'épiscopat au premier Concile du Vatican, Unam Sanctam* 37 (Paris: Les Éditions du Cerf, 1961), p. 301; *Decrees of the Ecumenical Councils*, vol. 2, p. 814 (DH 3061).

123. Mansi 52, 1103D–04A; cf. the revised disciplinary schema *De Episcopis:* Mansi 53, 721–22.

124. DH 3112–16; complete English text in *The Teaching of the Catholic Church*, pp. 230–33.

125. See J.-P. Torrell, *La théologie de l'épiscopat*, p. 301; for the first and second drafts see p. 300.

126. Matteo Liberatore, "La definizione dommatica dell'infallibilità pontificia," *Civiltà Cattolica* 7, 11 (1870), p. 178; cited in Hermann Josef Sieben, *Katholische Konzilsidee im 19. und 20. Jahrhundert* (Paderborn: Ferdinand Schöningh, 1993), p. 144.

127. "Il dottor Döllinger e la petizione dei vescovi al concilio," *Civiltà Cattolica* 7, 9 (1870), pp. 392–93.

128. Sieben, *Katholische Konzilsidee*, pp. 153–54.

129. See Gustave Thils, *L'Infaillibilité pontificale: source—conditions—limites* (Gembloux: Éditions J. Duculot, 1969), pp. 186–91.

130. Mansi 52, 1214AC; Thils, *L'Infaillibilité pontificale*, pp. 191–92.

131. Mansi 52, 1225BC.

132. Ibid., 23B–D and 36C; 52, 746AB, 764D–765A, and 766C; cf. 52, 1214D; also see Gustave Thils, *Primauté et infaillibilité du pontife Romain à Vatican I* (Leuven: Leuven University Press, 1989), pp. 190–91.

133. Mansi 52, 1213BC; Thils, *L'Infaillibilité pontificale*, pp. 220–21.

134. Mansi 52, 1212D–1213B and 1219A; Thils, *L'Infaillibilité pontificale*, pp. 212–16.

135. Mansi 52, 1213ABC.

136. Ibid., 1225B; See Thils, *L'Infaillibilité pontificale*, pp. 177–79 and 184.

137. Mansi 52, 1213C.

138. Ibid., 1226–27; see Thils, *L'Infaillibilité pontificale*, pp. 245–51, also cf. 161 and 207–9; Francis A. Sullivan, *Magisterium*, pp. 133 and 140; and his "Note: The 'Secondary Object' of Infallibility," in *Theological Studies* 54 (1993), pp. 538–39 and 544.

139. For the Latin texts of the drafts in parallel columns, see J.-P. Torrell, *La théologie de l'épiscopat*, p. 313.

140. See Thils, *L'Infaillibilité pontificale*, pp. 162–63.

141. *Summa* 2, 2, q. 1, a. 10, resp.; *De Potentia* 10, 4, ad 13.

142. Brian Tierney, *Origins of Papal Infallibility 1150–1350: A Study of the Concepts of Infallibility, Sovereignty and Tradition in the Middle Ages*, Second Impression with a Postscript (Leiden: E. J. Brill, 1988, orig. ed. 1972), pp. 93–109.

143. Ibid., pp. 116–17.

144. Ibid., pp. 120–21 and 125.

145. Ibid., pp. 173, 178–79, and 190–92.

146. Ibid., pp. 182–83.

147. Sullivan, *Magisterium*, pp. 92–93; also see Tierney, *Origins of Papal Infallibility*, pp. 238–51.

148. Tierney, *Origins of Papal Infallibility*, pp. 248–49; original text in *Guidonis Terreni Quaestio de magisterio infallibili Romani pontificis*, ed. Bartolomé M. Xiberta (Münster in Westfalen: Aschendorff, 1926), p. 28. According to the text on page 17, Terreni presumed that the pope would have sought the counsel of cardinals on such matters.

149. See Congar, *L'Église: De saint Augustin à l'époque moderne*, pp. 386–87.

150. Mansi 52, 22D–23A, 36C, 765AB, and 1213BC; Thils, *L'Infaillibilité pontificale*, pp. 216–21.

151. Mansi 52, 765A and 1227BC; Thils, *L'Infaillibilité pontificale*, pp. 159–60 and 220.

152. Mansi 52, 765B.

153. *Magisterium*, pp. 96–97.

154. J. Derek Holmes, *The Triumph of the Holy See*, pp. 135–36.

155. Ibid., p. 136.

156. For example, Vacant, Bellamy, Billot, Perriot, Fenton, and Salaverri: see G. Thils, *L'Infaillibilité pontificale*, pp. 179–82.

157. See Thils, *L'Infaillibilité pontificale*, pp. 182–83, also cf. 160–62; Umberto Betti, *La Costituzione dogmàtica "Pastor aeternus" del Concilio Vaticano I* (Rome: Pontificio Ateneo "Antonianum," 1961), pp. 646–47.

158. Franciscus W. Wernz, *Ius Decretalium*, Tome II, part 2: *Ius Constitutionis Ecclesiae Catholicae*, third edition (Prato: Libraria Giachetti, 1915), pp. 501 and 540.

159. From his letter to Lord Blachford, of February 5, 1875, in Dessain and Gornall, *The Letters and Diaries of John Henry Newman*, vol. 27, p. 212.

160. Yves Congar, "The Historical Development of Authority in the Church: Points for Christian Reflection" in *Problems of Authority*, ed. John M. Todd (Baltimore: Helicon Press, 1962), pp. 137 and 148–49.

161. I have adapted Thomas S. Kuhn's observations concerning the manner in which shifts in scientific paradigms are incorporated into text-books. See *The Structure of Scientific Revolutions*, second edition, enlarged (Chicago: University of Chicago Press, 1970), pp. 10, 17, and 137.

162. *The Reshaping of Catholicism: Current Changes in the Theology of Church* (San Francisco: Harper & Row, 1988), pp. 24–25.

163. John Henry Cardinal Newman, *Essays, Critical and Historical*, vol. 2 (London: Longmans, Green, and Co., 1891) p. 44, note.

164. *Immortale Dei* (1885) and *Libertas praestantissimum bonum* (1888).

165. In the encyclicals *Satis cognitum* (1896) and *Divinum illud munus* (1897).

Chapter 6

1. Abbott, *The Documents of Vatican II*, p. 712.

2. *Discorsi, messaggi, colloqui del Santo Padre Giovanni XXIII*, vol. III (Vatican City: Libreria Editrice Vaticana, 1967), p. 205.

3. Giancarlo Zizola, *The Utopia of Pope John XXIII* (Maryknoll, NY: Orbis Books, 1978) pp. 225–27.

4. Ibid., p. 113.

5. *The Reshaping of Catholicism: Current Challenges in the Theology of Church* (San Francisco: Harper & Row, 1988), pp. 20–33.

6. Unless otherwise noted, citations are from *Vatican Council II*, vol. 1, *The Conciliar and Post Conciliar Documents*, ed. Austin Flannery (Northport, NY: Costello Publishing, 1992); Latin text (also with English translation) of Vatican II documents is found in *Decrees of the Ecumenical Councils*, vol. 2, pp. 820–1135.

7. See C. Vagaggini, "Idee fondamentali della Costituzione," in *La Sacra Liturgia rinnovata dal Concilio*, ed. G. Barauna (Turin-Leumann: Elle Di Ci, 1965), pp. 62–63.

8. The ninth, tenth, and eleventh chapters, which eventually became separate documents, dealt with relationships between Church and State and religious tolerance, the necessity of proclaiming the gospel to all peoples and in the whole world, and ecumenism. There was also an appendix entitled "Virgin Mary, Mother of God and Mother of Men." See Gérard Philips, "Dogmatic Constitution on the Church: History of the Constitution," in *Commentary on the Documents of Vatican II*, vol. I, ed. Herbert Vorgrimler (New York: Herder & Herder, 1967), p. 106.

9. Ibid., pp. 107–9.

10. Ibid., p. 110.

11. Translation is mine: "veluti sacramentum seu signum et instrumentum intimae cum Deo unionis totiusque generis humani unitatis."

12. Aloys Grillmeier, "The Mystery of the Church," in *Commentary on the Documents of Vatican II*, p. 146.

13. *Notificatio: de scripto P. Leonardi Boff, OFM "Chiesa: Carisma e Potere," Acta Apostolicae Sedis* 77 (1985), pp. 756–62, here pp. 758–59; English text in *Origins* 14 (1985), pp. 685–86.

14. Francis A. Sullivan, *The Church We Believe In One, Holy, Catholic, and Apostolic* (New York/Mahwah, NJ: Paulist Press, 1988), p. 33.

15. Ibid., p. 25.

16. See Grillmeier, "The Mystery of the Church," in *Commentary on the Documents of Vatican II*, pp. 157–58.

17. *Theological Highlights of Vatican II* (New York/Glen Rock, NJ: Paulist Press, 1966), p. 121.

18. Translation is mine: "...in *Ecclesia sua varia ministeria instituit, quae ad bonum totius Corporis tendunt*" (section 18).

19. Gérard Philips, "Dogmatic Constitution on the Church: History of the Constitution," p. 129.

20. Ibid.; also see Karl Rahner, "The Hierarchical Structure of the Church, with Special Reference to the Episcopate; Articles 18–27," *Commentary on the Documents of Vatican II*, p. 196.

21. Translation is mine: "Non intelligitur autem de vago quodam *affectu*, sed de *realitate organica*, quae iuridicam formam exigit et simul caritate animator."

22. For example, Rahner in "The Hierarchical Structure of the Church," p. 203; and in Karl Rahner and Joseph Ratzinger, *The Episcopate and the Primacy, Quaestiones Disputatae* 4 (New York: Herder & Herder, 1962), pp. 97–100.

23. Thomas Aquinas, *Summa* 3, q. 73, a. 3.

24. "The Hierarchical Structure of the Church," p. 216.

25. See Paul VI, *motu proprio, Apostolica Solicitudo (Sept. 15, 1965) in Acta Apostolicae Sedis* 57 (1965), pp. 775–80.

26. *Cantate Domino* (Decree for the Jacobites), *Decrees of the Ecumenical Councils*, vol. 1, p. *578 (DH 1351).

27. John Henry Cardinal Newman, *The Arians of the Fourth Century* (London/New York: Longmans, Green, 1891), pp. 358 and 445.

28. John W. O'Malley, *Tradition and Transition: Historical Perspectives on Vatican II* (Wilmington, DE: Michael Glazier, 1989), p. 94.

29. Ratzinger, *Theological Highlights of Vatican II*, p. 39.

30. Ibid., pp. 8–9.

31. Ibid., pp. 34–35.

32. "La collegialitá episcopale: spiegazione teologica," in *La Chiesa del Vatican II*, edited by G. Barauna (Florence: Vallechi, 1965), pp. 745–47.

33. *Theological Highlights of Vatican II*, pp. 121–22.

34. Hermann J. Pottmeyer, "A New Phase in the Reception of Vatican II: Twenty Years of Interpretation of the Council," in *The Reception of Vatican II*, eds. Giuseppe Alberigo, J. P. Jossua, and J. A. Komonchak, tr. Matthew J. O'Connell (Washington, DC: The Catholic University of America Press, 1988), p. 37.

35. Ibid., p. 38.

36. See Joseph A. Komonchak, "The Local Church and the Church Catholic," *The Jurist* 52 (1992), p. 416

37. *Theology & Church*, p. 158.

38. Section 5, *Acta Apostolicae Sedis* 65 (1973), pp. 402–4; English translation in *Catholic Mind* 71 (1973), pp. 58–60.

39. Pottmeyer, "A New Phase in the Reception of Vatican II," p. 38.

40. Sections 89 and 95–96; *Acta Apostolicae Sedis* 87 (1995), pp. 921–82, here pp. 974 and 977–78; English text in *Origins, CNS Documentary Service* 25 (1995), pp. 49–72, here 68–70.

41. See Avery Dulles, *The Reshaping of Catholicism: Current Challenges in the Theology of Church* (San Francisco: Harper & Row, 1988), pp. 189–90.

42. *Litterae ad Catholicae Ecclesiae episcopos de aliquibus aspectibus Ecclesiae prout est communio, Acta Apostolicae Sedis* 85 (1993), pp. 838–65. English translation, and ecumenical responses, in *Catholic International* 3 (September, 1992), pp. 761–67.

43. "Church as Communion," nos. 1–6, *Catholic International*, pp. 761–63.

44. Ibid., nos. 10 and 11, pp. 764 and 765.

45. Ibid., no. 8, p. 763.

46. *Papal Primacy and the Episcopate* (New York: Crossroad, 1998), pp. 24–25.

47. Ibid., no. 7, p. 763, citing Second Vatican Council, *Lumen gentium* 23 and *Ad Gentes* 20.

48. Ibid., citing Second Vatican Council, *Christus Dominus* 11.

49. *Christus Dominus* 6.

50. "Church as Communion," no. 9, *Catholic International*, pp. 763–64.

51. *Lumen gentium* 23.

52. "Address to the Roman Curia," (20 Dec. 1990) no. 9; *Acta Apostolicae Sedis* 83 (1991), pp. 745–47.

53. "Church as Communion," no. 9, *Catholic International*, p. 764.

54. Ibid., no, 10, p. 764.

55. English translation from Susan K. Wood, "The Church as Communion," in *The Gift of the Church: A Textbook on Ecclesiology in Honor of Patrick Granfield, O.S.B.*, ed. Peter C. Phan (Collegeville, MN: Liturgical Press, 2000), p. 174.

56. "Church as Communion," no. 11, *Catholic International*, p. 764.

57. Ibid., no. 12, p. 765.

58. Ibid., nos. 13–14, p. 765.

59. Tillard, *The Bishop of Rome*, p. 189.

60. "Church as Communion," no. 15, *Catholic International*, pp. 765–66. Churches that are not in communion with the bishop of Rome, or that do not retain apostolic succession and a valid Eucharist, are said to be "wounded." Ibid., no. 17, p. 766.

61. *Theological Highlights of Vatican II*, pp. 8–9, and 35.

62. *The World of Late Antiquity*, p. 135.

63. William Henn, "Historical-Theological Synthesis of the Relation between Primacy and Episcopacy during the Second Millennium," *Il primato del successore de Pietro: Atti del simposio teologico, Roma, dicembre 1996* (Vatican City: Libreria Editrice Vaticana, 1997), pp. 219–20; cited by Buckley, *Papal Primacy and the Episcopate*, p. 14.

64. Miroslav Volf, *After Our Likeness: The Church as the Image of the Trinity* (Grand Rapids, MI: Eerdmans, 1998).

65. Ibid., pp. 29–72.

66. Ibid., pp. 204–13 and 278. In Volf's view, catholicity also includes "a willingness to accept other Christians and other churches precisely in their otherness."

67. "Church as Communion," no. 15, p. 766.

68. Ibid., p. 281.

69. Ibid., p. 282.

70. See, generally, Edward Schillebeeckx, *Jesus*, p. 579.

71. Ibid., p. 577.

72. Hans-Georg Gadamer, *Truth and Method*, p. 281.

Chapter 7

1. Karl Rahner, "A Fragmentary Aspect of a Theological Evaluation of the Concept of the Future," in *Theological Investigations*, vol. 10, *Writings of 1965–67*, trans. David Bourke (New York: Herder and Herder, 1973), p. 237.

2. Karl Rahner, "On the Theology of Hope," *Theological Investigations*, vol. 10, p. 257.

3. Kasper, *Theology and Church*, p. 163.

4. *City of God* 12, ch. 11; 20, chs. 7, 9, and 13.

5. Meier, *A Marginal Jew*, vol. 2, pp. 336–51, cf. 450–54.

6. *1 Clement* 23:3; 2 *Clement* 11:2.

7. *City of God* 12, ch. 11; 20, chs. 7, 9, and 13.

8. *The Catholicity of the Church* (Oxford: Clarendon Press, 1987), p. 90.

9. Ibid., p. 92.

10. O'Malley, *Tradition and Transition*, pp. 47–48, 67, 107, and 109.

11. *Keeping Hope Alive*, p. 59.

12. See Kasper, *Theology and Church*, pp. 32–34, 54–72.

13. *Gaudium et spes* 10, 18, 22, 32, 37, 38, 45, 78.

14. Karl Rahner, *On the Theology of Death* (New York: Herder and Herder, 1972; orig. 1961), p. 57.

15. Kasper, *Jesus the Christ*, pp. 118–19.

16. Schillebeeckx, *Christ*, p. 825.

17. See Kasper, *The God of Jesus Christ*, pp. 194–97.

18. Schillebeeckx, *Christ*, p. 830, cf. pp. 728–29.

19. Origen, *Homily on Ezekiel* 6, 6 and *Commentary on Matthew* 10, 23; Anselm, *Proslogion* 8.

20. Stillman Drake, ed. and trans., *Discoveries and Opinions of Galileo* (New York: Doubleday, 1957), p. 182; Kenneth Surin, *Theology and the Problem of Evil* (Oxford: Basil Blackwell, 1986), p. 40.

21. "Letter to Foscarini," in Jerome K. Langford, *Galileo, Science and the Church* (Ann Arbor, MI: University of Michigan Press, 1978), p. 61; James Brodrick, *The Life and Work of Blessed Robert Francis Cardinal Bellarmine*, S.J. (London: Burns, Oates and Washbourne, 1928), II, p. 359; Thomas S. Kuhn, *Copernican Revolution: Planetary Astronomy in the Development of Western Thought* (Cambridge, MA: Harvard University Press, 1957), p. 198.

22. See Thomas S. Kuhn, *Structure of Scientific Revolutions*, pp. 200–201. Along the same lines, see David Hume's 1776 *Dialogues Concerning Natural Religion*, 2nd ed., ed. Richard H. Popkin (Indianapolis: Hackett, 1998), pt. 2, pp. 21–22. Hume's character, Philo, expresses the transition in thinking that Kuhn analyzes.

23. Ibid., p. 175.

24. Kuhn, *Copernican Revolution*, p. 7; *Structure of Scientific Revolutions*, p. 140.

25. Surin, *Theology and the Problem of Evil*, p. 41.

26. Kuhn, *Structure of Scientific Revolutions*, pp. 175, 200–201.

27. Ibid., p. 19.

28. Pietro Redondi has proposed that the second condemnation was politically calculated to counter the threat that Galileo's physics posed to *Tridentine* eucharistic theology: *Galileo Heretic* (see chap 4, n.54), pp. 203–26, 326–32.

29. See A. J. Gurevich, *Categories of Medieval Culture*, tr. G. L. Campbell (London/Boston: Routledge & Kegan Paul, 1985), pp. 123–25.

30. *Summa contra gentiles* II, 46; *Summa theologiae* 1, 2, prologue; also 1, 2, q. 106, a. 1–4, q. 108 a. 1–4.

31. Karl Löwith, *The Meaning of History* (Chicago: University of Chicago Press, 1949), p. 65.

32. Daly, *Creation and Redemption*, p. 208.

33. See Kasper, *Theology and Church*, p. 71.

34. Schillebeeckx, *Church: The Human Story of God*, pp. 85–101 and 119–27.

35. "Was der Mensch sei, sagt nur die Geschichte." Wilhelm Dilthey, *Die drei Grundformen der Systeme in der ersten Hälfte des 19.Jahrhunderts*, in *Gesammelte Schriften*, 4 (Stuttgart: B. G. Teubner, 1959/Göttingen: Vandenhoeck & Ruprecht, 1968), p. 529; cited by Kasper, *Theology and Church*, p. 82.

36. Nainfa, *Costume of Prelates of the Catholic Church*, p. 124.

37. Abbott, *Documents of Vatican II*, p. 712.

38. Hermann J. Pottmeyer, "'Auctoritas suprema ideoque infallibilis,' Das Missverständnis der päpstlichen Unfehlbarkeit als Souveränität und seine historischen Bedingungen," *Konzil und Papst. Historische Beiträge zur Frage der höchsten Gewalt in der Kirche*, Festgabe für Hermann Tüchle, ed. Georg Schwaiger (Munich/Paderborn/Vienna: Schöningh, 1975), pp. 519–20.

39. Carl J. Peter, "A Rahner-Küng Debate and Ecumenical Possibilities," *Teaching Authority and Infallibility in the Church: Lutherans and Catholics in Dialogue VI*, eds. Paul C. Empie, T. Austin Murphy, and Joseph A. Burgess (Minneapolis: Augsburg, 1980), p. 165.

40. Joseph A. Burgess, "The Historical Background of Vatican I," *Teaching Authority and Infallibility in the Church*, p. 296; Hermann J. Pottmeyer, *Unfehlbarkeit und Souveränität. Die päpstliche Unfehlbarkeit im System der Ultramontanen Ekklesiologie des 19. Jahrhunderts*, Tübinger Theologische Studien 5 (Mainz: Matthias-Grünewald Verlag, 1975), p. 420, cf. pp. 408 and 416.

41. See Tillard, *The Bishop of Rome*, pp. 167–91.

42. Josef Ratzinger, "Free Expression and Obedience in the Church," in *The Church: Readings in Theology*, eds. Albert LaPierre et al. (New York: P. J. Kenedy, 1963), p. 212.

Epilogue

1. James R. Cain, *The Influence of the Cloister on the Apostolate of Congregations of Religious Women* (Rome: Lateran University, 1965), p. 6.

2. Ibid., pp. 14–35.

3. Ibid., pp. 37–50.

4. J. Grisar, *Die Ersten Anklagen im Rom Gegen Das Institut Maria Wards,* in *Miscellanea Historiae Pontificiae in Pontificia Universitate Gregoriana,* XXII (Rome: Gregorian University, 1959), pp. 203–4; cited by Cain, *Influence of the Cloister,* p. 42.

5. Cain, pp. 48–58.

6. "Commentary on the Declaration of the Sacred Congregation for the Doctrine of the Faith on the Question of Admission of Women to the Ministerial Priesthood," in *Women Priests: A Catholic Commentary on the Vatican Declaration,* eds. Leonard Swidler and Arlene Swidler (New York/Ramsey, NJ: Paulist Press, 1977), pp. 319–37, here p. 319.

7. *Declaratio circa quaestionem admissionis mulierum ad sacerdotium ministeriale (Inter insigniores), Acta Apostolicae Sedis* 69 (1997), pp. 98–116. English translation in *Women Priests,* pp. 37–49.

8. Sections 2 and 4 of the Apostolic letter, *Ordinatio sacerdotalis, Acta Apostolicae Sedis* 86 (1994), pp. 545–48, here pp. 546 and 548.

9. *Responsio ad dubium circa doctrinam in Ep. Ap. "Ordinatio Sacerdotalis" traditam, Acta Apostolicae Sedis* 87 (1995), p. 1114.

10. Francis A. Sullivan, *Creative Fidelity: Weighing and Interpreting Documents of the Magisterium* (New York/Mahwah, NJ: Paulist Press, 1996), p. 182.

Index of Modern Authors

Index of Selected Topics